ROUTLEDGE LIBRARY EDITIONS: SOVIET POLITICS

Volume 8

THE LIMITS OF DESTALINIZATION IN THE SOVIET UNION

THE LIMITS OF DESTALINIZATION IN THE SOVIET UNION

Political Rehabilitations in the Soviet Union since Stalin

ALBERT P. VAN GOUDOEVER

Translated by
FRANS HIJKOOP

Routledge
Taylor & Francis Group

LONDON AND NEW YORK

First published in 1986 by Croom Helm

This edition first published in 2024
by Routledge
4 Park Square, Milton Park, Abingdon, Oxon OX14 4RN

and by Routledge
605 Third Avenue, New York, NY 10158

Routledge is an imprint of the Taylor & Francis Group, an informa business

© 1986 Albert P. van Goudoever

British Library Cataloguing in Publication Data
A catalogue record for this book is available from the British Library

ISBN: 978-1-032-67165-9 (Set)
ISBN: 978-1-032-67612-8 (Volume 8) (hbk)
ISBN: 978-1-032-67614-2 (Volume 8) (pbk)
ISBN: 978-1-032-67613-5 (Volume 8) (ebk)

DOI: 10.4324/9781032676135

Publisher's Note
The publisher has gone to great lengths to ensure the quality of this reprint but points out that some imperfections in the original copies may be apparent.

Disclaimer
The publisher has made every effort to trace copyright holders and would welcome correspondence from those they have been unable to trace.

The Limits of Destalinization in the Soviet Union

Political Rehabilitations in the Soviet Union since Stalin

ALBERT P. VAN GOUDOEVER
translated by Frans Hijkoop

CROOM HELM
London & Sydney

© 1986 Albert P. van Goudoever
Croom Helm Ltd, Provident House, Burrell Row,
Beckenham, Kent BR3 1AT
Croom Helm Australia Pty Ltd, Suite 4, 6th Floor,
64-76 Kippax Street, Surry Hills, NSW 2010 Australia

British Library Cataloguing in Publication Data

Goudoever, Albert P. van
    The limits of destalinisation in the Soviet
    Union: political rehabilitations in the Soviet
    Union since Stalin.
    1. Soviet Union — Politics and government — 1953-
    I. Title   II. Angst voor het verleden. *English*
    320.947   JN6581
    ISBN 0-7099-2629-4

To Georgette

Printed and bound in Great Britain by Mackays of Chatham Ltd, Kent

CONTENTS

Contents

FIGURES AND TABLES

Figure

3.1 Biographical Articles in the Press, 1956-80

Tables

3.1   Reappearance in Publications (1)
3.2   Reappearance in Publications (2)
3.3   Reappearance in Publications (3)
3.4   Reappearance in Publications (4)
3.5   Reappearance in Publications (5)
3.6   Reappearance in Publications (6)
3.7   Reappearance in Publications (7)
3.8   Continuity of Recording of Biographical Headwords in
       Encyclopaedias
3.9   Continuity of Recording of Biographical Headwords in
       the Relevant Encyclopaedias
3.10 Number of New Names of Rehabilitated Persons in the
       Encyclopaedias, Compared to Encyclopaedias
       Published Earlier
3.11 Date of Party Entrance of Politically Rehabilitated
       Persons Newly Recorded in Encylopaedias
3.12 Social Origin of Politically Rehabilitated Persons Newly
       Recorded in Encyclopaedias
3.13 Social Classification According to Office of Politically
       Rehabilitated Persons Newly Recorded in
       Encyclopaedias
3.14 Nationality of Names of Politically Rehabilitated Persons
       Newly Recorded in Encyclopaedias
3.15 Number of Initiative Articles and Total Number of
       Commemorative Articles in the Press, 1956-80
3.16 Initiative Articles in the Press, 1956-61
3.17 Initiative Articles in the Press, 1962-7
3.18 Total Number of Commemorative Articles in *Pravda*
       and *Izvestia,* 1962-6

PREFACE

The study of political rehabilitations in the Soviet Union can go on for years yet. The absence of material in the form of original documents may give cause for complaint, but the Soviet press offers the researcher ample work. Every public rehabilitation of one of Stalin's victims can be investigated as an isolated case. Systematic examination nonetheless reveals that more incidental studies hardly affect the main conclusions. At this stage, I think the time has come to publish the results.

Now that my work has been completed, I should first like to express my gratitude to my friend Professor Dr Z.R. Dittrich, head of the department of East European Studies of the University of Utrecht. His stimulating guidance, a combination of mild tolerance towards my initial drafts and ineluctable directives in matters of content incessantly inspired further and more detailed examination of the material. It is a privilege to work with him.

I am greatly indebted to Professor Dr J.W. Bezemer of the University of Amsterdam. Through his incisive commentary he has made a substantial contribution to the present form and content of this book.

Dr M.C. Jansen of the International Instituut voor Sociale Geschiedenis in Amsterdam proved to be an excellent colleague. His substantial knowledge of the field and patient willingness to assist have guided me through two versions of the manuscript.

In studying the juridical aspects of the rehabilitations, the historian finds himself on thin ice. Dr G.P. van den Berg of the Documentatiebureau voor Oosteuropees Recht in Leiden gave me a series of minute instructions which kept me straight. My colleague P.D. 't Hart helped to make the demographic calculations more readily accessible to the reader.

The Faculty of Arts made a significant contribution by granting me a so-called 'Hugenholtz year', comparable to a sabbatical year. I was allowed by the Deutscher Akademischer Austauschdienst to visit a number of specialised institutes in the Federal Republic. I gratefully remember the work of the late Professor Dr G. Geilke of the Seminarabteilung für Ostrechtsforschung in Hamburg. I would also like to thank Dr Keith Bush of Radio Liberty in Munich. The library of the

Bundesinstitut für ostwissenschaftliche und internationale Studien in Cologne offered a valuable collection for this investigation. Much, however, was found at closer quarters, at the Oost-Europa Instituut in Amsterdam.

The Limits of Destalinisation was translated with great skill and meticulous care by Frans Hijkoop, whose specific field of study, English linguistics and literature, is not even remotely connected with the basic subject matter of this study. His ever increasing interest in the subject and his growing enthusiasm contributed to an excellent form of team work, for which I owe him a debt of gratitude. I am also very grateful to my eminent colleague in the United Kingdom Dr Maurice Pearton (Richmond College) for his readiness to check the manuscript on English usage in only a short time.

Ab van Goudoever

ACKNOWLEDGEMENT

This translation was made possible through a grant from the Netherlands Organisation for the Advancement of Pure Research.

NOTE ON TRANSCRIPTION

This study uses a scientific transcription of Russian. Every word and every name included can be accurately rewritten in the Cyrillic script. The system is used consistently, except for the spelling of such well-known names as Khrushchev, Trotsky, Bukharin and Brezhnev.

INTRODUCTION

After Stalin's death in 1953 a process of destalinisation was initiated in the Soviet Union. The most important part of this policy consisted of the reduction of the terror. Gradually, those victims of Stalin who had survived the camps began to reappear in society. Many of those who had been killed were rehabilitated posthumously. This study deals with the forms, aspects and significance of the phenomenon of rehabilitation in the Soviet Union between 1953 and 1980.

On the one hand, the study covers the political manipulation of the selection of victims qualified for rehabilitation and reinstatement in the communist party. It also reviews the formal and juridical procedures. On the other hand, the manner in which the commemoration of the communist non-survivors was handled in propaganda and historiography is also covered, including the posthumous manipulation of party-internal oppositions, of Bukharin, Trotsky and others. In addition to the results of this systematic and comparative inquiry, I have provided three studies of individual rehabilitations.

Soviet leaders attach great importance to the historical role of their predecessors. This is sometimes expressed by a complete re-evaluation, often in the form of a depreciation of former party leaders in the press and party historiography. The present glorification of the founder of the Soviet state, Lenin, contrasts sharply with the repudiation of the former first secretary of the party, Khrushchev. The variation in the appreciation of Stalin after his death similarly discloses a political preoccupation with the image of the deceased leader.

In a traditional historical perspective, then, it does not come as a surprise that the role of Brezhnev, who was venerated during the last ten years of his life, is reduced to barely identifiable proportions in official commemorations and historiography. Irrespective of the outcome of the power struggles within the politburo, Brezhnev's status is devalued posthumously. The fact that Brezhnev died while he was still in power and that he was not put aside in a political *coup* makes little difference. The new leader creates his own public image. The commemoration of his predecessor is useful only in that the latter can be presented as a scapegoat for problems and deficiencies.

The political manipulation of the role of historical key figures exemplifies one of the astonishing paradoxes of the Soviet state. The

1

ideology is based upon a strictly deterministic world-view, in which social developments are interpreted in terms of a dialectically evolving process inside the macro-economic and social sphere where personal initiative has little validity. Political practice nonetheless displays a reverse application of the theory.

The party leaders give strict guidance to socio-economic and political evolution and waste no time awaiting social processes. This culminated in Stalin's appearance. His 'third revolution' — collectivisation and industrialisation — exhibits an exceptionally ruthless interference from above. In accordance with his actions, Stalin's personal role was raised to an unprecedented level. A constant personality campaign had to be waged to ensure that Stalin was seen not only as a new Lenin, but even as a new infallible deity.

The permanent terror reached its climax in the great purge in the years between 1936 and 1939, with enormous numbers of people being prosecuted. Arbitrariness had grown to a point where anyone could be victimised. Repression was used against the army, the state bureaucracy, and the party itself. This 'Great Terror' represented the 'fourth revolution', during which Stalin reduced every citizen to a small wheel in a mechanical society run exclusively by himself. The very thought of opposing the system and Stalin in person had to be defused in advance.

This political practice manifests itself clearly in party historiography. From the beginning of the thirties historical study came to be replaced by a propagandistic manipulation of history. Historical deformation or mutilation formed part of it. Victims of the terror were denounced or simply ignored. This — frequently posthumous — policy was also maintained by Stalin for those who had committed suicide to escape repression, as well as for deceased party executives and intellectuals. He besmirched their memory or transferred their names to the 'memory-hole' of history. Even Lenin was affected.

Stalin's death promoted the scientific quality of historiography, yet the histories of the Soviet Union and the communist party are reserved for propaganda. Individuals receive an impressive amount of attention. The selection of names, to be mentioned honourably or otherwise, and the degree of esteem are assessed with great precision on a political level. The personal authority of such alleged regime opponents as Trotsky and Bukharin has been acknowledged grotesquely by the diversity of incriminating epithets appended to their names. Despite the relaxation of the political climate after Stalin's death, it is still common practice to determine, at the highest party level, the prestige of those allowed to be entered in historiography. Former inner-party oppositions are still characterised as pernicious. The past represents a functional ingredient of contemporary politics.

After Stalin's death a policy of destalinisation was initiated. The key to an explanation of the extremes of Stalinism and the replacement of the party by Stalin was found by the regime not in the social structure, but in the character of Stalin himself. The political tactics of his consecutive successors Khrushchev and Brezhnev emphasised this negation of economic determinism. They put a personal stamp on their administrations and did not shrink from personality cults. The communist party as a whole continued to claim a prominent role in social life, aiming to give guidance to evolution in a direction dictated from above, even if in a modern industrial society a different line of action would be more credible. The tension between political practice and deterministic ideology continues to exist.

The political changes also related to the fate of the victims of the terror. The majority of the survivors were released from the camps and returned to society, with rehabilitation taking place on a massive scale. Relatives of deceased victims were notified by the authorities about posthumous rehabilitations. At a private meeting of the twentieth party congress in February 1956, first secretary Khrushchev launched an attack against the personality cult of Stalin and the terror against the party. This so-called 'secret speech' set off a public policy of destalinisation.

The issue of Stalin's victims was hardly ever discussed in public. Party leaders who had been killed in the terror, however, were incidentally commemorated, and a number of prominent names from party history were registered without the customary denigration.

At the twenty-second party congress in October 1961, Khrushchev charged several of Stalin's former henchmen with co-responsibility for the terror: his ex-colleagues in the presidium of the party, Molotov, Malenkov and Kaganovič. Khrushchev had managed to expel them from the party leadership four years earlier. They were now used to introduce an intensive campaign of public destalinisation, in which Stalin was criticised and denounced with great vigour. In the press many leading figures from party history were honourably commemorated, and the facts concerning their fates in the terror were not concealed. This phenomenon of public rehabilitation lasted for several years, but died down after Khrushchev's fall in October

1964. His successors, Brezhnev, Kosygin, Podgornyj and Suslov maintained a policy of silence with respect to the terror, in which rehabilitations were deemed unfitting. The denunciation of Stalin, which constituted a central component of Khrushchev's administration, was superseded by a less biased treatment in the media. If rehabilitation took place at all in the seventies, it should be associated primarily with Stalin and Molotov.

A similar process of terror and rehabilitation took shape in Eastern European countries under Soviet supremacy.[1] In line with the policy of standardisation of the social structure of the Soviet Union, terror was methodically used in the postwar years and party leaders were prosecuted in show trials. Here, too, one may observe the release of convicts and the beginning of a process of rehabilitation. There are, however, some significant differences in the way this policy was put into effect.

The Polish party was actually abolished by Stalin after his purge of the entire party leadership. During the war, however, when he needed the party once again, the communists pressed Stalin personally for rehabilitations, certainly as early as 1944.[2] They had to wait for Stalin's death, however, before Poland became the first country, in 1955, to embark on the public rehabilitation of its deceased leaders. The Hungarian and Bulgarian parties soon followed. Here, even the victims of the show trials conducted in 1949 were rehabilitated posthumously: the Bulgarian party leader T. Kostov and his Hungarian colleague L. Rajk. These rehabilitations correlated with the Soviet détente towards Yugoslavia in 1955. One of the formal accusations at the Eastern European show trials was so-called Titoism, the demand for a line of action increasingly independent from the Soviet Union.

In 1956, the policy of destalinisation in Hungary and Poland led to a spontaneous liberalisation movement, culminating in the so-called Polish October and the Hungarian revolt. In both countries power went to new party leaders, former Stalin prisoners who were subsequently rehabilitated: W. Gomulka and J. Kádár.

Czechoslovakia and Romania did not follow suit. Political trials were conducted at a later stage and continued well after Stalin's death. The most prominent of these was the anti-Semitically biased show trial held against the former party secretary Slánský in Prague in 1952. First of all, under Kremlin pressure during the second wave of destalinisation after 1961, some party executives were publicly rehabilitated, albeit with moderate enthusiasm. It was not until 1968 that in both countries prominent victims of the terror were rehabilitated. In Romania rehabilitation was a marginal phenomenon, and prepared the way for the supremacy of party leader Ceauşescu.

A fundamental revolutionary change manifested itself in Czechoslovakia only. The process of rehabilitation was greatly affected by the Prague Spring, for the issue of the terror was a matter of conscience to the reform movement.[3] Rehabilitations were dealt with juridically, a unique phenomenon in Eastern Europe. The communist party conducted an investigation into the proceedings of the terror and the process of rehabilitation. Documentation, available to researchers in shortened form, contains much information on the meetings of the politburo. We have thus obtained a reasonably clear insight into the Czechoslovak rehabilitation phenomenon.

The structures of party and state and the political culture in Czechoslovakia and the Soviet Union are roughly comparable. The liberalisation in Czechoslovakia was the counterpart of the Soviet policy of destalinisation, although Prague adopted a more radical line of action. The party leadership in Czechoslovakia assumed power in the Stalin era and succeeded in averting destalinisation for a long time, maintaining a largely continuous policy until 1968. All this points to the conclusion that it is worth investigating the development of rehabilitation in Czechoslovakia, and using the results to clarify the process of rehabilitation in the Soviet Union.

No comprehensive publications on Soviet rehabilitations have appeared as yet. Political scientists have produced some articles on incidental rehabilitations and conducted a few unpublished inquiries.

Now that rehabilitations belong to the past, the time has come for historians to take action. It is their task to study the phenomenon as a whole and to put it in the context of the central contemporary issues of Soviet society, such as stalinism, the nationality question, and the dispute between the Soviet Union and China.

Notes

1. K.W. Fricke (*Warten auf Gerechtigkeit. Kommunistische Säuberungen und Rehabilitierungen. Bericht und Dokumentation* (Cologne, 1971)) gives a superficial idea of the Eastern European rehabilitations. His book, however, is useful because it contains a number of documents on terror and rehabilitation in the German Democratic Republic.

2. A. Polonsky and B. Drukier, *The Beginnings of Communist Rule in Poland, December 1943-June 1945* (London, 1980), Document no. 29, dated 28 August 1944, p. 268.

3. A. van Goudoever, 'De Praagse Lente: een verantwoording van de intelligentsia', *De Gids*, no. 136 (1973), pp. 356-9.

1 REHABILITATIONS: DEFINITIONS, DISCUSSIONS AND QUESTIONS

The Concept of Rehabilitation

According to dictionaries, the concept of rehabilitation can be interpreted in a general sense as 'the re-establishment of a person's reputation, reinstatement in any previous position or privilege'. The term may also be used to refer to 'the restoration to good repute by vindicating, by clearing a person of unjust or unfounded charges'.[1] Soviet works of reference supply a general definition of rehabilitation: 'restoration to good repute of an unjustly accused or calumniated person'.[2] The use of the adverb of condition 'unjustly' (*nepravil'no*) is of crucial importance. Rehabilitation is associated with the loss of reputation through unjust charges or slander. Since this study is concerned with persons who were thus victimised, it is this general description that will be used here, as the Russian definition corresponds sufficiently to one of the English descriptions.

There are various aspects of rehabilitation: (a) *formal*, juridical and social rehabilitation, including the possibility of restoration of party membership; (b) *public* rehabilitation; (c) *posthumous* rehabilitation.

Formal Rehabilitation

In the Netherlands, rehabilitation is no longer an institutional part of penal law, and it is for this reason that the term has no juridical meaning.[3] 'Rehabilitation' used to be defined in penal law as 'the restoration of a convict to his former juridical competence, after fulfilment of punishment'.[4] Soviet law includes a similar interpretation. The concept of rehabilitation may be viewed as 'the restoration of rights'.[5] A comprehensive definition throws some more light upon its basic meaning: 'abrogation of the consequences of legal action taken against a person after establishing the latter's violation of the law and the imposition of punishment'. Under Soviet law penalisation includes administrative and disciplinary punishments, juridical penalties, such as the deprivation of individual political and civil rights (deprivation of voting rights, prohibi-

7

tion from engaging in some activity or other, expulsion from certain areas, etc.).[6] We are concerned here with a purely formal practice, which enables ex-convicts to return to society and to exercise their full rights as citizens after the fulfilment of punishment. This aspect will be referred to in this study as '*the restoration of rights*'.

Under Khrushchev, the formal definition of rehabilitation was extended, corresponding to the general description suggested above: 'revision of all legal consequences of a judgment pertaining to a person who was unlawfully prosecuted, in consequence of the acknowledgement of innocence'.[7] This statement apparently refers to legal procedures which involved the reassessment of the arguments for a judgment and the possible deduction of innocence. This aspect will be examined as *individual formal rehabilitation* in greater detail below.[8]

The social aspects of rehabilitation manifest themselves in the regulations designed for rehabilitated victims who were prosecuted without justification. They involve compensation for lost wages and suffering inflicted, and include restoration to former positions, restitution of confiscated property, and financial settlement for pension-years. Irrespective of any material arrangements, these regulations reflect the realisation of a process of restoration of a subject's good name and reputation. The concept of *social rehabilitation* comprises all these characteristics.[9]

This study is predominantly concerned with the rehabilitation of former members of the communist party of the Soviet Union. Party members who were victimised by the terror had all lost their party membership. Rehabilitation of this group can be fully realised only if this party punishment is abrogated too; therefore, the term '*reinstatement in the party*' will be used.

Public Rehabilitation

The concept of public rehabilitation represents the reappearance of names of victims of the terror in the press, periodicals, works of reference, etc. Depending upon the type of publication, several characteristics of this form of rehabilitation can be distinguished. We are dealing here with the re-entry of biographical key words in encyclopaedias, registration of lists of names of such official publications as the party history, republication of certain papers, commemoration in the daily press, etc.

Names of victims are also sometimes honourably mentioned

without any sign of rehabilitation elsewhere. Such cases are referred to below as *informal rehabilitations.*[10] The famous Sovietologist Borys Levytsky reports that, in the early seventies, there was much discussion among Soviet historians about the introduction of a category of 'historical personalities' in the encyclopaedias and historiography. This category would then be used to classify principal party politicians like Trotsky and Bukharin, who have not been rehabilitated after victimisation in the terror. The new category would be used for the sake of historical accuracy.[11] It is nonetheless incorrect to advance the term 'historical rehabilitation', since no real case of rehabilitation is involved. A possible historiographical change in this particular sense, however, certainly forms part of the argument of this study.

Posthumous Rehabilitation

The concept of posthumous rehabilitation should be applied to those victims who did not survive the terror, either because they were executed or because they died in the deprived conditions in prisons or camps. Formal rehabilitation and reinstatement in the party are equally possible for this category and for the survivors of the terror. This type of rehabilitation is particularly significant in terms of public rehabilitation. Practically none of Stalin's prominent political victims survived the terror. Posthumous rehabilitations proved to be of importance with regard to the allotment of pension rights, compensation, etc. to dependants.

Study of the Literature

The phenomenon of public rehabilitation aroused the interest of western political scientists in the sixties. In that period, several articles were published and the manuscript of a dissertation on political rehabilitations was completed.[12] The final years under Khrushchev witnessed a large number of cases of public rehabilitation. Since the beginning of the seventies, however, the phenomenon has been left untouched in publications outside the Soviet Union. Inside the Soviet Union information about the formal rehabilitations began to emerge in dissident circles, through illegal publications which were distributed by *samizdat.*

Unlike other researchers, the American political scientist Jane Perlberg Shapiro has set up a comprehensive and systematic investigation into the phenomenon and has published her findings. Her views are based upon the notion of a powerful discontinuity of stalinism. She is therefore readily tempted to detect aspects of destalinisation and her definitions and types of rehabilitation tend to an optimistic interpretation. Because of her predominant concern with the registration of names in the press, her approach is basically formal. The contents of sources on rehabilitations play a minor part in her investigations.

Borys Levytsky has also devoted attention to the rehabilitations in his work. He compiled valuable documentation, supplemented by an analytical introduction. Levytsky's is a modest contribution, for the results of his investigations are not enriched with more specific argument. In Levytsky's views on the post-Stalin era, the continuity of stalinism and scepticism towards destalinisation dominate the other aspects.[13] He distinguishes between types of rehabilitation on the basis of the political views on the rehabilitated held by the regime, that is, the degree of actual political rehabilitation. This means that Levytsky, above all, takes account of the *contents* of publications on the rehabilitated in the Soviet press.

Apparently protected by one of the party leaders, the historian Roj Aleksandrovič Medvedev, a resident of Moscow and son of a victim of the terror, has published widely in the West. He continues along the same historiographical line as that adopted by Khrushchev through his criticisms on Stalin, the personality cult and the terror. Although Medvedev's attitude towards the Soviet past became increasingly censorious, his views are still strongly tied to the present system. As a result, he adopts a sympathetic attitude towards Khrushchev and the latter's policies. He presents a very *constructive* image of the rehabilitations, especially in his first contributions on the subject. Through his information about the daily routine of the fifties, Medvedev's is a substantial contribution to our knowledge of the formal rehabilitations.[14] His observations are probably based upon oral information offered to him by old Bolsheviks and politicians close to Khrushchev. Medvedev does not annotate these passages in his work; nor does he make an effort to provide a satisfactory explanation.

Another dissident, Anton Vladimirovič Antonov-Ovseenko, who belonged to the category of 'children of public enemies' and was therefore arrested, spent a long time in prison camp. His father, the famous besieger of the Winter Palace in 1917, was executed in 1938. Antonov-Ovseenko is a historian who, in principle, adopts the same methods as Medvedev. He, too, uses oral information from inside the party leadership. A.I. Mikojan, a former member of the party presidium who died in 1978, was probably one of his informants. In *The Time of Stalin. Portrait of a Tyranny*, Antonov-Ovseenko, unlike Medvedev, tackles the rehabilitations in an extremely critical and dismissive manner,[15] often employing sarcasm to give vent to his resentment.

Through their method of dealing with the rehabilitations, both dissidents fall into the category of chronicle writers.[16] Their information to some extent compensates for the secrecy maintained by the authorities and must be taken very seriously. The results of the activities of Medvedev and Antonov-Ovseenko will be incorporated in the preliminary examination in conjunction with a number of memoirs by survivors of the terror, also distributed in *samizdat*. The fairly recent, illegal historical periodical *Pamjat'* (*Memory*) presents a substantial source of information.[17]

Research has so far produced results on the chronological development and outcome of the rehabilitations, as well as a number of explanations of the phenomenon.

Chronological Development

The process of the rehabilitations is associated with the campaign of destalinisation, the attacks against Stalin and his personal regime. In the years between Stalin's death in March 1953 and the twentieth party congress in February 1956, Stalin's name virtually disappeared from the public stage, with the exception of the commemoration of the anniversary of the day of his death in 1954 and his birthday in 1955. In this period of *silent destalinisation*, rehabilitations generally took place without public notice.[18] Victims of the terror returned from the camps, beginning with the relatives of the party leaders.[19] There appears to be no consensus in the literature as to whether releases took place in small[20] or large batches.[21] The actual significance of this form of rehabilitation also remains obscure. Posthumous rehabilitations in this period primarily applied to prominent party executives, literary persons and persons with academic and cultural backgrounds. They concerned faithful stalinists who had been active in the thirties.[22]

The development towards open anti-stalinism was set off by Khrushchev through his well-known 'secret speech' at the twentieth party congress, in which he denounced Stalin and the latter's terror against the party. After the congress, public rehabilitations began to materialise in the press. The importance and long-term significance of the form in which public rehabilitations were realised are left undiscussed. There are several views on its further development. Shapiro detects a continuation of the rehabilitations in 1956 and 1957, despite the stagnation of the policy of destalinisation. She registers the first case of full rehabilitation in 1957. Subsequently, only a few additional rehabilitations took place until 1961, but those who had already been rehabilitated received an increasing amount of attention in the press.[23] Levytsky notices a decrease in rehabilitations between the end of 1956 and the beginning of 1957 and an intensification between June 1957 and the end of 1958. Between 1959 and 1961, the regime proved extremely cautious about spreading information concerning the thirties and the rehabilitated.[24]

The twenty-second party congress led to a new *intensification* of destalinisation. Many new cases of public rehabilitation can be discerned, especially in 1963.[25] Formal rehabilitation, however, took place only occasionally.[26] After Khrushchev's fall from power in October 1964, destalinisation declined rapidly and the number of public rehabilitations dwindled. The press nonetheless continued to pay attention to the rehabilitated, at least according to some writers.[27] In her last article on this matter, published in 1969, Shapiro takes an optimistic view of future rehabilitations.[28]

Others, however, observe the termination of the rehabilitations. In their view, the rehabilitation of Stalin and restalinisation in cultural policies are indicative of the lack of concern with the victims of the terror. They do not observe any initiatives on the part of the regime. Antonov-Ovseenko's commentaries, which are quite sharp and acrimonious, even reject the use of the term 'the rehabilitation era': 'Isn't that too high-faluting a term for the few years in which mercies were doled out with an eyedropper?'[29]

The Outcome of the Rehabilitations

The number of victims of the terror continues to create serious dissent among the experts, and there is no consensus on the number of rehabilitations. The totals mentioned are widely divergent and range from several hundreds of thousands to millions. As regards the rehabilitations of the members of the Central Committee between 1918 and 1938 who had been victimised by the terror, the national party leadership, Shapiro computed that, by 1967, 70 per cent of the victims had been rehabilitated. Nevertheless, she noticed a shortfall of rehabilitations in the federal republics.

Members of the politburos and secretaries of the federal republic parties were rehabilitated only marginally.[30] The American political scientist also indicates the inconsistency of the rehabilitations. Victims of the terror who could be classified on the basis of several characteristics as belonging to the same category were subjected to extremely divergent treatment in the process of rehabilitation. Shapiro examined whether this could be explained on the basis of the different types of charges which had led the victims to be arrested or sentenced at the time. No correlation between charges and the selection of rehabilitation appeared to exist.[31]

Studies generally present the same views on the categories of victims who were *not* rehabilitated. Political adversaries of the communist party were not rehabilitated, and belonging to one of the oppositions inside the party proved to be an obstacle to rehabilitation. Even so, here too one may observe an inconsistent type of policy, for, in spite of everything, some individual public rehabilitations did take place. This even happened to a number of victims of the show trial held in 1938 against the so-called 'front of Rightists and Trotskyists' (the most prominent among the accused were Bukharin, Rykov, Rakovskij and Jagoda). No explanation for this exception has been discovered.[32]

Rehabilitation of those victims of the terror who did not belong to the higher ranks of the communist party has attracted little notice in the professional journals. Levytsky mentions a category of lower party executives and intellectuals who have been formally, but not publicly, rehabilitated. Lastly, this sovietologist reminds us of the hundreds of thousands of peasants and workers who have never been rehabilitated.[33]

Explanations

It is commonly accepted that the rehabilitations cannot be accounted for in terms of moral considerations on the part of the party leaders. There was never any evidence of a desire to make a clean sweep and to settle the past. The selective character of the rehabilitations and the restricted information about the terror are indicative of a political explanation. The issue of the rehabilitations in the Soviet Union has so far been approached predominantly from the angle of political conflicts inside the party establishment and discussions commonly reflect the question of which of the party leaders partaking in the struggle for personal power are involved in a specific, individual, public and posthumous rehabilitation. Kremlinology may benefit considerably from the study of rehabilitations, in addition to the examination of the protocol, the external actions of political leaders, the extent of the personality cult and the clientele system.

The role of a rehabilitation in the struggle for power brings out a significant historical dimension: the special responsibility of certain political leaders for the clearing of the person to be rehabilitated. Very little, however, is made public about the routine of party meetings, so the reconstruction of inside relations is basically speculative. Some information nonetheless trickles out occasionally, as in the case of the crisis inside the party leadership in the middle of 1957, for instance.

In June 1957, the power struggle between Khrushchev and Molotov, Malenkov and Kaganovič reached its climax. At the plenary meeting of the Central Committee, Khrushchev emerged triumphant, partly because he managed to saddle his opponents with the responsibility for the massive terror of the thirties and forties. The issue of the rehabilitations in this case served as a lever. The involvement of Khrushchev's opponents was exposed. The rehabilitations were used for *political-tactical* reasons, to ensure Khrushchev's survival.[34]

In addition to this explanation, the phenomenon of the rehabilitations is embedded by experts in the general policy of *destalinisation*, more specifically of the attacks against Stalin's personal regime. The public rehabilitations are used as evidence of the terror to underline the detrimental effects of Stalin's dictatorship for the party. Shapiro observes several inconsistencies: a temporary reduction in anti-stalinism, while public rehabilitations continue to take place. She attributes this development to the conflicts inside the party leadership. Moreover, the rehabilitations continually serve to show the people that the regime renounces the use of terror as a means to keep itself in power. The policy of rehabilitations is used specifically to enhance the people's *support* of the party.[35] This explanation has been endorsed by several authors who point out the considerable pressure exerted on the party leadership: rehabilitations were demanded by relatives of the victims, by old Bolsheviks and historians, and by communist parties in several Eastern European countries. Although we present these groups as one here, they are discussed in various places in the literature. Most explicit on this topic is the Russian *émigré* and historian Nekrič, who observes a spontaneous mass movement for the rehabilitations.[36]

Both explanations are nonetheless inadequate for the developments in the years after Khrushchev. The current political leaders have not been directly involved in the terror, and the issue of co-responsibility has thus become redundant. At the time, this particular aspect supported Shapiro's optimism with regard to future rehabilitations.[37]

Recent scholarly contributions by western sovietologists conclude that we may currently be witnessing the decline of the anti-Stalin campaign and the rise of a *pro-Stalin* movement. Rehabilitations other than Stalin's will not come up for discussion here. This development is accounted for by the continuation of the authoritative and hierarchic structure of the system, and by the projection of nationalist sentiments on to Stalin.[38] Perspectives have shifted and the long-term effects of stalinism have become perceptible, and the phenomenon of the rehabilitations is therefore of topical interest. This is rather cynical, since it now emerges in the form of the rehabilitation of Stalin.

Questions

The formal, social rehabilitation, the restoration of rights as well as reinstatement in the party, are examined on the basis of new information by dissident writers, supplemented by juridical sources. The manner in which people were released from the camps and their subsequent treatment or, alternatively, the form and significance of the posthumous rehabilitation will take up a central position. Researches aim to clarify the issue of the relation between these aspects of rehabilitation and the reappearance in public of the names of rehabilitated persons.

It is essential to establish a comparison with the Czechoslovak sources, because these contain information concerning the role of the party in formal rehabilitations, the struggle for personal political power in the party leadership in relation to the rehabilitation policy, the role of 'pressure groups', etc.

The issue of the long-term *significance* of some form or other of public rehabilitation is important. What, in terms of publicity, could happen in addition to the mere recording of a biography in an encyclopaedia or in the press? What is the significance of mentioning the name of a rehabilitated person at the party congress? Static moments in time have in fact been regarded throughout as rehabilitations and the nature of publication has played hardly any part in the analyses. The various types of public rehabilitation, however, can be differentiated according to the nature of publicity. Useful in this respect are the different types of Soviet publication: mass editions versus small-scale editions, specialist press versus mass propaganda, national press as opposed to federal press, and public papers in addition to the press of specific social groups.

The *contents* of press reports which reflect a public rehabilitation, too, should be considered. Which are the historical settings put forward in contributions regarding rehabilitated persons, which moral standards are stressed by the authors of the articles? The phenomenon of public rehabilitations, too, is part of political *propaganda.* Aims and target groups are indicated by the contents of the press and the choice of periodical or publishing house, while quantitative data may be significant as well.

The source materials for the public rehabilitations, consisting of publications in the Soviet Union, increased to a large extent in the seventies. Apart from the obvious daily and periodical press, various new encyclopaedias were published. The degree to which rehabilitations were continued and the question of whether new initiatives for public rehabilitation were explored should be subjected to examination.

By including the published material of the seventies in our research, we put the question of contents and significance in a historical perspective. As a result, the obscurities and differences of opinion in the established professional literature may be disentangled. It may now also become apparent to what extent one can actually speak of full rehabilitations.

In addition to systematic investigations, the study of individual cases of rehabilitation is essential as well. This makes further insights possible which are not so much based upon formal evidence. The cases of rehabilitation selected here are generally taken to be full-scale rehabilitations: the former chairman of the Supreme Soviet of the Ukranian SSR, who was rehabilitated in his lifetime, *G.I. Petrovskij*; the historian, head of the political department in the Red Army and vice-people's commissar for education, *A.S. Bubnov*; and the supreme commander of the army operating in the Far East, Marshal *V.K. Bljucher.* Bubnov was executed in prison or in camp. Bljucher was tortured to death while being interrogated. Petrovskij takes up a place of his own. He is the only one among the (candidate) members of Stalin's politburo who survived political overthrow and reappeared in the media after years of holding a minor office. Particularly in this case, rehabilitation could be realised without much effort, which supplies a solid basis for putting the policy of rehabilitation to the test.

The investigation into the public rehabilitations is limited to the *political* figures in Soviet history who were purged from the party. Historical figures in the domain of science and the arts will not be discussed. Without exception, the communist politicians who are the focal point of this inquiry were leading party executives. They had raised no objections to the prosecutions of non-communists. Their ethical and humanitarian standards are determined by the exertion of power. They are, in my view, not entitled to take up a prominent place in history as promoters of world progress. The present book is not a plea for the rehabilitation of convicted communists. It aims to determine the extent to which the communist party itself has been capable of overcoming the terror of Stalin's regime. This can be tested by examining what the party did to rehabilitate those of its members who, under Soviet law, had been unjustly prosecuted.

Notes

1. See, for example, the *Oxford English Dictionary* and *Webster's Third New International Dictionary*.

2. *Slovar' sovremennogo russkogo literaturnogo jazyka*, vol. 20 (Moscow/Leningrad, 1961), p. 1051, and *Bol'šaja Sovetskaja Enciklopedija*, 2nd edn, vol. 36 (Moscow, 1955), p. 138 (henceforth *BSE²*). It is worth mentioning that the term 'rehabilitation' is not defined in a general sense in the third edition of the *Great Soviet Encyclopedia* (*Bol'šaja Sovetskaja Enciklopedija*, 3rd edn, vol. 21 (Moscow 1975), p. 516) (henceforth *BSE³*). S.I. Ožegov (*Slovar' russkogo jazyka* (Moscow, 1978), p. 618) does not mention the aspect of a false accusation in his recent concise dictionary. The definition provided in this work resembles the one used in *Tolkovyj slovar' russkogo jazyka*, vol. 3 (Moscow, 1939), pp. 1301-2. On account of these differences it seems probable that the definition quoted in the text was *temporary* and was used in the Soviet Union only during the fifties and sixties. The changes in the political climate after Khrushchev here express themselves in lexicography.

3. *Fockema Andreae's Rechtsgeleerd Handwoordenboek*, 4th edn (Alphen on the Rhine, 1977), p. 522.

4. Cf. *Woordenboek der Nederlandsche Taal*, vol. 12 (The Hague, 1972), pp. 1577-80: 'het herstel van een veroordeelde in zijn rechtsbevoegdheden, nadat de straf geboet is'.

5. *BSE³*, vol. 21, p. 516.

6. *BSE²*, vol. 36, p. 138. See also *Juridičeskij slovar'*, vol. 2 (Moscow, 1956),

18   *Rehabilitations*

pp. 317-18. *Enciklopedičeskij slovar' pravovych znanij* (Moscow, 1965) does not include the headword 'rehabilitation'.

7. *Slovar' sovremennogo russkogo literaturnogo jazyka*, vol. 20, p. 1051.

8. The term 'juridical rehabilitation' is not used because there is no legal regulation as regards rehabilitation in the Soviet Union. Cf. B. Levytsky, *The Stalinist Terror in the Thirties. Documentation from the Soviet Press* (Stanford, Cal., 1974), p. 14. In the literature on rehabilitations in the Soviet Union, this term was introduced by L. Labedz in 'Resurrection and Perdition', *Problems of Communism*, vol. 12, no. 2 (1963), p. 52; the term was adopted by J.P. Shapiro in 'Rehabilitation Policy and Political Conflict in the Soviet Union, 1953-1964', unpublished PhD thesis, Columbia University, 1967, p. 8. Labedz and Shapiro use 'juridical rehabilitation' to indicate the interference with cases of rehabilitation by the judicial authorities. Neither goes deeply into the juridical background. Shapiro (pp. 84-5, 107-8) does discuss the reforms within the judicial machinery in relation to the issue of the rehabilitations.

9. Shapiro ('Rehabilitation Policy', pp. 11-13) describes this aspect as 'physical rehabilitation'.

10. Shapiro ('Rehabilitation Policy', pp. 7-11) considers the reappearance of the name of a victim in publications to be indicative of a full rehabilitation. In this she distinguishes between two categories: public rehabilitation (i.e. favourable mention in the press after a 'juridical rehabilitation') and full public rehabilitation (i.e. official commemorations of rehabilitated victims of the purges and publication of their work). Levytsky (*Stalinist Terror*, p. 14) uses the term 'full rehabilitation' in the sense of Shapiro's 'full public rehabilitation'. It is highly questionable whether this form of rehabilitation is actually as complete as is suggested by the term. This issue will come up for discussion in the questions and conclusions of this study. I have avoided the use of 'full rehabilitation' because this term is used in Soviet publications to indicate a formal rehabilitation and reinstatement in the party.

11. Levytsky, *Stalinist Terror*, p. 14. Without further definition, Shapiro ('Rehabilitation Policy', p. 13) introduces the term 'historical rehabilitation'. She uses this term to indicate the phenomenon that, in historiography, the obligatory references to mistakes made in the past by non-rehabilitated victims of the terror are sometimes omitted. This was characterised above as informal rehabilitation.

12. Labedz, 'Resurrection and Perdition', pp. 48-59; S.A. Oppenheim, 'Rehabilitation in the Post-Stalinist Soviet Union', *The Western Political Quarterly*, vol. 20, no. 1 (Utah, 1967), pp. 97-115; J.P. Shapiro, 'Soviet Historiography and the Moscow Trials: After Thirty Years', *Russian Review*, vol. 27, no. 1 (1968), pp. 68-77; J.P. Shapiro, 'Rehabilitation Policy under the Post-Khrushchev Leadership', *Soviet Studies*, vol. 20, no. 4 (1969), pp. 490-8; J.P. Shapiro, 'Political Rehabilitation in Soviet Central Asian Party Organizations', *Central Asian Review*, vol. 14, no. 3 (1966), pp. 199-209. In addition, Shapiro's 'Rehabilitation Policy' (1967) and Levytsky's *Stalinist Terror* (1974), already referred to above, should be mentioned as well. In Eastern Europe, a Czechoslovak historical journal published a unique article: T. Reimanova, 'K rehabilitacím v SSSR (stručný přehled iem a charakteristik osob veřejně rehabilitovaných v tisku a publikacích v SSSR)', *Ceskoslovenský časopis historický*, no. 4 (1964), pp. 591-601. This article contains a list of names of rehabilitated persons in the Soviet Union.

B. Meissner (*Das Ende des Stalin-Mythos. Die Ergebnisse des 20. Parteikongresses des KPdSU* (Frankfurt-on-Main, 1956), pp. 41-3) presents a first classification in categories of rehabilitated persons. Of less interest are the following articles: U. Picht, 'Die Rehabilitierungen nach Stalins Tod', *Sowjetstudien*, no. 14 (1963), pp. 96-111; 'Rehabilitations: Soviet Dilemma', *The Interpreter* (August 1964), pp. 10-14.

13. The difference in interpretation between Shapiro and Levytsky is nicely

expressed in their views on the position taken by the Soviet leaders in the first years after Stalin's death. Levytsky (*Stalinist Terror*, p. 4) observes that no attempt was made to do away with the personality cult of Stalin, whereas Shapiro ('Rehabilitation Policy', p. 323) notices the disappearance of references to Stalin. The authors take a totally different view of the interpretation of Khrushchev's speech on 8 March 1963. Levytsky (*Stalinist Terror*, p. 12) deems the words of the first secretary to have been indicative of a revaluation of Stalin. Shapiro ('Rehabilitation Policy', pp. 241-2) regards the speech as a weak attempt to keep a check on destalinisation. Finally, Levytsky (*Stalinist Terror*, p. 12) observes a change in the policy of destalinisation in 1963, whereas Shapiro ('Rehabilitation Policy', p. 317) argues that the anti-Stalin campaign was continued even throughout 1964.

Levytsky's inquiry into the contents of the press on the rehabilitations is not further substantiated. Above all, Levytsky's fundamental questions focus upon stalinism. The anti-stalinist campaign in the press, Levytsky (*Stalinist Terror*, p. 17) concludes, is indicative of feelings of discontent among party officials. This dissatisfaction was caused by Stalin's nationalities policy, the overstatement of Stalin's military role, and the way in which the agricultural policy was carried out.

14. R. Medvedev, *Faut-il réhabiliter Staline?* (Paris, 1969); R.A. Medvedev and Z.A. Medvedev, *Khrushchev. The Years in Power* (New York, 1976); R.A. Medvedev, *Political Essays* (Nottingham, 1976); R. Medwedjew, 'Vom XX. zum XXII. Parteitag der KPdSU. Ein kurzer historischer Ueberblick' in R. Crusius and M. Wilke (eds.), *Entstalinisierung. Der XX. Parteitag der KPdSU und seine Folgen* (Frankfurt on Main, 1977), pp. 23-49; R.A. Medvedev, *On Stalin and Stalinism* (Oxford, 1979); R.A. Medvedev, *Khrushchev* (Oxford, 1982).

15. A. Antonov-Ovseenko, *Portret tirana* (New York, 1980), trans. *The Time of Stalin. Portrait of a Tyranny* (New York, 1981).

16. Both Medvedev and Antonov-Ovseenko are dissidents against their will. They belong to this group because they could not publish their historical works in the Soviet Union, although this was certainly their intention.

17. *Pamjat'. Istoričeskij sbornik*, nos. 1 (New York, 1978) and 2 (Paris, 1979). For a discussion of this periodical, see M.C. Jansen's review in *Internationale Spectator*, vol. 37, no. 1 (1983), pp. 37-9.

18. Shapiro, 'Rehabilitation Policy', p. 316; Oppenheim, 'Rehabilitation', p. 98.

19. Medvedev, *Khrushchev*, p. 64.

20. Antonov-Ovseenko, *Time of Stalin*, p. 328; Medvedev, *Khrushchev*, p. 83; Levytsky, *Stalinist Terror*, pp. 3 and 13; S.F. Cohen, 'The Stalin Question since Stalin' in S.F. Cohen (ed.), *An End to Silence. Uncensored Opinion in the Soviet Union, from Roy Medvedev's Underground Magazine Political Diary* (New York, 1982), p. 25.

21. Shapiro, 'Rehabilitation Policy', p. 311.

22. Levytsky, *Stalinist Terror*, pp. 3 and 13; Medvedev, *Khrushchev*, p. 83.

23. Shapiro, 'Rehabilitation Policy', pp. 311 and 325. As opposed to Shapiro, Labedz ('Resurrection and Perdition', p. 51) argues that, after 1956, the rehabilitations were delayed for six years.

24. Levytsky, *Stalinist Terror*, pp. 7 and 9.

25. Shapiro, 'Rehabilitation Policy', p. 317; Levytsky, *Stalinist Terror*, pp. 10 and 12; Medvedev, *Khrushchev*, p. 211; Oppenheim, 'Rehabilitation', p. 101.

26. Medvedev, *Khrushchev*, p. 212.

27. Shapiro, 'Rehabilitation Policy', p. 254; Shapiro, 'Rehabilitation Policy Post-Khrushchev', p. 498; Levytsky, *Stalinist Terror*, p. 12; Oppenheim, 'Rehabilitation', pp. 101-2.

28. Shapiro, 'Rehabilitation Policy Post-Khrushchev', p. 498.

29. Cohen, 'Stalin Question', pp. 42-3; Antonov-Ovseenko, *Time of Stalin*, p. 339.

30. Shapiro, 'Rehabilitation Policy', p. 249; Shapiro, 'Rehabilitation Policy Post-Khrushchev', pp. 490 and 498.

31. Shapiro, 'Rehabilitation Policy', pp. 311 and 314-16; Shapiro, 'Political Rehabilitation in Soviet Central Asian Party Organizations', p. 208.

32. Shapiro, 'Soviet Historiography and Moscow Trials'; Levytsky, *Stalinist Terror*, p. 13; Oppenheim, 'Rehabilitation', p. 106.

33. Levytsky, *Stalinist Terror*, pp. 13-14.

34. Labedz, 'Resurrection and Perdition', pp. 48 and 51; Levytsky, *Stalinist Terror*, pp. 5-6.

35. Shapiro, 'Rehabilitation Policy', pp. 324-6.

36. Levytsky, *Stalinist Terror*, p. 3; Shapiro, 'Rehabilitation Policy', p. 322; Medvedev, *Khrushchev*, p. 212; Cohen; 'Stalin Question', p. 25; M. Heller and A. Nekrich, *Geschichte der Sowjetunion* (2 vols., Königstein, 1982), vol. 2, pp. 211-12.

37. Shapiro, 'Rehabilitation Policy Post-Khrushchev', p. 498.

38. Cohen, 'Stalin Question', pp. 42ff; Levytsky, *Stalinist Terror*, pp. 33-4.

2 REHABILITATIONS BEHIND THE SCENES

Introduction

Those who were prosecuted during the terror in the Soviet Union or in Czechoslovakia could be rehabilitated in a number of ways. It was possible for the government to decree a general pardon, an amnesty which could be granted to all political convicts. A decree of individual pardon was possible too, in case the regime did not wish to adopt general measures. In both cases, rehabilitation would imply a remittance of further punishment and the release of the person involved. If confinement in prison or in camp was effectuated by a court judgement — which was hardly ever the case — the legal authorities could pass on to a revision of the trial and the sentence. If in such a case grave errors in terms of juridical proceedings or the enforcement of the law were detected, the sentence could be annulled and the person involved declared innocent. This would add up to the actual re-establishment of a person's good name and honour. A possible return into society, social rehabilitation or, in posthumous cases, public rehabilitation would be greatly facilitated after the revision of the sentence.

Former party members, who were expelled from the party by virtue of their arrest, could be reinstated in the party after a formal, individual rehabilitation. The Central Control Committee of the communist party may nonetheless follow a policy of reinstatement which does not automatically provide for rehabilitation in the party.

The policy of destalinisation led to, among other things, a substantial decrease of the role of the secret police. Prominent executives could be held responsible for the violations of the law under Stalin. At trials against leading executives, the past was investigated in order to reveal the unlawful practices of the secret police. Formal rehabilitations took place inside this framework.

The policy of rehabilitation is always determined by the politics of the communist party. As the party places itself outside society and controls both the administration of justice and the courts of law, it can also prescribe the policy of formal rehabilitation to be adopted by the executive bodies. It is therefore highly questionable

21

whether one should actually speak of non-political, purely formal rehabilitations. Fundamentally, they are always *political* rehabilitations.

The Process of Rehabilitation in Czechoslovakia

The Role of the Communist Party

During the Prague Spring, the party opened discussions on the political trials and rehabilitations. In April 1968 the Central Committee resolved to initiate a programme of social reform and instituted a committee with the assignment of completing rehabilitation within the party with regard to those party members who were convicted in political trials held between 1952 and 1954. The party made a serious effort to restore legal order.[1]

Chairman of the committee was Jan Piller, a member of the politburo since January 1968. In the course of its work, this committee came to the conclusion that it could not perform its duties properly unless the entire course of events at the time of the trials and the rehabilitations was analysed.

This extension of duties soon produced such alarming results that in the summer the politburo was warned of the explosive power of the impending final report.[2] The inner core of the party turned out to have been deeply involved in the terror and to have delayed the rehabilitations for many years. The social authority of the communist party was at stake.

The Piller committee reported during 1968. Documentation amounted to 1,500 pages and provided concrete recommendations to the Central Committee. The draft resolution proposed full, public rehabilitation of the victims of the political trials, disciplinary penalties for the responsible party executives and general measures to avoid repetition. However, due to the altered political situation after the invasion, the Central Committee decided to bury the Piller report in its archives in December 1968.[3] The text was smuggled out of the country and was published in abridged form in Vienna. In addition to this important, unique document, the memoirs of one of the members of the Piller committee, the historian Karel Kaplan, were published.[4]

Within the scope of this work, we do not wish to provide a comprehensive study of the Czechoslovak practice of rehabilitation, but it may serve as a model of the course of events inside the

Soviet Union. Through a knowledge of the Prague approach, many unsolved questions about Soviet rehabilitations can perhaps be answered or at least elucidated in several respects.

After Stalin's death, the communist party of Czechoslovakia (KSČ) had not made any alteration in the policy of the terror. The great show trial against the former party secretary R. Slánský and others, held in 1952, had a long aftermath. In 1953 and 1954, new political trials continued to take place.

Meanwhile, however, investigations into the terror were in progress in the neighbouring countries of Poland and Hungary. The result proved to affect Czechoslovakia, for the political trials in the Eastern European countries were interwoven. The Field brothers were alleged to form the international link between the United States and the pseudo-conspiracies in Hungary, Poland and Czechoslovakia.

These American citizens, who had helped victims of Nazism to escape, were convicted as imperialist agents and spies. In October and November respectively, Herman Field in Poland and Noël Field and his wife in Hungary were released and rehabilitated. Their formal rehabilitations affected the grounds of the trial against Slánský, because the charges no longer stood up.[5]

The party leaders of the KSČ had received a large number of complaints about the prosecutions. Initially, these complaints were ignored. Now that other countries had been revising legal sentences, however, a commission was set up to examine several cases concerning the punishment measures. The politburo took action on 10 January 1955: member of the politburo and Minister of Internal Affairs R. Barák was appointed chairman. The Piller report shows that the members of the commission had themselves been involved in the political trials, so they could not be impartial. One troublesome task restricted the field of operations of the Barák commission: the trial against Slánský *et al.* had to be left untouched. The work of this commission basically consisted of an 'attempt to silence those signs which disturbed the politburo's conscience'.[6] Matters had to be dealt with silently, which explains why in several cases the commission preferred amnesty, free pardon or reduction of punishment. For these there was no need of a revision of the sentence in court; a recommendation by the Minister of Justice to the head of state was sufficient. Bad publicity could thus be avoided, particularly concerning the Slánský case.

The Barák commission advised that other cases should be

handled in the same manner, even if there was evidence of innocence. Arguments were continually adapted to current political
needs. The trial against the 'bourgeois nationalists', for instance,
which included G. Husák as the most distinguished person among
the accused, was not revised in spite of irregularities in the
proceedings. Other sentences, too, against the 'Economists' and
the 'Trotskyists' were not challenged because there was some
doubt as to the Leninist character of the viewpoints held by the
people involved.[7]

In some cases where revision of the sentence had been recommended the commission supplied *new arguments* to uphold the
sentence in whole or in part. As Novotný later declared, the
Supreme Court was instructed to 'find other charges, so as to
justify the time spent in prison by the comrades involved'.[8]

This method was applied to the cases of, among others, J.
Smrkovský and M. Švermová, who were released on parole. One
may compare the case against I.M. Majskij in the Soviet Union
discussed below.[9]

Eventually, the trial against Slánský and others had to be re-
examined. On the grounds of a variety of accusations concerning
unlawful practices in the course of legal investigations and extorted
confessions, made especially by A. London and V. Hajdu, who
received life sentences at the Slánský trial, the police official B.
Doubek was taken into custody (July 1955). The whole system of
the political trials became clear to the committee through his statements: charges were unfounded, confessions were false, and trials
had been carried out according to a prearranged plan. No conspiracy against the state existed. The secret police were assigned to
construct a Czechoslovak equivalent to the Hungarian show trial
against L. Rajk. The Slánský case was put up for discussion in the
politburo, but, as in other cases, no instructions to revise the trial
were given. Several charges, such as the connections with the Field
brothers and Titoist espionage, had to be altered because both Tito
and the Fields had been rehabilitated. In order to justify the conviction of Slánský, a new charge was levelled. Slánský was now
claimed to be the 'Czechoslovak Berija'. He himself had put the
mechanism of the political trials into operation. Even while he was
in prison he managed 'to guide the investigations into his own case
in a direction which made many innocent people suffer'.[10]

In contrast to these views, the politburo nonetheless decided to
release two of the three people who had received life sentences in

the Slánský trial. London was released in the beginning of February 1956, Hajdu in the course of that same year.[11]

After the twentieth party congress of the communist party of the Soviet Union, the approach to the Slánský trial seemed to be changing in some respects. After consultation with Moscow, the Czechoslovak politburo resolved to establish a second committee under Barák which was commissioned to investigate the trial against Slánský. This committee, however, followed the course previously taken.

In his report addressed to the party conference of the KSČ in June 1956, party leader Novotný concluded that there were no grounds for rehabilitating Slánský.[12] Novotný was quite content with this decision because he considered Slánský a Zionist. The anti-Semitic element in the purges, as well as the poor relations between the communist countries and Israel, continued to play a part in Novotný's attitude.[13]

The task of the committee then consisted primarily of the *justification of former sentences* by putting forward additional charges. This was by no means an easy task. A large number of reports by sub-committees had to be revised because they paid too much attention to the innocence of the accused with regard to the charges, whereas more evidence was demanded for new accusations. More than once, the Piller report concludes, a political body of the party took over the task of the courts of law, which was strictly illegal.

Barák completed his task on 2 October 1957 with a brief report to the Central Committee. In 6,678 cases the victims or their relatives had requested revision of the sentence, and the Barák committee had examined another 300. From the total number of 6,978 cases, 263 (3.77 per cent) were submitted for revision; the remaining sentences were considered to be lawful. In 50 cases of revision sentences proved to be unfounded, whereas punishment turned out to have been too extreme in the remaining 213 cases. In 6 — non-specified — cases, formal rehabilitation was followed by reinstatement in the party. Not one of this group of 6 was restored to former office.

Those who were dissatisfied with the outcome of the rehabilitations were informed by J. Harus, chairman of the Central Control Committee, that the party reserved the right to decide on reinstatement in the party independently of a formal rehabilitation. Novotný pronounced those formally rehabilitated persons who had set their minds on compensation or restoration of office to be enemies of the party. On 12 November 1957, the politburo considered the process of rehabilitation to have been completed and decided to file the documents as closed.[14]

After the alleged resolution of the rehabilitation issue in 1957, the politburo continued to receive letters from victims of the trials or their relatives. In this correspondence the principal issue was the (il)legality of the entire purge mechanism. Every year, dozens of similar letters arrived, and individual requests for rehabilitation were put on the agenda of the politburo.[15] Subordinates did not dare assume responsibility in these matters, as they involved formerly influential party members.

The hearing of these cases caused a great deal of vexation, dissension and loss of time, because the members of the politburo refrained from taking any fundamental decision. They were afraid that they might lose power if the purges were publicly investigated. The politburo consequently decided to revise several less significant trials in the sense that high treason and espionage were to be replaced by sabotage and abuse of power as grounds for convictions. Sentences of acquittal were issued only very rarely. In addition, incidental releases on parole continued to be granted, usually after serving half the term of imprisonment. In this way, a large number of prisoners were gradually released without any revision of sentence.[16]

Eventually, the politburo decided to decree an *amnesty*. On 9 May 1960 this amnesty was announced on the occasion of the anniversary of the day of liberation. It applied to political prisoners, and the majority of the 8,708 prisoners were released.[17] Those convicted in the show trials also benefited from the amnesty. As is the case after the granting of a pardon, however, the people involved were released *on parole*, which meant that their former conviction would revive if they were found guilty of a criminal offence for a probationary period of ten years (art. 1). Supplementary penalties, moreover, such as deprivation of civil and pension rights, were usually continued. The maintenance of these additional penalties caused those who were released on licence to be regarded as third-rate citizens; for this reason many petitions for exemption from supplementary punishment were filed. In February 1961 the politburo agreed to meet these petitions in order to avoid further trouble.[18] Yet even as late as in 1968, in the context of the amnesty which was then decreed, special regulations were required to lift the restrictions of 1960.

One would have assumed that, by virtue of the politburo's decision to repeal the supplementary penalties, the former political prisoners had become citizens with full rights. Yet former political and economic offenders were affected by pension legislation. In 1958, a bill was passed which covered the possibility of reducing payments for this category.[19] Those who had spent more than two years in prison for political or economic offences were sent to a committee for social welfare at the District Council which was authorised to grant full or partial pensions. When a pension had been revoked or reduced, the committee was capable of reinstating it if the person involved had exerted himself to compensate for his offence by working in the interest of society (para. 3).

We are therefore dealing here with a *probation* treatment. It is clear that these formulations could give rise to extremely capricious treatment of potential petitioners. Those who were released by decree of amnesty or pardon were not considered innocent, because the trial had not been revised and the issue of guilt had not been settled. Restrictive regulations were in force and a return to society was seriously impeded. Basically, those involved felt they were *social outcasts* and they had to be reinstated to their former social status.[20]

The twenty-second party congress in the Soviet Union and the serious attacks against Stalin and the terror led to a renewed approach to the Czechoslovak trials, although not at once. Novotný confirmed the position previously adopted and once again accused Slánský of being responsible for unlawful practices.[21] In spite of the fact that several members of the Central Committee as well as a number of Soviet executives (possibly Ju. V. Andropov) insisted on obtaining full information, no change of policy became apparent. The ball was nonetheless set rolling in 1962 when Barák, Minister of Internal Affairs and member of the politburo, fell from power. At the beginning of 1962, Barák made preparations to attack Novotný, for which he planned to use Novotný's position on the rehabilitation issue. For this purpose he had concealed some documents, but Novotný was too quick for him and had Barák arrested and accused. The politburo gave orders to press for a 15-year sentence, but wished to avoid a political trial against Barák for 'internal political' reasons.[22]

Now the road was clear for the further changes which were so eagerly desired. If previously the politburo had lacked the political courage to have the trials substantially revised, it had now created the opportunity because one from their midst was at hand to serve as a scapegoat.

The risk taken by the party in raising the issue of the political trials can be illustrated by the case of Novotný. During the preparation of the Slánský trial, part of the interrogation of Artur London focused upon Novotný's personal attitude in the concentration camp at Mauthausen. According to information provided by Artur London in his memoirs, Novotný had kept himself aloof from the resistance movement, which earned him a lot of criticism from his comrades. London was interrogated about this several days before the trial began. A large file of material was already at hand at that time.[23]

This document cropped up in the private files of Barák, Novotný's opponent, in 1961-2. At the interrogation conducted by the Piller committee in 1968, Barák claimed it had been presented to him by a chief of the Soviet security service in Berlin in order to be used in the struggle for power, which he said he had joined at the instigation of the Soviet generals.[24]

After Barák's fall, the politburo was informed about his files. He had concealed material concerning Slánský and other documents which he should have surrendered, including documents about the preparation of the trials and comments on the political positions of several members of the politburo in earlier times.[25] The file on Novotný was one of these. Apparently, Novotný had been held in reserve during the preparation of the trials. If necessary, a certain amount of 'incriminating' material could have been used. A revision, however, could bring all this up for discussion, which may explain part of Novotný's hostile attitude towards the rehabilitations. Not unexpectedly, Novotný took a great interest in the file, and when Barák was put under arrest and his documents were examined, the president and party leader attended in person. The file in question was never seen again.[26] It is conceivable that such cases were in the first instance deemed as much of a threat to the inner core of the party as the issue of co-responsibility. After all, all were in the same boat and no one knew what traps were still hidden in the trial documents.

Even so, it took another seven months after Barák's fall (late in January 1962) for a commission for rehabilitations to be appointed: on 4 September 1962, under the leadership of politburo member Kolder. The committee had to have their report ready before the end of November for the results to be used at the twelfth party congress of the KSČ. The long wait for the committee to be installed and this sudden haste are accounted for in the Piller report: it is assumed that the terror had to be publicly exposed as a reaction to Chinese criticisms of the policy of de-stalinisation.[27]

The first report by the Kolder committee was indeed completed before the twelfth party congress (December 1962). Novotný informed the representatives of the tasks of the committee but avoided committing himself by speaking in general terms. He announced that, by and large, judgements on the period of the personality cult, which had been given in November 1962, had proved to be correct.[28]

After the congress, the Kolder committee continued to work along the same line: the material had to be used to support Novotný's views. No minutes were taken of the meetings of the committee.[29] The most important question which had to be solved was the issue of responsibility for the terror: which of the members of the politburo who had been in power at the time could be held responsible? Novotný did not share the views of the committee, which were reported to him before the twelfth party congress. He wanted to shift responsibility on to the former Minister of Justice, Čepička, who had fallen from power in 1956. In addition, he maintained that Slánský was guilty.

Despite the political restrictions which the Kolder committee had to cope with, some very important and substantial progress was made. The party leaders could no longer disclaim the fact that the trials had been unlawful and that punishment had to be remitted, and consequently that formal rehabilitation of the victims could not be circumvented. The issue of responsibility had been strongly emphasised and the consequences were inevitable.

The final report of the Kolder committee was presented at the plenary meeting of the Central Committee of the KSČ in April 1963.[30] The members of the Central Committee were allowed to glance through the text, but Novotný discouraged undesirable contributions to the discussion. The meeting passed a resolution releasing the victims of the political trials; in some cases a charge was submitted, such as abuse of power, which was not followed by a trial if the person involved had died or had received amnesty. The Supreme Court took care of further juridical treatment, an account of which was issued in August 1963.[31] The plenary meeting in April also arrived at several decisions with regard to party penalties which had been imposed on those who were now rehabilitated. With six others, Slánský remained expelled from the party. Reinstated in the party were Švermová, Smrkovský, Löbl, Novomeský, Clementis, Margolius and others. The party penalties of exclusion from the Central Committee and dismissal from office were maintained.

Lastly, the plenary April meeting agreed that the charge of bourgeois nationalism was *not* to be withdrawn for a number of rehabilitated persons. The Slovak party sections objected to this last resolution (the accusation of 'bourgeois nationalism' applied to the Slovaks). Owing to these objections, the party instituted a committee to examine the case in further detail. This resulted in the withdrawal of the charge in December 1963.[32]

Between the plenary meeting in April 1963 and 1968, 427 victims of the terror were reinstated in the party.[33] The restrictions which were established in 1963 were still binding. It was not until the Piller committee advanced its draft resolution that the decision of 1963 was replaced and full rehabilitation in the party for Slánský and others was given consideration.[34]

The Piller committee repeatedly underlined the important aspect of the correlation between the rehabilitation policy and foreign policy. Improved relations between Czechoslovakia and Yugoslavia in 1955-6 affected the process of rehabilitation in a constructive sense, since the charge of 'Titoism' was no longer valid and had to be dropped. When relations cooled in 1958 in reaction to the supposedly revisionist new party programme of the Yugoslavs, increasing vigilance was once again promoted. Possible reforms were consequently frozen.

The issue of the revision of trials against former social democrats depended upon the policy towards foreign socialists. Revision of these trials was set in motion during the period of détente between the KSČ and western social democrats, but the accusation of espionage re-emerged when this course was discontinued a year later.

The Polish revolt in Poznán (June 1956) and the Hungarian revolt in November 1956 led to a campaign for increasing vigilance and attacks against liberalism. On 19 November 1956, the politburo decided in this context to postpone conditional release of political prisoners and revision of political trials.[35]

The Piller report also indicates the concentration of *personal power.* Due to his tenure of leading positions between 1951 and 1968, Novotný had a special responsibility. He controlled all information and had the power to use it: he blocked several rehabilitations because he had had personal disputes with the people involved.

Finally, ideological rigidity, which was the result of the demand for absolute unity within the party, certainly acted as a brake on the rehabilitations.[36]

Czechoslovak Legislation on Rehabilitations in 1968

During the Prague Spring the issue of the rehabilitations was dealt with quite fundamentally.[37] First, an unconditional *amnesty* was decreed on 9 May 1968.[38] This applied to, among others, all crimes against the state committed before 1960 (art. 3) and involved 25 people. Probationary release on the grounds of earlier amnesty or pardon was abolished (art. 8); 37 people benefited from this arrangement. The previously mentioned deficiencies of these regulations had now been undone.

Of even greater importance was the extension of legislation. On 25 June 1968 a *bill of juridical rehabilitations* was passed, which was operative from 1 August and was to remain formally valid until the fundamental revision in the middle of 1970.[39] Since this is the only law on rehabilitation in postwar Eastern Europe, its contents merit some discussion.

The preamble and first article of the law specify its aim as the 'restoration of socialist legality' and 'the annulment of unlawful sentences'. It could not be allowed to serve real enemies of socialism, who had been justly convicted. The socialist legal order as established after 1958 was not to be endangered. Thus, the legislators proved themselves conscious of the inherent risks of a legal settlement of the rehabilitations, that is, rehabilitation of the wrong people and undermining of the existing criminal laws by the new legal standards.

The revision of trials applied to three categories: sentences by the Supreme Court between 1 August 1953 and 31 December 1956; sentences by the former State Court between 24 October 1948 and 31 December 1952; sentences by district courts or higher military courts between 1 January 1953 and 31 July 1965.

Cases of revision came up for hearing in *special senates*, in the first instance of district courts or higher military courts and secondly before the Supreme Court, consisting of three and five members respectively (arts. 3 and 4).

It was possible to instigate the procedure of revision on a large scale. Article 5 of the rehabilitation law granted the right to request revision of a sentence to the person convicted, his wife or first-degree-relatives, or their solicitor.[40] Since the legislative body wished to settle the affair as quickly as possible, it decided upon a period of one year for submitting requests: requests for revision were possible until 1 August 1969 (art. 6).

A special role in the guidance of the process of rehabilitation was allotted to the Union of Fighters against Fascism. As social counsellors, representatives of this organisation were entitled to attend the revisions, including the preliminary investigations. In each district, a section was ready at hand to provide this assistance (art. 11).

A legal sentence could be revised if it involved a conviction for criminal action against the state. For the period 1948-57, however, the accusation had to be politically motivated. Excluded from revision were crimes against socialist property, abuse of power, or disciplinary offences. The special senate verified the legal procedures using the criterion of violation of the law (art. 15) then in force. It could decide upon rehabilitation in the following cases: (a) incorrect assessment, particularly in case of artificially constructed charges and false evidence; (b) violation of regulations of procedure, particularly in relation to the extortion of confessions; (c) police provocation; (d) qualification of the action as a punishable act in violation of the penal code; (e) stricter qualification of the action than ensues from the law; (f) evident contradiction between punishment and its legal purpose, and disproportionately severe punishment in view of the public danger caused by the offence committed.

Revision of a sentence also had to be carried through if the person involved had died in the meantime. In such a case the entire juridical procedure had to be continued (art. 17). It was possible to appeal to the Supreme Court against the new sentence by the court (art. 19).

Compensation for the victims was settled in articles 26-33, and included compensation for loss of income (to a maximum of 20,000 Czechoslovak korunas (Kčs) per annum), for confiscated property, for damage to health, for costs of trial and legal assistance and for imposed fines. Non-convicted victims of unlawfully conducted preliminary investigations could also claim damages.

Amounts of up to 20,000 Kčs were paid in cash and, in case of higher payment, 20 per cent in cash and the rest in government bonds which ran for a period of ten years. Where the person involved had died, payment was issued to the widow or first-degree relatives.

Full compensation was given only if the person involved was absolved from all blame. In assessing pensions, terms of imprisonment which were the result of unlawful penalisation were included as terms of service.

Supplementary legislation was in preparation, but discussions ceased after the invasion. It covered practical issues such as the guarantee of a position which in terms of quality was equivalent to the position of the person involved before the purge, etc.[41]

Within three months after the law had been passed, it began to be carried out. On 17 September 94 judges were appointed in the rehabilitation senates. Announcements of rehabilitations appeared in the press.[42] Since then quantitative data about the results have been sporadically released.

On 13 December 1968, 9,000 requests had been filed,[43] on 1 July 1969 the total number was 17,832 (14,142 in the Czechoslovak federal republic and 3,690 in Slovakia)[44] and on 1 September, at the end of the (prolonged)[45] term of submission, at least 19,049,[46] possibly 23,306.[47] The computation of several correlations will be based on the lowest total. This yields a deceptive precision, for in reality this gives only a rough idea. At least 3,148 sympathetic settlements were decreed, 16.5 per cent of the number of requests.[48] This low percentage should not be attributed to an expected large number of refusals but to the slow workings of the senates. In the Czechoslovak federal republic, 1,419 of the 1,629 requests which were put forward for consideration were judged sympathetically, i.e. 87 per cent.

A faster pace was achieved in Slovakia; here 1,729 requests were granted out of a total of 3,690, i.e. 47 per cent. It is not possible on the basis of these figures to give credit to the Slovak party secretary Húsak for sympathy towards the rehabilitations, but his organisation was definitely in good order.[49]

Of the estimated number of 80,000 victims in the period 1948-65 it follows from the data that at least 3.75 per cent were rehabilitated, whereas approximately a quarter submitted a request for rehabilitation.[50] This last phenomenon was already hinted at by the Minister of Justice in April 1969. He suggested a number of explanations for the lack of large-scale interest in rehabilitation: scepticism about rehabilitation, the desire not to be reminded of the past, and a lingering sense of guilt.[51]

To cover the expenses for compensation of the victims or their relatives, the government decided to issue government bonds for a total amount of 1,800 million Kčs, a decision which was put into effect towards the end of December 1969.[52]

Further data, which, for example, could be used to estimate the average sums for compensation, are lacking. According to government decree, each person could be paid in cash to a maximum of 200,000 Kčs and the rest in bonds.[53] Prominent victims were eligible in any case. Husák received a quarter of a million Kčs. J. Slánská, widow of Slánský, demanded 1 million Kčs and received half that amount.[54]

No data are available on the period after 1970, but the process of rehabilitation was probably stopped before the end of 1969. As early as June the party press began to report once again that the revisions of the trials confirmed the guilt of those convicted and that only the penalties themselves turned out to have been too extreme.[55] Within the framework of 'normalisation', the expulsion of leaders of the Prague Spring was started in September 1969. Prosecutions against executives who had been called to account for their share in the purges in the fifties were dropped. At the end of November 1969 the chairman of the Central Control Board, V. Hájek, proclaimed that the rehabilitations had been discontinued.[56] On 31 March 1970, the committees for rehabilitation inside the social organisations of the national front, e.g. the Union of Fighters against Fascism, were dissolved.[57]

In the middle of 1970, finally, the law of juridical rehabilitations was 'normalised': a drastic revision was effected on 8 July.[58] Its contents may be characterised as a restriction on rehabilitation. Arbitrariness had been restored. The courts of law could refuse a request for revision of a sentence if the person involved was believed to have actually committed a punishable act; testimonies about the circumstances of the earlier course of legal proceedings were once again labelled as secret and were subjected to strict discretion; the rehabilitation senates were abolished; doors were opened to *dehabilitation*, that is to say, revocation of a rehabilitation.

Czechoslovak legislation on juridical rehabilitation was nothing more than an interlude. Ultimately, its outcome was fairly insignificant. Even so, the importance of this law should not be under-estimated. It has demonstrated what may happen if a ruling communist party takes the full consequences of destalinisation and attempts to overcome the past, and it provides a standard for measuring other parties' activities.

The Czechoslovak legislation was also important in that it estab-lished the right to demand revision of a sentence which was either passed on political grounds or effected after serious violation of legal procedure. In any case all (former) prisoners were given the opportunity to be rehabilitated, regardless of earlier charges.

Even compensation rights were confirmed, although compensa-tion money could not atone for personal grief. Possible arbitrari-ness in the revision of legal cases appeared to have been limited by the institution of the special senates at the law courts, whereas the public prosecutors were consciously allotted a minor role, really no more than a channel of communication.

Formally, no role whatsoever was assigned to the party bodies, even though the Union for Fighters against Fascism may be regarded as a substitute for the party. The party, of course, ulti-mately decided in what manner the laws were enforced. During the Prague Spring, however, the development towards a genuine con-stitutional state was well advanced. The draft resolution of the Central Committee, which was intended to complete the rehabili-tations, suggested that the lesson that was taught by the political trials and revisions was that 'the insistence on the independence of the judges and investigating judges was fully justifiable'.[59]

Conclusion

It is evident that the politburo directed the course of rehabilitation down to the smallest detail. The inner core of the party felt a powerful aversion to bringing up the purges at private meetings, let alone in public. Willingness to take decisions was limited. Only small steps were possible: silent release, conditional amnesty, adaptation of charges and limitation to formal rehabilitations. A considerable number of executives had themselves played an active part in the purges and were still in high office. Party leader and president A. Novotný may be regarded as the exponent of this group of ossified apparatchiks. The structure of stalinist society, moreover, had not changed in any fundamental sense. The party assumed the position of judge and exercised control over the legal authorities through the secret police. The Supreme Court and the prosecutor-general merely carried out orders from above.

The struggle for personal power, too, played an influential part. Rehabilitations formed a formidable weapon against party leaders who had been co-responsible for the terror: the personal battle between Novotný and Barák serves as an illustration here. The fight took place behind the scenes because publicity would be of no benefit to either of them. A show trial against Barák, the losing party, therefore never materialised. He was convicted, however, and used to serve as a scapegoat for violations of the law. Even so, Barák's conviction does not rule out the guilt of the triumphant Novotný — far from it.

The political line of action and the ideology of the party proved to be restraining factors in the process of rehabilitation. Rehabilitation was discontinued if the views of those convicted did not coincide with current party policies during the rehabilitation process. Charges which had led to conviction appeared to be particularly important with respect to the so-called 'bourgeois nationalists'. Rehabilitation of this category was delayed for a long time.

Relations between the party and the people were significant, because party leaders were apprehensive about possible repercussions of publicity about the terror which might endanger the position of the party within society. The course of events in Poland and Hungary confirmed this anxiety and party leaders decided to end the rehabilitation process. Still, the politburo was sensitive to public requests for rehabilitation if they came from relatives of prominent victims. Their requests were never examined by lower executives but were transferred to the politburo. Such cases were felt to put a burden on the agenda of meetings, but the party leaders gave in to pressure.

Developments abroad had a powerful effect on the process of rehabilitation. As other Eastern European countries had made a start with rehabilitation, Czechoslovakia could not but follow suit. The Hungarian revolt caused an immediate reaction in Prague, where the rehabilitation committee suspended its diffident activities. The progress of relations with Yugoslavia expressed itself in the policy of rehabilitation of the KSČ. The wave of public rehabilitations inside the Soviet Union after 1961, which the Piller committee related to the attack on the Chinese party, resulted in a revival of the rehabilitations. The genuinely full rehabilitations which had begun during the Prague Spring were not immediately cut off by the invasion in August 1968. Even in the Soviet Union this did not give rise to any suspicion. During talks with Czechoslovak leaders in the Kremlin after the invasion, Podgornyj assured them that rehabilitation could be continued within certain limits. He declared that the Czechoslovaks should attempt to attain the Soviet level of rehabilitations.[60] The subsequent 'normalisation', however, interfered with the process of rehabilitation. On the one hand, this was the result of a change in Soviet policy in favour of a moderate sort of restalinisation, and, on the other hand, of the strict regime of party leader Dubček's successor, Husák. The importance of the foreign political factor as an explanation for the rehabilitation process in Czechoslovakia, then, is considerable with respect to the period in which Novotný and Husák were in power. Developments in 1968 were clearly not influenced by foreign countries.

The Prague Spring proved that, although the party could arrive at an entirely different policy in principle, restrictions continued to exist in this case. The Piller report does not create adequate insight into the quantitative data on the victims and fails to distinguish between individual members of the party in the rehabilitations. The report does not include those who were not prosecuted through litigation. Rehabilitation policy concentrated on the group of victims in general and remained strictly juridical. The slow progress of revision of the trials quite logically led to a relatively small number of rehabilitations. A political decision on a generous rehabilitation of the victims was carefully avoided because it was not possible in terms of jurisdiction and because only a purely juridical examination of earlier legal proceedings could exempt the state from the risk of rehabilitating genuine criminals. The magnanimous gesture failed to materialise.

The Soviet Union: Formal Rehabilitations

Amnesty and Release

The political prisoners who had been convicted under Stalin's terror were not released until after the death of the dictator, although they had continually hoped for a decree of amnesty on some occasion or other. Speculation included the Day of the Victory, the Anniversary of the Revolution, or a session of the Supreme Soviet. 'The whisper of an amnesty sounds like the trumpets of archangels,' Solženicyn allows his political exile Kostoglotov to reflect.[61] Apparently the prisoners in the Gulag archipelago had not yet lost all hope and expected a spontaneous end to the terror.

At the tenth commemoration of the revolution in 1927, a limited amnesty was decreed, and the defeat of the Germans in 1945 was celebrated likewise.[62] And there had been some minor 'counter-currents' in the channels of the Gulag archipelago. In 1939, a small number of political prisoners were released from camps to serve in the army. In 1947, a number of prisoners had served the then customary sentence of ten years and were released, to be once again arrested or exiled sooner or later: *povtorniki,* those who are called up for reinternment.[63]

After Stalin's death an amnesty was decreed fairly promptly, on 27 March 1953, which extended beyond any earlier decrees.[64] This decree allowed not only amnesty but also established the necessity of reforming the penal code (art. 8). Even if this clearly indicated that the judicial machinery was to adopt a different course of action in the future, the range of the amnesty was limited.[65] The category of political prisoners was strictly excluded in accordance with article 7, which declared the decree to be non-applicable to those who had been convicted for counter-revolutionary activities. The preamble makes it clear that the so-called 'enemies of the people' are excluded as well, because these cases involve criminal activities which offer a substantial threat to the state. The amnesty was designed for ordinary criminals, who were released from prison or whose sentences were reduced by half. In the suggestive words of Solženicyn, the 'criminal scum' were released.[66]

It was not until the following year that an amnesty was decreed which applied to criminal and political prisoners. The restriction now was that the conviction had to have been imposed before the person involved had reached the age of 18 and that he had to have served a third of his sentence. By virtue of this decree, conditional remission of punishment was also possible.[67] In practice this led to, among other things, the release of the category of 'children of the enemies of the people', who had been taken into custody if they were twelve or over. One of the daughters of the famous Marshal Bljucher, for instance, benefited from this amnesty.[68]

Other groups of political prisoners who were released had ended up in the camps of Gulag during the Second World War.

On 17 September 1955, the Supreme Soviet granted an amnesty to the collaborators of the war: those who had been sentenced to ten years' imprisonment for helping the enemy or who had been punished for joining the German forces. A year later this amnesty was extended to soldiers who had surrendered to the Germans.[69]

In 1956 a number of national communities who had been deported during the war were rehabilitated: the Kabardino-Balkars, Chechen-Ingushi, Kalmyks, Karachai and Meskhi. From the following year, the remaining members of these communities were allowed to return to their original places of residence, a process which was continued in the years 1957-60.[70] The Meskhi, however, were not permitted to return.[71] The Volga Germans (1964) and the Crimean Tartars (1967) were not to be rehabilitated until much later, without obtaining permission to return.[72] This also holds for the deported Muslims from Georgia, who were rehabilitated in 1968.[73]

Estonians, Latvians and Lithuanians had been deported during the war in large numbers, but not as entire communities. They too were released in the first months of 1956.[74] It may be added that in 1954, 1955 and 1956 thousands of German, Austrian and Japanese prisoners of war as well as many Poles were sent home from the camps.[75] Prisoners from the Ukrainian and other liberation movements were not discharged.

From the above it will be clear that political prisoners received amnesty only to a limited extent. Most of those who profited from this had been convicted or deported during the war on account of their alleged or real collaboration with the Germans. Apparently, to grant these prisoners amnesty was not considered very dangerous to the state.

The party, though, was apprehensive of a decree of general amnesty which would also apply to a large group of prisoners who, before or after the war, had been convicted for internal political motives. A public resolution on the collective release of this group would imply that such notions as 'counter-revolutionary activities' and 'enemy of the people' were no longer useful. The party would thus thwart its own handling of its opponents, who were deemed always to be present. For this group, decrees of individual pardon were more appropriate.

Apart from the releases, which constituted a vital condition for the people involved, the importance of a decree of amnesty was fairly small. Juridically, amnesty provided no absolute security for the future, since it implied nothing more than a remission of punishment and a restoration of civil rights of the people involved ('snjat' sudimost' i vosstanovit' v pravach').[76] In this way, the potential innocence of a released person was not recognised by law. This implied that those who were released were lumbered with all the charges on which the earlier sentences were based. From a legal point of view, those who had received an amnesty remained as suspect as before.[77] In practice, prisoners released by amnesty were not always entirely free in their doings either. Many of them are known to have spent their lives in exile after release, since they were not allowed to return to their homes.[78] In such cases, the authorities employed an administrative measure: a number of places could be excluded as living areas on the basis of the decree on internal passports. In the jargon, this was referred to by the people involved as a 'minus'. About 1956, such restrictions were probably abrogated.[79]

In *samizdat*, several cases have been registered which clearly indicate the limited long-term meaning of the amnesty. A certain B.M. Samcharadze, pensioned as an invalid of the first category in 1946, was imprisoned in 1950 on a charge of 'treason'. He had, after all, spent the war in France! The fact that Samcharadze did not change sides there is indicated by impeccable testimonials from the French resistance. By virtue of the amnesty of September 1955 he was again released, and, one year later, once more received his pension regularly. Nevertheless, Samcharadze filed a petition for revision with the Military Collegium of the Supreme Court, which decided upon a rejection of the request in 1960.

Later on, Samcharadze became an active member of a group which dedicated itself to the issue of human rights, which, in view of his life story, is not entirely without logic. As a result, he was deprived of his pension in 1974. He was informed by the secret police, the KGB, that there were documents which indicated high treason on his part. It appears from this case that the charge of 1950 was not annulled by the amnesty and was preserved in police records. This old charge was used against Samcharadze as soon as he was felt to be a nuisance.[80]

Ukrainian dissident circles provide another example. It is a well-known fact that large numbers of Ukrainians were not released from the camps in the fifties. This also holds for Svjatoslav Josypovič Karavans'kyj, a writer who was sentenced to 25 years' imprisonment in 1954 on the charge of 'collaboration with fascists', because he had been active in occupied territory. As usual, this was enough to get him arrested, even if his activity had been directed against the enemy. In 1960 Karavans'kyj was released on account of the amnesty of 1955. Later he devoted himself to the struggle against russification in the Ukraine and wrote memoranda on this critical issue which he presented to the consuls of Poland and Czechoslovakia; this resulted in his arrest (1965). The amnesty was annulled and Karavans'kyj was forced to serve the original sentence.[81]

Amnesty for a former political prisoner could consequently be interpreted only as a *conditional* release. Unless he behaved himself, he was not left in peace. Punishment could be re-established at the subjective discretion of the authorities. Since release did not automatically entail a free choice of residence and released prisoners were not socially accepted without question, the effect of amnesty was limited for the people involved. Beyond any doubt, the group of former political prisoners continued to be suspected by the regime. This, however, not only holds for the — again, limited — group which received amnesty, but also for those who were released, individually.

Individual Formal Rehabilitation

Unlike amnesty or individual pardon, which do not determine the question of guilt, genuine rehabilitation is possible only if the original sentence is repealed. Legal procedures concerning rehabilitation of political delinquents are no different from those concerning criminal cases, since there are no specific laws or articles of law for political cases in the legislation.

One important category of victims poses a problem. Most people had been convicted on the basis of decisions taken by Special Senates at the Ministry of Internal Affairs ('Osoboe soveščanie pri NKVD'). These senates were instituted on 10 July 1934 and, according to the measures set out on 15 November 1934, were assigned to impose punishment on 'socially dangerous persons' without involving the courts of law.[82] Decisions were taken in the absence of the suspects, and there could be no appeal. In other words, there were neither legally valid procedures nor appropriate sentences. When these Special Senates were abolished on 1 September 1953, the Supreme Court and lower courts of law were instructed to check their activities. The cases of those who had been unlawfully punished had to be revised and the people involved rehabilitated.[83] It is not clear whether a juridical revision could be applied to cases which had been handled outside litigation. The fact that, in principle, this could indeed be the case is illustrated by the case study of Solženicyn, which will be discussed later.

In terms of procedure, revision of a sentence could be accomplished either on the grounds of the so-called protest right, or by means of a revision which involved a re-opening of the case as new evidence presented itself.[84] The first implied a re-opening of the case by *protesting* to the prosecutor-general of the Soviet Union or the President of the Supreme Court, or to the same functionaries on federal level. In 1954 and 1955, competence to issue a protest was extended and decentralised. The procedure exists within the framework of supervision (*nadzor*) by the *prokuratura* and the higher courts of law over the lower courts, and consisted of checking legal sentences in terms of legality and accuracy.[85] According to article 413 of the criminal procedure code of the RSFSR, possible grounds for annulment of an already operative sentence in the procedure of supervision were: inadequate or unlawful conduct of the preliminary investigations; violation of essential procedural regulations; violation or unjust enforcement of the law; evident inaccuracy of the sentence.[86] The decision to file a protest lay with the Public Prosecutor or the chairman of the higher courts.

The prisoner or his representative could file a complaint which could result in a protest by a duly authorised official body, but he had no rights in this matter.[87]

The second possibility of sentence annulment was offered by a revision of the case on the grounds of new evidence.[88] This could happen in cases of falsification of evidence, abuse on the part of the court of law, and circumstances which established the innocence of the person involved. In the event of the death of the prisoner, there was an explicit opportunity for passing on to a revision of the sentence.

A petition for rehabilitation could be filed by relatives or acquaintances of the deceased. It was common practice to bring such social organisations as unions and the party into play. Since citizens could not assert any right on the revision of trials, this method produced more results by virtue of the authority of such organisations. However, since the legal authorities do not of their own accord trace any cases of injustice, we are confronted here with a substantial element of arbitrariness. Chance may determine whether there is someone who remembers a missing person and sets off the mechanism of revision.

The communist party, too, interfered with the petitions, even though this was not formally recorded. If a petition for revision was approved of by the party, it was passed on through the *prokuratura* to the Military Collegium of the Supreme Court, because sentences by military tribunals were usually involved.[89]

After annulment of the sentence, the legal case could be completed on the grounds of the absence of a punishable act in the actions which were attributed to the accused and the defectiveness of evidence with respect to the conveyance of the charge to the court of law.[90] The document (*spravka*) which was given to the rehabilitated person or his relatives in evidence of revision contained several concise formulations which indicated the annulment of the sentence (*privogor otmenen*) and the completion of the case (*delo prekraščeno*) on account of the unproven nature of the charge (*nedokazannost' obvinenija*), the lack of evidence (*nedostatočnost' ulik/dokazatel'stv*), or the absence of a punishable act (*otsutstvie sostava prestuplenija*).[91]

From these 'pieces of evidence' of rehabilitation, one may infer that a distinction can be made between those who were regarded as innocent because their actions, which had led to conviction at the time, were not punishable, and those whose guilt could not be established.

In Soviet juridical literature, the theme of rehabilitation has not been adequately elucidated. Before 1964, only a single article came to light which was specifically concerned with this issue, so that for this period of juridical work of reference gives us the best insight.[92] Since 1964, however, a number of journal articles have been published in which several aspects of rehabilitation are discussed. For the present study, this discussion is somewhat academic in that we are dealing here with rehabilitation in cases which are still under consideration and in which no sentences have as yet been passed. Even so, the contents of the discussion are sufficiently interesting.

Apart from the fact that the literature sheds light upon the types of grounds which can be indicated for rehabilitation and describes details concerning legal interpretation which are irrelevant in the context of our investigations, there is one single item which is too striking to be ignored. For our purposes, the following question is essential: what is the meaning of the completion of a case on the aforementioned grounds? The answer provided by juridical experts is that the meaning can be taken only as a full restoration of rights of the person involved. There is no consensus, however, on the question of whether it is appropriate and desirable to use the motive 'on account of lack of evidence' for the completion of a case in cases of rehabilitation. This creates the impression that the innocence of the person involved is not incontestable. V.M. Savickij, in particular, pleaded in 1957 and in 1965 for consolidation of a rehabilitation where possible, on the basis of an article which mentions the absence of a punishable act in the actions of the accused.[93]

Since the argument also re-emerges in the literature later, it is clear that this *modus operandi* has not been accepted. The authoritative commentaries on the criminal procedure code, supplied by V.A. Boldyrev in 1963, have no difficulties whatsoever with the formulation objected to.[94]

By and large, the juridical aspects of the issue of rehabilitation appear to have inspired only a few discussions. In particular, the lack of case-studies in literature and jurisprudence indicate that hardly any general rules were interpreted in an accurate manner. The claim that a rehabilitation is complete as soon as there is proof of 'lack of evidence' in the case shows that the theoretical elaboration of the law is limited.

The release of political prisoners who stayed in camp or in prison in the Soviet Union was settled in the first instance by temporary special committees. We know that such committees functioned from June 1953.[95]

After the twentieth party congress, however, a hundred travelling committees were set up by Khrushchev himself. These were composed of representatives of the State Prosecutor's Office and the Central Committee of the party. In camps, prisons and places of exile these committees examined qualified cases and talked to the prisoners involved. On the basis of this inquiry an immediate decision was taken in the name of the Supreme Soviet on release, pardon or mitigation of punishment.

In complicated cases the person involved was simply released and advised to make a plea for rehabilitation himself.[96] This course could also be pursued by those who had left the camps but had as yet been forced to remain in exile or in 'permanent residence', a form of administrative punishment. According to Medvedev, some twenty special committees for exiles were functioning.[97]

There is no certainty as to the number of people who were released, and the time this took place, although 1956 is frequently mentioned as the year of mass rehabilitations and the memoirs are unanimous in this respect. Official party statements, however, point out different years. In his 'secret speech', Khrushchev mentioned 1954 as the year in which the camps rapidly emptied.[98] Official party histories mention 1954-5.[99] Nevertheless, one also comes across the official view that the process of rehabilitation was effected exclusively by the twentieth party congress.[100] This divergence of observations is probably occasioned by the priority of party members in the process of rehabilitation and the recognition of this fact as decisive for the entire process, or by ignorance of this phenomenon.

The intensity of releases dwindled rapidly after 1956. The process was continued in 1957, but after that hardly any cases are mentioned. At best, the work on posthumous revisions lasted until the beginning of the sixties, and only a few incidental cases have been reported afterwards.[101]

The data concerning numbers of rehabilitations have been specified only by Medvedev. Except for his biography of Khrushchev, in which the data are adjusted and more gradations are given, Medvedev uses the concept of 'rehabilitation' in the sense of revision of the trial which led to conviction.

According to Medvedev, who believes that a number of 12-13 million people had ended up in camps, 4,000 people were released in 1953, 12,000 in 1954-5, and 7-8 million in 1956-7. In addition, 5-6 million people were posthumously rehabilitated. Medvedev's most recent estimation comes down to a total number of 20 million rehabilitated persons.[102] This would mean that all victims had been rehabilitated.

This method of rehabilitation cannot but have been extremely superficial. Simple arithmetic at once reveals that the pace of working must have been tremendous. Assuming that one hundred committees rehabilitated 3 million political prisoners in six months (156 working days), each committee would have had to settle 192 cases every day. No matter how one juggles alternative figures, the proportion between the number of committees and the number of cases is such that we can only speak of instant execution of justice, not serious juridical examination.

Moreover, priority was given to former members of the party and to relatives of non-surviving party members. Socialist revolutionaries, Mensheviks and anarchists were released, Medvedev argues, but not rehabilitated.[103]

In view of the veil of inconsistencies and discrepancies in the policy of rehabilitation, it is quite inconceivable that the numbers given by Medvedev are accurate. This unreliability is indicated by a comparison with the figures on rehabilitation in the party (see below), which show that a small percentage of victims was rehabilitated. One may also have some serious doubts about Medvedev's 'millions' of releases in 1956, compared to Sakharov's 'hundreds of thousands'.[104]

Medvedev's extremely high figures can be accounted for by his approach: if we take into consideration that, in accordance with the official party histories, he suggests that all party members have been rehabilitated whereas other data deny this, it can be argued that Medvedev began working on the basis of an assumption, and not facts.[105] Furthermore, he equates rehabilitation with release.

As neither Medvedev's nor Sakharov's data are supplemented with more specific argument and therefore cannot be verified, we will have to look for methods of calculation. It is certain that rehabilitation was concomitant with restoration of rights, including voting rights. In principle, the electorate must have increased enormously after 1956-7, as millions of people are involved. It follows that for the election of the Supreme Soviet in 1958 a considerable increase in the electorate should be noticeable, or at any rate significantly greater than could be expected on the basis of the demographic increase of the part of the population that was entitled to vote (over 18). In Appendix A, a computation is made to measure this expected increase. Although the calculation is far from perfect because of lack of accurate data and may contain serious error, its result is interesting. Awaiting greater precision, the computation indicates that approximately *2 million* people entitled to vote were registered in excess of what could be expected on the basis of the demographic increase of the population. This means that rights had been restored to approximately 2 million people. In short, we are dealing here with a considerable number of people in the category of restoration of rights, but not nearly as many as is suggested by Medvedev. We could find no way to compute a convincing method to estimate data on the number of releases without restoration of rights.

Social Rehabilitation

From a social point of view, the rehabilitation of the victims of Stalin presents one of the most pressing and, at the same time, least accessible issues in the history of Soviet society. Not all material measures can be traced.[106] Nevertheless, the rights of the rehabilitated or their relatives can be examined in direct relation to the pronouncement of rehabilitation.

From the Soviet legislation it appears that these rights are encompassed in various regulations. A resolution dated 4 October 1956 could be traced, referring to the 'term of service of citizens whose punishments were mitigated after a procedure of legal supervision'.[107] Surplus terms of punishment were considered as *official terms of service*. The practical significance of this resolution expressed itself in the principle of calculation of the wages and pensions which were to be paid. It was stipulated with great emphasis that payment of lost wages or pensions for the term of unjustly imposed punishment was out of the question. Financial compensation for the infliction of grief was not mentioned at all. According to the memoirs of Šul′man, this did not prevent one or two 'eccentrics' from handing in official accounts, in which they even demanded compensation for lost professional careers.[108]

However, it is not true that the state provided no compensation whatsoever for a rehabilitated person. There was a regulation which in effect caused a sum of money, equivalent to two months' wages on the basis of the most recent position, to be paid to the person involved, or, in case of posthumous rehabilitation, to the latter's family.[109] Jurisprudence mentions a few cases of revision of a legal case which referred to this payment. From these it follows that, in the event of posthumous rehabilitation, the sum was paid to those who were part of the family of the person involved at the time of arrest.[110] The memoirs, too, mention the existence and practice of the regulation.[111]

In addition, a rehabilitated person was given priority in obtaining accommodation. Little is known about this. One single reminiscence describes the chicaneries of the authorities in such a case.[112] This source also informs us of the possible existence of a regulation for restoration to former office. Although this had been confirmed to the person involved, he had never been restored to his former office.[113] There is little more information concerning restoration to former privileges, to wit the right to use a *dača* under co-operative supervision. The Supreme Court rejected such demands and, in the aforementioned case, pronounced the co-operative itself entitled to take decisions.[114] The outcome of these issues is unknown.

It appears from various memoirs that it was not uncommon for a former political prisoner to be burdened with administrative expulsion after his release, a so-called 'minus'. In such a case, the person involved was denied access to a number of cities. This punishment was presumably abolished in the years 1956-7.[115]

The integration of former inhabitants of the Gulag archipelago into Soviet social life, or, in cases of posthumous rehabilitations, of their relatives, has been described by the Medvedevs as a full accommodation of these victims. Surviving relatives were permitted to return to their places of residence and were given priority in finding accommodation, widows of deceased victims received special pensions; rehabilitated workers were entitled to employment in compliance with their former positions; soldiers who had died in camp were honoured in a similar way to those who had perished at the front, with their widows receiving compensation and special pensions, according to a command of Marshal Žukov.[116] These authors seem to have no knowledge of the regulation concerning payment of two months' wages, no more than of the previously mentioned pension regulation. As no other sources are indicated and the 'privileges' of the rehabilitated are not accounted for by relevant laws or resolutions (except for the military cases), it can be deduced that the data provided by the Medvedevs are deficient.

The image they create does fit in with the sympathetic image of Khrushchev and therefore seems to be too rosy. This does not alter the fact that those who returned from the camps had to be assisted in finding accommodation and employment, since these were conditions upon which their social security depended. For this, people could probably only appeal to the civil authorities or the company they worked for before the purge. The material is too deficient to justify any conclusion on the way in which reintegration into social life was realised.

Information concerning the problems of social rehabilitation is too scarce to offer a well-founded judgement. Supplementary investigation into emigrant circles may possibly produce some results, but may also give cause to distortion by virtue of the predominance of Jewish emigrants: it seems highly probable that having a Jewish nationality in the Soviet Union created additional difficulties regarding rehabilitation.

What cannot be discussed here at all is restoration to good name and reputation, which is supposed to be the fundamental goal of full rehabilitation.[117] Savickij, to whom we have referred before, points out a fundamental gap in the law on this matter.[118]

In juridical circles, however, the subject continues to attract attention. We can take as one example M.F. Poljakova's dissertation, which was prepared under Savickij's supervision. It describes the compensation for inflicting injustice, starting from the UN covenant on civil and political rights, which was ratified by the Soviet Union in 1973. This lawyer suggests that the right to compensation be settled through civil law.[119]

We have nonetheless a long way to go before such ideas can be realised, and the debate on aspects of rehabilitation has not had any visible effects for a long time. Consequently, it seems justifiable to take a pessimistic view of future changes.

Reinstatement in the Communist Party

Reinstatement in the party (*vosstanovlenie v partiju*) constituted a fundamental element of the rehabilitation of party members. Until then one was not considered to be fully rehabilitated (*polnost'ju reabilitirovan*).[120] After all, victims had been either expelled from the party before their conviction or execution or had lost their party membership on account of the conviction.

Restoration to the membership of the party was no new activity. As early as the twenties and thirties, it was not uncommon for people who had been expelled from the party as 'opposition' to be reinstated after bowing to the party. Sometimes, as in the cases of Kamenev and Zinov'ev, this happened more than once. In the case of the small counter-currents from the Gulag archipelago, too, rehabilitation in the party took place (see below).

A number of non-specified cases of rehabilitation in the party are mentioned in the literature. The wife of Molotov was the first to be released and reinstated in the party. The brother of Kaganovič, M.M. Kaganovič, was restored posthumously to party membership.[121] Khrushchev supplies the names of several army officers and Ukrainians: A.A. Novikov, A.I. Todorskij (who returned from camp in 1955), A.P. Dovženko, M.I. Potapov, I.N. Muzyčenko, P.G. Ponedelin, and relatives of Kosior, Kosarev and Korytnyj.[122] Also known is the group of medical doctors of the Kremlin hospital who were released in 1953, as were a number of

Georgians.[123] These rehabilitations are ascribed to Berija's pursuit of power.

A few months after Stalin's death, a group of Ukrainian partisans, who had taken action independently of the Ukrainian staff and who had been put in prison later by the Soviet regime, were rehabilitated. In 1954, it was publicly announced that their case had been conducted using unjust methods. The Central Committee of the Ukrainian party had the sentences repealed and restored the wrongly accused to their party membership. The Ukrainians received preferential treatment, for in Belorussia the same category of person was not rehabilitated until 1960.[124]

These early examples of rehabilitation in the party are *politically motivated*, on the parts of both Berija and Khrushchev. They represent incidental cases which indicate in which circles Khrushchev attempted to find support, namely the Ukrainian party leaders and the army. In order to strengthen his grip on the Ministry of Internal Affairs, Berija removed the police officials responsible for the recent purges.

Formally, the Party Control Committee at the Central Committee was the obvious official body to deal with requests for reinstatement in the party. It was part of its duty to serve as a court of appeal with respect to decisions taken by committees concerning expulsions and disciplinary measures.[125] The committee was obliged by statute to publish its findings. According to article 10 of the party statutes of 1952, the names of expelled party members as well as cases of reinstatement in the party had to be made public. This, however, was never done. According to estimates by dissidents, the total number of party members purged in the second half of the thirties amounted to 1.0 to 1.2 million, of whom 50,000 to 80,000 were released.[126] The Party Control Committee examined at least 70,000 cases.[127]

At the public session of the twentieth party congress, no policy of reinstatement became noticeable, for there was no mention of it in the report by the Control Committee. Khrushchev, however, mentions a party committee under supervision of the presidium in his 'secret speech'. This committee was assigned to investigate the possible outcome of repression against the majority of the Central Committee as elected at the seventeenth congress. It was assumed to have been set up after the 'exposure of the gang of Berija',[128] was conducted by P.N. Pospelov and had become active in 1954: 7,679 people had been reinstated in the party.[129] It nonetheless looks as if Khrushchev's statement was incomplete.

At the twenty-second party congress, E.N. Serdjuk, vice-chairman of the Party Control Committee, announced that 'as chairman of a committee for investigation of violations of socialist legality Molotov did everything possible to conceal the truth from the party'.[130] Since Medvedev was aware of the existence of a Pospelov-Molotov committee, which, in his view, had been established in the beginning of 1955, we may assume that we are dealing here with the same committee.[131] Why specifically these two personalities?

In the case of *Molotov*, it seems surprising that he in particular, having played such an active part in the purges, became chairman of a committee for rehabilitation. Among the members of the presidium, Molotov was the oldest party member and had held influential offices since 1921. He had been personally acquainted with the most prominent victims and was familiar with the political background. In addition, as a member of Stalin's staff he had been closely involved in the purges. This implied that Molotov must surely have been able to rehabilitate a selection of victims, chosen in such a way that no damage was done either to himself or to the party. Before 1956, the question was not to set up a fundamental investigation into the excesses of stalinism, but to rectify marginal deficiencies.

A similar course of events can be observed in 1939, when a presidium committee allowed a minor number of prisoners to return into society. Party secretary A.A. Andreev was chairman of this special committee, which was instructed to examine the activities of the NKVD.[132] Andreev was chairman of the Party Control Committee from 1939 to 1952, but was also closely involved in the purges in earlier days. He signed the sentence of Osip Mandel'štam and was 'one of the most important links in Stalin's terrorist policy'.[133] Considering this background, Molotov's chairmanship is no longer a surprise.

The second personality mentioned, *P.N. Pospelov*, was one of the party secretaries and leading ideologists. As a conservative historian and faithful stalinist, he could be trusted with a matter as delicate as the inquiry into abuse of power.[134] In view of his position in the party hierarchy, Pospelov could only have taken a second place next to Molotov in the committee. His former office as director of the Marx–Engels–Lenin Institute from 1942 to 1952 offered an appropriate background to be able to determine which political selection should be applied to those who were to be rehabilitated. This institution represented the place of preparation of many rehabilitations. Like the Central Party Control Committee,[135] it had to that end appointed surviving old Bolsheviks such as G.I. Petrovskij.[136]

One of Khrushchev's protégés, *A.V. Snegov*, was also a member of this committee for rehabilitation. This old Bolshevik had spent years in prison camp. In December 1953 he was a witness at the trial against Berija. A few months later, he was released and reinstated in the party. Khrushchev saw to it that he was granted the rank of lieutenant-colonel and had him appointed deputy chief of the Gulag, and at the same time a member of the Ministry of Internal Affairs, the MVD. Snegov now also became a member of the rehabilitation committee. He is reported to have set out to release as many people as possible from the camps.[137]

If the twentieth party congress did not as yet mention rehabilitations by the Committee for Party Control, in 1957 the chairman, N.M. Švernik, remarked in relation to the 'anti-party group' that his committee 'had examined many personal files of former party members who had been rehabilitated by the juridical bodies'.[138] In a comprehensive report at the twenty-first party congress (1959), Švernik went a little further into the matter.

> The twentieth party congress called upon the party to rectify completely the violations of revolutionary legality which were perpetrated during the period of the personality cult. Heeding these instructions of the Party Congress, the territory committees, province committees, Central Committees of the Union-republic Communist Parties, and the Party Control Committee under the Party Central Committee restored to party membership persons who had been expelled from the party in the past for alleged heinous political crimes.[139]

Švernik observed that 'all communists who were convicted without grounds had been restored to the membership of the party'.[140] He could also mention the social groups to which most of the victims belonged: 'It was mainly party, Soviet, economic, military and other executive personnel who were subjected to unwarranted expulsion from the party'.[141] Thus he echoed Khrushchev's 'secret speech', this time in public. No wonder, then, that Švernik stuck a feather in Khrushchev's cap: 'The files in the cases of individuals rehabilitated through the courts and restored to party membership have completely confirmed Khrushchev's conclusions.'[142] The conciseness of his report may be applauded, yet the observer would have been grateful for more details.

Two years later, Švernik came up with a new public statement, with concrete information on the complete work which the party committee had conducted between 1956 and 1961: 70,000 appeals had been investigated, and more than 15,000 people had been reinstated to party membership. The political charges against many of these members had been unfounded.[143] Švernik mentioned a final report. As a matter of fact, very little is known about reinstatement of Stalin's victims in the party after the twenty-second party congress.

The total number of purged party members, according to Sacharov, amounts to 1.2 million.[144] In comparison, the numbers mentioned by Švernik are small. It is certain, however, that reinstatement in the party also took place on a lower level than that of the Central Committee.

Yet it is hard to believe that former political prisoners were reinstated in the party on a large scale by the lower party bodies. The working methods of the communist party have always excelled in shifting responsibility. What lower party secretary would dare to take responsibility for mass reinstatement? One may compare the fact that the lower courts conducted no more cases of revision than the Supreme Court.[145] Unfortunately, no cases are known of reinstatement in the party below top level, so that one can only assume that the reinstatement policy was ineffective.

From the reports of the chairman of the Central Committee for Party Control one might conclude that restoration to party membership took place on a *limited scale.* Only slightly over 20 per cent of the petitions were granted. The small chance of regaining party membership may have been an important factor in the lack of interest in filing petitions on the part of the victims or their relatives. The survivors exhibit a powerful scepsis and suspicion towards the party establishment, itself guilty of the purges. In other, but very similar, circumstances this feeling was expressed by Imre Nagy, in his final words: 'I am convinced that history will condemn my murderers. However, there is one thing I could not suffer: that the rehabilitation is pronounced by those who kill me.'[146]

One may easily imagine that the relatives or acquaintances of deceased victims have little faith in the sincerity of the intentions of the party. Aino Kuusinen quite cynically quotes a well-known saying from life in camp: 'Christians believe in resurrection after death, communists believe in rehabilitation after death.'[147]

A critical comment must be made on the notion that, in terms of proper procedure, revision of the sentence is required before the party may reflect upon rehabilitation. The committees which travelled from camp to camp, after all, comprised a party component because one of their members participated on behalf of the party. These committees were appointed by the party secretary himself. We cannot therefore regard this as a purely juridical matter.

Unmistakably, the more important the persons to be rehabilitated were in the party, or the more they had personal acquaintances in high office, the greater the influence of the party. It is certain that rehabilitation of the victims from the Tuchačevskij trial was not possible until after the presidium had taken a decision.[148] For the rehabilitation of the victims from the Polish party leadership, the Komintern was even temporarily revived: at the twentieth party congress a committee was formed consisting of members of the CPSU and the parties of Bulgaria, Italy and Finland, which at the time had condemned the Poles and were now assigned to inaugurate their rehabilitation.[149] There was no question of prior juridical rehabilitation. Moreover, in addition to Czechoslovak practice, the course of events at the rehabilitations of Rajk in Hungary and Kostov in Bulgaria indicates that in these important cases the party always took the first decision and thus introduced the rehabilitation.[150] Customarily, the party set up committees under supervision of a very high official to examine these cases, whereupon the presidium took a decision. Here, too, one may perceive a remarkable relation between the process of purging and the revision of sentences in political cases. At political trials, the party usually determined the sentence in advance; at the revision of sentences it determined the outcome.

Bukharin

The history of the partial rehabilitation of N.I. Bukharin, who was once referred to by Lenin as the 'favourite of the party', clearly reveals the extent to which political susceptibility, ideological dogmatism and the personality element interfere with the process of rehabilitation. As the prime accused at the show trial against 'the united bloc of Rights and Trotskyists', Bukharin was convicted and executed in March 1938. The sentence found him guilty of leading a conspiracy against the Soviet state. There was supposed to be a link between this conspiracy, Trotsky and imperialist powers. Various assassinations were said to have been planned, of Lenin amongst others in 1918, and four murders were supposed to have been carried out, on Gor'kij, Menžinskij, Kujbyšev and Peškov. In addition, the pursuit of separation of parts of the USSR from the Union and sabotage and espionage, as well as a plan to undermine the Soviet Union by a consciously anti-Leninist line of action, had been advanced as grounds for conviction.

The so-called 'right-wing and Trotskyist bloc', as the group of accused were referred to at the trial against Bukharin, was still a headword in the *Great Soviet Encyclopaedia (BSE)* in 1955. After that, it no longer occurred in this sense. It is worth while comparing this text to the same headword in the first edition of the *BSE*,[151] in which the entire proceedings of the trial were carefully followed. In 1955, however, a number of omissions can be observed. Stalin no longer served as a potential victim of the so-called conspiracy. Among those who were said to have been assassinated, Gor'kij's son, Peškov, was omitted. The episode of the assault on Lenin was no longer described as a combined conspiracy between Bukharin, Trotsky and the Socialist Revolutionaries. Concrete acts of sabotage were no longer included, even though this charge was maintained. Not one of the individual members of the 'bloc' was mentioned individually with respect to a 'crime'. In the enumeration of the members of the 'bloc', the so-called 'provocateurs' of the Ochrana (the tsarist secret police) were missing. Even Tuchačevskij was not mentioned as a conspirator. Finally, the accusation of separation of Middle Asian and Transcaucasian republics was omitted.

Such alterations could not possibly be accounted for by the editorial staff itself because of the inherent changes of the contents of the trial. The political responsibility should probably be ascribed to party leaders, just as the Czechoslovak party leaders had effected the changes in the Slánský trial. The conclusion, then, is that before June 1935 a *partial revision* of the show trial against Bukharin and others was effected in compliance with instructions from the party presidium. Soon afterwards, a sympathetic statement concerning Bukharin was issued by Khrushchev, who, in his 'secret speech', read from Lenin's last will and quoted the familiar passages on Bukharin as the party favourite and ideologist who had failed to grasp the finer points of dialectics. This document was published in the Soviet press after the twentieth party congress.[152]

The party leaders again discussed the trial of Bukharin in 1958. According to Z. Medvedev, some twenty cases of rehabilitation of convicts from the Bukharin trial and several other former leaders came up for discussion at a presidium session.[153] As representatives of foreign parties, M. Thorez and H. Pollit, of the French and British communist parties respectively, were also present. This was considered to be necessary on account of the possible world-wide effect of a potential announcement of Bukharin's rehabilitation and the possible loss of members or sympathisers within the French party.

For this session, the Supreme Court and the prosecutor-general had prepared a document which established Bukharin's innocence. The consent of the presidium was now needed for a definite rehabilitation. Khrushchev pronounced himself in favour of rehabilitation, but Thorez and Pollit objected.[154] Apparently, Khrushchev was unable to secure a majority in the presidium, for the outcome of the meeting was against Bukharin. The rehabilitation of a number of others was nonetheless granted, certainly in the cases of Krestinskij and Ivanov, and probably also of Grin'ko, Zelenskij, Levin and Pletnev. Ikramov had already been rehabilitated by the end of 1957.[155] Accordingly, the *History of the Soviet Union*, edition of 1960, mentions that a series of innocent people had been put on trial.[156]

In March 1961 Bukharin's widow Larina and his son Ju. Larin filed a petition for rehabilitation. Bukharin's 'last will', in which he describes his loyalty to the party, served to support this. The request was not answered by the party. Even so, at the end of 1962 there seemed to be new developments which indicated that the case had come up for discussion in the presidium. The *New York Times* mentioned rumours about impending rehabilitation of Bukharin.[157] The only concrete event occurring in 1962 was party secretary P.N. Pospelov's announcement at a congress of historians that Bukharin had never been a spy or a terrorist.[158] This implied that the charges concerning foreign contacts and assassination or preparations to that end had been annulled. In view of Pospelov's position, he may be looked upon as the mouthpiece of the party leaders at the time. The sentence had apparently been revised, yet only the spying and terrorism charges had been dropped, the rest remaining intact: a partial revision, not an annulment of the sentence.

In the light of the course of events in Czechoslovakia, this method is no surprise. Apart from Pospelov's rather casual announcement, this decision received no other publicity.

However, this line was resumed by the historians and the old Bolsheviks. Two veteran comrades of Lenin, Stasova and Karpinskij, filed a request for rehabilitation, supported by A. Rudenko and R. Katanjan, at the beginning of 1965.[159] Both Stasova and Karpinskij were people of considerable prestige in the party, so their request had to be taken very seriously. Their timing seems a little awkward, after Khrushchev's fall, but can be accounted for by the political irresolution of the new party leaders. In March and May of 1965, new rumours about Bukharin's possible rehabilitation circulated. A spokesman of the state press committee reinforced these rumours by announcing that the publishing house Nauka intended to publish the *ABC of Communism* in 1966.[160]

This book was written by Bukharin and Preobraženskij in 1919, that is, in the days in which he still belonged to the left wing of the party. Preobraženskij, who was later purged as a Trotskyist, has never been rehabilitated and, as far as we know, has never come up for consideration in the presidium either. The announcement in question probably represented no more than a vague design, or straws in the wind to test how the western press would react. This time, too, further rehabilitation of Bukharin certainly did not transpire. Both Karpinskij and Stasova died soon afterwards, in 1965 and 1966 respectively. Stasova left her memoirs, which were published in a censored form in 1969 and did not contain any suggestions about Bukharin.[161]

It was not until just before and during the twenty-fifth party congress in 1976 that Larina and Larin again attempted to induce the party leaders to proceed to full rehabilitation of Bukharin. They asked the politburo and Brezhnev personally for reinstatement in the party and the Academy of Sciences. As the request made no mention of a revision, the petitioners apparently believed that such a revision had already been established. This time, albeit with an 18-month delay, the party issued a reply. The chief of a department of the Party Control Committee, G.S. Klimov, telephoned Larin in June 1977 to announce that he had been instructed to report that Larin's request for rehabilitation of

Bukharin in the party and as a member of the Academy of Sciences of the Soviet Union could not be granted. The charges of the criminal acts for which he had been convicted still existed.

In reaction to Larin's argument that Krestinskij, Ikramov, Chodžaev and others had been rehabilitated, Klimov replied that the vast majority of the convicts at the trial had not been rehabilitated. As Larin specifically asked whether Klimov seriously believed that Gor'kij had been killed by Nikolai Ivanovič (Bukharin), Klimov referred him to the law courts and the prosecutor-general, where he had a right to take action, but advised him against it. The case was supposed to be too complicated.[162] After receiving this information, Larin and Larina handed in a petition to the Supreme Court. After a year, apparently without having received any notice from these institutions, Larin requested the secretary of the Italian communist party to start a campaign for Bukharin's rehabilitation. On 15-16 March 1978 an apologia on Bukharin by Roj Medvedev was published in *La Stampa*. The campaign, which was begun by the Bertrand Russell Foundation in the second half of 1978, lasted for six months but did not bear any fruit.[163] The party maintained silence.

Only in a *Pravda* review, which dealt with Trotsky and Bukharin, was it noticed with reference to an old book that 'the ideological annihilation of both had made a significant contribution to the reinforcement of the international communist movement'.[164] The position of the party had not been destabilised by the campaign.

Despite the omission of the entry 'Right-wing and Trotskyist bloc' from the encyclopaedias and the disappearance of the accusation of treason and conspiracy from the party history, Bukharin's views as well as his political activities are still subject to severe criticism. He is still regarded as the unfaithful communist who obstructed the party line.[165] Nadežda Mandel'štam's comment on the treatment of Bukharin's memory was extremely dejected: 'They will not rehabilitate him ... Then everything would have to change. I am not sure if that is possible in a dead country.'[166]

Political Trials after 1953 in Relation to Rehabilitations

The trials that were conducted from Stalin's death until 1956 against officials of the secret police resulted each time in rehabilitation of victims from the party.

We may infer from the previous passage that the selection of names of beneficiaries was entirely a party matter. First, at the trial against Berija (December 1953) an effort at rehabilitation was made by mentioning in the charge that 'M.S. Kedrov, party member since 1902, member of the Čeka presidium and of the OGPU board under F.E. Dzeržinskij respectively, had been killed by Berija and his accessories.'[167] As other, non-specified murders are mentioned in this document, it seems likely that additional names of victims were known, so it is sensible to examine this selection in further detail. Kedrov was a character from the police machinery who had not played any part of public significance since the late twenties. Consequently, the mere mention of his name could not be associated with the leaders of the secret police in the thirties. It is not inconceivable that, to offset Berija, the party leaders wished to provide an example of a 'good' chief of police who had become Berija's victim. This could serve to counterbalance the defamation of the reputation of the police, which was then at issue. Kedrov, then, serves as a symbol for the secret police from the Dzeržinskij era, the era of the 'uncorrupted' police body.

Furthermore, there is another side to the matter: considering the material put forward by Khrushchev, Berija's guilt in Kedrov's death had been proved to be incontrovertible.[168] None of the remaining leaders were deemed to be accessories. Kedrov's rehabilitation could do no harm. Even so, Berija and others were convicted without mention of this murder as one of the grounds for conviction.[169] It may be inferred that there was no consensus among the party leaders as to the question of whether formal rehabilitations should be drawn into the trial against Berija. Incidentally, Kedrov was indeed considered to have been rehabilitated on the grounds of the aforementioned accusation.[170]

Other trials against prominent executives of the secret police unveiled a number of rehabilitations, albeit initially in exceedingly obscure terms. The case against the Undersecretary of State Security, Rjumin, in July 1954, revealed that his victims, among whom were a group of medical doctors (i.e. the Kremlin doctors), had been 'fully rehabilitated'.[171] This, however, had already been announced at the time of Rjumin's arrest.[172]

Likewise, the victims of the so-called 'Leningrad affair' were fully rehabilitated at the trial against Abakumov, Minister of State Security from 1946 to 1951, and others in December 1954.[173] It was not until the end of 1955 that actual names were released at a similar trial: the trial against the chiefs of the Transcaucasian security service, Rapava, Ruchadze and others. Four prominent Georgians from the thirties were mentioned as victims in press reports. Consequently, they must have been rehabilitated, even though this had not been announced. We are dealing here with

> terrorist acts of violence against M. Orachelašvili, secretary of the Transcaucasian party committee, his wife M. Orachelašvili, people's commissar for education in Georgia, Buačidze, commander of the Georgian division, Begija, director of the Marx–Engels–Lenin Institute in Tbilisi, and others.[174]

In April 1956, at least some twenty names of victims of the party and government of Azerbaidžan were released in the same manner at the trial against the former secretary of Azerbaidžan, Bagirov, and others: R. Achundov, L. Mirzojan, A.G. Karaev, G. Musabekov, M.D. Guseinov, G. Vezirov, D. Buniat-Zade, S.M. Efendiev, U. Rachmanov, to mention only the names of first secretaries, prime ministers and a president.[175] With the end of political trials of leading police officials, this method of rehabilitation came to a halt.

From the four trials which were conducted after the case against Berija, there appears to be a difference in reticence and in the selection of victims who were rehabilitated. The *Pravda* news service concerning the first two central trials supplied no specification of names. In the first case, it vaguely referred to the medical doctors, in the second to a well-known case, the Leningrad affair. The Transcaucasian trials, on which no reports had been issued in the national press, presented very explicit examples of victims, and prominent historical personalities were included in the selection without hesitation. Here, the trials involved victims from the years 1937-8 and even before, from 1936, for the purges under Berija in the Transcaucasian districts had already begun at that time.

There is nonetheless a direct link between the Transcaucasian trials and the trial of Berija: the death of Sergo Ordžonikidze, a prominent member of the politburo and an old Bolshevik. Ordžonikidze's 'suicide' in February 1937 had at the time been attributed to a heart attack, and a state funeral and a seven-day commemoration in the press had been bestowed upon him. Ordžonikidze, in short, was not publicly regarded as a victim of the purges and was not posthumously calumniated. In retrospect, however, his death heralded Stalin's wholesale attack on the party itself. At the trial against Berija, it was mentioned in the charge that Berija had secretly plotted against Ordžonikidze and had thus been indirectly guilty of the latter's death.[176] Rapava, Ruchadze and others were found guilty of complicity. They accumulated libellous material and terrorised the family and friends of Ordžonikidze.[177] 'Intrigues' appear to have been extended over a number of years. Bagirov, finally, had taken part in the plot against Ordžonikidze by ordering the extortion of false testimonies against him.[178]

We are not concerned here with Ordžonikidze's rehabilitation, but with the restoration of truth regarding his death. The struggle for power in the highest ranks of the party in Khrushchev's days is involved here. The Ordžonikidze issue was raised at both the twentieth and the twenty-second party congresses. At the latter congress, it was mentioned in relation to the issue of co-responsibility of the 'anti-party group' for the terror. Robert Conquest has already pointed out that it was specifically directed against Malenkov, just as the revival of the Leningrad affair was used against Malenkov.[179]

From this survey, we may conclude that the authorities were extremely reluctant to use the political trials against the secret police as a means of rehabilitation. As no press campaign attended this, no more than a *symbolic rehabilitation* of legality and prosecution of the offenders could be noticed. It was not very clear what these people had actually done wrong. The remarkable thing about the case against Berija is that charges are promoted to facts even if the sentence does not mention these: the names of Kedrov and Ordžonikidze had been omitted from the sentence.

The way in which the rehabilitation of victims was handled at these trials reveals a clear-cut political background, which is illustrated by the use of the Leningrad affair and the Ordžonikidze issue. The series of names of victims in Transcaucasia goes beyond the political background mentioned. Apparently the party leaders in Georgia and Azerbaidžan exerted themselves to rectify their own party history and were permitted to do so on higher authority. There were several reasons for this. In his career Berija had made important progress in these areas especially, which resulted in his ultimate position. Repression was extraordinarily severe, so the restoration of faith in the party in these areas had to be attended by the direct exposure of at least some injustice. All of this fitted in with the policy of the central party authorities of using Berija as a universal scapegoat.

Case-studies

No genuine examples of a complete description of a case rehabilitation can be detected in official Soviet publications. More details are supplied in the underground literature and occasionally some accounts of rehabilitations are published. Some examples will be discussed below.

Aino Kuusinen is the former wife of the prominent Finnish communist who even became a member of the party presidium in the fifties. On 15 July 1955 she filed a petition for revision of her sentences, which dated back to 1939 and 1950. On 12 October 1955 she was informed that both charges had been repealed on account of the absence of a criminal act. Later on she received money from the Central Committee and was invited to a 'rehabilitation dinner' in her honour by the personnel department of the general staff, for whom she had worked in the military espionage service.[180]

The rehabilitation of the writer *A.I. Solženicyn*, who was still a maths teacher at the time, provides an additional example. In 1945 he was sentenced to eight years' confinement in camp by a Special Senate of the NKVD. He was juridically rehabilitated by the Military Collegium of the Supreme Court on 6 February 1956. Solženicyn had filed a request for rehabilitation, whereupon a procedure for revision had been initiated by means of a protest against the sentence by the judge-advocate. The court summoned witnesses and was informed of the military service record of the person involved. The sentence read: 'annulment of the sentence on account of lack of evidence'. Among other things, it was taken into consideration that Solženicyn's activities at the time were not criminal.[181] The act of rehabilitation proved to be fairly circumstantial, while the hearing of witnesses is illustrative of a serious approach. From the text it clearly follows that Solženicyn's record of military service and his decorations carried great weight.

A strange course of events could be observed at the revision of the charges against the famous diplomat *I.M. Majskij*. At the end of February 1953 he was arrested and accused of espionage for the UK. Though rather late, Stalin had adopted a suspicious attitude towards the trip to England and the United States by a diplomatic mission under Molotov in 1942. Majskij's arrest consequently introduced an attack against Molotov. Stalin's death, however, put things in a different light. The legal authorities involved Majskij in the case against Berija, which had been at issue since the middle of

1953, and he pleaded guilty to the charge. Berija was said to have been willing to appoint Majskij, who was still in prison at the time, to be his Minister of Internal Affairs after Berija's alleged bid for power. As Berija had really intended to release Majskij from prison — cf. the Kremlin doctors — it was not difficult to establish a link between them. Majskij was lucky not to be sentenced at the so-called trial against Berija, and did not appear in court until the summer of 1955, after two and a half years of solitary confinement.[182] He was accused of treason and anti-Soviet activities. Majskij conducted his own defence and managed to accomplish a withdrawal of the charge, yet he was still not released. Apparently it was felt to be embarrassing to release him without further ado, so a new charge was put forward. Majskij was accused of having been remiss in his duties as ambassador in London. He was finally sentenced to six years' imprisonment. A petition for pardon was granted at once by the Supreme Court of the RSFSR, which shows that the revision was a farce. Later on, the legal sentence was also annulled and Majskij was fully rehabilitated as a citizen. In Majskij's own view, Vorošilov and Bulganin played a beneficial part in the hearing of his case; the former because he too was suspected of espionage for the UK by Stalin.[183]

The Majskij case indicates how difficult the development towards a legal procedure in the hearing of political cases has been and how inconsistent the choice of solutions was: first a conviction, then a pardon and rehabilitation.

In her memoirs, *Nadežda Mandel'štam* reports that she, like the widow of the poet Babel' and the daughter of the stage director Mejerchol'd, filed a request at the time of the twentieth congress for the rehabilitation of her husband, the great poet Osip Mandel'štam. She had been advised to do so by Il'ja Erenburg. The secretary of the Union of Writers, candidate member of the Central Committee A.A. Surkov, met her with an unprecedentedly cordial welcome and after only a few weeks she received a declaration of acquittal in the Mandel'štam case dating from 1938. Later on, however, a request for additional annulment of Mandel'štam's arrest in 1934 was rejected. This happened in the days of the Hungarian revolt, which apparently had a direct impact upon the rehabilitation climate. Surkov nonetheless proceeded to the additional rehabilitation of Mandel'štam's literary work, although it took quite some time before this was once again printed. Nadežda Mandel'štam received a sum of 5,000 roubles in compensation and the case was thus completed. Hence her complaint that Mandel'štam was granted only a second-rate rehabilitation.[184]

The problems which could face dependants with respect to posthumous rehabilitation of a relative are described in an unpublished letter to *Pravda*, towards the end of 1977 or early in 1978. In 1938, one *F.I. Lapik* was arrested and sentenced to ten years' imprisonment without right of correspondence, whereupon nothing had been heard of him. In 1953, his son asked the KGB for information and was told that this father was still alive somewhere on the northern isles. After a year the request was repeated, but the answer was the same, apart from adding that it was best not to continue searching, for the person involved was an evil man. The police nonetheless advised addressing the state. The result was disappointing. In 1955, the relatives received a death certificate (Lapik had died on 19 December 1941) and a document which indicated that he had been rehabilitated on account of the absence of a criminal act in his case. In the letter to *Pravda*, the relatives lodged a complaint against police methods and announced that news had recently been received that Lapik was still alive after all. The relatives were now bullied by the KGB, which finally began its own search. The family feared arrest and therefore handed the story on to *samizdat*.[185]

The case of *M.B. Šul'man* shows that rehabilitation in the party too, may be full of gaps.[186] He was the only survivor from a group of 83 people who belonged to the set of Jan Gamarnik, the political chief of the army, in 1937. Šul'man was rehabilitated and restored to party membership in 1955, but with a note of interruption in membership between 1937 and 1955, the term of his imprisonment. Šul'man lodged a complaint on this point, arguing that he had remained a communist even while in camp, but he neither managed to unravel the reason for this new punishment nor succeeded in accomplishing a different decision.

Even less successful was *E. Osipov*, another rehabilitated victim, who had at the time been convicted for taking part in an oppositional group and for Trotskyism. For bureaucratic reasons, his petition for rehabilitation in the party was left unexamined for a long time. In his account he mentions various comrades whose requests were not successful until they made use of their personal relations (*blat*). He himself was forced to manage without them. When his petition was finally considered in the bureau of the Leningrad committee, first secretary I.V. Spiridonov remarked: 'I suggest we do not reinstate this comrade in the party considering his excessive activities in the opposition, and to reject his request for reinstatement in view of his protracted stay outside the party ranks.'[187] This case is illustrative of the real reason for keeping the man out of the party, i.e. oppositional history, and of the excessive formal motive upon which the rejection is based.

Conclusion

The formal regulations concerning rehabilitation in the Soviet Union are highly inadequate. The degree of publicity of government decrees in this matter is practically zero. Those who deem themselves entitled to rehabilitation or who have been rehabilitated can find no adequate information in either legislation or jurisprudence to inform themselves of their possible rights and titles. They are in effect dependent on the executive officials.

The juridical procedures which must be followed for rehabilitation are none too clear. Requests are passed on through various party and state bodies to the legal authorities. The petitioner for rehabilitation can only be patient and has no right to demand revision of the sentence. No action is taken unless one brings up the case oneself. The legal authorities conduct a full-scale wait-and-see policy. From the debates among Soviet lawyers it appears that the grounds selected for proceeding to juridical rehabilitation may be contestable too, that is, in the case of annulment of the sentence on account of insufficient evidence.

The formal rules for social rehabilitation, in so far as they have been traced, indicate that this must be preceded by juridical rehabilitation. Those who were merely released without evidence of rehabilitation have probably been treated in the same way as people who benefited from amnesty: they are not treated as first-class citizens and continue to be persecuted by such administrative measures as expulsion. It is not impossible that the authorities regard such cases as conditional releases, since the sentence has not been changed.

On account of a total lack of data, restoration to former office will have to be left unexamined. As everyone, released and rehabilitated alike, needed some job to avoid being arrested for parasitism — no reports are known on this matter — the former political prisoners would probably have been integrated somewhere in the production process or have been granted pensions. It is still open to question whether the authorities in these cases took note of the positions formerly occupied by the persons involved. Former soldiers possibly received preferential treatment.

The communist party played a dominating part in the process of rehabilitation. Up until 1956, rehabilitation policy was arbitrary. A minor number of political prisoners were rehabilitated, in which cases party members were given priority. The combined committees which were in charge of selection were probably instructed first of all to trace this group. A constant preoccupation with the party and lack of concern for non-party people is clear from various memoirs and Khrushchev's 'secret speech'. The masses received attention only after the twentieth party congress.

No conclusion can be drawn with respect to the number of releases and the number of rehabilitations or the relation between these figures. The mingling of both notions is mentioned in the literature as an important cause for the widely divergent figures. Some certainty has been obtained with respect to the party data. From these it appears that one out of every five requests for restoration to party membership was granted. This means that the party adhered in principle to the justness of the purges. As such requests were not filed until after juridical rehabilitation, the small number of party rehabilitations indicates that the party adopted the extremely formalistic view that state bodies were capable of error, yet that the party was not responsible for this. The political trials after 1953 revealed a pattern of great hesitation with respect to the names of rehabilitated persons. It is evident that rehabilitation of victims of the accused was not the aim, but the consequence, of the trial. Considering the variations in press interest, the political trials in Transcaucasia were also meant to increase public faith in the party.

The party tried to have political prisoners reinstated as silently as possible. Until the twenty-second party congress, no attention whatsoever was paid to the phenomenon in the press.

Until 1956, leaders inside the party who had shared great responsibility for the purges were involved in rehabilitation policy: Berija and Molotov. As both were well acquainted with the machinery of the purges, they must have been quite eager to cover up a large number of cases. The fact that both can be regarded as future victims of impending purges may also have been of importance. The machinery of the purges had been put into operation by Stalin as early as 1953, and it was in their interest to put an end to it. Confessions which had been extorted from prisoners were used to make new arrests. This mechanism had to be stopped. To this end, replacement of the highest ranks of the secret police, new instructions for the legal bodies, and rehabilitation of prisoners were possible means.

Notes

1. For general background information, see Z. Suda, *Zealots and Rebels. A History of the Ruling Communist Party of Czechoslovakia* (Stanford, Cal., 1980), and J. Pelikán (ed.), *Das unterdrückte Dossier. Bericht des ZK des KPTsch über politische Prozesse und 'Rehabilitierungen' in der Tschechoslowakei 1949-1968* (Vienna, 1970), p. 303. Also known as the *Piller-rapport.*
2. *Piller-rapport*, p. 11.
3. P. Windsor and A. Roberts *Czechoslovakia 1968. Reform, Repression and Resistance* (London, 1969), p. 108; Suda (*Zealots and Rebels*, p. 325) wrongly argues that the Piller committee reported its findings to the Central Committee in April 1968.
4. K. Kaplan, *Dans les archives du Comité Central. 30 Ans de secrets du Bloc soviétique* (Paris, 1978). Additional sources are J. Pelikan, *Pervertierte Justiz* (Vienna, 1972) and various memoirs by survivors, such as A. London, *Ich Gestehe. Der Prozess um Rudolf Slansky* (Hamburg, 1970), E. Löbl and D. Pokorńy, *Die Revolution rehabilitiert ihre Kinder. Hinter den Kulissen des Slánský-Prozesses* (Vienna, 1968), and J. Slanska, *De Waarheid over Mijn Man* (Leiden, 1969).
5. *Piller-rapport*, pp. 81, 87 and 127.
6. Ibid., p. 161.
7. Ibid., pp. 161-7.
8. Ibid., p. 169.
9. J. Smrkovský, member of the politburo between 1946 and 1951, was given a life sentence in 1951. He was released on probation in 1955 and was reinstated in the party eight years later. In 1968 he became a member of the politburo and chairman of the National Assembly. M. Švermová, widow of the war hero Jan Šverma, was a member of the politburo between 1946 and 1951 and acted as deputy secretary-general between 1949 and 1951. She was arrested in 1951 and was given a life sentence in 1954. She was released in 1956 and formally rehabilitated in 1963, yet she continued to be excluded from the Central Committee.
10. *Piller-rapport*, pp. 172 and 175-6.
11. Ibid., pp. 178 and 414; London, *Ich Gestehe*, pp. 452-3. The third person to receive a life sentence, E. Löbl, was released on probation in May 1960.
12. *Piller-rapport*, pp. 184-5.
13. Ibid., pp. 179 and 214.
14. Ibid., pp. 214-17.
15. Ibid., pp. 225-7.
16. Ibid.
17. *Sbírka Zákonu ČSSR* (henceforth *Sb. Zak.*), no. 20 (10 May 1960), resolution dated 9 May 1960.
18. *Piller-rapport*, pp. 228-9.
19. Sb. Zak., no. 16 (23 July 1958), law no. 40, dated 3 July 1958.
20. J. Škvorecký (ed.), *Nachrichten aus der CSSR. Dokumentation der Wochenzeitung 'Literárni listy' des Tschechoslowakischen Schrif-tstellerverbandes*

Prag, Februar-August 1968 (Frankfurt-on-Main, 1968), p. 310.
21. *Rudé Právo*, 21 November 1961. In a similar way, party leader Gheorghiu-Dej succeeded in preventing the rehabilitation of Ana Pauker in the Romanian party. See Gh. Gheorghiu-Dej, *Articole si cuvintari 1961-1962* (Bucharest, 1963), pp. 197-210.
22. *Piller-rapport*, pp. 232-4.
23. London, *Ich Gestehe*, p. 335; Löbl and Pokorný, *Die Revolution rehabilitiert ihre Kinder*, p. 63.
24. Kaplan, *Dans les archives*, pp. 84-5.
25. *Piller-rapport*, pp. 232-3.
26. Kaplan, *Dans les archives*, pp. 83-4.
27. *Piller-rapport*, p. 237.
28. Ibid., p. 247.
29. Ibid., pp. 248-9.
30. Ibid., pp. 251-5.
31. *Rudé Právo*, 22 August 1963. See *Bulletin der Internationalen Juristen-Kommission*, no. 17 (1963), pp. 45-7, and *Wiener Quellenhefte zur Ostkunde. Reihe Recht* (henceforth *WQO*), ČS (1963), pp. 16-18.
32. *Piller-rapport*, pp. 257-9.
33. Ibid., p. 258.
34. Ibid., pp. 373-4.
35. Ibid., pp. 198, 220 and 335.
36. Ibid., pp. 282-9.
37. For political discussions on the issue of the rehabilitations, see H. Gordon Skilling, *Czechoslovakia's Interrupted Revolution* (Princeton, 1976), pp. 373-411.
38. *Sb. Zak.*, no. 18 (9 May 1968), resolution dated 9 May 1968. Translation in *Die wichtigsten Gesetzgebungsakte in den Ländern Ost-, Südosteuropas und in den Ostasiatischen Volksdemokratien, WGO*, vol. 10 (1968), pp. 105-8. For a specification of the number of people who were granted amnesty, see the statistical yearbook of Czechoslovakia. The numbers are subdivided for each article and are provided separately for the Czech and the Slovak federal republics. See *Judicial Statistics of the Czechoslovak SR as Contained in the Statistické ročenky ČSSR 1968-1980* (Leiden, 1983), p. 12.
39. 'Zákon o soudní rehabilitaci', *Sb. Zak.*, no. 26 (28 June 1968), law no. 82 dated 25 June 1968. Translated in *WGO* (ČSSR), vol. 10 (1968), pp. 305-16. For commentaries, see M. Jestřáb and V. Hladil, *Soudni rehabilitace. Komentár k zákonu c. 82/1968 Sb. o soudni rehabilitaci* (Prague, 1969), and 'Das Tschechoslowakische Wiedergutmachungsgesetz', *Osteuropa Recht*, no. 2 (1969), pp. 143-8.
40. A complaint lodged by a former, divorced wife of a victim was not considered. This interpretation of the law was a rather harsh one because, during the purges, the wives of 'people's enemies' were often pressed into divorcing their husbands. Cf. Jestřáb and Hladil, *Soudni rehabilitace*, p. 40.
41. Gordon Skilling, *Interrupted Revolution*, pp. 395-6.
42. *Politika*, no. 5 (26 September 1968); V.V. Kusin, *From Dubček to Charter 77. A Study of 'Normalisation in Czechoslovakia, 1968-1978* (Edinburgh, 1978), pp. 53-4.
43. Windsor and Roberts, *Czechoslovakia*, p. 108.
44. *Rudé Právo*, 24 July 1969.
45. H. Slapnicka, 'Politische Verurteilungen und Rehabilitierungen in der Tschechoslowakei', *Osteuropa*, vol. 6 (1970), p. 417, which wrongly states an extension until 1 August (the legal period).
46. In *Rudé Právo* (26 October 1969), only the final numbers for the Czech federal republic are presented. No information is provided for Slovakia for July

and August 1969.

47. *Deutscher Ostdienst*, 15 April 1970; quoted in Fricke, *Warten auf Gerechtigkeit*, p. 61. As this edition puts forward a total number of rehabilitations (1,250) which is certainly far too low, I have decided to consider the numbers of requests mentioned as also incorrect.

48. *Rudé Právo*, 24 July and 26 October 1969: 1,729 in Slovakia, and 1,419 in the ČSR. It should be noted that, in the Czech republic, the number of favourable decisions already amounted to 1,742 on 1 July. I have used the specification of October because this clearly reflected the final result.

49. *Radio Free Europe Research*, Czechoslovakia, no. 29 (8 April 1969), p. 3, and Czechoslovakia, no. 17 (20 June 1969), p. 6.

50. V.V. Kusin, 'A Note on K 231', *Soviet Studies*, vol. 24, no. 1 (1972), p. 78.

51. Slapnicka, 'Politische Verurteilungen', p. 417.

52. *Sb. Zak.*, no. 25 (30 June 1969), resolution no. 65, dated 6 June 1969; *Sb. Zak.*, no. 39 (30 July 1969), announcement, p. 418. See *WGO*, vol. 12 (1970), p. 9.

53. Slapnicka, 'Politische Verurteilungen', p. 412.

54. Statement by Dr Karel Kaplan in Munich to author.

55. See, for example, M. Jakes, 'Zájem strany vyžaduje uvědomělou disciplinu', *Rudé Právo*, 13 June 1970; in addition, V. Hájek, 'V bojis oportunismem prosadit leninské principy stranickéno života', *Rudé Právo*, 23 September 1969, and J. Hecko, 'Rehabilitace ano, ale takto ne!' *Rudé Právo*, 25 October 1969.

56. Slapnicka, 'Politische Verurteilungen', p. 418.

57. *Radio Free Europe Research*, Czechoslovakia, no. 16 (17 April 1970), pp. 7-9.

58. *Sb. Zak.*, no. 22 (17 July 1970), law no. 70, dated 8 July 1970. See *WGO*, vol. 12 (1970), p. 261; M. Tramer, 'Die Novellierung des Tschechoslowakischen Rehabilitierungsgesetzes', *Osteuropa Recht*, no. 1 (1971), pp. 24-30.

59. *Piller-rapport*, p. 380.

60. Statement by Dr Karel Kaplan to author.

61. A.I. Solzhenitzyn, *Cancer Ward* (Harmondsworth, 1971), p. 282; cf. E. Ginzburg, *Krutoj maršrut. Tjur' ma-lager' -ssylka*, vol. 2 (Milano, 1979), p. 323.

62. *Juridičeskij slovar'*, vol. 1 (1956), p. 32.

63. See Solženicyn, *Gulag Archipel*: Solschenizyn, *Der Archipel Gulag, 1918-1956* (3 vols., Berne, 1974-6), vol. 1, pp. 83 and 92-3 (publication outside Soviet Union); N. Mandelštam, *Memoires* (Amsterdam, 1971), p. 435; A. Nekrič, *Otrešis ot stracha. Vospominanija istorika* (London, 1979), pp. 22-4; Ginzburg, *Krutoj maršrut*, vol. 2, pp. 258-9; T.I. Til', 'Social-demokratičeskoe dviženie molodeži 1920-ch godov', *Pamjat'*, vol. 3, pp. 248 and 255-7.

64. *Pravda*, 28 March 1953; *Sbornik zakonov SSSR*, vol. 2, pp. 627-8.

65. R. Maurach, 'Das sowjetische Amnestiegesetz', *Osteuropa*, no. 3 (1953), p. 166. How limited the amnesty actually was became evident, for instance, in the appeal procedures of the case of I.F. Gladov, who had been sentenced for violation of art. 193 (sub. 17), and who had been granted amnesty in March 1953, in the course of which the record of his previous convictions was destroyed and he continued to receive a pension. In 1959, the Military Board decided to maintain the sentence, though without enforcement of the punishment; the amnesty and the pension were cancelled. See *Sbornik postanovlenij plenuma i opredelinij kollegij Verchovnogo Suda SSSR po voprosam ugolovnogo procesa 1946-1962 gg.* (Moscow, 1964), pp. 7-8.

66. Solzhenitzyn, *Cancer Ward*, p. 241; cf. Ginzburg, *Krutoj maršrut*, vol. 2, p. 327.

67. *Ugolovnyj kodeks RSFSR* (Moscow, 1957), p. 142; Shapiro, 'Rehabilitation Policy', p. 62.

68. *Leningradskaja Pravda*, 4 October 1964.

69. *Vedomosti Verchovnogo Soveta SSSR* (henceforth *VVS SSSR*), no. 17 (4 October 1955), *ukaz* (Edict) 345, dated 17 September 1955. The resolution was extended to former Russian prisoners of war by decree (*postanovlenie*) 411, dated 20 September 1956: *VVS SSSR*, no. 19 (25 September 1956). Cf. *Bjulleten' Verchovnogo Suda SSSR*, no. 3 (1959), pp. 13-14. The amnesty of 17 September 1955 was also granted to E.G. Karabanov, whose case was still being examined. Later he lodged several complaints and demanded a full rehabilitation. In 1959 things reached a stage where the General Prosecutor filed a protest with the Supreme Court which eventually returned the case for renewed examination.

70. *VVS SSSR*, no. 4 (24 February 1957), *zakon* (law) dated 11 February 1957, in which reference is made to the *ukaz* of 9 January 1957; *BSE²*, vol. 51, pp. 127, 135, 141 and insert; A.M. Nekrič, *The Punished Peoples. The Deportation and Fate of Soviet Minorities at the End of the Second World War* (New York, 1978). The resolution of 9 January 1957 concerned the constitution of an autonomous *oblast'* (region) for the Kalmyks, the change of the Čerkessy ASSR into the Karačai-Čerkessy ASSR, acknowledement of the Kabardino-Balkar ASSR and of the Čečen-Inguši ASSR within the RSFSR. On 11 January 1957 and 10 April 1957 the Čečen-Inguši ASSR was again expanded by adding territory which had been given to Georgia and Northern Ossetia respectively. On 26 July 1958 the autonomous province of the Kalmyks attained the status of ASSR. See G. Geilke, 'Rechtsfragen der Rückkehr zwangsausgesiedelter Bevölkerungen in Ländern des Ostblocks' in K. Rabl (ed.), *Das Recht auf die Heimat*, vol. 3 (Munich, 1959), p. 133. In 1955, a beginning of rehabilitation for the Čečen-Inguši could be noticed: national schools, a national newspaper, the use of the national language by a Society for the Propagation of Political-Scientific Knowledge, an amateur theatre. See *Kazachstanskaja Pravda*, 17 May 1955, 16 September 1955, 3 December 1955, quoted by W. Kolarz, 'Die Rehabilitierung der liquidierten Sowjetvölker', *Osteuropa*, no. 6 (1957), p. 416.

71. For the unpublished resolutions of 28 April 1956 and 31 October 1957 see P. Reddaway (ed.), *Uncensored Russia. The Human Rights Movement in the Soviet Union. The Annotated Text of the Unofficial Moscow Journal 'A Chronicle of Current Events'*, nos. 1-11 (London, 1972), p. 270.

72. Resolution of the Supreme Soviet, dated 29 August 1964, *VVS SSSR*, no. 52 (28 December 1964), position 592; resolution of the Supreme Soviet, dated 5 September 1967, *VVS SSSR*, no. 36 (8 September 1967), position 493-4, also in *Pravda Vostoka*, 9 September 1967. To some extent, concessions were made to the Volga Germans by virtue of a resolution (dated 13 December 1955) regarding the abolition of restrictions on their legal status. In the Altai area a newspaper written in German was published, while later on, in 1957, the traditional German settlement areas established their own national schools. See Geilke, 'Rechtsfragen', pp. 129-31.

73. *VVS SSSR*, no. 23 (5 June 1968), position 188, resolution dated 30 May 1968; G. Geilke, 'Rehabilitierung deportierter Mohammedaner', *WGO*, vol. 10 (1968), p. 164. Cf. Reddaway, *Uncensored Russia*, p. 271. We are dealing here with restoration of rights for Turks, Kurds, Chemšils and Azerbajdžani, who originally lived in the Adžar ASSR (Batum) and in various areas in Georgia.

74. *Sovetskaja Litva*, 22 March 1956; *Sovetskaja Latvija*, 11 January 1956; *Sovetskaja Estonija*, 13 January 1956. According to S.S. Margulis (vospominanija, *Pamjat'*, vol. 2, pp. 564-6), the Lithuanians were released in 1953, but they had to stay in Jakutsk as exiles until 1956.

75. *VVS SSSR*, no. 17 (4 October 1955), position 351, resolution dated 28

September 1955; *VVS SSSR*, no. 6 (1955); *VVS SSSR*, no. 47 (1957), st. 222, agreement dated 25 March 1957; *VVS SSSR*, no. 24 (21 December 1956), st. 528, *ukaz* dated 13 December 1956. Cf. 'Amnestie und Begnadigung', *WGO*, vol. 7 (1965), pp. 26-33. In 'Japaner klagen gegen undankbares Vaterland' (*Frankfurter Rundschau*, no. 101, 2 May 1981, p. 11), which deals with the demands of former Japanese convicts in labour camps in Siberia, P.W. Crome observes that the Japanese state paid their wages because such labour had been acknowledged as part of Japanese reparations to the Soviet Union.

76. See the papers of B.M. Samcharadze, dated 25 December 1973, *AS* 2206-10.

77. D.A. Loeber, 'Sozialistische Gesetzlichkeit im Zeichen des XX. Parteikongresses der KPdSU', *Osteuropa Recht*, vol. 2, no. 2 (1956), p. 248.

78. L. Konson, 'Lagernye istorii', *Kontinent*, no. 30 (1981), pp. 259-74; O.I. Jasevič, 'Iz vospominanija', *Pamjat'*, vol. 1, pp. 156-7; M.B. Bajtal'skij, *Političeskÿ dnevnick*, no. 37 (October 1967), also included in Cohen, *End to Silence*, pp. 98-100.

79. See the biographical notes in Til', 'Social-demokratičeskoe dviženie molodeži 1920-ch godov', *Pamjat'*, vol. 3, pp. 247-8. pp. 269-79.

80. *AS* 2206-10.

81. *Chronika*, no. 13 (28 April 1970); V. Chornovil, *The Chornovil Papers* (New York, 1968), pp. 166-170; V. Moroz, *Among the Snows* (London, 1971), p. 55.

82. *Sbornik normativnych aktov po sovetskomu ispravitel'no-trudovomu pravu (1917-1959 gg.). Istorija zakonodatel'stva* (Moscow, 1959), p. 304.

83. G. Ginsburgs, 'Structural and Functional Evolution of the Soviet Judiciary since Stalin's Death 1953-1956', *Soviet Studies*, vol. 13 (1961-2), p. 283; H.J. Berman, 'Soviet Law Reform — Dateline Moscow 1957', *The Yale Law Journal*, vol. 66 (1957), p. 1192; Antonov-Ovseenko, *Time of Stalin*, p. 322.

84. *Juridičeskij slovar'*, vol. 2 (1956), pp. 317-18. M. Fincke (*Die aufsichtliche Ueberprüfung rechtskräftiger Strafurteile im Sovjet-recht*, (Herrenalb, 1966), p. 111) wrongly claims that a rehabilitation is possible only through the right of protest.

85. 'Zakon o sudoustrojstve SSSR, sojuznych i avtonomnych respublik, ot 16 avgusta 1938 g.', *Sbornik zakonov 1938-1956*, pp. 100-1. By virtue of the *ukaz* of 14 August 1954, the legal capacity to protest against a valid sentence was altered in the sense that the president of the court as well as the public prosecutor, to the level of the *oblast'*, also obtained the right to protest. See *VVS SSSR*, no. 17 (1954). Cf. N. Valters, 'Urteilsüberprüfung im Aufsichtsverfahren I', *Osteuropa Recht*, no. 1 (1955), p. 38. This implied a decentralisation through which possible rehabilitation procedures could be carried out much more rapidly. The legal examination of the appeal was assigned to the presidium-to-be of the court involved, thus restoring the same situation as before 1938. By virtue of the *ukaz* of 25 April 1955, the regulations were made somewhat more refined, because in this it prevented involving in the revisions the same judges who had dealt with the cases at the time. See *VVS SSSR*, no. 7 (1955); V.G. Lebedinskij and Ju. A. Kalenov, *Prokurorskij nadzor v SSSR* (Moscow, 1957), pp. 172-3; cf. Valters, 'Urteilsüberprüfung im Aufsichtsverfahren II', *Osteuropa Recht*, no. 1 (1956), pp. 200-1; Fincke, *Aufsichtliche Ueberprüfung*, pp. 113-14.

86. *Ugolovno-processual'nyj Kodeks RSFSR* (Moscow, 1953), art. 413 (henceforth *UPK 1953*).

87. *Zakon o sudoustrojstve*, art. 16; cf. Fincke, *Aufsichtliche Ueberprüfung*, pp. 17 and 171, and R.D. Rachunov, *Peresmotr prigovorov i opredelenij v prezidiumach sudov* (Moscow, 1965), p. 64.

88. *UPK 1953*, arts. 373-9.

89. Medwedew, 'Vom XX. zum XXII. Parteitag', p. 38; Loeber, 'Sozialistische Gesetzlichkeit', p. 248; Antonov-Ovseenko, *Portret tirana*, p. 336.

90. *UPK 1953*, art. 4, sub. 5, and art. 204, sub. b; S.M. Savickij, 'Po povodu ugolovno-processual'nych garantij prava nevinovnogo na reabilitaciju', *Sovetskoe Gosudarstvo i Pravo*, no. 9 (1965), pp. 49-50. See the case of Semenov, who was sentenced to ten years' imprisonment in 1944 for a major crime. His sentence was repealed on 15 May 1954 because the accused had died (*UPK*, art. 4, sub. 1). After the President of the Supreme Court had lodged a protest, the sentence was changed by the court and the case was considered closed because the charges could not be substantiated (16 August 1962). See *Sbornik postanovlenji Koll. VS SSSR 1946-1962*, p. 5.

91. See, for example, *Subednaja praktika Verchovnogo Suda SSSR*, no. 4 (1956), pp. 6-7 and 43-4; *BVS SSSR*, no. 1 (1958), pp. 16-7; no. 3 (1959), pp. 13-4; 'K biografii G.A. Levitskogo', *Pamjat'*, vol. 4, pp. 466-9; Ginzburg, *Krutoj maršrut*, vol. 2, p. 365; author's correspondence with Inez Rubin in Jerusalem (see also I. Rubin, 'Manipulatie met biografische gegevens. De oriëntalistiek in de Sovjet Unie', *Internationale Spectator*, vol. 36, no. 4 (1982), pp. 204-8); in addition, see the case-studies below.

92. V.M. Savickij, 'O zakonnosti i obosnovannosti prekraščenija ugolovnych del', *Sovetskaja Justicija*, no. 3 (1957), pp. 48-54.

93. Ibid., pp. 50-1; Savickij, 'Po povodu ugolovno-processual'nych garantij prava nevinovnogo na reabilitaciju', p. 52.

94. V.A. Boldyrev (ed.), *Naučno-praktičeskij kometarij k uglovno-processual'nomu kodesku RSFSR* (Moscow, 1963), p. 381; G. Čanguli, 'Nedokazannost' učastija obvinjaemogo v soveršenii prestuplenija kak processual'noe osnovanie k prekraščeniju ugolovnogo dela v stadii predvaritel'nogo sledstvija', *Socialističeskaja Zakonnost'*, no. 3 (1965), p. 59. For the dispute in the following years, see Ja. O. Motilovker, 'Osnovanija prekraščenija ugolovnogo dela po reabilitirujuščim lico motivam', *Sovetskoe Gosudarstvo i Pravo*, no. 9 (1972), p. 92; M.F. Poljakova, 'Reabilitacija nevinovnych: garantij česti i dostoinstva ličnosti', *Sovetskoe Gosudarstvo i Pravo*, no. 10 (1976), pp. 121-2; M.F. Poljakova, *Imuščestvennye problemy reabilitacii po sovetskumo pravu. Avtoreferat* (Moscow, 1977). The author is greatly indebted to Dr D.A. Loeber for sending a copy of this avtoreferat.

95. Nekrič, *Otrešis' ot stracha*, p. 120; S.S. Margulis, 'Iz vospominanija', *Pamjat'*, vol. 2, p. 551; Antonov-Ovseenko, *Portret tirana*, p. 359; Medvedev, *Khrushchev*, p. 83.

96. P.P. Kuskov, 'Istorija letčika', *Pamjat'*, vol. 3, p. 413; Medvedev, 'Vom XX. zum XXII. Parteitag', p. 38.

97. Ginzburg, *Krutoj maršrut*, vol. 2, pp. 350f; Medvedev, *Khrushchev*, p. 97.

98. Krushchev, 'Secret speech', *Current Soviet Policies*, vol. 3 (New York, 1960), p. 179 (henceforth *CSP*).

99. *Istorija Kommunističeskoj Partii Sovetskogo Sojuza*, 2nd edn (Moscow, 1959), p. 484; V.G. Esajasvili (ed.), *Očerki istorii Kommunističeskoj Partii Gruzii* (2 vols., Tbilisi, 1957-63), p. 159. M. Agurskij, 'My Father and the Great Terror', *Soviet Jewish Affairs*, vol. 5 (1975), pp. 2 and 93.

100. *Partijnaja Žizn'*, 4 November 1956; *BSE²*, vol. 12, p. 557.

101. See, for example, the case of Armand Maloumian, *Frankfurter Allgemeine Zeitung*, 7 May 1979: cf. A. Maloumian, *Les fils du Goulag* (Paris, 1976); in addition, see B.V. Mazurin, *Pamjat'*, vol. 2, no. 21, p. 159, and the old Bolshevik S.E. Cuckaev, *Sovetskaja Istoričeskaja Enciklopedija*, vol. 16 (Moscow, 1976), p. 102; Reddaway, *Uncensored Russia*, pp. 35 and 382.

102. R.A. and Z.A. Medvedev, *Khrushchev. The Years in Power*, pp. 19-20; Medvedev, *Khrushchev*, p. 260. The data presented by the Medvedevs are fully

adopted by Nekrich, *Sowjetunion*, pp. 212-13.

103. Medvedev, 'Vom XX. zum XXII. Parteitag', p. 38; Til',
'Social-demokratičeskoe dviženie molodeži 1920-ch godov', *Pamjat'*, vol. 3, pp.
269-79; E. Olickaja, *Moi vospominanija* (Frankfurt-on-Main, 1971); I.
Kachovskaja, 'Letter to the Central Committee', *Političeskij Dnevnik 1964-1970*
(2 vols. Amsterdam 1972-5), vol. 1, pp. 705-26.

104. A.D. Sakharov, *Sakharov Speaks* (London, 1974), p. 83; R.A and Z.A.
Medvedev, *A Question of Madness* (London, 1971), p. 198.

105. Medvedev, *Political Essays*, p. 85; *Istorija KPSS* (1959), p. 484; *Istorija
KPSS* (1980), p. 558.

106. E. Efimov, 'Pravovye voprosy vosstanovlenija trudovogo staža
reabilitirovannym graždanam', *Socialističeskaja Zakonnost'*, vol. 41, no. 9 (1964),
pp. 42-5.

107. *Postanovlenie*, 4 October 1956, no. 1369; *SPP*, no. 2 (1957), position 10.

108. M.B. Šul'man, 'Moja žizn' v pis'mach-novellach', *Pamjat'*, vol. 1, p. 189.

109. *Juridičeskij slovar'*, vol. 2 (1956), p. 318; Efimov, 'Pravovye voprosy
vosstanovlenija trudogo staža', pp. 42 and 44.

110. We are dealing here with the case of a certain A.E. Čikovani who was
posthumously rehabilitated in October 1955, as a result of which his wife received
two months' wages, amounting to a total of 5,400 roubles. As this was his first
marriage, this payment was protested against by the children from his first
marriage. In 1959 the Supreme Court disallowed their claim, because they had not
been part of Čikovani's household at the time of the latter's *repressija*. See *BVS*,
no. 3 (1959), pp. 12-13.

111. Margulis, 'Iz vospominanija', *Pamjat'*, vol. 2, p. 552.

112. Šul'man, 'Moja žizn'', pp. 190-1.

113. Ibid., p. 202.

114. *SP*, no. 4 (1956), pp. 6-7.

115. See *Pamjat'*, vol. 1, pp. 156-7; Šul'man, 'Moja žizn'', p. 191; L. Konson,
'Lagernye istorii', *Kontinent*, no. 30 (1981), pp. 259-74; M.B. Bajtal'skij,
Političeskij Dnevnik, no. 37 (October 1967), also in Cohen, *End to Silence*, pp.
98-100; Antonov-Ovseenko, *Portret tirana*, 'Avtor o sebe'; Reddaway,
Uncensored Russia, p. 392.

116. R.A. and Z.A. Medvedev, *Khrushchev. The Years in Power*, pp. 14-20;
Shapiro, 'Rehabilitation Policy', p. 6.

117. *Juridičeskij slovar'*, vol. 2 (1956), p. 318.

118. Savickij, 'Po povodu ugolovno-processual'nych garantij prava
nevinovnogo na reabilitaciju', p. 48.

119. M.F. Poljakova, *Imuščestvennye problemy reabilitacii po sovetskomu
pravu*, pp. 6 and 14.

120. R.A. Medvedev, *K sudu istorii. Genezis i posledstvija Stalinizma*, 2nd edn
(New York, 1974), p. 364.

121. Medvedev, *Khrushchev*, p. 64. Subsequent biographical data do not
confirm M.M. Kaganovič's reinstatement. Perhaps he was dehabilitated after his
brother's fall from power.

122. S. Talbot (ed.), *Khrushchev Remembers* (Boston, 1970), pp. 181 and
369; Medvedev, 'Vom XX. zum XXII. Parteitag', p. 34. Svetlana Korytnaja, a
daughter of the secretary of the Ukranian Komsomol, committed suicide because
she was afraid to return. See Nekrič, *Otrešis' ot stracha*, p. 24.

123. R. Conquest, *Power and Policy in the USSR. The Study of Soviet
Dynastics* (London, 1961), pp. 203-4; W. Leonhard, *The Kremlin since Stalin*
(London, 1962), p. 64.

124. B. Lewytzkyj, *Die Sowjetukraine 1944-1962* (Cologne, 1964), p. 125.

125. *Ustav KPSS* (1952), art. 35 (*Pravda*, 14 October 1952).

126. Sakharov (*Sakharov Speaks*, p. 84) mentions a number of 1.2 million victims of the purges and 50,000 releases; Medvedev (*Political Essays* (Nottingham, 1976, p. 85) mentions 1 million victims and 60,000-80,000 releases. The latter indicates that 94 per cent of the victims have been posthumously rehabilitated.

127. Švernik's speech at the twenty-first party congress, Ch. Saikowski and L. Griulow (eds.), *CSP*, vol. 3, p. 141.

128. *CSP*, vol. 2 (New York, 1957), p. 175.

129. Talbot, *Khrushchev Remembers*, p. 345; H. Carrère d'Encausse, 'Le XXème Congrés du PC de l'URSS', *Le Vingtième Congrès, Mythes et Réalités de l'Europe de l'Est en 1956* (Paris, 1977), p. 19.

130. *CSP*, vol. 4 (New York, 1962), p. 217.

131. Medvedev, 'Vom XX. zum XXII. Parteitag', p. 29.

132. R.A. Medvedev, *Let History Judge. The Origins and Consequences of Stalinism* (London, 1971), p. 244. One case is actually described in the memoirs of L. Panteleev ('Dve vstreči', *Pamjat'*, vol. 3, note p. 321): A.I. Ljubarskaja, a writer of children's books, was released in 1939 after revision of her trial (*po peresmotru dela*). See also M.B. Bajtal'skij, *Političeskij Dnevnik*, no. 37 (October 1967), also included in Cohen, *End to Silence*, pp. 98-100. Cf. Solschenizyn, *Der Archipel Gulag*, vol. 1, p. 430.

133. Mandelštam, *Memoires*, p. 403. Cf. Medvedev, *Let History Judge*, p. 247. In his 'secret speech', Khrushchev remarked that Andreev had received a complaint from M.S. Kedrov from prison but had not acted on it. At the same time, he described Stalin's decision to expel Andreev from the presidium as 'one of the most unbridled acts of arbitrariness'. See *CSP*, vol. 2 (New York, 1957), pp. 184 and 187. A fine piece of total inconsistency.

134. Medvedevs, *Khrushchev. The Years in Power*, pp. 67-8.

135. S. Allilueva, *Only One Year* (London, 1969), p. 134.

136. F.F. Bega and V.G. Aleksandrov, *Petrovskij* (Moscow, 1963), pp. 310-1.

137. Medvedev, *Khrushchev*, p. 69; V. Bukovsky, *To Build a Castle. My Life as a Dissenter* (London, 1978), pp. 108-9.

138. *Pravda*, 7 July 1957.

139. *CSP*, vol. 3, p. 141.

140. Ibid.

141. Ibid.

142. Ibid.

143. *CSP*, vol. 4, p. 169.

144. *Sakharov Speaks*, p. 84.

145. Ginsburgs, 'Structural and Functional Evolution of the Soviet Judiciary since Stalin's Death 1953-1956', pp. 296-7.

146. S. Kopásci, *Die ungarische Tragödie, Wie der Aufstand von 1956 liquidiert wurde* (Stuttgart, 1979), p. 281. Cf. Ginzburg, *Krutoj maršrut*, p. 364, and A. Kuusinen, *Der Gott stürzt seine Engel* (Vienna, 1972), p. 152.

147. Kuusinen, *Gott stürzt seine Engel*, p. 152.

148. *Dvadcat' vtoroj s"ezd KPPS, 17-31 oktjabrja 1961 goda. Stenografičeskij otčet*, vol. 1 (Moscow, 1962), p. 396.

149. *Trybuna Ludu*, 19 February 1956; *Pravda*, 21 February 1956.

150. L. Rajk was rehabilitated in June 1955; Kostov's case was revised by the party on 11 April 1956, and by the Supreme Court on 6 November 1956. See Fricke, *Warten auf Gerechtigkeit*, pp. 35 and 43. See also the *Piller-rapport*, passim.

151. *BSE*[1], vol. 46, pp. 668-70; *BSE*[2], vol. 34, p. 363.

152. 'Neopublikovannye dokumenty V.I. Lenina', *Kommunist*, no. 9 (1956) pp. 15-26.

153. See Z. Medvedev's letter in K. Coates, *The Case of Nikolai Bukharin* (Nottingham, 1978), p. 102; Antonov-Ovseenko, *Time of Stalin*, pp. 333-4.

154. Z. Medvedev in *Tribune* (London), 15 September 1978.

155. Ikramov, see note 151, p. 167 Grin'ko, see *Ukrainska Rad'jans'ka Enciklopedija*, vol. 1 (1959), p. 517; Zelenskij, see *Odinnadcadtyj s" ezd RKP (b)*. *Mart-aprel' 1922 g. Stenografičeskij otčet* (1961), p. 820; Levin and Pletnev, see Shapiro, 'Soviet Historiography and Moscow Trials', p. 74; Krestinskij, see *Ist. Arch.*, no. 4 (1959). p. 55; Ivanov, *Vosmoj s" ezd RKP (b)* (1959), p. 586; Ch. G. Rakovskij was rehabilitated in Romania only in 1977, as far as his work in the Romanian socialist movement until 1917 is concerned. See A.P. van Goudoever, 'Cristian Racovski and Nashe Slovo', *Romanian History 1848-1918. Essays from the First Dutch-Romanian Colloquium of Historians Utrecht 1977* (Groningen, 1979), p. 112.

156. *Geschichte der Sowjetunion* (1960), p. 498.

157. *AS* 3032; Medvedev, *Let History Judge*, p. 183; *New York Times*, 19 October 1962; Medvedev, *Bukharin. The Last Years* (New York, 1980), pp. 164-5.

158. See R. Conquest, *Russia after Khrushchev* (New York, 1965), p. 44.

159. *AS* 1060; Antonov-Ovseenko (*Time of Stalin*, p. 334) mistakenly gives the year of this request as 1961.

160. *The Economist*, 6 March 1965; *New York Times*, 1 March 1965.

161. E.D. Stasova, *Vospominanija* (Moscow, 1969).

162. For Klimov's report, see *AS* 3032. Also included in Coates, *Case of Bukharin*, p. 14.

163. Y. Blanc and D. Kaisergruber (eds.), *L'affaire Boukharine ou Le recours de la mémoire* (Paris, 1979), pp. 175-8; see also M.C. Jansen, 'Boecharin', *Ruslandbulletin*, no. 5 (1981), pp. 5-6 and 36-8.

164. *Pravda*, 27 May 1979.

165. Dr A. Stam (Utrecht) drew my attention to the *Beijing Review*, no. 15 (13 April 1981). It reported that a Chinese translation of Bukharin's 'The Economics of the Period of Transition', which he had written in 1920, had been published. Although the *Beijing Review* puts forward several critical comments, Bukharin's article is felt to be useful in its discussion of the relationship between city and countryside and of the socialist production process. At the time of a policy of de-maoisation the Chinese apparently had less difficulty in — partially — rehabilitating Bukharin than their Soviet Russian colleagues during destalinisation.

166. N. Mandelštam, 'Hier ist alles tot', *Kontinent*, no. 1 (1983), p. 65.

167. *Pravda*, 17 December 1953.

168. *CSP*, vol. 2, p. 184; Talbot, *Khrushchev Remembers*, p. 373.

169. *Pravda*, 24 December 1953.

170. I.V. Viktorov, 'Vernyj syn partii', *VI KPSS*, no. 11 (1963), pp. 105-7.

171. *Pravda*, 23 July 1954.

172. Ibid., 6 April 1953.

173. Ibid., 24 December 1954. The Leningrad affair refers to the purge of the supporters of Ždanov in Leningrad in 1949: Voznesenskij, Kuznecov, Popkov and others.

174. *Zarja Vostoka*, 22 November 1955.

175. *Bakinskij Rabočij*, 27 May 1956. The other names are: G. Sultanov, A. Sultanova, L. Dovlatov, L. Aruatamov, M.V. Barinov, G. Rachmanov, I. Menjailov, M. Plešakov, I. Knaškin, I. Ul'janov, B. Aliev, Chalilov and Džuvarlinskij.

176. *Pravda*, 17 December 1953.

177. *Zarja Vostoka*, 22 November 1955.

178. Bakinskij Rabočij, 27 May 1956.

179. Conquest, *Power and Policy in the USSR*, pp. 289-90. The fact that, apparently in expectation of the results of the twenty-second party congress, the commemoration of Ordžonikidze's 75th birthday, which should have been celebrated on 27 October, actually took place one month too late, indicates that, politically, Ordžonikidze's death continued to be an extremely delicate matter even as late as in 1961. See *Pravda*, 26 November 1961.

180. Kuusinen, *Gott stürzt seine Engel*, pp. 299 and 306.

181. Solzhenitzyn, *A Documentary Record*, ed. L. Labedz (Harmondsworth, 1972), pp. 21-3.

182. Cf. R. Pimenov's review (*Pamjat'*, vol. 1, pp. 444-5) of A. Sifrin, *Četvertoe izmerenie* (Frankfurt-on-Main, 1973): Šifrin was arrested in May 1953 and was accused of espionage for the United States of America and for Israel. As a 'Berievcev' he is supposed to have had no part in the general mitigation of punishment.

183. Nekrič, *Otrešis' ot stracha*, pp. 125-34.

184. Mandelštam, *Memoires*, pp. 422-3.

185. *Otkrytoe pis'mo v redakciju gazety 'Pravda' ot Lapik Filippa Filippoviča*, *AS* 3316.

186. Šul'man, 'Moja žizn' v pis'mach-novellach', *Pamjat'*, vol. 1, p. 187.

187. 'Iz rasskazov E. Osipova', *Pamjat'*, vol. 1, pp. 348-50.

3 PUBLIC POSTHUMOUS REHABILITATIONS IN THE SOVIET UNION

Sources

Introduction

The procedure of formal and social rehabilitation took place in silence between the person involved, or his relatives, and the regime. In addition, public rehabilitation was possible through the mass media or historiography. Any random test demonstrates that those of Stalin's victims who benefited from the latter possibility once played an historic part or were prominent members of the party.

Further investigation confirms that there has been no question of systematic concern for other victims, such as ordinary party members, let alone for those who belonged to oppositional parties or religious groups. Nor was any attention paid to ordinary citizens who did not rank among these categories. Even though articles on personal life stories of ordinary people who distinguished themselves as partisans in the war or obtained some exceptional results in the domain of production are quite common in the Soviet press, a different course has been adopted in this matter.

In public rehabilitation of victims of the terror, selections were consciously made from the ranks of former party leaders, old Bolsheviks, or prominent executives who had played an influential part in one of the social sectors (the state machinery, the police, the army, industry, science or the arts).

The various forms in which names of Stalin's victims reappeared publicly will be discussed below, classified according to the importance of the publication: speeches at party congresses, works of reference, daily press, periodicals, source publications, specialist works, etc. The nature of the publication and its distribution will be taken into account, as will the issue of whether the publication in question was published by the national or the federal press. For each separate type of publication, the significance of the rehabilitation presented will be examined. Furthermore, we will look for consistency in the public rehabilitation of individual cases.

Wherever possible, groups of rehabilitated persons will be identified and the frequency of public rehabilitations will be established.

Demarcation

Rehabilitation in the news media covers the public rehabilitation of those who were the victims of elimination, conviction, arrest or concentration camps. In cases of posthumous rehabilitation, the people involved died in prison or in camp as a result of the purges. In addition to these 'physical' victims, public rehabilitation also includes those who were vilified after a natural death. One may think of General S.S. Kamenev, Divisional Commander Ja. F. Balachonov, the Azerbaidžanian S.A. Ogli Agamali, party opponents N.B. Ejsmont and V.V. Lominadze; all died between 1930 and 1936.

These cases must be incorporated into the investigations. However, it would go beyond the scope of this study to include those persons who died a natural death in the twenties and on whom silence has been maintained since. After all, these is no relation between these persons and Stalin's terror. Of genuine importance are those who escaped the terror by committing suicide, but who were over-taken posthumously by slander. These include the Ukrainian leaders N.A. Skrypnik (as early as 1933) and P.P. Ljubčenko, the Belo-russian leader A.V. Červjakov, the former leader of the unions M.P. Tomskij, and General Ja. B. Gamarnik. These people have been included in the investigation as well.

From Soviet publicity relating to the rehabilitations a limited number of leaders of Eastern European communist parties have emerged, who were incorporated in our inquiry: the Poles A. Warski, M.G. Bronski, F. Ja. Grzelszczak, A. Kostrzewa, P.L. Lapinski, G. Walecki, S. Budzyński, Ju. Lenski; the Czech R. Slánský; the Hungarians L. Rajk and B. Kun; the Romanians A. Pauker, A. Dobrogeanu-Gherea and L. Pătrășcanu; and the Bulgarian T. Kostov. By virtue of their considerable activity in the Soviet Union such persons as Ch. G. Rakovskij and Ja. S. Ganeckij automatically belong to the list of names which have to be examined.

Finally, there is a category which defies any classification: those who have almost certainly been victimised by Stalin, but who have not been slandered and, on the contrary, continue to be greatly honoured: S.M. Kirov and G.K. Ordžonikidze. Both received a state funeral and their memory was held in great honour. The special circumstances of their deaths, however, provoke an examination of their vicissitudes in historiography and the media. These cases, however, have too much of a place of their own to be used in the systematic inquiries.

Historical personalities who played a most distinguished part in science, such as the historian M.N. Pokrovskij and the lawyer P.I. Stučka, can also be counted among the victims of slander. In these cases, their scientific work rather than the people themselves is subjected to slander. Both died in 1932 and are not physical victims of Stalin.

There was no historical personality of note who was not affected in some way or other by Stalin's interference with historiography. The famous Russian marxists proved no exceptions: Plechanov was hardly ever discussed and Lenin's works were profaned. The political and historiographical treatment of these men provides evidence of rehabilitation also in post-Stalin times: a rehabilitation which undoubtedly contains some political aspects. Such cases have not been included in the systematic publication inquiry. The cases of partial rehabilitation of the ideas of Pokrovskij and Stučka have also been omitted from the inquiry. They are more suited to the framework of an investigation into the restoration of historical studies or jurisprudence.

In short, the following publication inquiry examines the way in which the Soviet press once again drew attention to the historical party personalities who had been denounced under Stalin. Not all key figures, however, are involved.

Scientists, artists and writers have not been included in the systematic inquiry unless they also played some political part or had held political positions before their subsequent careers. For these professional categories, specific works of reference and literature are available. Possible rehabilitations can only be studied in conjunction with the contents of relevant artistic or scientific accomplishment. This study confines itself to historical-political personalities.

By virtue of this criterion, the following well-known rehabilitated victims, for example, are excluded from the investigation: the director and actor S.M. Michoëls, the poet I.A. Babel', the dramatist V.M. Kiršon and the biologist N.I. Vavilov. Included in the investigation on the basis of the criteria mentioned earlier are:

the writer and union leader A.K. Gastev and the historians and
party executives V.G. Knorin and V.I. Nevskij.

Published Material

The sources at our disposal are diverse, but have in common that
they are all publications that were printed in the Soviet Union. In
this investigation, use has been made of the records of party
congresses since 1956, the party histories, works of reference, the
daily press, historical periodicals, biographies, memoirs, reprinted
works and source editions. All sources were checked on the names
of rehabilitated persons they included.

Among the records of party congresses only those of the
twentieth and twenty-second party congress are significant,
because the records of other post-stalinist congresses contain no
information on rehabilitated persons. The second, revised second,
third, fourth and fifth editions of the party histories were edited in
the same manner, as were the survey of the party history in the
second edition of the *Great Soviet Encyclopaedia* (*Bol'shaja
Sovetskaja Enciklopedija*) and the history of the Soviet Union in
the edition of 1959. Biographical headwords were examined in the
following works of reference: the *Leningrad Handbook* (*LES*,
1957), the *Great Soviet Encyclopaedia*, second and third editions
(*BSE*), the *Concise Soviet Encyclopaedia*, third edition (*MSE*), the
Ukrainian Encyclopaedia (*URE*), the historical and military encyclopaedias (*SIE* and *SVE* respectively), the *Diplomatic Dictionary*,
second and third editions (*DS*), and the *Encyclopaedic Dictionary*,
second and third editions (*ES*).

The daily press from 1956 to 1980 was examined by means of
the bibliography of press articles, *Letopis' Gazetnych Statej* (for
specification, see pp. 117-20 and Appendix D), and, with respect
to the national daily press between 1956 and 1960, also for
incidental records of names of victims of Stalin, in so far as these
were included in the personal files of the American broadcasting
station in Munich, Radio Liberty, which were kept reasonably up
to date for this period.

The following historical periodicals were checked on biographi-
cal articles on rehabilitated persons: *Voprosy Istorii, Istoričeskij
Archiv, Voprosy Istorii KPSS, Voenno-istoričeskij Žurnal,
Istoričeskie Zapiski.*

A systematic search for informal records of names of victims
was conducted in *Voprosy Istorii* for the period 1953-7, when a

reasonable degree of initiative could be observed in the process of rehabilitation.

Biographies and new editions of the works or memoirs of victims were traced for each person through bibliographies.

Of some importance, furthermore, are the biographical notes, very brief summaries of personal data, in the new edition (since 1958) of the records of the first eleven party congresses and in the fifth edition of Lenin's complete works (1958-65). These editions also contain notes on historical personalities who have definitely not been rehabilitated (see Appendix C).

We can thus obtain more insight into the consistency of further mention in publications of the name of a victim once he is mentioned in a positive sense. It is possible to determine when a biographical note, a headword in a work of reference, a recording in the party history, a biography or a reprinted work of a rehabilitated person first appeared. In addition, we can observe the existing degrees of rehabilitation and also which personalities received less notice.

By means of the differentiation for each publication we can determine whether the initiatives for publishing biographical material were taken in certain federal republics or in specific social groups.

To begin with, the question of the significance of a first mention of the names of victims needs to be answered: are we dealing in these cases with full rehabilitation, or are they straws in the wind?

The Significance of a Public Rehabilitation

Nothing is known about the relation between the mention of names of victims in the press, the appearance of a biographical note, the registration of a name in a source edition and formal rehabilitation. It is commonly assumed that a biographical article in the (daily or periodical) press or in a work of reference implies that the person in question is fully rehabilitated. They are sometimes referred to as 'rehabilitation articles', and the rehabilitation is dated on the day of publication. In my view, a biographical article is correctly assumed to reflect a form of rehabilitation, but it puts no date on this. A large number of articles of this type were published because it was the turn of the alphabetical letter in a work of reference, because the nth commemoration of the anniversary (every five years) provided the opportunity, etc.

How unreliable these criteria are is indicated by cases in which the year of formal rehabilitation is known. Let us compare these to the time of the first sympathetic mention in the press, the first biographical note, the first article on the person in question in the press, the first encyclopaedic headword including the latter's name, a complete biography or biographical pamphlet, and recording in an official (party) history (see Table 3.1). From this survey, there clearly emerges a discrepancy between the date of rehabilitation and subsequent treatment in the press. We notice that formal rehabilitation did not immediately result in mention in the press, nor that on the first occasion an encyclopaedic article was included. It does not appear to be necessary for a name to reappear first in a work of reference before it is mentioned sympathetically, or a biographical note is issued.

The table clearly shows a gradual increase in reverence, but not in a similar manner or degree. Formal rehabilitation actually appears to have taken place before the emergence of sympathetic mention. The case of Enukidze supplies a test: in two places in *Istoričeskij Archiv* his name is given a footnote, without including any qualification.[1] His biography was included in two congress records: as a non-rehabilitated person in the beginning of 1960, and as a rehabilitated person late in 1960. The contents of these biographical notes must therefore be interpreted with great care (see 'Memories of Lenin', pp. 150-1).

Finally, there appears to be a difference in time between formal rehabilitation and first sympathetic mention. In the literature, such

Table 3.1: Reappearance in Publications (1)

Name and Formal Rehabilitation	A	B	C	D	E	F	G
M.S. Kedrov (1953)	1956	1957	1958	1963	1963	1957	1956
A.V. Kosarev (1954)	1956	1958	1958	1963	—	1958	1963
N.A. Voznesenskij (1954)	1955	1957	1958	1958	1963	1957	1963
M.D. Orachelašvili (1955)	1957	—	1958	1963	1965	—	—
E.I. Kviring (1956)	1956	1960	1961	1963	1968	1962	—
A.S. Enukidze (1959)	—	1960	1964	1962	—	—	—

A: first sympathetic mention
B: first biographical note
C: first recording of the name as encyclopaedic headword
D: first press article on person in question
E: publication of biography
F: recording in a party history
G: publication of the work or memoirs of the person in question

first mentions are often considered to carry political weight. This is certainly not impossible. Yet it is at least as probable that political conflicts actually originated in the formal rehabilitation, i.e. at an earlier stage than is indicated by the first mention.

Party Congresses Under Khrushchev and the Rehabilitation of Party Leaders

The Twentieth Party Congress

The 'secret speech' delivered by Khrushchev at the end of the twentieth party congress in February 1956 is among the most important sources for political rehabilitations.[2] With some reservations, the famous speech of the first secretary can be counted among the public documents, although the text has not been published in the Soviet Union. All party members, together with prominent non-party people, were nonetheless informed of the contents of the speech at meetings; a document was designed for the guidance of party staffs, including an instruction to destroy the paper after deliberation; the leaders of other communist parties obtained detailed information. All this indicates that the party as well as the social elite and even the foreign communists were well informed about Khrushchev's 'secret speech'.[3]

We are concerned here with the question of the significance of the mentioning of names of Stalin's victims by Khrushchev: can each of these persons be considered to have been fully rehabilitated straight away? The selection is also of importance.

Khrushchev's information on the injustice caused by Stalin, which was probably taken from the Pospelov report, was based predominantly on letters addressed to the Central Committee or Stalin by prominent victims at the time of their imprisonment. In these, they complained about their arrest or about ill treatment. The report included some supporting testimonies. Regarding the limited number of people brought forward by way of example, Khrushchev remarked that they had been 'fully rehabilitated'.[4]

The general pattern of restoration of these persons in historiography is clear: practically all were mentioned positively as early as 1956 or were entered in the encyclopaedia in 1957 or in 1958. Entry in the party history followed immediately afterwards. Biographical articles were devoted to them in the press in the period 1962-5, when work by most of them was published as well.

Table 3.2: Reappearance in Publications (2)[a]

Name and Formal Rehabilitation	A	B	C	D	E	F	G
V. Ja. Čubar' (1956)	1956	—	1957	1957	1963	1956	1964
R.I. Ejche (1956)	1957	1958	1957	1965	—	1962	—
A.V. Kosarev (1954)	1956	1958	1958	1963	—	1958	1963
S.V. Kosior (1956)	1956	1957	1958	1964	1964	1957	1964
P.P. Postyšev (1956)	1956	1957	1958	1958	1962	1957	1957
Ja. E. Rudzutak (1955)	1956	1957	1958	1962	1963	1959	1964

Note: a. See Table 3.1 for explanation of categories A-G.

In several cases, articles were published in the federal press beforehand. A different, less complete post-rehabilitation treatment was given to R.I. Ejche, of Latvian origin and active in Western Siberia since 1922, where he played a dominating part in industrialisation. Neither in *Pravda*·nor in *Izvestija* was he ever commemorated, even though he had been part of the politburo as a candidate member in 1935. He was brought forward on a federal level as a revolutionary in 1917 and was mentioned in the lists of names of Latvians who had been of great importance to the Soviet Union. There is no obvious explanation for Ejche's historiographical treatment.

Khrushchev's selection from the series of possible examples of victims of the terror was evident: Čubar', Ejche, Kosior, Postyšev and Rudzutak were members of Stalin's politburo, who had been arrested while still in office in 1937 and 1938. Also part of this group was Ežov, who nevertheless now served as a scapegoat in Khrushchev's secret speech, being held responsible for the actions of the secret police during the terror. Kosarev was not among the leaders, but was the head of the Komsomol. For his rehabilitation, as for Kosior's, Khrushchev had personally exerted himself.[5]

Khrushchev also mentioned the rehabilitation of victims of the Leningrad affair, dating back to 1954. He was primarily concerned with Voznesenskij and Kuznecov, while the others were mentioned only once.[6] Considering the data shown in Table 3.3, it can be argued that rehabilitation took place only in the case of Voznesenskij. Again, however, it was not automatic.

As the Leningrad affair was now being attributed entirely to Berija and Abakumov, the case of M.S. Kedrov too was presented in detail by Khrushchev and ascribed to Berija, as well as the affair of the

Kremlin doctors from 1953 and the Mingrelian affair (the purge of Georgian party and police cadres in 1951).

The removal of the people's commissar for public health Kaminskij and of the Transcaucasian party secretary Kartvelišvili (assistant of Ordžonikidze) were put forward as early signs of Berija's criminal conduct. Implicitly, Khrushchev indicated that both had been rehabilitated, with the result shown in Table 3.4. In contrast to the first group that Khrushchev adduced, these two names were included in works of reference at a later stage. Yet until 1961 Kartvelišvili was not honoured as a Georgian, but as an activist in the Ukrainian party during the war. The Georgian party history still shows a large gap concerning Kartvelišvili after 1962.[7]

Khrushchev further discussed the construction of the case against executives from the Ural area, under supervision of the party secretary of Sverdlov' *oblast'*, I.D. Kabakov. The significance of mentioning the latter's name proved to be small, for only one sympathetic mention dating from 1958 was discovered, whereas the name does not crop up in any encyclopaedia. Since 1962 the party history has mentioned him as a contributor to *Pravda* in 1912. Even so, Kabakov had been a man of distinction, as is testified by his record in the first edition of the *BSE*.

Table 3.3: Reappearance in Publications (3)[a]

Name	A	B	C	D	E	F
A.A. Kuznecov	1957	1958	1965	—	1959	—
P.S. Popkov	1957	1975	—	—	—	—
M.I. Rodionov	—	—	—	—	1960	—
N.A. Voznesenskij	1957	1958	1958	1963	1957	1963

Note: a. See Table 3.1. for explanation of categories A-F.

Table 3.4: Reappearance in Publications (4)[a]

Name and Formal Rehabilitation	A	B	C	D	E	F	G
G.N. Kaminskij	1956	1958	1965	1963	1966	1962	1965
L.I. Kartvelišvili (1955)	1958	1961	1962	1962	—	1962	—

Note: a. See Table 3.1 for explanation of categories A-G.

Finally, a number of names were mentioned in the quotations from the documents which Khrushchev advanced as evidence, and one or two names he referred to very casually. Table 3.5, which includes these names, supplies deceptive data, since both well-known and unknown party members are mentioned. Therefore, the names of Čudova-Šapošnikova (wife of M.S. Čudov) and Baturina (mother of I.M. Golubev), on whom we have no data, are left out.[8] The latter was mentioned as a fellow victim of Kedrov, together with I.M. Golubev, for whom only a biographical note in 1963 was found.

We are dealing here with a group of executives who, in the case against Komarov, were linked up with each other into a so-called Leningrad centre. This group was purged in 1937. Despite the fact that there were party secretaries from Leningrad (Smorodin, Ugarov, Pozern, Čudov) among these persons and Komarov had served as people's commissar, Khrushchev's mention of the affair has had little long-term significance, as can be seen from Table 3.5.

In relation to the Ejche case, Khrushchev mentioned two leaders from the domain of heavy industry who have been given rather divergent treatment in publications since 1956: Mežlauk reappeared in full fairly soon, whereas Ruchimovič had to wait until after the twenty-second party congress. There was possibly some connection with the death of his principal, Ordžonikidze.

Khrushchev had used two old Bolsheviks to serve as witnesses. Both had been convicted and, after Stalin's death, rehabilitated: Rozenbljum and A.V. Snegov. The latter was already actively engaged in the process of rehabilitation. Khrushchev also mentioned other survivors. These were leading army officers who had been released from prison and had distinguished themselves in the Second World War: Rokossovskij, Gorbatov, Mereckov and Podlas. Like Snegov, Gorbatov afterwards devoted his time to the

Table 3.5: Reappearance in Publications (5)[a]

Name	A	B	C	D	E	F	G
N.P. Komarov (reh. 1955)	—	1960	1963	—	—	—	—
M.S. Čudov	—	1957	1958	—	—	—	—
B.P. Pozern	—	1957	1959	—	—	—	—
P.I. Smorodin	—	1957	1959	1967	1965	—	—
A.I. Ugarov	—	—	1973	—	—	—	—

Note: a. See Table 3.1 for explanation of categories A-G.

Table 3.6: Reappearance in Publications (6)[a]

Name	A	B	C	D	E	F	G
V.I. Mežlauk	1956	1958	1959	1963	—	1962	—
M.L. Ruchimovič	1956	1964	1963	1979	—	—	—

Note: a. See Table 3.1 for explanation of categories A-G.

history of other victims of Stalin and wrote their biographies.

Of the deported national communities, the party leader mentioned the Kalmyks, Karačai, Čečen-Inguši and Balkars, without referring to rehabilitation.

It is of some importance to note that Khrushchev did not grant rehabilitation to another victim: A.S. Enukidze. The party leader observed of Enukidze that he had signed the decree regarding the intensification of the terror on 1 December 1934. This represented 'the basis for massive abuse of socialist legality'.[9]

In Table 3.1 we saw that the rehabilitation of Enukidze did not take place until 1959. Khrushchev's words contained a reason for the belated rehabilitation: Enukidze was co-responsible for the great purge. Furthermore, he had already been expelled from the party in 1935, which may have supplied Khrushchev with a criterion not to regard him as a victim of the personality cult (for similar cases, see below).

At the show trials, Enukidze's name frequently emerged as the one who organised the 'treacherous actions'. When he was criticised in the middle of 1935, Khrushchev was one of the most prominent critics.

In 1956, there was no need to repeat the charges against Enukidze, as Khrushchev's whole story would lose credibility. It is possibly for this reason that he pointed out Enukidze's co-responsibility for the terror, as a warning that the limit of the possibilities of rehabilitation had been reached. This reading basically implies that the presidium had posthumously pronounced a *new charge* in the debate on the case of Enukidze, which is not inconceivable in view of Czechoslovak experience (cf. the posthumous changes in the sentence of Slánský).

As a reminder, it should be mentioned that Khrushchev to some extent elaborated upon 'Berija's intrigues against Ordžonikidze' by pointing out the prosecution of the latter's relatives and the execution of his brother, in consequence of which Ordžonikidze 'was put in a position in which he was forced to commit suicide'. This did not clarify much, but it once again made clear the extent to which Ordžonikidze's death must have formed a key element in the terror.

From the inquiry into the historiography of those persons who were mentioned by Khrushchev in his 'secret speech', it follows that only a small number of them were granted full rehabilitation in publications. Even within the group of rehabilitated politburo members, one can find a gap: Ejche. In particular, the figures who were mentioned rather casually and who are not explicitly reported as rehabilitated reappear in the literature at a later stage than the politburo group, and rehabilitation is significantly less complete. For some cases the excuse of 'irrelevance' may be advanced, but eventually most of the names can be found in a national encyclopaedia.

In all, Khrushchev mentioned 23 names of physical victims. In 19 cases more is known through coverage in various publications. From data on their elimination, it appears that a number of persons were killed at practically the same time. From 23 to 26 February 1939, Čubar', Kosarev, Kosior, Postyšev and Pozern; from 27 to 29 July 1938, Rudzutak, Mežlauk and Ruchimovič.

According to Robert Conquest, such coincidences of dates of death indicate that the NKVD combined these victims into a group, tied them together, and executed them as conspirators.[10] One wonders whether all the victims of these 'trials' also received simultaneous rehabilitation. Rehabilitation of some, after all, undermined the whole of the 'trial'. As Table 3.1 shows, formal rehabilitation occurred at different dates, at least for some individuals.

If Conquest's theory is correct, we will have to assume that the cases were examined individually, irrespective of the fact that with rehabilitation of one case the other convictions of the trial should have been revised.

At the congress, *Mikojan* was the only one who openly discussed the issue of the terror. Even though he expressed himself in covert terms, his speech was so spectacular that it was published a day later than scheduled. Mikojan, too, mentioned two victims of Stalin from the Pospelov report: the Ukrainian party secretary S.V. Kosior and V.A. Antonov-Ovseenko, one of those who stormed the Winter Palace in October 1917:

some complicated and contradictory events from the civil war
1918-1920 have been interpreted by various historians not as
changes in class relations in some period or other, but as so-
called sabotage on the part of several party leaders in those
days, who were wrongly pronounced to be public enemies many
years after the described events. Antonov-Ovseenko and
Kosior, for example, were presented in this fashion. Let the
Ukrainian historians themselves write this history.[11]

Mikojan criticised a recent book on Ukrainian history written by
the eminent historian A.V. Licholat and favourably reviewed by
Voprosy Istorii.[12] Mikojan's observation achieved results, for in its
March issue the historical periodical published a new review,
which was written by two Bolsheviks, one of whom was Khrush-
chev's protégé A.V. Snegov. In a now very critical discussion of
Licholat's work, the reviewers reiterated the names mentioned by
Mikojan and added those of A.S. Bubnov and N.A. Skrypnik.[13]
Mentioning Antonov-Ovseenko and Kosior unequivocally repre-
sented a public rehabilitation (see Table 3.7).

As a matter of fact, this reference to Kosior, stalinist and
politburo member of immaculate character, was less surprising
than the choice of Antonov-Ovseenko as an example of a leader
who was unjustly stigmatised as an 'enemy of the people'. Antonov-Ovseenko, after all, had a long record in the opposition inside
the party and was regarded as a 'Trotskyist' after 1923 until he
bowed to the party in 1928.[14] Before that time he served as
supreme commander in the Ukraine during the civil war and in
1922-4 he held the office of political chief of the army, from which
he was discharged. After 1928, Antonov-Ovseenko held various
diplomatic posts. As consul-general in Barcelona he was one of the
most prominent Soviet representatives in the Spanish Civil War.
He compensated for his oppositional past by fiercely prosecuting

Table 3.7: Reappearance in Publications (7)[a]

Name	A	B	C	D	E	F	G
V.A. Antonov-Ovseenko	1956	1957	1958	1963	1965	1957	1956
S.V. Kosior	1956	1957	1958	1964	1964	1957	1964

Note: a. See Table 3.1 for explanation of categories A-G.

the Trotskyists. Of paramount importance, however, were his actions during the October revolution: as direct executor of the *coup* he arrested the interim government in the Winter Palace, and he was a member of the army and naval college in the first Soviet government. Articles devoted to him in the press after 1956 describe his activities in the period of revolution and Civil War. He was honoured as a military man rather than as a party man.[15] His legendary reputation from that period must have formed the reason for restoring his name so soon. Apparently, his dissident past was not deemed to be an objection as he had followed the party line in an unexceptionable manner after his submission.

The twentieth party congress revealed a series of surprises. Khrushchev pointed out the rehabilitation of former leaders of the party, the army and the state. Mikojan — possibly by way of experiment[16] — referred to the Ukrainian purges and opened up a range of possibilities of rehabilitation for less faithful party people, provided that they had played an important part during the revolution or Civil War and that their commemoration was useful in terms of legend creation.

In his speech, Khrushchev showed little interest in Ukrainians, at least in the context of activities in the Ukraine area. Perhaps he avoided this subject because in the past, as party secretary of the Ukraine, he had been co-responsible for the purges. He also disregarded the rehabilitations which had already taken place in federal republics, especially in Transcaucasia, with the exception of Kartvelišvili (see pp. 58-61).

Yet the nationalities were not ignored in Khrushchev's speech. He even paid a great deal of attention to the Latvian Ejche and discussed the case of the Latvian Rudzutak separately.

The series of names put forward in a positive sense by Khrushchev included no name which could be associated with one of the party opposition. Accordingly, he explicitly praised Stalin's combat against the left-wing and right-wing oppositions and against bourgeois nationalism.

His criticisms of the terror were limited to the events after 1934, particularly in 1937-8. Victims who had not been part of the party were not referred to in any way. Khrushchev also carefully avoided alluding to false charges of *Zionism*, even though he did mention the rehabilitation of the Kremlin doctors. By means of this omission he protected the trial against Slánský.[17] Furthermore, he also refrained from mentioning purges in other parties, despite the fact that the rehabilitation of the Polish communist party as well as of the Hungarian Béla Kun took place at the time of the congress. To some extent, Khrushchev's recognition of Tito as a worthy communist whose mistakes had been exaggerated by Stalin takes up a place of its own. Nevertheless, he did not refer to acknowledgement of Titoism or unjust prosecution of so-called Titoists.

From the attention which was paid in publications to persons who were mentioned by Khrushchev, it appears that no systematic approach was used. At various moments, a biography or some other type of notice was devoted to those who were mentioned. A large number of names, however, were included in works of reference in the years 1957-9. Nevertheless, there were some important exceptions. Therefore, the privilege of being mentioned by Khrushchev was not a precedent which automatically resulted in public rehabilitation in the press.

The Twenty-Second Party Congress

As the process of formal rehabilitation of Stalin's victims was deemed to have finished in 1959, given the speech of the chairman of the Central Control Board N.M. Švernik at the special twenty-first party congress, a new initiative in this domain could not be expected at the twenty-second congress.

Nor could it be inferred from occasional commemorative articles published in the regional and the army press that such an initiative was imminent. On the contrary, since April 1961 practically no articles on rehabilitation had appeared in the entire Soviet press.

Nevertheless, at the beginning of the congress, on 17 October 1961, the issue of rehabilitation came up for discussion in relation to attacks against the anti-party group. According to Roj Medvedev, Khrushchev unexpectedly turned the renewed attack against Molotov, Malenkov, Kaganovič and others into a point for discussion.[18] Suslov is claimed to have felt it to be nonsensical to criticise the 'political corpse' of the anti-party group, yet Khrushchev managed to impose his way; the speakers at the congress changed their texts at the last minute and inserted passages which contained some reflections upon this theme.

What was the function of the rehabilitations at the congress?

In his Central Committee report Khrushchev went further into the execution of the resolutions of the twentieth congress with respect to the 'subduing of the consequences of the personality cult and the development of leninist norms of party life and principles of party leadership, as well as the increased readiness to fight of the party'.[19] He praised the party (read: himself) at length for the adjustments that had been imposed upon the excesses of Stalin's actions. He thereby presented himself as the true successor of Lenin by appealing to the latter's authority more than once. Discussing the consequences of the personality cult, he mentioned mistakes and abuse of power. Stronger terms he did not use. Deficiencies of the system were not observed by him: instead he found 'examples of most glaring violations of socialist legality, abuse of power, examples of arbitrary action and repression against many honest people, including prominent executives of party and state'. After the exposure of Berija, the party leader had discovered this and decided to tell the truth, as Khrushchev put it. The risk of provoking 'feelings of bitterness and even dissatisfaction' had been taken willingly, and now see what happened: 'progress on the way to communism accelerated'.[20]

After this conclusion, Khrushchev proceeded to expose the opponents to his course of action. First of all, the '*anti-party group*', Molotov, Kaganovič, Malenkov and Vorošilov, whose actions against the condemnation of the personality cult had to be interpreted in terms of their personal responsibility for massive repression. The group managed to persuade Bulganin, Pervuchin, Saburov and Šepilov to launch an attack against the course of the twentieth congress, which was averted by the Central Committee in June 1957: so far Khrushchev's account recapitulated what had already been said in public. At this point, however, a second opponent to party policy regarding the personality cult emerged in his speech: the *Albanian People's Republic*, which was considered to be the mouthpiece of the Chinese point of view. After the Albanian party had long followed the CPSU in criticising the personality cult, the party leaders had changed course in 1960.

Khrushchev observed that the Albanian leaders now once again put the methods of the personality cult into effect (in defiance of the interests of the people). They were even claimed to be ready to drag the CPSU along with them. But as a counterbalance Khrushchev used the internationalist duty of the CPSU to induce the Albanians to toe the line.[21]

Khrushchev subsequently described how disadvantageous the personality cult had been to party life and how sucessful the new party line proved to be in overcoming its consequences.

It is remarkable that Khrushchev mentioned no actual examples in his report, and confined himself to generalities and vague accusations. He kept his powder dry and, at the following sessions of the congress, had a number of assistants supply him with the necesary ammunition in the form of stories on the victims, so as to bring everything together with great zest and passion in his conclusion, in a charge against the anti-party group and the Albanians. The contributions of Khrushchev's supporters, which were pronounced between 19 and 27 October, became more elaborate and more specific on the issue of the anti-party group and Albania after the departure of the Chinese delegation on 23 October. Speakers who did not belong to this faction, too, devoted more attention to the subject. The proposition to expel the group from the party also came up for consideration in this second phase.

From the speeches, it does not immediately appear as if the speakers were unprepared for the theme of the personality cult. It is evident, though, that initially practically every contribution briefly referred to the twentieth congress and the restoration of leninist norms in party life. If later in the speech there was a more elaborate discussion of the personality cult (Stalin's name was mentioned only incidentally), it quite frequently occurred at some illogical point.

The intensity with which the party leaders busied themselves with the 'anti-party group' and Albania constitutes a gauge for determining who supported Khrushchev. The lack of support in this matter from party secretaries from the Central Asian republics and Transcaucasia, except Armenia, is remarkable. The attacks were focused upon Molotov, Malenkov and Kaganovič.

Although *Molotov* was generally pointed out as the most important figure in the 'anti-party group', the ideologist, the politician who in the 1950s constantly resisted the decisions of the Central Committee, the personal responsibility for the terror was attributed in particular to Malenkov and Kaganovič. These two former members of the presidium were also blamed for shortfalls in the economy, which will not be discussed here.

The purges in Belorussia in the years 1935-6 were blamed in the first instance on *Malenkov*. Among his victims, according to the first secretary of this federal republic K.I. Mazurov, was the chairman of the Belorussian Soviet of People's Commissars, N.M. Goloded.[22] In addition, he was accused of contriving the Leningrad affair. This point was discussed by the first secretary of the

Leningrad *oblast'* committee I.V. Spiridonov, who, however, mentioned no names. He claimed to refer to the repressions in the period 1935-7 and apparently alluded to the wave of purges in the city after the assassination of Kirov.[23] The first secretary of the *oblast'* Gor'kij, L.N. Efremov, was the first to associate Malenkov's name with the Leningrad affair.[24] Still more details were provided by the chief of the KGB, A.N. Šelepin, who mentioned the most important victims, including their functions: Kuznecov and Voznesenskij.[25] The police chief also charged Malenkov with responsibility for the Armenian purges. Before him, the first secretary of Armenia, Ja. N. Zarobjan, had already referred to 'the activities of Malenkov against the Armenian party'.[26]

Kaganovič was charged with the purges in the Ukraine in 1947 by the Ukrainian party secretary N.V. Podgornyj.[27] Kaganovič was also blamed for the purge of the Kuban district by D.S. Poljanskij Prime Minister of the RSFSR.[28] The Minister of Transport of the Soviet Union, B.P. Beščev, further pointed out the large number of arrests in the railway sector, which had been effected through Kaganovič.[29] The chairman of the Central Control Commission, Švernik, also mentioned examples of Kaganovič's work in Čeljabinsk, Ivanovo and Yaroslavl.[30]

Šelepin imparted details regarding one of the Armenian victims: the first secretary Chandžjan was murdered by *Berija* in person in 1936.[31] Berija was also blamed for the purges of Lithuanian staff executives by the first secretary of Lithuania, A. Ju. Snečkus.[32] A link between Berija's actions and those of the anti-party group was merely hinted at.

Although all previously mentioned speakers at the congress did their bit to accomplish Khrushchev's aim of exposing the anti-party group, no one discussed the crimes of the group at such length and in such detail as the KGB chief, Šelepin. He threw some light upon the system of the terror:

in November 1937, Stalin, Molotov and Kaganovič allowed a group of comrades ... to be handed over to the court. The majority of them were executed. Among the innocently executed and posthumously rehabilitated persons were such excellent party and state executives as the comrades Postyšev, Kosior, Ejche, Rudzutak, Čubar, people's commissar for justice Krylenko, secretary of the Central Executive Committee of the

Soviet Union Unšlicht, people's commissar for education Bubnov and others.[33]

All these names had already been recorded in the *Great Soviet Encyclopaedia*, yet the fact that they had been executed was still officially unknown.

Šelepin subsequently quoted a letter from the famous general I.E. Jakir, who, from prison, had written a request to Vorošilov and Ežov for support to his family — without success, for in reply to this letter Vorošilov wrote that he doubted Jakir's honesty. Šelepin also read from a letter on an old Bolshevik, G.I. Lomov-Oppokov, a left-wing communist from 1918, addressed to Stalin in June 1937, in which Lomov-Oppokov was depicted as Bukharinist. In reply to Stalin's question about what action should be taken, Molotov reacted by noting that 'the pig' should be arrested at once. Molotov's responsibility was emphasised still further by his approval of the purge of I.D. Kabakov (secretary of the Ural district), K.V. Uchanov and Krutov (chairman of the executive committee of the Far East province). Lomov-Oppokov's rehabilitation was new, Kabakov was also mentioned by Khrushchev in 1956, Uchanov was included in the *BSE*, and Krutov was unknown.

Finally, Šelepin also expanded on the Leningrad affair and the Armenian purges. People he discussed had already been rehabilitated, so only the details were new.[34]

The soldiers and specifically the victims of the Tuchačevskij trial were dealt with exclusively by the Minister of Culture, E.A. Furceva. She supplied a brief report on a lengthy presidium meeting, held a short time before the plenary session in June 1957, which involved a discussion of 'the full rehabilitation, including the restoration to party membership, of the prominent army leaders Tuchačevskij, Jakir, Uborevič, Egorov, Ejdeman, Kork and others'.[35]

At stake was the demonstration of duplicity on the part of Molotov, Malenkov and Kaganovič, because they had voted in favour. For the sake of completeness, we will also mention several supporters of the Khrushchev line who supplied additional arguments.

Vice-premier N.G. Ignatov criticised the anti-party group in the domain of economics. He further described the course of proceedings during the plenary session in June 1957, how Khrushchev and

Mikojan were permitted together with Vorošilov and Bulganin to engage in a discussion with members of the Central Committee, who wished to obtain full particulars of the matter. In addition, he proposed removing Molotov, Kaganovič and Malenkov from the party.[36]

N.A. Muchitdinov, general party secretary and Uzbekian by nationality, discussed the repression which had taken place in the federal republics and referred to collaboration between the anti-party group and types like Bagirov, tried in April 1956 (see pp. 60).[37]

The head of the Agitprop department at the Central Committee, L. F. Il'ičev, devoted a great deal of attention to the issue of Voznesenskij's book on the war economy and to the work of the historian M.N. Pokrovskij. Both had indeed made mistakes in their work, he said, but this was no reason to ban their publications and to besmirch their names. He further quoted from an article written by Molotov for *Kommunist* in 1960, but which had not been printed, to demonstrate how incompatible the latter's views were with those of the Central Committee.[38]

The general editor of *Pravda*, P.A. Satjukov, discussed the abuse of power by the anti-party group and mentioned Rudzutak and Čubar' as its victims. [39] Satjukov quoted from Molotov's letter to the congress, in which he characterised the new party programme as directed against the revolution.

The attack on *Albania* was continued after Khrushchev's report, and two major points can be discerned in it: (a) an objection to the violation of proletarian internationalism and to the 'adventurist course' of the Albanian party; and (b) a protest against Albanian objections to the condemnation of the Stalin cult. Khrushchev then attacked Albania on account of its obstinate course in internal and foreign policies. Various guest speakers — Gomulka, Thorez, Ulbricht, Gheorghiu-Dej Živkov and, very cautiously, Tsedenbal — criticised Albania with respect to the first point. Kádár, Novotný, Kim Il Sung, Ho Sji Min and, of course, Zhou En-lai refrained from criticism. Togliatti criticised both the lack of internationalism and the internal regime in Albania.

President Brezhnev was the first to criticise Albania and its internal policy, but he was greatly surpassed in harshness by A.I. Mikojan.[40] The latter launched a sharp attack on the anti-party group, in particular on Molotov as the ideologist of conservatism and dogmatism, after which he moved on to the terror in Albania.

He mentioned some explicit examples, pointing at the 'repression of Liri Belišova, member of the politburo, Maqo Çomo, minister and member of the Central Committee, and the party veteran Koço Taško, who had been recently removed from the party and had subsequently been exposed to repression', that is, they had been executed.[41]

Although there were clearly some speakers who did not partake in the criticism of Stalin, Molotov and Hoxha, Khrushchev, in his final statement, felt sufficiently supported to dwell upon the victims of Stalin, the anti-party group and Albanian practice.[42] Dealing with the last subject, Khrushchev alluded to the example of the two executions of 1960, those of Liri Belišova-Gega and Koço Taško.

He ascribed the executions to the fact that the victims had disagreed with party leaders and had been advocates of the Soviet line. The CPSU was claimed to have intervened in Tirana without avail.

In addition, Khrushchev devoted a long passage to the period of the personality cult in the Soviet Union. He discussed the questionable circumstances under which Kirov and Ordžonikidze had died, the charges against Tuchačevskij and others, and the deaths of Jakir and Stalin's brother-in-law Svanidze. He was cynical with respect to Kaganovič's request not to be punished in the vengeful manner which was customary in Stalin's days, but he was forgiving towards Vorošilov, who had immediately adopted a self-critical and repentant attitude in June 1957. For those who mended their ways, it was possible to be accepted once again. The Albanians, it could be read from this message, could return into the Soviet camp without harm.

After Khrushchev's conclusions, further speeches were held on 30 October which related to the removal of Stalin's corpse from the mausoleum. In a series of speeches by supporters of Khrushchev, various details of the terror were described to the congress. The Leningrad secretary Spiridonov, who had so modestly brought up the subject of the personality cult on the first day of the congress, now announced that repression in his city in 1935-7 and in 1949-50 had taken place directly on Stalin's orders.[43] As the party leaders from Georgia still failed to attack Stalin or his assistants, a 'representative of the Georgian party', G.D. Dzavachišvili, had been found willing to describe the damage his party had suffered: 'M. Orachelašvili, M. Kachiani, Š. Eliava, L. Gogoberidze, S. Buačidze, Lakoba, Kartvelišvili, and many others died innocent. They have been posthumously rehabilitated.'[44] None of these names were new in the rehabilitation literature: four were mentioned as rehabilitated as early as 1956[45] and the other names were mentioned favourably in a first part of the Georgian party history,[46] or were known from the 'secret speech'. Yet not one of them had been commemorated in the daily press, while only Orachelašvili could be found in encyclopaedias, so that this open announcement was indeed important.

The script of this part of the congress included a 'moving contribution': a former victim, D.A. Lazurkina, told how Lenin had manifested himself to her; he was apparently annoyed by the fact that Stalin lay next to him in the mausoleum.[47] She also mentioned two names of victims, Čudov and Kodackij, of whose arrests Ždanov was supposed to have been guilty. The former had been known from the 'secret speech' and the encyclopaedia for a long time, the latter had remained obscure after 1917.

Of interest is the performance of the first vice-chairman of the Central Control Committee, Z.I. Serdjuk, who came up with considerably more interesting statements than his chief Švernik in the first series of discussions. Like Šelepin, he supplied insight into the mechanism of the terror by mentioning the list of categories of victims used by the party leaders. Furthermore, he quoted an example from the purges in Ivanovo, where the party secretary, Epanečnikov, and the chief of the Agitprop department, Michajlov, were purged by a single stroke of the pen as soon as the purging team, under the supervision of Kaganovič, had arrived. This example was brought to life by a female textile worker from Ivanovo, Ju. M. Večerova, who characterised Kaganovič's activities in 1937 as a 'black whirlwind' ('černyj smerč').[48]

The outcome of the 'debate', of course, had already been settled: Stalin would be removed from the mausoleum.

In addition to Khrushchev, the chief of the KGB, A.N. Šelepin, put forward a great deal of incriminating material with respect to the 'anti-party group' at the twentieth congress. Beyond doubt, this executive had ready access to the most relevant files, yet, because of his position, he was also the one who could most easily work in a selective manner. Unbiased and objectivising reflection upon the terror could not be expected from his. Šelepin was a 'party careerman', who had led the Komsomol until 1958 and in that position had often collaborated with Khrushchev. He could not be associated with the great purges which had given the KGB machinery such a bad reputation. During his three years as police chief, Šelepin worked together with the party historian B.N. Ponomarev on investigating rehabilitation, the results of which he presented to the congress.[49] Two weeks after the twenty-second congress, Šelepin was promoted to party secretary. V.E. Semičastnyj succeeded him as chief of the KGB.

It is not so surprising that Šelepin discussed the terror at greater length than the others. Possibly Khrushchev wished to demonstrate that he was in control of the secret police by having Šelepin describe details which discredited the image of the police machinery. Perhaps he also wanted to create the impression that such a terror would henceforth be out of the question.

Compared with the 'secret speech' at the twentieth congress, the list of names of rehabilitated persons in Khrushchev's concluding statement was unimpressive. He did not repeat the names of deceased leaders from the federal republics who had been mentioned in the speeches. He did mention Tuchačevskij *et al.* — the single addition to his speech from five years before. Incidentally, he did not refer to all the historical personalities mentioned then. Khrushchev exhibited a special interest in Jakir, whom he had known well and whose son had appealed to him in 1961 with a request for information and public rehabilitation.

His elaboration on Jakir is typical of Khrushchev's approach: the case which most appealed to him personally was quoted as an example. This concern with Jakir possibly explains why the latter's memories of the civil war were printed as early as in 1957.

The significance of the speeches at the twenty-second party congress lies in the public examination of the issue of the terror against the party.

Names of victims were openly mentioned and details on their fates were reported. In 1956, this remained an open secret and between 1956 and 1960 silence was maintained on the subject. Information on rehabilitated persons remained limited to their activities during the revolution and the Civil War, so that the public heard nothing about their ultimate fates. This new step in the rehabilitation process could not be taken without an accompanying step in the process of destalinisation. The scapegoat Stalin and his accessaries Molotov *et al.* were dealt with: in Stalin's case by removing his mortal remains from the mausoleum and interring them in front of the Kremlin wall next to Kalinin, Sverdlov,

Frunze, Ždanov and Dzeržinskij.

In addition, it was decided that the names of cities, mountains, companies and so forth which had been named after Stalin would be changed.[50] However, things did not reach a stage where Khrushchev's proposition to raise a momument for the victims was accepted. The 'anti-party group' was not expelled from the party by the congress.

It was not until 1962 that Molotov was silently erased from the party file. The 'anti-party group' was denigrated in historiography. Molotov, Malenkov and Kaganovič were treated as non-persons. Their biographies were not included in the works of reference which appeared in the sixties.[51]

So far, however, it was evident that the decision of the twenty-second party congress to remove Stalin from the mausoleum and to ban his name from public life had symbolically paved the way for posthumous reappearance of his victims in publications.

Khrushchev's chief motive for broaching the personality cult and springing it upon the congress seems to have been to rouse *anti-Chinese sentiment.* The link between the terror and the activities of the Albanian leaders represents a systematic attempt to isolate the Chinese party. Therefore, the attack had to be unexpected, for otherwise the Chinese delegation would not have attended.

The incessant harping on the co-responsibility of Molotov, Malenkov and Kaganovič cautioned the Soviet party not to adopt the same course. What purpose, then, was served by mentionng concrete examples?

Generally, it was Khrushchev's style to illustrate the effects of the personality cult. Examples were evidently meant as warnings: Stalin's close assistants were eliminated in the same merciless manner as lower executives. In a country like China, where a similar personality cult existed, top executives ran the same risk. The reading of the concept of *kul't ličnosti,* personality cult, is exclusively concerned with the terror: denigration, slander, execution or depiction as a non-person. Consequently, the term 'personality cult' can be interpreted as an equivalent of 'terror'.

In terms of historiography, it was important that the period of the terror was now interpreted in a wider sense. In the 'secret speech' of 1956 the unjustified terror had actually been deemed limited to the period after 1937, going by Khrushchev's examples, but at the twenty-second congress explicit use was made of cases from the period 1934-7. This time, therefore, it was acknowledged that, before Stalin's full-scale attack upon the party leadership in 1937, massive regional purges had taken place, not only in Leningrad, but also in Armenia and Belorussia.

No direct attacks were made by means of the rehabilitations on the political leaders attending either the twentieth party congress or the twenty-second party congress. Former executives from the highest party ranks were selected as scapegoats. Before the respective congresses, both Berija and the 'anti-party group' had already been rendered politically harmless. It now remained to be seen whether, like these, the ghost of stalinism was also a thing of the past. Khrushchev may have met with sufficient support for his destalinisation in the party, yet many speakers at the twenty-second congress referred only scarcely, or not at all, to the terror. This was a bad sign for his future politics.

Works of Reference and Party Histories

Encyclopaedias

The importance of the encyclopaedia as a source of information on rehabilitations is considerable. Not only do a large number of names and biographies come to our notice for the first time in this manner, but other facts, such as date of death, are mentioned. Obviously, the recording of a historical character in an encyclopaedia indicates the kind of importance attached to the person in question by the party, and may even be reflected in the number of lines, the size of the portrait, and the selection of facts. By checking the works of reference in which people are included we can determine the degree of consistency of the recording policy, and to what extent a person can be deemed to be a figure of general importance, of importance for a federal republic, or for a social sector. As early as the twenties and the thirties, a number of historical characters, particularly the old Bolsheviks, were deemed to be so important that they were recorded in works of reference. By determining who reappeared in similar works of reference and who did not, selection can be established with some ease. The relative percentage of rehabilitation, furthermore, emerges from the numbers.

The importance which the party leaders attach to works of

reference became evident from the changes which were made after publication of several volumes in the Stalin period and in the years immediately following his death. Subscribers were sent new pages, with a request to remove the old pages with a pair of scissors or a sharp knife. This happened regularly, when someone had been purged, with the first edition of the *Great Soviet Encyclopaedia*.[52] The second edition, too, was not completely untouched, even after Stalin's death: the headwords 'Berija' and 'Kao Kang' at least were replaced. The volume containing the name 'Stalin' was not published until after subsequent volumes had already been issued. Thus the problem of possible alterations was forestalled.

Usually the list of biographical entries was approved by the politburo during the compilation of encyclopaedias; the names of executives of other communist parties were also submitted for approval to the respective party leaderships. [53] This makes the list of names in a work of reference into a representative mirror of the views prevailing among potential leaders.

The process of rehabilitation in encyclopaedias can be monitored for post-stalinist times by the various editions published. New editions of the *Great*[54] and *Concise*[55] Soviet encyclopaedias, the *Literary Encyclopaedia*[56] and the *Encyclopaedic Dictionary*[57] were supplemented with a separate *Historical Encyclopaedia*[58] and editions of the federal republics.[59] The *Diplomatic Dictionary*[60] and *Military Encyclopaedia*,[61] in addition, are relevant for our research.

The most important, and in the main centrally published, works of reference were examined by headword for our investigation and will be discussed below. The list of names is recorded in Appendix B. The number of lines devoted to each person has not been registered because the precise value of this information is unclear. It was noted only in extremely divergent cases; for instance, the headword 'Slánský' in the third edition of the *Great Soviet Encyclopaedia*, volume 23 (1976), comprises no more than twelve lines: far too few for a former secretary-general of the Czechoslovak party.

The Great Soviet Encyclopaedia.   In the last volumes of the second edition, the *Great Soviet Encyclopaedia* (*BSE*) began to include, albeit scantily, headwords on purged prominent executives. This was the case from volume 47, imprimatur 19 April 1957. In 1956 and 1957, these people's names had been incidentally mentioned in headwords concerned with a party congress or a battle. A relevant supplement to the biographical headwords was provided by the publication of a volume of 'supplementary information': volume 51, which was approved on 28 April 1958. This included a series of 30 rehabilitated victims from politics, which adds up to a total of 37 for this category in the BSE^2. Information on them, certainly with respect to the dates of death, is still in poor supply. The biographies are no more than enumerations of offices and contain no information on the purges and rehabilitations of the persons involved.

By and large, the names of victims recorded in BSE^2, had, at some time or other, already been mentioned in a positive sense, either in a work of reference on Leningrad (*LES*), or in a collection of memoirs on Lenin, in *Voprosy Istorii*, in the daily press (sometimes with a concise biography), or had been referred to by Khrushchev or Mikojan during the twentieth party congress (see Table 3.10). Volume 50 of the BSE^2, in which the history of the party and the Soviet Union were discussed, already included several names as well. It thus appears that the encyclopaedia took no initiative with respect to the biographies.

The consistency by which the selection of the *BSE* was preserved in subsequent encyclopaedias was considerable: 81 per cent reappeared in the MSE^3, 95 per cent in the *SIE*, and 100 per cent in the third edition of the *BSE* (Table 3.8). However, the selection of the BSE^3 included only 15 per cent of the names of executives who later became physical victims of Stalin in the first edition of the BSE^{62} and the encyclopaedia *Granat*[63] (Table 3.9). Numerous opponents in the twenties who were mentioned in these were not included in the recent editions (see Appendix C).

We can ascertain that several categories are missing. Persons of less weight in Khrushchev's speech, for instance, were not included, for instance the group of names used to establish Berija's crimes (see Tables 3.4 and 3.5). The rehabilitations that took place during the trials against the police officials (1953-6) were not systematically recorded either (see pp. 58-61).

The Leningrad Handbook.   At the same time that the *Great Soviet Encyclopaedia* began to devote biographical headwords to Stalin's victims, the *Encyclopaedic Handbook for Leningrad* (*LES*), which received its imprimatur on 21 October 1957, was published.[64] This one-volume work of which 75,000 copies were distributed, can be counted among the mass editions. The history of the city and area of Leningrad was used as a starting-point and on this basis revolutionaries and executives were selected for recording in the book. Out of the 24 political victims of Stalin mentioned, 17 were active as revolutionaries in what was then known as St Petersburg (or Petrograd); they were part of the party before 1917.[65] Not one of them was then a member of the Central Committee. Six of the victims recorded were at some time secretaries of the Leningrad party organisation.[66] Of interest was the mention of two union leaders, who had both belonged to right-wing oppositions yet had not been expelled from the party.[67] Five people belonged to the secret police.[68] In addition, several figures of national interest were mentioned who had had little importance in Leningrad.[69] Among them was Marshal Tuchačevskij.

The *Leningrad Handbook* provided several names which had not been mentioned on an earlier occasion. Apart from the first biographical data on Tuchačevskij, G.I. Bokij and M.I. Lacis were new names. Both had been active in the secret police.

The Leningrad affair, which must have represented a delicate matter for such a publication, was reflected in the tiny number of lines devoted to its victims: Voznesenskij, Kuznecov and Popkov.

The consistency of mention of all these names in subsequent encyclopaedias varies: see Table 3.8. It is only since the publication of the *Historical Encyclopaedia* that most of the names can be found again. This underlines the regional nature of the selection at the time of publication; the publication does not play a further part in the analysis.

The Concise Soviet Encyclopaedia.   Following the final volumes of the *BSE²*, a start was made immediately on a smaller and entirely revised encyclopaedia, which came to consist of ten volumes: the *Concise Soviet Encyclopaedia (MSE)*, third edition (1958-60). The number of new names of Stalin's victims included in this does not differ much from the previous works of reference: 61 in all, 27 of which were recorded as a headword for the first time. As we saw above, only a few names which were recorded in the *LES* reappeared. The list from the *BSE²*, too, was not taken over as a whole: 7 names of victims are missing. Since later encyclopaedic publications contain these names and the daily press published commemorative articles, there is no reason to examine these cases in further detail.

The Historical Soviet Encyclopaedia. The *SIE* was published in 16 volumes between 1961 and 1976. This work of reference is extremely valuable for the investigation because it supplies data on rehabilitation. Even though the information remains limited to merely recording rehabilitation and does not usually make any mention of date or motive, the fact of publication in itself is remarkable. Indication of rehabilitation has occurred consistently in the *SIE*, and the publisher has not made any alterations in this respect over the years. Actually, this might have been expected because the new edition of the *Great Soviet Encyclopaedia* did not adopt the practice of indicating rehabilitations in the seventies.

The formula which has been chosen can usually be found at the end of the relevant biographical headword and connects unlawful repression with the rehabilitation:

v period kul'ta ličnosti byl nezakonno repressirovan i posmertno reabilitirovan (experienced unlawful repression at the time of the personality cult and was posthumously rehabilitated.)

In addition, the *SIE* draws its importance from the recording of an extensive number of names of rehabilitated, of whom 117 appeared in an encyclopaedia for the first time. Further analysis will take place below.

With Soviet publications it is important to study two dates: the date the manuscript was presented to the compositor and the date the censor gave his consent to the printer. In the case of the *SIE*, it appears that the relevant interval for the initial ten volumes (1961-67) was six to eight months. For subsequent volumes, a whole year is quite normal. Apparently, a more accurate check took place, or more authorities were called in. This is confirmed by a review of the entire encyclopaedia in *Pravda*, which pointed out that 'in the first ten volumes some influence of biased and other mistakes is still detectable'.[70] One example of such a relic from Khrushchev's days is the article on *kul't ličnosti* included in volume 8 (1965). This headword did not appear again in a work of reference. The number of newly recorded names of rehabilitated people, however, does not appear to have been reduced after volume 10, as might have been expected on the basis of the more meticulous screening. Several names which were not taken over from other encyclopaedias reappear in the *BSE³*, so that a conclusion of dehabilitation is unjustified.[71] A possible effect upon the selection of names will come up for discussion in a more detailed analysis.

From a few cases it appears that the process of rehabilitation has not restricted itself to the victims from the Stalin era: a case of execution on false charges from 1921 was revised as well. It involved the commander of the second cavalry army, F.K. Mironov. In 1960, he was fully rehabilitated, juridically as well as in the party.[72] Despite his relatively minor political importance, it took six years before his name was included in the encyclopaedia.

The Great Soviet Encyclopaedia Revised.   A new edition of the *BSE* was produced at a rapid pace in the seventies: 30 volumes from 1970 to 1978. Compared to earlier encyclopaedias, the number of names of rehabilitated was augmented by 90 people. Some names not recorded by the *Historical Encyclopaedia* now reappeared. Moreover, a new selection took place and 23 people were no longer included.

In the cases where names no longer appear, those involved generally do not disappear from other works of reference, so that no actual revision of the process of rehabilitation is apparent. Several intriguing mentions involve people who are not included in the list of computations because they do not belong to a category of physical victims within the party. The former Menshevik and director of the Marx-Engels Institution in the twenties, D.B. Rjazanov, who has definitely not been formally rehabilitated, serves as an illustration. In the article on him, there is still reference to his alleged relation to the so-called Menshevik Centre, which was condemned at the so-called Mensheviks trial (1931), which would not have happened in case of formal rehabilitation. Furthermore, a place is found for such dissident characters as M.M. Laševič, expelled from the party as a Trotskyist in 1927, as well as V.V. Lominadze, an opponent from the thirties (both died before the great purge and required no formal rehabilitation). A similar case, albeit surrounded by more dispute, involves the lawyer E.B. Pašukanis, who died in 1932. Lastly, a number of rehabilitations from Eastern European countries have penetrated the *BSE³*. The Romanians L. Pătrăşcanu and A. Pauker, the Czechoslovak R. Slánský, all rehabilitated in their respective countries in 1968, are incorporated with a brief article. It is curious that L. Rajk, who had been rehabilitated in Hungary in 1955 and could subsequently be found in Soviet works of reference, is no longer present in the *BSE³*. No plausible explanation for this presents itself. By and large, these cases are indicative of a somewhat more liberal policy with regard to rehabilitations of people seriously incriminated in the past.

Encyclopaedias in the Federal Republics.   In various federal republics, comprehensive encyclopaedias in the national languages were published in the seventies.[73] Because of the language barrier, no systematic inquiry into public rehabilitations in these editions has been conducted. By means of several random tests, we may obtain some idea. These new encyclopaedias supply no information on the terror in the biographical entries. Only the Estonian encyclopaedia mentions, in addition to the names of rehabilitated victims, that they had been prosecuted and posthumously rehabilitated. The completeness of encyclopaedias of the federal republics has been checked in the Belorussian, Ukrainian, Estonian and Kazachstanian encyclopaedias. In each of these works names emerge of purged, national communist heroes who have not been included in a national encyclopaedia.

At the same time, various names are missing, so that in the national encyclopaedias, too, completeness in public rehabilitations has as yet not been achieved. In the Estonian encyclopaedia, for instance, member of the politburo R. Mirring is recorded for the first time as a headword, yet the revolutionary P. Oras, the orgburo members A. Orlov-Saar and J. Paulmann and the politburo member J. Kreuks have been omitted.[74] In the Kazachstan encyclopaedia, two national party leaders are mentioned for the first time: O.K. Žandosov and M.K. Myrzagaliev. The names of S. Džakupov, U. Džandosov, I.Ju. Kabulov and M.M. Čumbalov are missing.[75]

The Belorussian encyclopaedia mentions a very large number of names of rehabilitated victims of the terror. The first two volumes have been examined systematically.[76] Many virtually unknown figures in the history of the Soviet Union are mentioned, such as L. Abramovič, I.A. Adamovič, N.L. Aksjučyc, A.A. Al'seuski, etc. Even so, the names of several people's commissars are missing: A. Balicki and Z. Pryščepau.[77] The same holds for the new edition of the Ukrainian encyclopaedia: there are many new names (I.K. Amosov, N.A. Alekseev, M.S. Bogdanov, S.F. Buzdalin), but there are also omissions: V.K. Averin, E.M. Adamovič.[78]

Since 1973 the name of V.M. Molotov again crops up as a headword in the encyclopaedias. The memory of his past in the so-called 'anti-party group' is still mentioned in 1973 and 1974, but then disappears altogether. It is evident that Molotov has again been rehabilitated, but not at a level high enough for his 90th birthday in 1980 to be commemorated in the press. Considering this information, the news that Molotov was reinstated in the party in July 1984 seems less surprising than the world press would have us believe.[79]

An attempt to rehabilitate Malenkov as well, however, failed. In 1973, the Estonian encyclopaedia recorded the headword 'Malenkov', but other editions did not follow suit. Apparently there was some opposition in the party to Malenkov's rehabilitation.

The Military Encyclopaedia.   Finally, in the seventies an important national encyclopaedia was published: the *Soviet Military Encyclopaedia* (*SVE*). The names of various generals who had died in the thirties could be found in a work of reference for the first time. Several were publicly rehabilitated for the first time: P.E. Knjagnickij, G.E. Langemak, I.A. Onufriev and N.V. Sollogub. Much longer is the list of names of military commanders who had been apportioned public rehabilitation in the daily paper of the Ministry of Defence, *Krasnaja Zvezda*, or in the military-historical periodical *Voenno-istoričeskij Žurnal*, yet whose names were omitted from the new encyclopaedia.[80]

In the second half of the fifties and in the sixties, it seemed that the military leaders, by publishing so much biographical material, led the way in public rehabilitation. In the seventies, this tendency apparently reversed. Perhaps the explanation lies in the changes in the military and party leadership: Marshal Grečko was succeeded as Minister of Defence by a civilian, Ustinov, and the head of the KGB, Andropov, entered the politburo. The political influence of the generals was thus reduced, whereas the secret police gained more power. Therefore, the opportunities for continuation of public rehabilitation of Stalin's military victims diminished.

Quantitative and Comparative Analysis of Rehabilitations in the Encyclopaedias.   The policy for recording names of rehabilitated persons in works of reference can only be reconstructed to some extent through quantification of data. In general, the continuity of recording in an encyclopaedia has been considerable. Finally, practically all names turn up in the *BSE³* once recording as a headword has taken place. The *Historical Encyclopaedia* has exhibited the smallest degree of consistency in recording names which had already been included earlier in an encyclopaedia (Table 3.8).

In terms of the selection of biographical headwords, the works of reference published since 1956 do not follow such important earlier works of reference as the first edition of the *BSE* and the so-called *Granat Encyclopaedia*. The first work, published between 1926 and 1947, began with the letters A and Ja, beginning and end of the Russian alphabet, in simultaneous publication.

Names which are in the middle of the alphabet therefore came up during or after the purges, so that this part displays the largest gaps. In the *Granat Encyclopaedia* several volumes were included in the years 1926-8 which are entirely filled with autobiographies of important Soviet leaders. This edition quite dependably indicates the major Soviet leaders. For these two editions, percentages of recording in the new encyclopaedias are highly parallel, as will be clear from Table 3.9.

Taking into account a certain degree of inaccuracy, it may be claimed that the authors of the new encyclopaedias have taken over some 15, 50 and 60 per cent respectively from the earlier works of reference. The difference between the *Historical Encyclopaedia (SIE)* and *BSE³* is sufficiently significant for us to be able to conclude that the process of rehabilitation has continued in this manner. Among those not as yet included are prominent historical figures from the oppositions of the twenties and victims of the large trials (and not all of them, for several have indeed been rehabilitated).

Table 3.8: Continuity of Recording of Biographical Headwords in Encyclopaedias[a]

First Recording of Headword in	Reappearing Headword in			
	BSE²	*MSE³*	*SIE*	*BSE³*
LES	34	39	91	95
BSE²	—	81	95	100
MSE³	—	—	84	98
SIE	—	—	—	88

Note: a. Expressed in percentages of the number of names of politically rehabilitated persons for each encyclopaedia.

Table 3.9: Continuity of Recording of Biographical Headwords in
the Relevant Encyclopaedias[a]

Recording of Headword in	Percentage of Reappearing Headwords in		
	BSE[2]	*SIE*	*BSE*[3]
BSE[1b]	14.9	51.2	59.5
Granat[b]	14.6	45.9	60.4

Notes: a. Expressed in percentages of the total number of names of purged or
rehabilitated people for each encyclopaedia.
b. Number of confirmed victims in *BSE*[1] 121; in *Granat* 96 (see Appendices B and C).

The various encyclopaedias published after 1965 are relevant to
our research, as demonstrated in Table 3.10. The *SIE* contributed
the most. For the total survey the *BSE*[3] is the work of reference
which contains most data. Actually, the *Concise Soviet Encyclopaedia* (*MSE*) is disappointing. Its policy on public rehabilitation is
still very reticent.

We can assume that various social factors in the biographies
of rehabilitated persons formed a criterion for selection. Therefore,
a distinction has been made between the date of party entrance,
social origin, the most prominent office held and the nationality of
the rehabilitated. These categories will also be examined in the
context of party purges.

The majority of the group of rehabilitated appear to have been
members of the party before 1917, so we are dealing here with old
Bolsheviks (see Table 3.11). Both in the smaller and in the larger
numbers the pattern is relatively consistent, with no evidently
different selection policy being conducted in over the years. The
shift which manifests itself in the category of Bolsheviks before
1917 between *SIE* and *BSE*[3] confirms the result of Table 3.9, i.e.
that the *BSE*[3] has drawn from earlier encyclopaedias. This selection indicates that the party was particularly interested in bringing
figures from the past back into public. There was, after all, so
much choice of victims that a selection of younger persons was not
inconceivable.

Theoretically, it could have been postulated that a solid social
background, that is, descent from a workers' family, would also
carry some weight in selecting for rehabilitation in the works of
reference. However, the investigation shows that this played no
part (see Table 3.12). Even peasant origin has a higher score than
the working classes. It does not come as a surprise that nearly half

Table 3.10: Number of New Names of Rehabilitated Persons in the
Encyclopaedias, Compared to Encyclopaedias Published Earlier

	New Headword		Total Number of Names of Rehabilitated for Each Encyclopaedia	
	No.	%	No.	% New
BSE²	37	13.7	37	100
MSE³	27	10.0	60	45
SIE	117	43.2	193	61
BSE³	90	33.2	276	33
Total	271	100.0		

Table 3.11: Date of Party Entrance of Politically Rehabilitated
Persons Newly Recorded in Encyclopaedias

Membership of the Party	*BSE²*		*MSE³*		*SIE*		*BSE³*		*Total*	
	No.	%	No.	%	No.	%	No.	%	No.	%
Before 1917	22	59	15	55	62	53	58	64	157	58
1917-18	10	27	9	33	29	25	20	22	68	25
After 1918	3	8	3	11	21	18	11	12	38	14
Unknown	2	5	—	—	5	4	1	1	8	3
Total	37	100	27	100	117	100	90	100	271	100

of the rehabilitated have a bourgeois background given that, as we saw in Table 3.11, so many were party members before 1917: at the time, the Bolshevik party was an intellectuals' party *par excellence*. The *BSE³* shows a variation in favour of the working classes, an increase of 10 per cent compared to the *SIE*. In this edition, the recording of social background in biographies was attended to with apparent accuracy, as a result of which the idea of a conscious criterion of a working-class background gains credibility. Since the increase in this category is at the expense of the bourgeois element, this notion is reinforced.

The relationship between selection of rehabilitated people and their social position is sufficiently transparent in the sense that only persons of considerable status are included. It is, however, important to know from which social sector they derive, and this aspect is explored in Table 3.13. The executives in the state bureaucracy represent nearly half the total number of newly recorded names. People from this sector were included in the works of reference in growing numbers. Those who were recorded in the first instance

Table 3.12: Social Origin of Politically Rehabilitated Persons Newly Recorded in Encyclopaedias

Social Origin	BSE²		MSE³		SIE		BSE³		Total	
	No.	%	No.	%	No.	%	No.	%	No.	%
Worker	6	16	2	7	17	15	23	25	48	18
Peasant	9	24	7	26	28	24	22	24	66	24
Others[a]	14	38	15	55	56	48	36	40	121	45
Unknown	8	22	3	11	16	14	9	10	36	13
Total	37	100	27	100	117	100	90	100	271	100

Note: a. The category 'others' contains professions which cannot be ranked as 'worker' or 'peasant' and which are usually characterised as so-called 'bourgeois': executives, merchants, artisans, nobility.

Table 3.13: Social Classification According to Office of Politically Rehabilitated Persons Newly Recorded in Encyclopaedias[a]

Social Sector	BSE²		MSE³		SIE		BSE³		Total	
	No.	%	No.	%	No.	%	No.	%	No.	%
Party	14	38	1	4	21	18	19	21	55	20
State	6	16	12	44	52	44	54	60	124	46
Army	9	24	10	37	27	23	11	12	57	21
Diplomacy	1	3	2	7	3	3	3	9	3	
Foreigner or Komintern	4	11	—	—	14	12	3	3	21	8
Miscellaneous	3	8	2	7	—	—	—	—	5	2
Total	37	100	27	100	117	100	90	100	271	100

Note: a. In case of change of career, the position held in the thirties predominates.

were, to be sure, predominantly party executives. Nevertheless, the *MSE* in particular displays an extraordinarily small share of new names from the party machinery. The only party man to be newly mentioned is secretary A. Ikramov, who had been convicted during the trial against Bukharin and others. His name was the first among this special group of victims to be recorded in a work of reference. The party sector recovered in subsequent editions and attained the average level.

Special attention should be paid to the number of biographical entries of higher military men, which, proportionally, exhibited a distinct decrease for the first time in the *BSE³*. In the second edition of the *BSE*, this group comprised 35 per cent of the total number. The names of Tuchačevskij, Egorov and Bljucher complete the category 'marshals of the Soviet Union who have been purged'. The same applied to the heads of the Political Department of the army, through the names of Antonov-Ovseenko, Bubnov and Gamarnik. It may be added that their notorious successor and purger of the army L.Z. Mechlis in his turn sank into oblivion, though not until after 1961.

The social backgrounds of these 13 (former) military men appeared to be different from the rest of the BSE^2 total group of 37. Of the military leaders, 7 had not become party members until 1917-18. These included 5 officers from the army of the Czar, of whom 1 was a career soldier (Tuchačevskij). Only Egorov descended from the working classes.

In conclusion, we can claim that the selection of names in the volumes of the second edition of the *BSE*, published from 1957 to 1958, contained a disproportionately large number of military men. In the selection of military men less notice was taken of early party memberships than was the case with other names. The conclusion is that the army had a voice of its own in the selection of names for rehabilitation in works of reference in the fifties.

Finally, the nationalities of those involved may have played a part in selection. In the case of Russians, Belorussians and Ukrainians, this cannot be established accurately. Only if a person was known not to belong to the Russian nationality did we use a determination of ethnic group other than Russian. Other cases are classified as Russian. Given this restriction, Table 3.14 shows that in absolute number the Russians are clearly dominant and are followed only at great distance by the Ukrainians. A relatively large number of Latvians have been recorded, and, in addition, many Georgians, Armenians and Poles are mentioned. The number of names of Jewish communists is insignificant, considering the party structure before the purges. The other nationalities are so divided that one gets the impression that the compilers of the encyclopaedias had to provide a distribution of a number of entries among the non-Slavonic nationalities; in the *SIE* and BSE^3 the total came to about as many as were available for Great Russians.

The Revision of Party Histories

The new edition of the *Istorija KPSS*, the history of the communist party of the Soviet Union, which was meant to succeed the official party history since 1938, the *Short Course*, was published in

Table 3.14: Nationality of Names of Politically Rehabilitated Persons Newly Recorded in Encyclopaedias

Nationality[a]	BSE²		MSE³		SIE		BSE³		Total	
	No.	%	No.	%	No.	%	No.	%	No.	%
Russian	13	35	9	33	42	36	34	38	98	36
Ukrainian	8	22	3	11	13	11	14	16	38	14
White Russian	1	3	—	—	4	3	4	4	9	3
Latvian	3	8	3	11	8	7	6	7	20	7
Estonian	—	—	1	4	4	3	1	1	6	2
Lithuanian	1	3	1	4	2	2	2	2	6	2
Georgian	1	3	—	—	8	7	1	1	10	4
Armenian	1	3	1	4	3	3	4	4	9	3
Azerbajdžan	—	—	1	4	4	3	1	1	6	2
Kazach	—	—	1	4	—	—	—	—	1	0.5
Uzbek	—	—	1	4	2	2	1	1	4	2
Turkmen	—	—	—	—	1	1	2	2	3	1
Tadžik	—	—	—	—	1	1	1	1	2	1
Cossack	—	—	3	11	3	3	2	2	8	3
Jewish	2	5	—	—	5	4	5	6	12	4
Polish	2	5	1	4	—	—	6	7	9	3
Kirghiz	—	—	—	—	—	—	1	1	1	0.5
Miscellaneous	5	14	2	7	16	14	5	6	28	10
Unknown	—	—	—	—	1	1	—	—	1	0.5
Total	37	100	27	100	117	100	90	100	271	100.0

Note: a. Determination of nationality on the basis of name, place of birth and possible reference in encyclopaedic article.

1959.[81] One of the most striking properties of this edition is the absence of historical personalities. It mentions very few names compared to the *Short Course*, which is full of names of politicians, albeit usually in an entirely negative sense. This edition was revised in 1962 and, towards the end of that same year, the 'second, extended edition' of the party history was published.[82] In this, more names were presented than in the edition of 1959. In general, small lists of 'excellent party workers' of both unincriminated and rehabilitated people were mentioned more frequently, in places where the 1959 edition had not yet supplied specification (e.g. with respect to the meritorious party executives who had waged the battle against the Mensheviks,[83] the new members of the party organisation in St Petersburg,[84] the *Pravda* group,[85] and the committee for agricultural collectivisation).[86]

In the new edition, the names of Stalin and Molotov were now recorded in a negative context as well, or omitted in the passage on their work in the Civil War, i.e. on the military-revolutionary committee of the Northern Caucasus,[87] yet their names continued to be included in small lists of appreciated people.[88] Other figures from the party leadership in the declining years of Stalin disappeared from the new edition, such as Kaganovič,[89] Mechlis,[90] and Ščadenko,[91] all of whom had been clearly co-responsible for the terror. Vorošilov retained his positive mention, yet this time it was Tuchačevskij who was honoured for the suppression of the revolt in Kronštadt.[92] Vorošilov was only mentioned as leader of the delegates to the tenth party congress who personally made a stand against the insurgents.

To illustrate the changes in the positive lists of names, we will enumerate here the Bolsheviks who returned from exile in 1917. In 1962, a number of people who had been subjected to purging, posthumous degradation or incrimination were added to the list. These names are italicised: *Bubnov*, Dzeržinskij, Džaparidze, *Kosior*, Kujbyšev, Ordžonikidze, *Pjatnickij*, *Rudzutak*, Sverdlov, *Skrypnik*, Stalin, Šaumjan, Jaroslavskij and the former Duma representatives Badaev, Muranov, Petrovskij and Samojlov. Even Skrypnik, a complicated historiographical case, was mentioned quite often in 1962.[93]

There clearly appears to be a difference here between the editions of the party history in 1959 and 1962: the first is simply much more sparing with names than the second, even in those cases where the progress of rehabilitation does not impede the mention of additional names.

An evident addition in 1962 is the use of the names of the high military officials Tuchačevskij, Uborevič, and Jakir in the series 'heroes from the civil war' as well as Egorov, who is described as a 'former Czarist officer'.[94] In 1959, these names had been excluded from the official party history, even though the encyclopaedias had already recorded them: the *BSE*[2] had honoured Tuchačevskij since 1957, among other places under the revised entry 'KPSS'.[95] The other generals had already been included in the *BSE*[2] as well.

The party history of 1959 supplied no details on the personality cult. Berija and Ežov were mentioned as co-responsible persons. The revised edition provided a supplement to this by mentioning Ordžonikidze's suicide (this was the first time it had been mentioned in a work of reference) and the victims of Stalin: Postyšev and Kaminskij, who were reported to have protested against the terror.[96] Bljucher, Egorov, Tuchačevskij, Uborevič and Jakir were presented as military victims; the Leningrad affair was elucidated through the names of Voznesenskij, Kuznecov and Rodionov. Our attention is drawn to the fact that nothing was changed in the series of names of party people as regards the national minorities. Only the Ukrainian Skrypnik is mentioned.[97] It thus appears that there was a lack of willingness to acknowledge contributions to the party by leaders of the national communities.

The next revision, the third edition, had been lost in its first version: this edition was published in October 1969, only to be impounded by the KGB before the public could get access to it.[98] It was said to be especially connected to material relating to the repression, which referred to victims having been killed and the detrimental effect of the purging on the army. These relatively simple statements were rejected, an ominous sign. A draft for the ninth volume of the *History of the Soviet Union* had been prepared by the Academy of Social Sciences in 1964. At the time, a number of rather more far-reaching suggestions were made, yet without result, for a paragraph on the illegality of the show trials including examples and quotations was not permitted.[99]

In 1970 the third edition finally came on to the market.[100] Now Khrushchev's name had disappeared from the lists, while Stalin and Molotov had been revalued.[101] However, the former right-wing opposition leader A.I. Rykov was also mentioned as a participant in the third party congress without further comment.[102] In a similar manner, V.P. Nogin, previously regarded as an 'opportunist', was included.[103] A.P. Smirnov, who had been part of the Tolmačev-Ejsmont opposition in the thirties and who had been expelled from the Central Committee, was also present in the new edition[104], as was K.J. Bauman, who had served as a scapegoat for the excesses of collectivisation.[105]

The list of victims of the terror, that is to say, the non-militaries, was expanded: Bubnov, Kosior, Krylenko, Postyšev, Rudzutak, Čubar', Ejche, Jakovlev, Kosarev, Čaplin.[106]

This, however, does not come up for discussion until the topic '20th congress', and does not appear under that of terror. Ordžonikidze and Kaminskij were now presented as those who had opposed the terror.[107] What precisely happened to the victims was not clearly described, while the death of Ordžonikidze was ignored altogether.

The third edition thus demonstrates a smaller degree of interest in the system of the terror and its contents, while more names of its victims are mentioned, but in the context of the appreciative passages on the recovery from the personality cult. The selection of names mentioned here and there is more balanced in this edition than in the earlier, although the common practice of allotting a prominent role to the ruling leaders in too premature a stage in history has not been avoided.The shades of intent with which members of former oppositions are mentioned in places which bear no relation to dissident activity is a common property of the historiography in the years after Khrushchev. In subsequent editions of the party history, the fourth edition from 1973, this approach has been maintained on the same level and has not been extended.

Commemorations in the Press

Introduction

Since 1956 biographical outlines of Stalin's victims have been published in the Soviet daily press. Such contributions could not be published without approval of the party authorities, so that one may speak of an open or public rehabilitation. An investigation of the daily press must analyse its meaning, determine the relation between formal rehabilitation and public rehabilitation, assess the number of national and regional publications and, finally, supply a general framework of interpretation.

This investigation has limited itself to biographies and posthumously rehabilitated persons. Furthermore, it deals exclusively with executives in the party, state or army who were party members. Artists, literary men and scientists who played no public part have not been included.

We have examined not only the national dailies *Pravda* and *Izvestija*, but also the most important Russian-language dailies of the federal republics. Papers of the unions and of the Ministries of Education, Defence, etc. have been included as well, in so far as these were referred to in the biographical source for articles in the press *Letopis' Gazetnych Statej*. Data have been checked until 1980.

The commemorative articles in the press have furthermore been differentiated by means of a separate evaluation of the first published commemoration of a personality. By including such articles, the paper in question and therefore the relevant party section has shown initiative, or at least the initiative was approved by the authorities in Moscow. In the subsequent investigation the term 'initiative article' will be used for this. In cases where articles were published simultaneously in several papers for the first time, the national press has been registered as initiator. In the case of simultaneous publication in *Pravda* and *Izvestija*, initiative has been ascribed to *Pravda*, because one is dealing here with a co-ordinated action of the party.

In these press articles, announcements on rehabilitation of the people involved remain opaque. The precise date is recorded only rarely, yet in sufficient measure to be able to conclude that formal rehabilitations took place particularly in the period 1954-9. Rehabilitation is nonetheless mentioned in general terms, in formulae such as 'The communist party and the people restored the creditable memory of sons of the country who died innocent.' Restoration to good reputation is quite often presented as a resurrection, as it were a cynical paraphrase of Aino Kuusinen's aphorism quoted above (p. 54): 'he is alive and in our midst'. Detailed accounts of arrests and the course of proceedings at the convictions rarely occurred in the daily press.

In general, much more information was published in the periodicals. Many biographies of rehabilitated people, including some information on the arrests of those involved, were published in *Voprosy Istorii KPSS* and in *Voenno-istoričeskij Žurnal* in the years 1963-4.[108] In addition, the large number of biographies in book form also constituted a source of information.

Since 1962 a series of scapegoats, said to have been especially responsible for the purges, have been presented in the press. Constantly involved are Berija and the members of the so-called anti-party group Molotov, Malenkov, Kaganovič or police officials who had been convicted in the period 1954-6 (Ruchadze, Rapava).

Those rehabilitated are often presented as exemplary, and not just as good communists and patriots of the ordinary type. This model function has not been reserved purely for former victims of Stalin, for such exemplary conduct is also mentioned in other cases. This exemplary function is often reflected in the title of the article. Commemorations are then announced as 'a true son of the party', 'a true son of the country', 'the legendary hero N.', 'soldier of the revolution', etc. Such articles are customarily published on the occasion of the 60th, 65th, 70th, 80th, 90th or 100th birthday of the rehabilitated. For important historical personalities, commemorative meetings are organised as well, at which prominent party people, relatives of the victims and old Bolsheviks give speeches. A brief report is published in the historical professional press or in the dailies. Commemorative articles also appear in series, like the commemorations of the revolution, the foundation of the Red Army, or the Order of the Red Banner.

In addition, series are published in the Soviet press under the headings 'fighters for the revolution', 'ardent fighters for the victory of communism', 'veterans of the revolution'. In such a series, where articles are often published at considerable intervals, commemorations emerge of both rehabilitated people and survivors of the terror.

The simultaneous commemoration of several personalities in various daily papers or in the entire press causes a distortion of the quantitative picture. This phenomenon was initiated in 1963 by a rush of articles as a result of the 70th commemoration of the birthday of Marshal Tuchačevskij (15 February) and the 60th of N.A. Voznesenskij, victim of the Leningrad affair (1 December). In 1963, A.S. Bubnov and A.V. Kosarev were commemorated in nine papers, whereas seven papers devoted attention to V.I. Mežlauk and I.S. Unšlicht. In 1964, S.V. Kosior and V.K. Bljucher were commemorated in the entire press, and articles were published on P.E. Dybenko in eight dailies and on Ja. Gamarnik in five papers. In 1965, the phenomenon began to diminish. At that time V.G. Knorin was commemorated in six papers and five articles were devoted to N.V. Krylenko. Soldiers I.E. Jakir and I.P. Uborevič were each apportioned six articles in 1966. A year later, corps commander Gaj was honoured in nine papers. Later on, P.E. Dybenko (1969), Ja. Berzin (1971), and G.D. Gaj (1977) came to public attention in a similar manner.

Press interest in the rehabilitated pales into insignificance beside the public commemorations of a number of prominent communists who were not victims of Stalin. A great deal of press interest is reserved for, to take some examples, Kalinin, chairman of the Central Executive Committee, Frunze, people's commissar for defence, and Dzeržinskij, chief of the Čeka.

The Press between 1956 and 1961

Between the twentieth and twenty-second party congresses commemorative articles were published almost exclusively in the daily papers of various federal republics and in the press of the

Table 3.15: Number of Initiative Articles and Total Number of
Commemorative Articles in the Press, 1956-80 (see Appendix D)

Year	Initiative Articles	Total Number of Commemorative Articles
1956	3	3
1957	19	21
1958	16	18
1959	4	7
1960	12	14
1961	6	10
1962	16	52
1963	48	131
1964	66	165
1965	31	66
1966	24	54
1967	23	78
1968	8	31
1969	6	35
1970	6	27
1971	10	31
1972	4	13
1973	6	28
1974	3	28
1975	6	37
1976	12	35
1977	4	51
1978	3	26
1979	3	26
1980	1	22

Ministry of Defence. Press interest is far from uniform (see Table
3.16). A differentiated approach for each republic can be
detected: in the Central Asian republics hardly any commemorative articles were published in this period, in the Transcaucasian
press the Georgian papers did not participate and the Armenian
press did not embark upon articles on the rehabilitated until an
advanced stage. After 1958, the number of articles rapidly
decreased, with the exception of the press in Armenia. The press in
the Baltic countries surpassed all in this period.

In the course of 1956 a prominent victim of Stalin was
commemorated in the respective presses of the Baltic federal
republics: the Latvian Jan Rudzutak (member, later a candidate
member of the politburo of the CPSU in 1926-32 and 1932-7)[109];
the Estonian Jan Anvel't (leader of the Estonian Revolutionary
Commune in 1918-19, later a Komintern executive)[110], and the
Lithuanian Zigmas Angaretis (secretary of the International

Figure 3.1: Biographical Articles in the Press, 1956-80 (see Table 3.15)

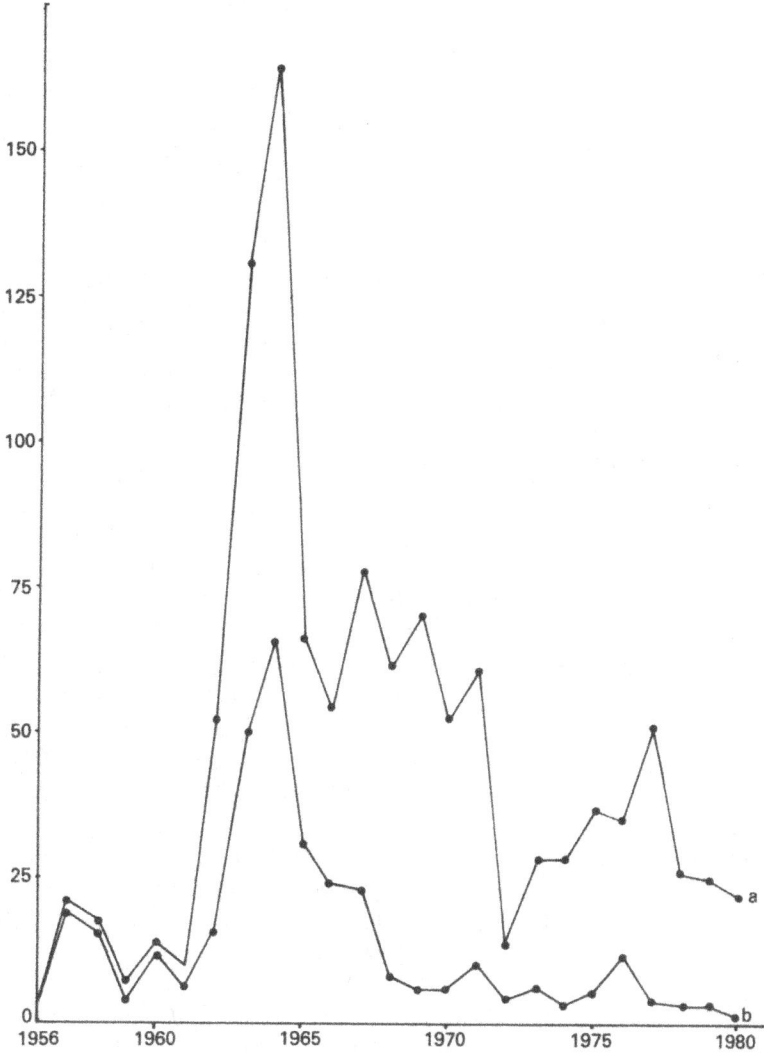

Note: a. Number of commemorative articles.
b. Number of initiative articles.

Table 3.16: Initiative Articles in the Press, 1956-61

	1956	1957	1958	1959	1960	1961
Bakinskij Rab.	—	2	2	2	1	—
Kommunist (Arm.)	—	1	—	—	8	2
Krasnaja Zvezda	—	2	1	1	1	1
Sov. Estonija	1	5	1	—	—	—
Sov. Latvija	1	5	7	—	—	1
Sov. Litva	1	—	1	—	—	1
Other	—	4	4	1	2	1
Total	3	19	16	4	12	6

Control Committee of the Komintern in 1926-35).[111] The latter two were honoured by commemoration of their birthdays, Rudzutak in relation to the celebration of the October revolution.

The articles did not breathe a word about the people involved having been purged and eliminated. The public was led to understand that here were virtuous sons of the working people who had dedicated their lives to the people. They were good revolutionary leninists, even though one or two things could be held against Angaretis.[112] All three of them were explicitly presented as true communists of their nationalities, which in the cases of Anvel't and Angaretis forms a remarkable contrast to the accusation of nationalism made against them during the purges.[113]

The Baltic press, particularly in Latvia and Estonia, continued the publication of commemorative articles in the years 1957-8. Many more of these were published here than elsewhere in the Soviet Union, and always involved personalities of the respective nationalities. In addition, these were the only papers in the Soviet press which sometimes, by referring to a 'tragic death', indicated that victims of the terror were involved.[114] The death of Robert Ejche, Latvian and candidate member of the politburo of the CPSU, was at this stage explicitly imputed to the 'gang of Berija'.[115] Apparently, the idea was to cultivate national pride. So far, hardly any historical personality could be found in the Baltic federal republics who had played a prominent part in the Soviet Union during the Interbellum and who had stayed alive. There were enough martyrs who had died in the underground communist movement, but the actual leaders fell victim to the Great Terror.[116]

The priority of these publications in the Baltic areas, through which the relevant communist parties, as it were, regained their national leaders, does not represent the only evidence. The amnesty for collaborators mentioned in Chapter 2 in general reflected a benevolent attitude of the central authorities towards the population of these countries.[117]

In 1957, the daily paper of the Ministry of Defence, *Krasnaja Zvezda*, began to devote a biographical article to one of the purged generals every year. A tentative beginning was made by reviewing the personal history of the Ukrainian first-rank army commander I.I. Fed'ko together with those of two accredited heroes from the Civil War, Vostrecov and Fabricius, who had died before the great purge.[118] In these, the peasant and working-class backgrounds of these soldiers were referred to and their different ethnic origins emphasised.

The first typical commemorative article, characteristic of the approach to Stalin's victims, was devoted to Marshal V.K. Bljucher (1890-1938), and was written by one of his former assistants.[119] The largest part of the article deals with Bljucher's legendary expedition through the southern Urals in the Civil War. Other important moments from the military career of the marshal were briefly touched upon without going into detail. The author paid a good deal of attention to the plain background of his hero, to the latter's admirable character traits, and to the many orders granted him.

With great emphasis, he pointed out that Bljucher had risen from the rank of soldier to marshal. No information was given on Bljucher's fate since August 1938: the reader would get the idea that he was still alive, were it not for the use of the past tense. The Bljucher case will be examined in further detail in a case-study below.

Bljucher was by far the most important military man to be commemorated in *Krasnaja Zvezda* in these years. The other generals in the series, R.I. Berzin, V.I. Šorin and D.P. Žloba, had acquired great fame in the Civil War, yet after the middle of the twenties they were no longer active in the army.[120] The same holds for the former supreme commander S.S. Kamenev.[121] Apparently, the political delicacy of the commemoration of these generals was less significant than that of higher officers who had been in command in the thirties (despite the fact that Berzin was expelled from the army as a Trotskyist in 1927). It was not until the twenty-second party congress that the barriers to commemoration of these commanders were removed.

It is remarkable that practically every article was written by a former assistant to the general involved. This is mentioned explicitly: on the one hand, a certain reliability of the contribution is thus suggested, while, on the other, requests for public rehabilitation by old Bolsheviks and surviving high officials are forestalled. The fact that these authors nonetheless compromise themselves appears from the deficiencies in the articles, the non-recording of years of death and circumstances of the purges, gaps in careers, etc.

The series of names mentioned in *Krasnaja Zvezda* is not identical with the series recorded in the encyclopaedias of the same period: Berzin and Žloba do not appear until later. Encyclopaedic contributions concerning those who were associated with Tuchačevskij did not get subsequent commemorative articles in the press.

It is true that in *Krasnaja Zvezda* not many biographies of this type were published, yet the paper expressed the wish to write more on Stalin's victims from the army. The director of the army archives provided a series of names which had been famous in the past, but which were now virtually unknown. As 'great defenders of the socialist mother country' he mentioned, among others, Bljucher, Žloba, Kovtjuch, Primakov, Kutjakov and Levandovskij, and, as 'military commanders', among others, Vacetis, Kedrov, Antonov-Ovseenko and Dybenko.[122] A remarkable series, even though many names are still missing, because one of the victims of the Tuchačevskij trial, i.e. Primakov, is bracketed together with some of the judges in this trial, Bljucher and Dybenko. Although the Tuchačevskij trial had been revised and those involved had been formally rehabilitated, the time had not yet come for freely recording their names in the press. It is also remarkable that in this series such little room is reserved for Vacetis, once supreme commander of the Red Army.

Finally, a number of soldiers appear to have been commemorated not in *Krasnaja Zvezda* but in the press of a federal republic. In such cases, the nationality rather than the profession of the person involved is considered to be of importance. From the inconsistency with which names of Stalin's victims are published in the press, it appears that no central list of names was published on the basis of which the press had to act: there was a prohibition against press articles on victims of the trial against Tuchačevskij *et al.* As became evident in the previous paragraph, matters could be carried further only in encyclopaedias.

The sudden explosion of commemorative articles in the Armenian press in 1960 (see Table 3.16) can possibly be explained by the change of leadership in this Soviet republic.

The first party secretary S.A. Tovmasjan was removed in August 1960 and succeeded by Ja.N. Zarobjan, without any apparent reason. The publication of six of the eight commemorative articles took place after this dismissal.

These biographical outlines were presented in October and November 1960 in relation to the fortieth anniversary of Soviet Armenia.[123] The contents of the articles conformed to this by examining predominantly the activities of the people involved at the time of the Civil War. Reference was not made to the nationality issue or to potential scapegoats. In the case of Armenia, too, it may be argued that the principal function of commemorative articles consisted in the presentation of good communist Armenians, who devoted themselves to the unification of Armenia with Soviet Russia.

The Press between 1961 and 1965

The quantitative survey of commemorative articles in the press (Table 3.15 and Figure 3.1) shows a peak in the years 1963 and 1964. Both the number of articles and the number of initiative articles are significantly greater in this period than in other years. The role of the national papers *Pravda* and *Izvestija* is considerable at this time (Table 3.17), but in the remaining years of the period under examination their role can be disregarded, with the exception of 1962.

In that year, the commemoration campaign was initiated under the auspices of the national press, after a start in December 1961 by the publication of the first newspaper article on Marshal Tuchačevskij in *Izvestija*.[124] In expectation of the twenty-second party congress, practically nothing of the kind had been published since April of that year. Even Ordžonikidze's birthday at the time of the congress was hardly commemorated, even though this commemoration was usually an illustrious one.[125]

Shortly before the congress, the water had been tested by publishing an article on one of the victims of the Tuchačevskij trial, army commander I.P. Uborevič, in *Sovetskaja Litva*.[126] In addition to the Ordžonikidze case this trial formed a central topic for discussion at the twenty-second congress.

The party congress resulted in an extensive campaign in which

Table 3.17: Initiative Articles in the Press, 1962-7

	1962	1963	1964	1965	1966	1967
Izvestija	2	7	6	—	1	1
Pravda	4	5	4	1	—	1
Bakinskij Rab.	1	1	4	4	5	—
Kazachst. Pravda	—	1	6	2	—	1
Kommunist (Arm.)	1	3	5	5	5	4
Komm. Tadžik.	—	—	7	1	1	1
Krasnaja Zvezda	3	12	9	3	—	1
Pravda Ukrainy	—	4	3	1	3	3
Pravda Vostoka	—	1	—	2	—	3
Sov. Belorussija	—	1	1	3	—	—
Sov. Latvija	1	3	4	—	—	1
Sov. Rossija	—	—	4	1	2	1
Turkm. Iskra	—	—	2	2	—	—
Zarja Vostoka	—	3	—	3	4	4
Other	4	7	11	3	3	3
Total	16	48	66	31	24	23

Stalin's terror was publicly exposed in detail. Within this frame-work, commemoration of the victims was initiated. Even if in 1962 the campaign as yet continued to take place on a limited scale, from February 1963 newspaper readers were confronted quite frequently with the rehabilitated victims of Stalin. From January 1965, however, a strong decline can be observed. The level of commemoration in *Pravda* and *Izvestija* has remained low ever since and hardly any further initiative has been taken.

In press articles published after the twenty-second party congress there were usually formulas from which the reader learnt some things about the terror:[127]

— v konce 30-ch godov po klevetničeskomo donosu tragičeski pogib (died at the end of the thirties after slanderous denuncia-tion);

— žizn' ego tragičeski oborvalas' v period kul'ta ličnosti Stalina (his life was tragically ended at the time of the personality cult of Stalin);

— žizn' ego tragičeski oborvalas' v konce trinadcatych godov. On byl oklevetan, arestovan i bezžalostno uničtožen v razgar repressij, prisuščich vremena kul'ta Stalina (his life was tragic-ally ended at the end of the thirties. He was calumniated,

arrested and destroyed without mercy at the height of the prosecutions which were characteristic of the time of the glorification
of Stalin);

— tragičeski pogib v ... godu. On stal žertvoj bezzakonija i
proizvola v period kul'ta ličnosti (he died tragically in the year
... He became the victim of lawlessness and arbitrariness at the
time of the personality cult).

The last example in particular was a very common formulation
in short biographies. The euphemistic phrasing is quite opaque.
The period of the personality cult is in many cases taken to be the
years after 1936 only, not the preceding period.

From the middle of 1956 onwards, information on the tragic
deaths of victims was occasionally omitted, and disappeared
almost completely in 1966. At the most, the formula 'the life of N.
was tragically ended in 1937' sometimes occurred. Rehabilitation
was mentioned only rarely in articles after 1965. After 1968, the
recording of a 'tragic end' is highly exceptional. The reader can no
longer infer from biographical articles in the press that he is
dealing with a victim of the terror. Only in the period 1962-5 was
attention paid to the era of the terror. The years 1963 and 1964
excelled in the large number of commemorative articles in which
this was done.

The explanation for the boom in commemorations in 1963-4 in
the daily and periodical press as well as in the form of special
conferences and meetings lies in the political function of the
phenomenon. The large scale of the campaign disallows an explanation in the sphere of a personal struggle for power in which
involvement in the purges served as a weapon.

Perhaps the idea was to create an image of a party, which, after
purification through the recognition of the disgraceful past, makes
an attempt to establish true communism, in accordance with the
party programme of 1961. Nevertheless, the biographical texts on
the rehabilitated contain no references to such a design. To
surmount the consequences of the personality cult was indeed held
to be a prerequisite for the realisation of the programme, as will be
illustrated below, yet the press campaign did not have this as
a goal.

The commemorations possibly had to appease oppositions. Old,
surviving Bolsheviks and children of prominent victims played an

important part in the campaign as authors of articles and as speakers at commemorative gatherings. Several distinguished figures, such as politburo member Mikojan and Marshal Mereckov also attracted notice by their considerable activity. In cases where formal rehabilitations had been completed, the pressure of this group alone cannot have carried sufficient weight to cause the party leadership to embark upon such a large-scale campaign. The party leaders would have responded with incidental public rehabilitations. This circumstance, though, may in some cases serve as an explanation.

Possibly, the campaign was directed against the group of apparatchiks who were not pleased with Khrushchev's destalinisation. In subsequent years, after all, this group appeared to be important. These latent adherents to the so-called 'anti-party group' may have been a target of the campaign of public rehabilitations. This hypothesis is supported by the connection between the campaign and the course of proceedings at the twenty-second party congress.

Above all, however, relations with China should be taken into account in the explanation. It has already been argued above that the Sino-Soviet conflict proved to be of paramount importance during the twenty-second congress (see pp. 100-101).

The climax in the campaign of public rehabilitations occurred in the years 1963-4, at approximately the same time as a sharpening of reciprocal abuse. The issue of the personality cult became a matter of controversy in this period in particular. This cannot have been mere coincidence and its significance must be examined further.

The theme of the personality cult emerged in Sino-Soviet polemics as one of the '25 items' put forward for discussion by China (June 1963). Under item 20 it was recalled that, on the pretext of 'fighting against the personality cult', there had been rude interference with internal affairs of other parties.[128] These had been forced to replace their leaders. The 'Public letter' of the communist party of the Soviet Union to Beijing on 14 July 1963 went into this matter in great detail.[129] That the Soviet population was now materially well off and that the 'atmosphere of fear, suspicion and uncertainty had disappeared' was ascribed to the subdual of the consequences of the personality cult.[130]

Ask people whose fathers and mothers were victims of the

repression at the time of the personality cult what it means to receive recognition that their fathers, mothers and brothers were honest people and that they themselves are no outcasts in our society, but first-rate sons and daughters of the Soviet mother country.[131]

Only on this basis, the argument went, could communism continue to be built up in accordance with the new party programme. The Soviet party perceived a flourishing of the personality cult in China at this time. The ideological principle for this cult was seen in the use of an incorrect conception of dictatorship of the proletariat. This involved the adoption of Stalin's theory that class struggle assumes a sharper form as socialism draws nearer.

China, in its turn, observed a still extant hostile class inside the Soviet Union and claimed that Moscow took risks by using the conception of 'people's state'. This had been discussed in item 18 of the '25 items'.[132]

Later on in the dispute, in February 1964, Suslov once again attacked Chinese views by pointing out that Stalin's theory of a sharpened class struggle was intended to justify grave violations of socialist legality.[133] His party had in the meantime dissociated itself from this. Chinese commentary, however, merely revealed a firmer point of view.[134]

In the course of the years 1963-4 the polemic on the theme of the personality cult became more and more concrete and virulent. Moscow reproached Mao Ze-dong for founding his internal politics on the personality cult and for extending his cult over the entire communist movement.[135] Beijing primarily blamed Khrushchev for denouncing Stalin and heaping abuse upon him. Thus, he insulted marxism-leninism and also the Soviet people, while he played into the hands of imperialism. In their analysis of the causes of Khrushchev's fall from power, this was the first consideration in the Chinese commentary.[136]

Suslov established an explicit connection between the personality cult, terror, rehabilitations and Chinese policies in a long passage of his speech before the Central Committee of the CPSU on 14 February 1964. The Kremlin needed more than six weeks to decide upon its publication, which may form an indication of the amount of explosive political power carried by the speech. In addition to various aspects which have already been discussed above, he underlined that the personality cult was nothing other than the method of physical repression of party members who were suspected by Stalin of disagreeing with him.

Arbitrariness had descended upon the choice of the party when socialism had already been accomplished. Stalin turned the weapons of dictatorship of the proletariat against the proper executives, according to Suslov. 'Even though numerous examples of Stalin's abuse of power during the period of the personality cult are generally known by now ... the Chinese leaders refer to mass repression as if we are dealing with irrelevant excesses.'[137] Subsequently, Suslov discussed the responsibility of Molotov, Kaganovič and Malenkov for the terror against prominent party members. He explained that 'the Chinese leaders wished to restore such inhuman practices and thus do harm to the interests of the people and the cause of socialism'.[138] Illustrated on the basis of biographical outlines on Stalin's victims, Suslov's speech sheds light on the relation between the Sino-Soviet dispute and the campaign against Stalin's terror. Even so, we are dealing here with a temporary ingredient of the polemic. After Khrushchev's fall from power the rehabilitation campaign was slackened and references to the personality cult diminished. Playing off Stalin's victims against China was a tactical method which should be associated specifically with Khrushchev.

The End of the Destalinisation Policy

The press campaign was revoked in 1965. Considerably fewer commemorative articles were published (see Table 3.17). From 1965 onwards, the national press gave only sporadic attention to Stalin's victims. References to the personality cult diminished in 1965 and virtually disappeared in 1966. Although the conflict with China went on, continuation of the polemic using arguments about the terror and the personality cult was abandoned. The cause of this change was twofold: Khrushchev's fall from power and changing relations inside the party.

Table 3.18: Total Number of Commemorative Articles in *Pravda* and *Izvestija*, 1962-6

	1962	1963	1964	1965	1966
Pravda	7	10	11	2	3
Izvestija	12	15	15	4	1
Total	19	25	26	6	4

In the spring of 1965 the army leadership began to press for rehabilitation of Stalin as a military man, and exerted pressure on the party to revise the destalinisation policy.[139] In September-October 1965 the party decided upon a change in policy: it emphasised cultural politics. Furthermore, the arrests of Sinjavskij and Daniel' implied the end of liberal tendencies.[140] The policy of public rehabilitations was also changed.

This became apparent from an article in *Pravda*, written by the chief of a newly established department for education and sciences at the Central Committee, S.P. Trapeznikov. In this he observed that destalinisation had been carried too far and that several of the rehabilitated had deserved no rehabilitation whatsoever. He felt that the personality cult had received too much attention at the expense of the contributions of ordinary citizens to the process of building up socialism. Trapeznikov argued that the nature of socialism had not been affected at all by the Stalin cult. Damage was said to have been limited to some social sectors. He charged Khrushchev, as became customary after his fall from power, with subjectivism and voluntarism.

Scientists, too, were supposed to be guilty of these charges by according certain people too much influence on history. 'Now and then people were praised who had played no significant part in the [historical] processes and had sometimes adopted opposite positions in the struggle.'[141] Unfortunately, Trapeznikov provides no example in his article.

This he did do, however, at meetings of which no public reports were published. It can be established for certain that he challenged the rehabilitation of F.F. Raskol'nikov, a Soviet diplomat who had disobeyed the order to return home in 1938. He was subsequently removed from the party and deprived of his citizenship; he died in Nice in 1939. His 'Public letter to Stalin', which presented a serious accusation, was published posthumously. Trapeznikov considered Raskol'nikov's rehabilitation to be unjustified, because he regarded the letter as treason. Even though Raskol'nikov was not formally 'dehabilitated' until 1969, this was a characteristic example.[142]

Trapeznikov's article in *Pravda* was a result of the decisions taken by the Central Committee at a session in September 1965. As the twenty-third party congress drew near, this critical note became more predominant. In a major article in *Pravda*, the concept of 'personality cult' was attacked.[143] The term 'period of the personality cult' was incorrect and un-marxist. This was a 'subjectivist influence'. The fact that several personalities had been allotted a greater role in history was ascribed to 'unprincipled conjuncturism'. In the articles, Soviet historians were summoned to fight against 'bourgeois nationalism, chauvinism, cosmopolitism, and anti-patriotism.'[144] After the twenty-third congress, a Georgian party secretary, D.G. Sturua, rephrased the meaning of this in powerful terms: 'Under the banner of the battle against the consequences of the personality cult, Trotskyism, right-wing deviations, bourgeois nationalism, and other anti-leninist ideological tendencies were rehabilitated.'[145]

From closer examination of the initiative articles which were published after Khrushchev's fall from power, it appears that more attention was devoted to officials of the secret police. Up to this point only a few 'čekists' had been commemorated in the press, such as Deribas, Kedrov, Lacis and Peters.[146] In the period 1965-7 a series of police chiefs were publicly rehabilitated. D'jakov, Džakupov, Gruodis, Lukašin, Masančin and Mikeladze were praised as good disciples of Dzeržinskij.[147] Their creditable features were integrity, respect for socialist legality, and loyalty to the party. Motives for rehabilitation of the secret police can be inferred from an article on the Kazach police chief Džakupov:

> There are people who, in relation to the subduing of the conse-
> quences of the personality cult, did not jib at besmirching the
> čekist framework as a whole. They do so despite the fact that
> the twentieth party congress explained that many faithful sons
> of the party and the people who served in the security machin-
> ery bravely challenged the policy of unjustified repression by
> Ežov and Berija and paid dearly for their attempts to reach
> Stalin's deaf ears.[148]

It is then reported how Džakupov resisted the arrest of, among others, the poet Sejfullin.

The motivation for the rehabilitation of Džakupov confirms the theory that party officials aspired to rehabilitation after Khrush-chev's fall from power. It is also noteworthy in this context that the Central Asian press, which did not begin to pay attention to persons of local origin until after Khrushchev's fall, concentrated on local police chiefs. Even the rehabilitations of 1965-7 show traces of resistance to the policy of destalinisation in the previous years. These publications even attest to restalinisation.

The explanation for this rejection of the policy of destalinisation does not essentially lie in personal rivalries inside the party leadership. More likely, we are dealing here with frustrations among the lower ranks in the party. At the twenty-third party congress, the future party secretary M.S. Solomencev was quite explicit about this. He spoke out against disrespectful criticism and objected to the defamation of party officials. He argued that the latter should be treated with respect.[149]

In February 1966 the trial against the dissidents Daniel' and Sinjavskij took place. Many rumours of an impending rehabilitation of Stalin circulated. Several important intellectuals and old Bolsheviks wrote collective letters to the party leaders to protest against the imminent trend. The return of Vorošilov, whose name had been associated with the 'anti-party group', to the Central Committee as well as Mikojan's departure from the politburo were signs of a volte-face in the party.

Apparently, the artificial separation between Stalin and the party in the interpretation of the Stalin era had produced insufficient results. Party officials sensed an offence in the vehemence of the attack on Stalin. To them, the denigration of Stalin meant the same as besmirching party and mother country, which affected them personally. Khrushchev underestimated the degree of aversion in the party to publicising the terror. Possibly, the campaign of public commemorations served as a boomerang, the catalyst which initiated Khrushchev's decline.

Central Asia, 1964-7

In the years 1964-5, the Central Asian press also devoted attention to its own deceased national leaders.[150] Such articles had been published incidentally towards the end of the fifties, whereas rehabilitations had been publicly accounted for in Uzbekistan only.[151] This time, however, 22 initiative articles were published in two years, after which the rate of occurrence decreased to incidental publication.

Most of the articles emphasise the struggle against the national movements, in particular against the Basmači movement. One may infer from this that it was possible to be an excellent communist, to be quite capable of collaborating with the ethnic Russians, and yet be a good son of one's nation.[152] An isolated initiative article on a Russian, D.V. Polujan, is primarily intended to indicate that the

Table 3.19: Number of Initiative Articles in the Central Asian Press, 1964-5

	1964	1965
Kommunist Tadžik.	7	1
Kazachst. Pravda	6	2
Sov. Kirgizija	—	1
Turkm. Iskra	2	2
Pravda Vostoka	—	2
Total	15	8

Russian people are not enemies of the other ethnic communities in the Soviet Union.[153]

Several articles, published in 1965 and 1967, clearly reflect foreign policy. Since the middle of the sixties, Soviet foreign policy had been increasingly directed towards the Third World. Simultaneously, closer relations with Turkey were pursued. The Central Asian republics, particularly Uzbekistan, were presented as examples of the Soviet model of development and modernisation, demonstrating at the same time how Turkish national culture was respected.[154] To competent observers, the contrast with the treatment of this group in Eastern Turkestan (China) was evident.[155] The rivalry between the Soviet Union and China emerged in these articles as well.

The presentation of Central Asia as a window to the Third World is nicely illustrated in the article on F. Chodžaev, chairman of the Central Executive Committee of the Uzbek SSR from 1927 to 1938.[156] Chodžaev had, at the show trial in 1938, been sentenced for bourgeois nationalism and attempted separation from the Soviet Union. Before he became a communist in 1920, the merchant's son Chodžaev was part of the nationalistic movement of Uzbeks, the party of Young Buchara which revolted against the emir in 1917. This background is made into a virtue in the commemorative article. Chodžaev is shown as a model. Of bourgeois descent, mentality and party, he had managed to overcome this completely and become an excellent communist. The leaders of the young Afro-Asian countries could take example from his progress.

On the occasion of another commemoration, that of K.S. Atabaev, chairman of the 'sovnarkom' of the Turkmenian SSR 1925-37, the Central Asian events are also presented as exemplary.[157] Atabaev had already distanced himself successfully from bourgeois nationalism before 1917. The 'brotherly assistance of the Russian proletariat' is furthermore presented as an important factor. These particulars were recorded only in the press of the relevant republics. At the same time, Chodžaev and Atabaev were commemorated in the central press, yet here references to bourgeois nationalism are missing and no reference is made to any exemplary function.[158]

Bourgeois Nationalism

From a political point of view, the theme of 'bourgeois nationalism' has always been extremely delicate in Soviet Russia. The fact that historical characters with such a past could be publicly rehabilitated has been illustrated above. However, it is not surprising that at the same time warnings were issued against nationalism in the press. In view of the specific characteristics of the Central Asian population, particularly that of religion, local nationalism could become politically dangerous through possible foreign relations; more specifically, relations with pan-Turkish and/or pan-Islamic movements. Warnings against such relations were also included in commemorative articles, as in the article on the chairman of the Uzbek sovnarkom in 1937 Sultan Segizbaev[159] and, above all, in the article of Turar Ryskulov,[160] one of the leading communists in Turkestan in the first half of the twenties. Ryskulov had become chairman of the Central Executive Committee of Turkestan in 1920 and had subsequently attempted to build up a united Turkish republic in Central Asia, which earned him a reprimand from Lenin. In 1921 he was summoned to Moscow to learn the right approach in other offices, and was afterwards allowed to return. In 1923-4 he was chairman of the sovnarkom of the Turkestan ASSR.

The commemorative article reported this story, yet appended a warning. Pan-Turkish and pan-Islamic movements were informed that the memory of Ryskulov was not useful for propaganda, because, after the deviation mentioned, he had proved himself to be an ardent Bolshevik who had no longer deflected from the party line. Three weeks after publication of the article, a commemoration of Ryskulov was published in *Izvestija* which did not contain this warning.[161] This time, too, no need was felt at the centre to refer with emphasis to pan-Turkish movements in view of the policy of establishing closer relations with Turkey.[162]

In general, the party has only with great caution rehabilitated people who had been charged with a 'bourgeois nationalist' past. Out of the 25 cases registered by Conquest, only 10 were commemorated in the press. The relevant articles are spread out over the period 1958-70, so there is no sign of a co-ordinated action.[163]

The first so-called 'bourgeois nationalist' who was commemorated in public was the Ukrainian N.A. Skrypnik. Soon after the twenty-second party congress, articles were published both in the Ukraine and in the central press on the occasion of the commemoration of his 90th birthday (January 1962).[164] Ukrainian by birth, Skrypnik was one of the founders of the Ukrainian Soviet republic. He had held various offices as people's commissar since 1918. In the twenties, he had advocated the conception of the Ukraine as a constituent republic in the Soviet Union. He had opposed Stalin's scheme of autonomisation, which entailed incorporation of the Ukraine into the existing Russian Federation. He had constantly defended the rights of the federal republics against Moscow centralism, which caused him to be severely criticised in 1933.[165] Skrypnik was even accused of bourgeois nationalism. He did not await the impending purge and committed suicide. Extensive denunciation followed posthumously, but in 1956 and subsequent years his name emerged first in a neutral, then in an accusing, sense.[166] This points to a dispute behind the scenes regarding his public rehabilitation. Formal juridical rehabilitation was not required because there had been neither trial nor execution. From Skrypnik's commemoration in 1962, it appears that the advocates of public rehabilitation had won. Beyond doubt, Khrushchev's assistant in matters of rehabilitation, A. Snegov, who wrote sympathetic articles on Skrypnik in 1956 as well as in 1962, was among these.[167] The contents of the commemorative articles were of especial interest to the reader because Stalin's nationalities policy was challenged. Little was said about the actual activities and ideas of Skrypnik. Thus, a sign was given that rehabilitation of 'bourgeois nationalists' was possible, provided that this was attended to with great judiciousness.

Details on the politics and writings of several 'bourgeois nationalists' were nonetheless not allowed to be published if they involved the nationality issue. This does also apply to the various cases of public rehabilitation in this group.

The Press between 1965 and 1980

In the period 1965-80 the quantity of commemorative articles is generally small, while initiative articles were published in scant numbers (see Figure 3.1, Tables 3.15 and 3.17, and Appendix D). In the years 1967 and 1977, the number of articles on the rehabilitated is larger than in the years before and after.

The explanation for these exceptions does not lie in a special political configuration, but in the celebration of half a century and sixty years of revolution respectively. Numerous press articles were devoted to old Bolsheviks, among whom were many obscure, but surviving, people. In the rush of the celebration of the revolution, the commemorative articles did not make any special impression.

Qualitatively, the level of commemoration was low as well in the seventies. In biographical articles, the careers of the people involved after 1921 were hardly mentioned, whereas their past as revolutionaries and fighters in the Civil War attracted all the attention. Apparently, the regime was capable of finding exemplary leaders of party and state in the present, yet it had to fall back on times long past for revolutionary zeal and Bolshevik romanticism. This trend was pervasive throughout mass propaganda. Popular biographies were printed in hundreds of thousands of copies (see case-study on Petrovskij below).

Even though one would not expect initiative articles in the seventies, these nonetheless occurred. They did not include historical personalities of interest and their standing in the party was relatively poor. They were often party officials.[168] The link of publication of these articles to a more general propagandistic aim appeared most strongly in the Armenian press. A campaign against corruption was held there, in which examples from the past were put forward. Incorruptibility and integrity were the virtues which were extolled.

In this period, the fact that victims of Stalin were involved and that rehabilitation had taken place is withheld from the reader. Indications as to the purging of the person involved are in some places indicated in terms like 'he died in the prime of his life', 'the ardent activity of the famous son of the people was ended in the ... year of his life'. Only those readers who were familiar with the issue of the terror could learn something from the specification of age or the recording of the year 1937 or 1938.

In the seventies, the question of 'to whom commemorative

articles are still being devoted' appears to be more relevant than the issue of whether there are new cases of rehabilitation.

As regards *Pravda*, it appears from the list of names that only those personalities who had already experienced a form of public rehabilitation before 1960 were commemorated.[169] We are dealing here with old Bolsheviks who are deemed to have become party members at an early stage.[170] Those involved are generally not burdened with an oppositional past.[171] No one was specifically bound to the history of one federal republic. This, then, is a rough characterisation of the selection for these 'iron commemorations'.[172] In *Izvestija* other personalities are commemorated, contrary to the publications in 1963-4 when both papers often paid attention to the same figures. The supplementary series contains names which were once associated with bourgeois nationalism (Ryskulov, Skrypnik) and other more problematic cases (Steklov, Bauman, Enukidze). The image of the government paper *Izvestija* is therefore slightly more liberal than that of the party paper *Pravda*. The frequency of commemoration of individual cases, moreover, is lower than in the sixties. At that time, commemoration could take place every five years, whereas in the period after 1967 only the 50th, 60th, 75th, 80th, 90th and 100th birthdays were commemorated.

As centenaries in Soviet society are readily used to launch into extensive commemorations, the eighties will supply an interesting picture of historical personalities whom the regime still considers to be of importance. After all, the élite of the thirties is then due to receive such commemorations.

The minor degree of interest in rehabilitation in the seventies fits in with the revaluation of Stalin. The tendency towards a certain restalinisation in ideology and cultural politics, which was becoming apparent in the years 1965 and 1966, definitely persisted in 1969.[173] Various contributions in *Kommunist* and *Oktjabr'* pressed for a more sympathetic approach to Stalin. The party secretariat prepared a large-scale campaign in commemoration of Stalin's 90th birthday. It seems that only the pressure from foreign communist parties, particularly the Polish and Hungarian parties, has prevented the politburo from an over-effusive commemoration of Stalin.[174] The placement of Stalin's bust near his tomb behind the Mausoleum, however, was a clear symbol of the altered attitude of the party towards the former leader.

In the seventies, negative aspects of Stalin's personality and politics occur only marginally in the literature. Stalin is once more the benefactor of the people and of socialism. He is the great national leader. Even the terror in the thirties is once again justified in some papers.[175]

Conclusion

Public rehabilitations and commemorations of victims of the terror in the press serve various political aims. There is actually no question of an independent campaign. Articles are placed within the framework of commemorations of the revolution, of the alliance of a federal republic with the Soviet Union, and of other important events. The articles are often part of a series in which they do not attract notice as rehabilitation articles. Before 1961 and after 1965, only insiders can tell whether biographical articles deal with victims of Stalin.

Biographical press articles are not published for the sake of rehabilitations in themselves. The moral motive of common humanitarian principles is entirely missing. The party prides itself upon the fact that these commemorations of victims attest to the consistent manner in which the party has once and for all finished with the terror. The selection of public rehabilitations in itself disproves this claim. Compared to other commemorations, press interest in Stalin's victims is relatively small.

Public rehabilitations in the press did not take place in accordance with a nationally determined, uniform pattern. A certain degree of differentiation of the Soviet press emerges from the investigation. There indeed appears to be a general framework within which the press moves. The national party leaders determine when to provide information on the terror and whether articles on Stalin's victims may be published at all in the press. In the months preceding the twenty-second party congress, this was apparently not permitted. Within these margins, however, there are relevant differences between the national press and the press of federal republics as well as between periodicals of the individual federal republics. Considerable differentiation can be noticed in terms of intensity as well as in the contents of the commemorative articles.

With the exception of the Ministry of Defence as mouthpiece of the military machinery, no important part in public rehabilitation has been played by social groups which have their own press organ.

In the years 1963 and 1964 only, the national papers *Pravda* and *Izvestija* played an important part in the initiation of commemorations of victims of the terror. This means that the party leaders left the initiative to parties of the federal republics and to the military leaders, even though the selection of names would usually be subject to Kremlin approval. This illustrates the need to make allowance for the feelings of non-Russian nationalities.

Communists of a particular nationality and Russian communists who joined hands fraternally illustrated the bonds between the Soviet nationalities. A clear demarcation, however, took shape with respect to those national communists who had been accused of bourgeois nationalism before the period of the great terror. They could not be written about in positive terms. A number of stalinist executives who had been accused of bourgeois nationalism were nonetheless publicly rehabilitated.

The amount of press interest in the commemoration of Stalin's victims was small, Virtually no major articles were published. The number of commemorative articles was relatively large in 1963 and 1964, especially in relation to the numbers of biographical articles published before and after. This series of public rehabilitations and commemorations formed part of the press campaign on Stalin's terror. The objective of this campaign was to convince the Chinese comrades that by following Mao they were on a wrong course.

Finally, initiatives for public rehabilitations in the period 1965-7 appear to have been taken so as to slow down the campaign on the terror, because the campaign was considered offensive to party executives. Several parties of federal republics which had taken a minimal part in the policy of destalinisation, especially in Central Asia, rehabilitated officials of the secret police. Such actions fit in with a campaign of restalinisation rather than destalinisation. Not every public rehabilitation is a demonstration of the intention of the communist party to overcome Stalin, the personality cult and the terror.

Informal Rehabilitation

Introduction

The work of Soviet historians was extremely difficult if it

concerned the purged. Historiography on the Soviet Union after 1934 had never been studied. A large number of documents from the period after 1941 had not been published,[176] and documents which were published, like those of the Council of People's Commissars, the Council of Labour and Defence, and the Central Executive Committee, were difficult to consult: they had been removed from libraries or were accessible only to high-ranking officials.[177] Still other documents, like those of Lenin, the government, the party congresses and the collected works of Stalin's assistants, were not easily accessible because of the absence of new editions.[178] Memoirs of old Bolsheviks had been spoiled by omission of certain passages, even as late as 1955.[179]

Soviet historians have nonetheless contributed to informal rehabilitation of the purged; but the question presents itself of whether they described the purged in sympathetic terms of their own accord, or only after a sign from higher up. We have investigated the way in which this informal rehabilitation emerges from historical periodicals. The investigation has been limited to the period around 1956: there were no large-scale public rehabilitations then, whereas formal procedures were in full swing. The inquiry has furthermore been limited to the periodicals *Voprosy Istorii* and *Istoričeskij Archiv*.

Voprosy Istorii

Records of names of Stalin's victims in the historical periodical *Voprosy Istorii* (circulation 1955-7 approximately 50,000 copies), published by the Academy of Social Sciences, did not occur in 1953 and 1954. Even so, names of old Bolsheviks who had survived the terror were re-entered and their memories of Lenin were again included in the paper (e.g. of G.I. Petrovskij, B.M. Volin and E.D. Stasova).[180] More use was also made of names of prominent party executives who had not been victimised, who had died before the terror and had not been calumniated posthumously, but whose names were simply never, or only rarely, mentioned. Examples are A.V. Lunačarskij and M.I. Vasil'ev-Južin.[181]

It was also relatively easy once again to mention, without deprecating epithets, a category of personalities who had died from natural causes and had been slandered posthumously. The historian M.N. Pokrovskij and the lawyer D.I. Kurskij, for example, were mentioned as revolutionaries.[182]

A good example in this category is P.A. Krasikov, the prominent lawyer and atheist activist who had been unjustly removed from his office as deputy chairman of the Supreme Court in 1938 and who had died of natural causes a year later. After his death, not a word was said about him until after Stalin's death.[183] *Voprosy Istorii* recorded his name in April 1955 and again described him as 'a prominent Bolshevik' in June 1955.[184] In subsequent issues, his name was mentioned repeatedly in lists of prominent Bolsheviks. This sympathetic approach, however, was limited to Krasikov's revolutionary activities.

The first victim of Stalin to be recorded in positive terms was the old Bolshevik I.I. Radčenko (1874-1942), a brother in arms of Lenin from the days of the St Petersburg Union of Struggle for the Liberation of the Working Classes. After the revolution, he held high offices in state economic bodies, yet had no significant function in the party. In the April issue of 1955, *Voprosy Istorii* published his memories of Lenin as a result of the commemoration of the revolution of 1905, to which this issue was predominantly devoted. Radčenko's memories, however, dealt with the period 1918-22.[185] The article was printed without a commentary on the author. Additional memories of Lenin were published from 1954 onwards, among which were a new series of collected memoirs.[186] Their selection and therefore also the publication of Radčenko's posthumous contribution could, in view of the importance of publicity on Lenin, only have been effected on a very high level and probably in the presidium. Until 1956, the selection was still small, for it was decided not to provide a more extensive edition of 'Memories of Lenin' until after the twentieth party congress.[187]

In 1955, *Voprosy Istorii* came up with only two further recordings of victims. Even the few names of rehabilitated victims which had been made public in relation to the trials against the secret police did not find their way into historiography immediately. It is also true, however, that in this category the most important name was used once again: N.A. Voznesenskij (1903-50), party economist, in 1941 first deputy chairman of the sovnarkom and member of the State Committee for Defence; since 1941 he had also been part of the politburo, of which he became a full member in 1947. In 1949, he was purged in the so-called Leningrad affair: the elimination of the supporters of Ždanov by Malenkov and Berija. Voznesenskij was formally rehabilitated during the trial against Abakumov in December 1954.

In the February issue of *Voprosy Istorii* in 1955, however, he was not mentioned among the members of the State Committee of Defence.[188] It was not until December 1955 that his name was mentioned in a positive sense in the periodical, when his book on Soviet economics during the Second World War was commended:

> in 1948 the work 'The war economics of the USSR in the period of the patriotic war' by N. Voznesenskij was published. The book shows the benefits of socialist economics, which guaranteed the victory over German imperialism. The work is worthy of praise because of its concrete historical testimonies and the general and differentiated numerical data. The author correctly emphasises that the 'great unity of the nations of the Soviet Union in the patriotic war, which the entire world admired, had grown on the basis of the victory of socialist production methods and the annihilation of the exploiting classes in the USSR'.[189]

This sentence has been interpreted by Sovietologists as a blow directed against Suslov, who had severely criticised both book and author in *Pravda* on 24 December 1952.[190] The rehabilitation persisted, for, in the subsequent issue, *Voprosy Istorii* quoted a speech of Voznesenskij before the Supreme Soviet which dealt with the postwar five-year plan. His name was mentioned as the speaker, though without stating his office.[191]

As Khrushchev also went into his case at great length during the twentieth party congress, Voznesenskij's historiographical treatment could be expected to be uncontroversial from then on. Even so, the *Leningrad Handbook*,[192] a work of reference which was particularly suited to provide an extensive biography of Voznesenskij, devoted only a few lines to him and did not even print a photograph. None of the victims of the Leningrad affair, for that matter, were granted the scope that could be expected. The entire affair was in fact ignored after Khrushchev's speech, until in 1963 various prominent papers took notice of it. Even at that time Voznesenskij's book was accompanied by critical comments.

It is still assumed that this was the work of Suslov and Kozlov.[193] The case has continued to be complicated, even after Khrushchev's fall from power. Except for Kuznecov and Voznesenskij, none of the victims of the Leningrad affair were granted a place in works of reference. Only Popkov was admitted to the *BSE* in 1975. As recently as 1978, Voznesenskij's 75th birthday was 'forgotten' in the press.[194]

Furthermore, there was some argument in *Voprosy Istorii* concerning Béla Kun in favour of the latter's rehabilitation, resulting in the publication of a relatively favourable evaluation in November 1955.[195] The number of names of victims in the historical periodical in 1955 is therefore extraordinarily small. The very modest start in April was not continued until the end of the year. This time, however, the trend persisted. The historian M.N. Pokrovskij, who had died in 1932 and had subsequently been denounced, received the relatively favourable comment that he had been the first historian to pass on to a marxist interpretation, even though he made some vulgarising mistakes doing this.[196] It was now the task of Soviet historians to examine the good sides of Pokrovskij's work.[197]

One day before the twentieth party congress, the February issue of *Voprosy Istorii* was approved for printing by the censor (13 February 1956). This issue contained contributions on the party congresses between 1917 and 1921 and on the union dispute in 1920-1. A number of names of Stalin's victims now appeared for the first time. To be sure, short shrift was given to Bukharin and Preobraženskij, on the basis of quotations from Stalin and Molotov, while the opposition of the democratic centralists Sapronov, Jurenev and Maksimovskij was exposed as an anti-party group. The Workers' opposition, including Šljapnikov as well as Trotsky and Bukharin, was accused of anti-leninism in the dispute on the position of the union in 1920-1. The names of Tomskij, Zinov'ev and Kamenev were suppressed, even though they had supported Lenin's view on the unions. Other disciples of Lenin at the time, among them the later stalinists Rudzutak and Lozovsky who had died in the terror, as well as Petrovskij, were judged favourably. Despite the critical approach to various opponents, the authors complained that little was known about them. All the same, now at least some things had been clarified regarding the various alternatives from the famous dispute and the opposition to Lenin had not been dismissed as treason.[198] In *Partijnaja Žizn'* this approach was criticised: it was 'after all unnecessary to quote Šljapnikov'.[199]

In an article on the Ukraine, G.I. Petrovskij and V.Ja. Čubar' were praised to the skies. Both names were also presented in the editorial review of recent brochures which discussed the congresses and conferences of the communist party of the Soviet Union.[200] The editorial staff criticised the fact that these did not mention speeches of important party leaders.

Apart from those already mentioned, the editors put the following people forward: S.V. Kosior, P.P. Postyšev, A.V. Kosarev, G.N. Kaminskij, S.A. Lozovskij, Ja.B. Gamarnik, N.P. Čaplin, as well as a number of names of non-purged stalinists who had not been mentioned in the relevant brochures either.

In general, interest in the role of persons in the historical process was considered too small. Because both victims and non-victims were listed, it was not made clear to the reader what was going on. If by chance the reader had heard Khrushchev's 'secret speech' at the twentieth congress, however, much more would have been clear, especially with respect to the names of victims: except for three of them, exactly these names were presented as fully rehabilitated by the party leader.

The publication of *Voprosy Istorii* cannot have been completely unrelated to Khrushchev's congress speech. Chief editor Pankratova, member of the Central Committee, who was responsible for the inclusion of the series of names in her periodical, must have been allowed access either to this speech, or to the Pospelov report which formed its basis. The latter seems more probable, considering the three extra names,[201] whose significance we will examine (see Table 3.20). It appears that the historiographical development of these names is comparable to that of the names mentioned by Khrushchev (see Tables 3.1-3.3). Therefore, we assume that the Pospelov report spoke favourably about Čaplin, Gamarnik and Lozovskij.

So far, the course followed by *Voprosy Istorii* regarding the victims of Stalin was not very original: the views of the party leadership were adopted. The cases of N.A. Voznesenskij and Béla Kun demonstrated how re-entry of the names of historical personalities was gradually effected just after or just before formal

Table 3.20: Reappearance in Publications (8)[a]

	A	B	C	D	E	F
N.P. Čaplin	1956	—	1957	1962	—	1969
Ja.B. Gamarnik	1956	—	1958	1962	1964	1962
S.A. Lozovskij	1956	1957	1958	1963	—	—

Note: a. See Table 3.1 for explanation of categories A-F.

rehabilitation. People who had been 'merely' denounced without physical elimination were dealt with somewhat more easily, yet in very small measure (see the case of P.A. Krasikov) and not on the journal's own initiative.

The twentieth party congress formed a definite turning point in the appearance of names and victims in *Voprosy Istorii*. After the congress, some time passed before the results of the decision taken there on the suppression of the consequences of the personality cult became visible in the periodical.

Preparations for the expansion of the series of names which would be presented to the public were made, but the editorial staff awaited the decision of party leaders. As soon as *Pravda*, on 24 March 1956, had publicly exposed the personality cult and the unjustified repression, however, the road was clear. On 29 March, the third issue of *Voprosy Istorii* in 1956 received the imprimatur. There was sufficient support from higher up for an editorial policy which wished to take an active part in public rehabilitation.

In an important editorial, the editorial staff redefined the research tasks for party historians. By way of introduction to a critical review of the *Kratkij kurs*, the *Short Course* of the history of the communist party, the only party history since 1938, it was announced in the article that as a result of the personality cult the work of a 'prominent party historian such as E.M. Jaroslavskij was called in question and the authors of other works on party history — A.S. Bubnov, V.G. Knorin, V.I. Nevskij, N.N. Popov — were slandered and their work was withdrawn from circulation'.[202]

The name of G.E. Zinov'ev, who had been one of the first to write a survey of the party history, could have been added. In the list given above a clear distinction was made between Jaroslavskij as 'prominent historian' and the others, who received no further qualification. No rehabilitation was formally needed for his case, as he had remained in office until his death (1943) and had not incurred any accusations.

In the same editorial, an additional series of names was presented. After a critical comment upon the exaggerated role of Stalin in the Civil War as presented in recent historiography, historians were invited to show the leading role of the party, the heroic role of the worker, 'to show the services of prominent commanders and political workers of the Red Army (and not only V.I. Stalin)'.[203] In the recent literature, according to the editorial, names were missing: V.A. Antonov-Ovseenko, V.K. Bljucher,

A.S. Bubnov, Ja.B. Gamarnik, A.I. Egorov, S.S. Kamenev, M.S. Kedrov, M.L. Ruchimovič, I.S. Unšlicht and 'many other comrades who made no small effort for the reinforcement of the Red Army and its successful operations'.[204]

The historiographical treatment of these names can be represented in a table (see Table 3.21). It appears from this table that practically all those mentioned received a short biography in an encyclopaedia within two years after the article in *Voprosy Istorii.* Knorin, Popov and Ruchimovič met with delay.[205] Jaroslavskij's name and work, on the other hand, had reappeared very quickly in publications because he represented no historiographical problem.

We have already seen several of the names mentioned here occur in one of the earlier sources above: Antonov-Ovseenko, Bljucher, Gamarnik, Kedrov and Ruchimovič. The editorial staff of *Voprosy Istorii* has in fact expanded the series. Conspicuous is the double recording of A.S. Bubnov; for this reason, and on account of the latter's greatly varied career, a case-study will be devoted to his rehabilitation below. Of importance also is the recording of A.I. Egorov, of whom it is known for certain that he was not formally rehabilitated until 1957. His name, similar to that

Table 3.21: Reappearance in Publications of Historians and Soldiers who are Mentioned in the Editorial of *Voprosy Istorii*[a]

	A	B	C	D	E	F	G
Historians							
A.S. Bubnov	1956	1957	1958	1963	1963	1957	1956
E.M. Jaroslavskij	1953	1957	1955	1958	1960	1946	1955
V.G. Knorin	1956	1958	1965	1965	1970	1962	—
V.I. Nevskij	1955	1957	1959	1966	—	—	1956
M.M. Popov	1956	1960	1963	1971	—	1956	—
Soldiers							
V.A. Antonov-Ovseenko	1956	1957	1958	1963	1965	1957	1956
A.S. Bubnov (see above)							
V.K. Bljucher	1956	1958	1958	1957	1960	1957	1958
Ja.B. Gamarnik	1956	—	1958	1962	1964	1962	—
S.S. Kamenev	1956	1957	1958	1959	—	1957	1957
M.S. Kedrov	1953	1957	1958	1963	1963	1957	1956
M.L. Ruchimovič	1956	1964	1964	1969	—	—	—
A.I. Egorov	1956	1960	1958	1963	—	1957	—
I.S. Unšlicht	1956	1957	1958	1964	—	1957	—

Note: a. See Table 3.1 for explanation of categories A-G.

of Ruchimovič, had not yet been released for use in publications.

Mentioning the series of historians was not accepted by every-one. There was a powerful countercurrent against their work. The periodical of the Central Committee, *Partijnaja Žizn'*, published a hostile article, in which it was argued that the party histories of Knorin, Bubnov, Popov, Nevskij and Jaroslavskij, which were so highly commended by *Voprosy Istorii*, 'definitely offer some inte-resting things, but are no better than the *Kratkij kurs'*.[206]

The author also expressed a different view on Licholat's book on the Ukraine (see p. 89 above), which had been reviewed for the second time, now negatively, in the same issue of the historical periodical. He held a considerably more favourable opinion of Licholat and indicated that Bubnov, together with Pjatakov, had taken up an anti-leninist position. By persisting in the rejection of the early party historians, the author put himself in the stalinist tra-dition, yet at the same time adhered to the newly prescribed rejection of the *Short Course*.

The author of the relevant commentary in *Partijnaja Žizn'*, E.I. Bugaev, was the assistant chief editor of the paper and also depart-mental head of the party secretariat, as it were 'the mouthpiece of the ideological machinery of the party', and possibly also of the party secretary and ideologist Suslov.

Voprosy Istorii defended itself weakly and denied having recommended the party histories in question, but had meant to say that one should indeed have knowledge of them. The names of the earlier historians, however, did not recur in the debate, while the names of the military did not come up for discussion at all. Bugaev's article was nonetheless directed primarily against a con-tribution in the April issue of *Voprosy Istorii* by assistant chief editor E.N. Burdžalov, in which the role of the Mensheviks during the Revolution was slightly revalued. This has been examined in great detail by N.W. Heer,[207] so that the outcome of the discussion will suffice: *Voprosy Istorii* had to give up the role of pioneer in the process of revision of the Soviet history. In January 1957 the Central Committee established a new, private periodical for party history, *Voprosy Istorii KPSS*; E.N. Burdžalov was dismissed.[208]

No initiative on the part of the historians themselves emerges from this survey of informal rehabilitations in *Voprosy Istorii*. Those who were once again mentioned in a favourable sense had already been mentioned elsewhere or had been formally rehabili-tated by the party. The dispute with *Partijnaja Žizn'* proves that there was no regulation regarding the proper historical approach to rehabilitated victims. Several historians had gone too far or not far enough in the comments on the historical personalities discussed by them. The correcting influence of the propaganda machine of the Central Committee prevented such 'deviations'. The conclusion that each person mentioned without further commentary can therefore be considered to be fully rehabilitated must be rejected.

There are victims who receive no consistent positive or negative qualification in the press, such as A. Skrypnik, M.N. Tuchačevskij and I.I. Vacetis. There is also the question of a more differentiated treatment of former dissidents in the party, the so-called oppositions, for whom milder terms than 'treason' are employed. This in no way reflected a rehabilitation.

Istoričeskij Archiv

As *Voprosy Istorii* added no further biographical information to the recordings of persons in articles, it is important to examine another historical periodical in which this did happen.

Such a periodical is *Istoričeskij Archiv* (circulation 1955-7 4,000-4,400). A lot of source material on the Soviet period, supplied with explanatory and biographical notes, had been published in it since 1956.

In the fourth issue (July-August) of 1956 names of victims of the terror (the generals I.T. Smilga and V.I. Šorin) were mentioned for the first time, though without annotation.[209] However, in the following issue (September-October 1956) the first biographical notes appeared. They dealt with G.I. Petrovskij and F.I. Gološčekin[210] in a publication of Sverdlov's letters from exile before the revolution. Both belonged to the party leadership at the time and were part of the Central Committee. In the same issue, M.G. Rošal', an old Bolshevik, published memoirs on the Bolsheviks of Helsinki at the time of the revolution of 1917. He mentioned favourably the names of several of those who had been purged — V.V. Šmidt, N.K. Antipov, A.F. Il'in-Ženevskij, I.N. Stark, V.A. Antonov-Ovseenko and P.E. Dybenko — without explanatory note.[211] Except for Stark, within one year these names can be found in memoirs or works of reference. The diplomat Stark followed several years later in the diplomats' handbook.[212]

Istoričeskij Archiv's last issue of 1956 was largely devoted to documents on Plechanov. This was a great bonus for historians, because Plechanov had received only minor attention in Stalin's time. In addition, N.I. Podvojskij's memoirs on Lenin in 1917 were published, including biographical notes on V.P. Miljutin (some formal data without dates), Antonov-Ovseenko and Kollontaj.[213] Hesitation towards Miljutin can be accounted for by his past. Before he attained senior positions in economics, he had resigned from the sovnarkom in November 1917 because he was in favour of a coalition government. Until 1910, moreover, he belonged to the Mensheviks. In other words, a small part of his biography paralleled those of Rykov, Kamenev, Zinov'ev and Nogin.[214]

In 1957, the periodical included the important publication of an inquiry which was held among the party members in 1927. The questions related to the activities of the party members between February and October 1917 and during the first days of Soviet dominion. Furthermore, they had to give accounts of their meetings with Lenin.

These documents were recorded by *Istoričeskij Archiv* accompanied by short biographical introductions.[215] At the same time, a similar, indeed nearly identical, collection was published in a separate volume.[216] In this way, a large number of names were once again permitted to appear in publications. Many figures are hardly known. From the dates of death it may be inferred that they are very probably victims of the terror who were often not sufficiently important to return in an encyclopaedia or a commemorative article. Those who can be found in publications fairly soon afterwards, like G.P. Ačkanov, F.I. Gološčekin, P.E. Dybenko, M.S. Kedrov and G.I. Lomov-Oppokov, were important officials. Others did not turn up until the seventies in the encyclopaedia *BSE*: A.A. Korostelev, S.S. Pestkovskij, Ja.Ch. Peters and I.V. Civcivadze. During 1957 a number of names were gradually recorded in *Istoričeskij Archiv* and supplied with favourable qualifications in the footnotes. They often concerned people who had been mentioned elsewhere for the first time. Names of people who had apparently not yet been rehabilitated were mentioned too. In these cases, the footnotes stated his function, or his dates of birth and death, or said nothing at all about the person involved.

Memories of Lenin

An important publication in which Soviet citizens could read about Stalin's victims was the three-volume edition of the *Memories of*

Lenin, upon which the Central Committee decided in the course of 1956.[217] The first volume received the imprimatur on 17 May 1956. It contained, among other things, the memoirs of M.S. Kedrov, the only victimised person to appear in the book. In the second volume (imprimatur 21 February 1957), many more were added and this time information was also provided on the authors of the contributions by means of an index providing some biographical data. This is what mattered: a number of these notes concluded with the formula 'in 1937 he became the victim of hostile slander and he was rehabilitated later' ('v 1937 g. stal žertvoj vražeskoj klevety, vposledstvii reabilitirovan'). This was all that was said about the authors who had been victimised by the terror and who had now been formally rehabilitated. The 13 names included complete strangers from times long past and prominent stalinists.[218]

This insertion of biographical data was not continued in the third volume (1960). Nothing has been written on purging and rehabilitation anywhere in works of reference, document editions or memoirs since before the twenty-second congress. Apparently party leaders had no wish to give any publicity whatsoever to the terror in this manner. The fact that this happened all the same in this edition is indicative of a lack of regulations until the beginning of 1957.

Conclusion

By and large, historians have played no initiating part in political rehabilitations. Usually, the mentioning of names of victims of Stalin was preceded by their formal rehabilitation. However, formal rehabilitation did not as a matter of course lead to public rehabilitation.

The way in which *Voprosy Istorii* reintroduced a number of people from the past was not acceptable to the propaganda department of the party machinery. As the general editorial staff certainly did not operate without political protection, the conflict between the propaganda department and the editors mirrored a conflict inside the highest ranks of the party. Therefore, the initiative taken by *Voprosy Istorii* in public rehabilitation has not been merely a concern of historians and members of the editorial staff.

More initiative became apparent in *Istoričeskij Archiv* because, in this journal, victims are presented without formal rehabilitation.

The extremely cautious manner in which this happened — hardly any biographical data were supplied — as well as the limited circulation of the periodical cause this initiative to be marginal.

The collection *Memories of Lenin*, volume 2, was highly remarkable because it was the only publication since the period prior to 1961 which offered data on purges and rehabilitation. Published as a mass edition, this work reached a fairly wide audience. This frankness was not continued in the third volume. As this concerned a publication by the Institution for Marxism-Leninism in which various old Bolsheviks participated, we are probably dealing in this case with an initiative from lower down, albeit that political protection from above was indispensable. The role of one of these old Bolsheviks will be further examined in the case-study on Petrovskij.

This investigation has also extended to those who were not typical victims of the terror. Every historical figure in the Stalin era was subject to suppression and possibly slander. It was relatively easy to single out these people, but these cases, too, appear to have been handled extremely cautiously and selectively. It is thus shown how delicate these matters were. In terms of public rehabilitation, in fact, there was relatively little distinction between physical victims, those who were posthumously slandered, and those who were suppressed.

Opposition within the Party and the Rehabilitations

Introduction

The selection of historical figures who could be rehabilitated took place also on the basis of the political conduct of those involved. Faithful stalinists who had always toed the line consequently stood a reasonable chance of being rehabilitated. Those who had once belonged to an opposition as yet risked a negative judgement and therefore no rehabilitation because of their political deviation. It thus appeared from the course of events in Czechoslovakia that being rehabilitated was more difficult for those whose 'leninism' was doubted than for others. Consequently, it is important to examine which oppositions or deviations from the party line in the Soviet Union were still considered to be so harmful that their supporters were not rehabilitated. Subsequently, the oppositions will be studied, first by checking the official historiography in surveys of the party history and in works of reference, and secondly by determining the progress of rehabilitation of individual opposition members.

The 'Left Communism'

The fight and annihilation of 'left communism' in 1918 was a relevant theme in the various party histories. In 1938, 'left communism' was defined as 'fight against Lenin, accomplices of Trotsky, conspiracy against the Soviet government and secret hostility towards the communist party'.[219]

After 1959, this view was altered somewhat. Ideas on the German terms of peace in February 1918, that of Trotsky and his solution of 'neither war nor peace' and that of Bukharin and his view of a 'revolutionary war' were this time rejected in the editions of the party history. They condemned their conduct as 'Trotsky's and Bukharin's adventurist tactics, which would be disastrous for the Soviet republic'.[220]

The debate in the Central Committee on the final German ultimatum on 23 February 1918 was presented as a dispute between Lenin and the 'left communists', after which the latter continued their course towards disruption of the party. However, the edition of 1962 was changed here to bring out the 'hesitant' conduct of Stalin in this matter, who, after being reproached by Lenin, joined the leader. Subsequent editions no longer repeat this passage.[221] The activities of the 'left communists' against the peace treaty of Brest-Litovsk were qualified as 'disastrous for the party'. The fact that they continued to voice their opinion after the decision to sign was condemned as 'disruptive anti-party activity'. The Left Socialist Revolutionaries were said to have approached Bukharin with a plan for dislodging Lenin together, and forming a coalition government of both movements. Since 1962, however, this passage has been supplemented by the observation that Bukharin did not accept this proposal, yet that the episode illustrated how dangerous the fight of the faction of 'left communists' was.[222]

Analogous to the changes in the party history was the treatment of 'left communism' in works of reference. In the second edition of the *BSE* in the middle of the fifties, the headword 'left communism' was defined as 'a group hostile to the communist party which wished to conduct a criminal policy by drawing the young Soviet republic into a war with imperialist Germany'.[223] Bukharin, Radek and Pjatakov were 'sworn enemies of the party' and their politics were 'treacherous'. These observations were based upon material from the show trial in 1938. The group was depicted as a permanent action group within the party against the party.[224] In later encyclopaedias, the term 'left communism' was interpreted as 'left-wing opportunist, operating from a petty bourgeois revolutionary disposition'.[225]

Although only a small group had been maintained by name as belonging to the 'left communists' in *Istorija KPSS* (Bukharin, Urickij, Lomov, Bubnov, Osinskij, Sapronov and Stukov), the *SIE* and the *BSE³* supplied a long list of names in which notorious dissidents were mentioned side by side with pillars of the party previously deemed beyond suspicion.

In terms of content, the *SIE* was still equally severe by referring to the 'Trotskyist adventurist thesis on the revolutionary war', while in the *BSE³* left-wing communism was treated (by the same author B.M. Morozov) without abuse, though larded with strong condemnations by Lenin.

In the party history, 'left communism' changes from a treacherious deviation into an excusable sin. In *Istorija KPSS* it was reported from 1962 that the 'left communists', after admitting their mistakes, had once again actively resumed their work in accordance with the leninist norms of party life. Kujbyšev, Kosior and Jaroslavskij,[226] whose names had not been recorded when the negative aspects of left-wing communism had been discussed, are suddenly mentioned as examples. The *SIE* goes much further in this by mentioning many more names in this context.

Compared to other oppositions, a relatively large number of 'left communists' have been rehabilitated: a clear sign of the forgiving attitude of the party towards this group. A list of 25 names of victims — former 'left communists' — shows that 10, among whom 3 were leaders, reappeared in works of reference (N.M. Antonov, G.I. Bokij, A.S. Bubnov, A. Lomov-Oppokov, Ju.M. Lenskij, N. Osinskij-Obolenskij, V.N. Mancev, I.S. Unšlicht, B.Z. Šumjackij and V.N. Jakovleva). Those who belonged to left-wing communism and had died without having been prosecuted either before 1936 or after 1944 were recorded without difficulty in the works of reference (I. Armand, M.I. Vasil'ev-Saratovskij, M.S. Zemljačka, A.M. Kollontaj, V.V. Kujbyšev, M.N. Pokrovskij, I.I. Skvorcov-Stepanov, A.A. Sol'c, M.S. Urickij, G.A. Usievic, P.K. Šternberg, M.V. Frunze and E.M. Jaroslavskij). The rest are the non-rehabilitated left-wing communists, among whom are such leading figures as Bukharin, Preobraženskij and Pjatakov. In addition, S.N. Ravič, K.B. Radek. T.V. Sapronov, G.I. Safarov, V.M. Smirnov, V.I. Šorin, I.N. Stukov and G.I. Mjasnikov also appear. Most of these figures were expelled from the party as Trotskyists or democratic centralists in 1927 and/or sentenced during a show trial. They had continued their oppositional activity until long after 1918 and were therefore also part of later dissident groups.

The 'Workers' Opposition' and the 'Decists'

In general, Soviet historiography has remained very ill disposed towards the 'workers' opposition'. Views on the role of the unions in economics which were common in this group conflicted with the regulations of the party after settlement of the dispute on the position of the unions in 1921. The leaders of the 'workers' opposition', S.P. Medvedev, G.I. Mjasnikov and A.G. Šljapnikov, as well as the prominent supporters I.I. Kutuzov and A.P. Tolokoncev, have not even been formally rehabilitated.[227] Their names have not been included in any work of reference, while they are only mentioned in relation to opposition in the official party histories.[228] In so far as less distinguished supporters could be traced in document editions, it became evident that they should not be considered to have been formally rehabilitated. Only three figures have been formally and publicly rehabilitated: A.S. Kiselev, N.A. Kubjak and A.G. Pravdin.[229] A fourth, Ju.K. Milonov, was dehabilitated after rehabilitation.[230]

A prominent exception is formed by the historiography on Aleksandra M. Kollontaj. She had joined the 'workers' opposition' at a relatively advanced stage, but belonged to the leaders on the strength of her activities in politics and publications. Even though Stalin could have placed Kollontaj in a category of political victims without difficulty, he left her in peace. This happened to various prominent female old Bolsheviks (among whom were E.D. Stasova and R.S. Zemljačka). In spite of the fact that the *Kratkij Kurs* reminded readers of her dissident past,[231] her name continued to be mentioned in works of reference.[232] After 1956, however, attention was also paid to Kollontaj's work. Documents, memoirs and numerous commemorative articles were published.[233] Anthologies from her work were published in the seventies.

It appears from the material that Kollontaj was honoured as a revolutionary, propagandist and diplomat. Except for a few quotations from negative commentaries by Lenin, no place is reserved for her feminism and her role in the 'workers' opposition'. Here the question of why Kollontaj's opposition did not stand in the way of a sympathetic approach is important. In the biographical material, her oppositional activity is repeatedly stated to have been short-lived. It is observed with great emphasis how much she had taken Lenin's criticisms to heart, how she had acknowledged her mistakes and how she had declared herself to be loyal to the party line.[234] Kollontaj had continued her work as a diplomat under Stalin and had not been purged. For this reason historiography could regard her as an honoured person and declare her activity in the 'workers' opposition' to be an incidental aberration.

The opposition of Democratic centralist (Decists), too, is rejected altogether in the present literature.[235] Out of the ten Decists who were victims of the terror, three have been publicly rehabilitated: A.S. Bubnov, N. Osinskij and K.K. Jurenev.[236] None of those who continued the opposition until the fifteenth party congress and who were then expelled from the party have been rehabilitated.[237]

The 'Right Opposition'

A great deal of attention was devoted in the *Kratkij kurs* to the 'right opposition', the group of opponents to Stalin's policy of collectivisation and industrialisation which was removed from the party leadership in 1929. Bukharin was regarded as an accomplice of Trotsky, who as yet operated secretly. It was not until the party launched the attack upon the kulaks that the 'right opposition' threw off its mask and defended the kulaks: they were 'right opportunist capitulants'.[238] Except for the fact that they did not class Bukharinists and Trotskyists together, the editions of the party history from 1959 and later largely maintained this approach. Bukharin was reported to have introduced the slogan 'enrich yourself' as early as 1925. The group of 'right capitulants' was said to have been formed in those days. At the time of the fight against the Trotskyists and the Zinovjevists, when these represented the chief danger to the party, the right-wingers even formally participated in the anti-Trotskyist fight. With the transition to the attack upon the kulaks, Bukharin, Rykov and Tomskij took public action against the party: against the growth of heavy industry, against the high pace of industrialisation, against the elimination of capitalist elements in economics, and against anti-kulak action.[239] They denied the possibility of building up socialism in the Soviet Union. According to the party history, their politics could have led to the restoration of capitalism. This was also apparent in international communism. The 'right' was on the same line as the 'reformism' of the Second International and was regarded at the Komintern congress in 1928 and subsequently also by the Central Committee as the chief danger. Despite the severe criticisms, the 'right' formed an anti-party faction. When Bukharin entered into communication with the Trotskyists[240] through Kamenev, Bukharin and Tomskij were removed from their prominent posts because of 'capitulant ideology and anti-party activities in the unions'.

At the plenary meeting of November 1929, the ideas of the 'right capitulants' were described as incompatible with their presence in the party. Bukharin was expelled from the politburo as the initiator. Rykov and Tomskij were given serious warnings. After that, they indeed delivered statements of loyalty, yet they showed their 'Janus faces' from then on by continuing their opposition in secret. From 1962 onwards, the editions of the party histories were less severe about this: 'They did not fulfil their promises and waited.'[241] The term 'Janus face' was omitted.

In the various editions of the *Great Encyclopaedia* we can perceive distinct changes in the views on the 'right opposition'. Under the headword 'right restorers', the first edition (1940) uses the definition 'right capitulants, who, from an anti-leninist group, change into a visionless gang of political Janus faces, spies, saboteurs and murderers, acting under orders of foreign intelligence services'.[242] Their anti-party activity prevailed from 1907 until their expulsion in 1937. In the second edition (1955),[243] the terminology is toned down to some extent, though without mitigating the condemnation. This time the headword was 'Right deviation in the VKP(b)'. They were called opportunists, and stand accused of being the chief danger at the time of the large-scale attempt to attain socialism. They were in favour of annihilation of the attainments of the proletarian revolution and headed for restoration of capitalism. Together with the Trotskyists and the Zinovjevists, they were agents of Menshevism, their hangers-on and successors, and agents of foreign intelligence services. Even though the beginning of their activities was not fixed at so premature a date as in the first edition, it nonetheless resulted in a combination with the various oppositions of the thirties. The show trial of 1938 was still quoted. It is also true, however, that from

1955 onwards Bukharin's name is once again mentioned without straightforward criticism in the *BSE* as speaker at several party congresses.

The *SIE* and the third edition of the *BSE* no longer refer to the collaboration with Trotskyists and Zinovjevists under 'Right deviation', but they observe that, since 1917, the right-wingers had been political waverers all along.[244] During 1928-30 they were opportunists and followed an anti-leninist course. They continued their oppositional activity even after they had been criticised. However, they are no longer accused of having wished to restore capitalism and the quotation 'enrich yourself' is omitted. Initials and offices of Bukharin, Rykov, Tomskij, Frumkin and Uglanov are mentioned in the article. Stalin, too, gets his place: in the *SIE* as a name in the alphabetical list of figures who have made a positive contribution to the fight against right-wing opposition, in the *BSE³* as a pioneer mentioned as such earlier.

Of the 16 party executives who are counted among the 'right opposition' in the six-volume party history, only M.I. Frumkin has been rehabilitated.[245] If we expand the list by means of data from other sources,[246] the name Frumkin can be supplemented with the names of V.M. Michajlov, V.V. Šmidt, A.I. Dogadov, A.P. Smirnov and V.I. Polonskij. The majority of these figures were publicly commemorated in 1967. A common characteristic of these rehabilitated people is that every one of them had held an important position in the unions in the twenties. Their rehabilitation was possibly an attempt to arrive at rehabilitation of the union leader M.P. Tomskij. This perhaps explains the discovery of a sympathetic mention of his name.[247]

The 'Left Opposition'

The collective label 'left opposition' indicates various oppositional groups, which eventually formed a common target of the Stalin-Bukharin tandem which was in power in the twenties. We are dealing here with Trotsky, Zinov'ev, Kamenev and their supporters, who operated successively under the names of 'left opposition', 'new opposition' and 'united opposition'. The group of democratic centralists under Sapronov also formed part of this. At the fifteenth party congress (1927), the opposition was disposed of summarily by depriving a large number of opponents (75 Trotskyists and 23 Decists) of their party membership.[248]

In general, practically no inclination to rehabilitate these groups existed. On the contrary, even greater attention was paid to the dangers of Trotskyism both in the press and in works of reference, in relation to the neo-Trotskyist movements in the world.[249] Trotsky himself has remained the 'nastiest enemy of leninism'.[250] There has never been any question of rehabilitating Trotsky in the Soviet Union,[251] not even by way of rumour, even though Isaac Deutscher entertained some hopes in 1962.[252] Even so, the tone of historiography has become somewhat milder. Denigrating epithets are omitted and source records can go the length of mentioning 't. [comrade] Trockij' in footnotes.[253] The usual charges of treason, open anti-Soviet activity, terrorism and aspiration to restoration of capitalism, to which the *Kratkij kurs* paid so much attention, are dropped. The Soviet state, in brief, no longer regards him as a criminal. The approach, however, has remained completely nega-tive, although the accusation of criminal activity has disappeared. Trotsky is still deemed to have been willing to undermine the party in order to establish his own personal power. His politics are ignored or denounced.[254]

Zinov'ev and Kamenev are treated in almost the same manner in historiography. They have not been rehabilitated, although sug-gestions to that end was raised in several places.[255] In their cases, too, the accusations of treason and of the murder on Kirov have been withdrawn. These were the charges which had led to their condemnation at the show trial against the so-called Muscovite Centre (1936). The disappearance of references to these 'crimes' can be placed in the period 1960-1.[256] Apparently a revision of the trial has taken place. Zinov'ev and Kamenev have continued to be depicted as opponents to the party line, although they are used much less often as scapegoats than Trotsky. Tactical and political mistakes, in particular, are ascribed to this pair, and they are blamed for opportunism and irresolution.[257]

Only a few of those who can be counted among the 'left oppo-sition' have been rehabilitated.[258] These are V.A. Antonov-Ovseenko, A.G. Beloborodov, N.N. Krestinskij and E.A. Ešba. The first three ceased their opposition in time and were not expelled from the party at the fifteenth party congress as Ešba was. He is the only victim of the terror from this group who has been rehabilitated. The recording of his name in works of reference, however, lacks consistency.[259] The case is comparable to that of M.M. Laševič, who, after his expulsion from the party, submitted and was reinstated. He died from natural causes in 1928.[260]

Laševič, too, was a non-person in Stalin's time. Even though no rehabilitation was formally required, for a long time he was treated in the same way as the other opposition members. His public rehabilitation did not take place until 1967. Finally, the only survivor of the party members expelled as Trotskyists, S.I. Kavtaradze, has been included in works of reference. He had been rehabilitated as early as 1940 and had become departmental head at the people's commissariat for foreign affairs. He did not sink into oblivion and was held in esteem as an old Bolshevik after 1953.[261] Thus, only 3 of the 98 figures expelled from the party at the congress in 1927 have re-emerged in the press and works of reference.

All this leads to the conclusion that formal expulsion from the party in 1927 formed a substantial obstacle to rehabilitation. Although a number of party opponents were again reinstated after public atonement, expulsion nonetheless followed once more later on.

Conclusion

Of those victims of the terror who belonged to the opposition in the party, only a small number were rehabilitated. When this happened, it was emphasised that they had acknowledged their mistakes and had faithfully followed the general party line afterwards. Members of the opposition group who were not purged or who survived the terror could be re-entered in publications more easily, but this was not a matter of course. The expulsions in 1927 and convictions in the show trials of 1936 and 1937 appear to be important barriers to any form of rehabilitation.

It is possible that a number of figures who belonged to the opposition have indeed been formally rehabilitated, as became evident in the cases of several of the accused of the show trial in 1938, but few were destined for rehabilitation in the party and posthumous reinstatement, let alone public rehabilitation.

A partial explanation for the selection of personalities who were fully rehabilitated in spite of everything can perhaps be found in the activities of relatives of those involved, who stubbornly continued to trouble the party leaders for rehabilitation. This did not always work: Bukharin's relatives, among others, did not succeed.

For other cases, the explanation is fairly specific: witness, for instance, the case of Ikramov. The selection of victims of the show trials who were rehabilitated probably took place during meetings of the presidium in the years 1958-60. A number of charges were withdrawn. Some people who took part in oppositions before 1923 had been considered rehabilitated since 1956, like Bubnov and Antonov-Ovseenko. They have been regularly commemorated without restriction ever since. A few others were granted rehabilitation at an advanced stage and, in addition, were commemorated in the press of a federal republic only. New names have been presented in publications up to the seventies.

The defective rehabilitation of party oppositions causes the historiography of the party to be seriously handicapped. This appears from a survey of the rehabilitations of victims of the terror who were part of the highest official party and state bodies. In the highest party ranks, 20 to 25 per cent of the members have not been rehabilitated (see Table 3.22).

Those inside the secretariat, the politburo, the orgburo and the sovnarkom are often the same politicians. In the category of non-rehabilitated victims of the terror, we are actually dealing with 14 people: N.I. Bukharin, G.E. Evdokimov, N.I. Ežov, L.B. Kamenev, I.M. Moskvin, E.A. Preobraženskij, A.I. Rykov, L.P. Serebrjakov, G.Ja. Sokol'nikov, M.P. Tomskij, L.D. Trotsky, N.A. Uglanov, P.A. Zaluckij and G.E. Zinov'ev. Except for the notorious police chief and henchman of Stalin's terror, Ežov, these are former opposition members in the party.

Non-rehabilitated victims from the Central Committee are, in addition to a number of little-known figures, the chief of the secret police from 1934 to 1936, G.G. Jagoda, and the most prominent accused of the show trial in 1937, G.L. Pjatakov.

Table 3.22: Rehabilitation of Members of the Most Important Soviet Administrative Bodies

Administrative Body	Members in the Period 1917-39	Victims of the Terror		Non-rehabilitated Victims	
	No.	No.	%	No.	%
Secretariat	27	15	55.5	6	22.2'
Politburo	34	17	50	9	26.5
Orgburo	64	42	66	13	20.3
Sovnarkom (chairmen and vice-chairmen)	18	10	55.5	2	11.1
Central Committee (full members)	71	49	70	11	15.5

Notes

1. *Ist. Arch.*, no. 1 (1957), p. 42, note 20; *Ist. Arch.*, no. 1 (1959), p. 32.
2. 'Secret speech', *CSP*, vol. 2, pp. 172-88.
3. Medvedev, 'Vom XX. zum XXII. Parteitag', p. 34; Carrère d'Encausse, 'XX-ème Congrès, p. 21.
4. For an account of the sources, see the data presented in Appendix B. For the table I have used the same mentions as in Table 3.1. The year of a first favourable mention has been determined on the basis of references in the press rather than on the basis of references by Khrushchev during his 'secret speech'.
5. Medvedev, 'Vom XX. zum XXII. Parteitag', p. 34.
6. See Appendix B. Even though Khrushchev mentioned 1954 as the year of rehabilitation, a reliable reference has been found which indicates that Voznesenskij's rehabilitation took place in 1955.
7. *Očerki istorii KP Gruzii*, vol. 1, pp. 61 and 158.
8. In Appendices B and C only politically well-known figures have been listed.
9. 'Secret speech', p. 176.
10. Conquest, 'The Historiography of the Purges', *Survey*, vol. 22, no. 1 (1976), pp. 156-64.
11. *Pravda*, 18 February 1956.
12. A.V. Licholat, *Razgrom nacionalističeskoj kontrrevoljutsii na Ukraine 1917-1922 gg.* (Moscow, 1954), and the review in *Voprosy Istorii*, no. 4 (1954), pp. 145-52 (henceforth *VI*).
13. E.S. Oslikovskaja and A.V. Snegov, 'Za pravdivoe osveščenie istorii proletarskoj revoljutsii', *VI*, no. 3 (1956), pp. 140-1.
14. Submission of Antonov-Ovseenko on 4 April 1928. See A.V. Rakitin, *Imenem revoljucii (Očerki o V.A. Antonove-Ovseenko)* (Moscow, 1965), p. 158.
15. In the *Istorija KPSS* (1959) Antonov-Ovseenko had not yet been included; this happened in the 3rd edition (1969, p. 265). The *BSE* (*BSE²*, no. 50, p. 209) mentions his name in the survey of the history of the Soviet Union.
16. Carrère d'Encausse, 'XX-ème Congrès', p. 21.
17. *Piller-rapport*, p. 332.
18. Medvedev, 'Vom XX. zum XXII. Parteitag', p. 44.
19. *Dvadcat' vtoroj s"ezd*, vol. 1, pp. 102-13.
20. Ibid.
21. Ibid.
22. Ibid., pp. 290-1.
23. Ibid., p. 284.
24. Ibid., p. 400.
25. Ibid., vol. 2, p. 404.
26. Ibid., vol. 1, p. 602.
27. Ibid., p. 208.
28. Ibid., vol. 2, p. 43.
29. Ibid., p. 497.
30. Ibid.
31. Ibid.
32. Ibid., p. 49.
33. Ibid., p. 403.
34. Ibid., p. 404.
35. Ibid., vol. 1, p. 396.
36. Ibid., vol. 2, p. 104.
37. Ibid., pp. 148-9.
38. Ibid., pp. 184-6.

39. Ibid., p. 352.

40. Ibid., vol. 1, pp. 343-4.

41. Ibid., p. 459. Cf. *Zëri i popullit*, 1 September 1960, translated in W.E. Griffith, *Albania and the Sino-Soviet Rift* (Cambridge, Mass., 1963).

42. *Dvadcat' vtoroj s"ezd*, vol. 2, pp. 577-81.

43. Ibid., vol. 3, p. 114.

44. Ibid., pp. 117-18.

45. *Zarja Vostoka*, 23 August 1956, pp. 2-3.

46. *Očerki istorii KP Gruzii*, vol. 1, pp. 238, 304 and 367.

47. *Dvadcat' vtoroj s"ezd*, vol. 3, pp. 119-20.

48. Ibid., pp. 150-9.

49. *Pravda*, 10-12 November 1961.

50. R.M. Slusser, 'A.N. Shelepin' in G. Simmonds (ed.), *Soviet Leaders* (New York, 1967), p. 91.

51. See Appendix B.

52. Mandelštam, *Memoires*, p. 393.

53. Statement by Dr Kaplan to author.

54. *Bol'šaja Sovetskaja Enciklopedija*, 3rd edn (1970-9) (henceforth *BSE³*).

55. *Malaja Sovetskaja Enciklopedija*, 3rd edn (1958-60) (henceforth *MSE³*).

56. *Kratkaja Literaturnaja Enciklopedija* 1962-78) (henceforth *KLE*).

57. *Enciklopedičeskij Slovar'*, 2nd edn (1953-5) (referred to as *ES²*); 3rd edn (1963-6) (henceforth *ES³*).

58. *Sovetskaja Istoričeskaja Enciklopedija* (1961-76) (henceforth *SIE*).

59. *Ukrainskaja Rad'jans'kaja Enciklopedija* (1959-65) (henceforth *URE*). The second edition was also published in a Russian translation: *Ukrainskaja Sovetskaja Enciklopedija* (1978-) (henceforth *USE*). Since the end of the 1960s, in addition, a number of works of reference have been published in several federal republics. See Bibliography.

60. *Diplomatičeskij Slovar'*, 2nd and 3rd edns. (henceforth *DS²* and *DS³* respectively).

61. *Sovetskaja Voennaja Enciklopedija* (1976-80) (henceforth *SVE*).

62. *Bol'saja Sovetskaja Enciklopedija*, 1st edn (1926-47) (henceforth *BSE¹*).

63. *Enciklopedičeskij Slovar' Russkogo bibliografičeskogo instituta 'Granat'* (1927-9) (henceforth *Granat*).

64. *Leningrad. Enciklopedičeskij Spravočnik* (1957) (henceforth *LES*).

65. We are dealing here with Antipov, Antonov-Ovseenko, Blagonravov, Bokij, Dybenko, Il'in-Ženevskij, Krylenko, Lacis, Mechonošin, Nevskij, Pozern, Radčenko, Ugarov, Čubar', Čudov, Šmidt and Šotman. We have no further information on T.V. Baranovskij and E.M. Izotov.

66. Antipov, Pozern, Smorodin, Čudov, Kuznecov and Popkov.

67. F.Ja. Ugarov was temporarily associated with Bukharin towards the end of the 1920s. V.V. Šmidt was part of the Ejsmont-Tolmačev opposition, for which he was given a warning in 1933.

68. Antipov, Lacis, Nevskij; also Bokij and Blagonravov, both of whom embarked upon a long career with the secret police in Petrograd.

69. Čubar', Voznesenskij and Tuchačevskij.

70. *Pravda*, 28 June 1976, p. 2.

71. Ja.I. Alksnis, A.Ja. Arosev, V. Kostrzeva, P.S. Popkov, S. Sejfullin, A.P. Serebrovskij, S.M. Ter-Gabrieljan, V.A. Trifonov, T.S. Chvesin. Only in the *BSE³* is the Pole R.I. Černjak no longer included.

72. *SIE*, vol. 9, pp. 492-3. The rehabilitation by the Supreme Court took place on 15 November 1960, while his party membership (which dated back to 1920) was restored by the political directorate of the army on 9 December 1960. See the case in *Samizdat Register* (vol. 1, London, 1977, pp. 73-91), as well as the parallel

case of B.M. Dumenko in Medvedev, *Let History Judge*, p. 396, *Znamja*, no. 3 (1965) and *Novyj Mir*, no. 2 (1966), pp. 237-50.

73. See the bibliographies in Soviet publications and encyclopaedias. In the course of the 1970s, a large number of additional national encyclopaedias began to be published in the federal republics, e.g. in Armenia, Azerbajdžan, Georgia, Turkmenistan and Uzbekistan.

74. Headword 'Eestima KP', *Eesti Nougude Entsüklopeedia*, vol. 2, p. 35 (henceforth *ENE*).

75. Headword 'RKP', *Kazak Sovet Enciklopedijasy*, vol. 9, pp. 497f (henceforth *KSE*).

76. *BelSE*; cf. the review of volume 1 in *Times Literary Supplement*, 30 June 1972, pp. 743-4.

77. I.S. Lubachko, *Belorussia under Soviet Rule 1917-1957* (Lexington, Mass., 1972), p. 94.

78. Since 1978 the edition discussed here has been published in both a Ukrainian and a Russian edition.

79. Molotov was not mentioned in *ES³*, *SIE*, *MSE³*, *DS²*, *DS³*, *LME* and *ESM*. The index of the *BSE²* did not refer to the biographical headword in volume 28. The Estonian encyclopaedia *ENE* (vol. 5, p. 205), approved by the censor on 19 December 1972, included a biographical entry which contained information neither on Molotov's activities in the 'anti-party group' nor on the end of his career. This edition (*ENE*, vol. 5, pp. 53-4) also included an article devoted to Malenkov. The *BelSE* (vol. 7, p. 289, 'Molatau'), which had been approved by the censor on 16 March 1973, also contained a biography of Molotov. This ends with the following sentence: 'Expelled from the presidium and the Central Committee in 1957 for setting up an anti-party faction, removed from the party in 1962.' In *BSE³* (vol. 16, pp. 484-5) the text under 'Molotov' ends as follows: 'He retired in 1962.' The 'anti-party group' is not mentioned at all. This volume was approved on 11 April 1974. Since then, Molotov's name has been included in various encyclopaedias, most recently in *SES* (1980, p. 833) and *LTE* (vol. 7, 1981, p. 593). See A.P. van Goudoever, 'De Sovjet Scheurkalender 1980 and de Politiek', *Spiegel Historiael*, no. 15 (1980), p. 648.

80. In vols. 1-7 the following names are missing: Amelin, Appoga, Blaževič, Borisenko, Bulin, Bjuler, Vajner, Vajnuch-Vajnjarch, Vakulič, Vesnik, Gajlit, Galler, Galling, Germanovič, Gordon, Gorjačev, Golikov, Gribov, Grjaznov, Deribas, Kakurin, Kalmykov, Kangelari, Karaev, Kaširin, Kvjatek, Koževnikov, Kosič, Krapivjanskij, Kuk, Kučinskij, Longva, Medvedev, Meženinov, Mezis, Movčin, Mjasnikov, Osepjan, Ošlej, Peremytov, Rogovskij, Sablin, Sergeev and Slavin. See Appendix B.

81. *Istorija Kommunističeskoj Partii Sovetskogo Sojuza* (Moscow, 1959) (henceforth *Ist. KPSS* (1959).

82. *Istorija Kommunističeskoj Partii Sovetskogo Sojuza* (Moscow, 1962) (henceforth *Ist. KPSS* (1962)).

83. *Ist. KPSS* (1959), p. 71; *Ist KPSS* (1962), p. 74.

84. *Ist. KPSS* (1959), p. 143; *Ist. KPSS* (1962), p. 148.

85. *Ist. KPSS* (1959), p. 156; *Ist. KPSS* (1962), p. 163.

86. *Ist. KPSS* (1959), p. 417; *Ist. KPSS* (1962), p. 437.

87. *Ist. KPSS* (1959), p. 295; *Ist. KPSS* (1962), pp. 315-16.

88. *Ist. KPSS* (1962), pp. 136 and 161.

89. Ibid., p. 404.

90. Ibid., p. 314.

91. Ibid.

92. *Ist. KPSS* (1959), p. 322; *Ist. KPSS* (1962), p. 337.

93. *Ist. KPSS* (1959), p. 199; *Ist. KPSS* (1962), p. 208.

94. *Ist. KPSS* (1959), pp. 280-1; *Ist. KPSS* (1962), pp. 293-4.
95. *BSE²*, vol. 50, pp. 218, 260, 419 and 423.
96. *Ist. KPSS* (1959), pp. 483-4; *Ist. KPSS* (1962), p. 505.
97. *Ist. KPSS* (1959), p. 251; *Ist. KPSS* (1962), p. 262.
98. L. Grünwald, 'Zur Geschichte der "Geschichte" der KPdSU', *Osteuropa*, no. 6 (1973), p. 438.
99. Medvedev, *Let History Judge*, p. 182.
100. *Istorija Kommunističeskoj Partii Sovetskogo Sojuza* (Moscow, 1969) (henceforth *Ist. KPSS* (1969).
101. *Ist. KPSS* (1969), pp. 122-3, 147 and 369.
102. Ibid., p. 76.
103. Ibid., p. 105.
104. Ibid., p. 144.
105. Ibid., p. 397; cf. Conquest, *The Great Terror* (Harmondsworth, 1971), p. 359.
106. *Ist. KPSS* (1969), p. 567.
107. Ibid., p. 452.
108. Between 1963 and 1967, a number of commemorative articles were published in *VI KPSS*; in *Voenno-istoričeskij Žurnal* this happened in the period 1962-9. No such articles had been published before the periods mentioned, while afterwards they were published only occasionally. The following table shows the actual number of articles:

Number of Commemorative Articles Dealing with Rehabilitated Persons in *VI KPSS* and *Voenno-istoričeskij Žurnal*

	1962	1963	1964	1965	1966	1967	1968	1969
VI KPSS	—	15	9	8	4	2	—	—
Voenno-ist.	6	22	18	14	14	5	2	4

109. *Sov. Latvija*, 25 October 1956, p. 3.
110. *Sov. Estonija*, 18 April 1956, p. 3.
111. *Sov. Litva*, 14 June 1956, p. 2.
112. *Sov. Litva* (14 June 1956, p. 2) reported that 'owing to a lack of experience, however, the Lithuanian leaders, among whom Angaretis, made some mistakes in 1919 with regard to the necessity of tightening the bonds between farmers and workers'.
113. As an alternative interpretation, one may also suggest that Anvel't and Angaretis were important members of the International Control Committee of the Komintern, while Rudzutak supervised the Central Control Committee of the CPSU between 1932 and 1936. These official bodies kept an eye on the purity of the party and guarded against deviations. Rehabilitating the people mentioned provided a means of demonstrating that these control committees had done a fine job and that the purges before 1936 were sound. Such an explanation derives from the combined functions of those involved, but is not factually supported by comments in the articles published. Consequently, the explanation offered in the main text is preferable.
114. *Sov. Litva*, 21 February 1958, p. 2, and *Sov. Latvija*, 31 July 1957, p. 2. We are dealing here with references to V.K. Putna and V.G. Knorin respectively.
115. *Sov. Latvija*, 14 February 1957, p. 2.
116. This specific interest in people especially from Estonia and Latvia is disproportionate to the comparative over-representation of Latvians in the CPSU

during the 1920s. See T.H. Rigby, *Communist Party Membership in the USSR 1917-1967* (Princeton, 1968), p. 366.

117. This connection comes up for discussion in an article written by the Lithuanian prosecutor-general G. Bacharov, which was published in *Sov. Litva*, 1 August 1956, p. 3.

118. *Krasnaja Zvezda*, 9 July 1957, p. 3.

119. Ibid., 10 August 1957, p. 3.

120. Ibid., 14 February 1958; ibid., 19 February 1959, p. 3; ibid., 21 September 1960, p. 3.

121. Ibid., 4 April 1961, p. 4.

122. Ibid., 17 August 1957, p. 2.

123. They were published in *Kommunist (Armenii)* and dealt with the following people: D.A. Saverdjan (6 January 1960 (no. 4), p. 2), A.B. Chalatov (3 June 1960 (no. 131), p. 3), D.A. Ter-Simonjan (28 August 1960 (no. 205), p. 2), S.M. Ter-Gabrieljan (20 October 1960 (no. 250), p. 3), A.E. Ter-Vartanjan (1 November 1960 (no. 260), p. 2), A.T. Atojan (16 November 1960 (no. 271), p. 2), O.A. Pogosjan (20 November 1960 (no. 275), p. 2) and I.G. Laz'jan (23 November 1960 (no. 277), p. 2).

124. *Izvestija*, 29 December 1961, p. 6.

125. On 28 October 1961, commemorative articles on Ordžonikidze were published in *Trud* and *Zarja Vostoka* only. *Pravda* did not publish a similar article until 26 November 1961. The traditional commemorative meeting in the Museum of the Revolution did not take place until then. To some extent, this was compensated for in February 1962 when a number of articles in commemoration of the death of Ordžonikidze, 25 years earlier, were published. See *Ekon. Gazeta*, 12 February 1962, p. 5; *Literaturnaja Gazeta*, 17 February 1962 no. 21, p. 2; *Pravda*, 18 February 1962, p. 5; and *Kommunist (Arm.)*, 18 February 1962 (no. n.a.).

126. *Sov. Litva*, 6 October 1961, p. 4. The article commemorated the 65th birthday of Uborevič, though not without ten months' delay, which supports the idea that we are dealing here with an experiment. A subsequent article on this *komandarm* (general) was published shortly afterwards in *Krasnaja Zvezda*, 24 December 1961, p. 4.

127. Appendix B refers to biographical articles in *SIE* and *VI KPSS* which contained these formulas.

128. *Peking Review*, 21 June 1963 (no. 17).

129. *Pravda*, 14 July 1963, p. 3.

130. Ibid. This particular point was also mentioned by Suslov (*Pravda*, 3 April 1964, p. 7).

131. *Pravda*, 14 July 1963, p. 3.

132. *Peking Review*, 21 June 1963 (no. 17).

133. *Pravda*, 3 April 1964, p. 7.

134. *Peking Review*, 17 July 1964 (no. 29).

135. *Kommunist*, 18 October 1963.

136. *Peking Review*, 20 September 1963 (no. 38); ibid. 8 May 1964 (no. 19); ibid., 27 November 1964 (no. 48).

137. *Pravda*, 3 April 1964, p. 7.

138. Ibid.

139. E.F. Pruck, 'Die Umwertung Stalins und Chruschtschows in wehrkundlicher Sicht', *Osteuropa*, no. 15 (1965), pp. 807-12; B. Lewytzkyj, 'Chronik Sowjetunion', *Osteuropa*, no. 16 (1966), p. 267.

140. B. Meissner, 'Sowjetrussland zwischen Restauration und Reform', *Osteuropa*, no. 16 (1966), p. 267.

141. *Pravda*, 8 October 1965, pp. 3 and 4.

142. H.L. Verhaar, 'De "dehabilitatie" van Raskol'nikov', *Internationale*

Spectator, vol. 8 (1971), pp. 1759-71. The public rehabilitation of Raskol'nikov had taken place in 1963. According to the dissident historian L. Petrovskij, this was connected with criticisms of Mao which Chinese deserters were allowed to air in the Russian press at this time. Raskol'nikov's example of criticism of Stalin could legitimate this, while, on the other hand, his conduct could hardly be called unjustified any longer. See Verhaar, 'De "dehabilitatie" van Raskol'nikov', p. 1770.

143. *Pravda*, 30 January 1966, p. 2.

144. Ibid. See also the commemoration of the stalinist cultural politician A.A. Ždanov in *Pravda*, 30 January 1966, p. 4.

145. *Zarja Vostoka*, 10 March 1966, p. 2; cf. Meissner, 'Sowjetrussland zwischen Restauration und Reform (II)', *Osteuropa*, no. 16 (1966), p. 417.

146. See *Krasnaja Zvezda*, 11 October 1963, p. 2, and 24 February 1963, p. 3 respectively; *Sov. Litva*, 12 February 1958; *Sov. Latvija*, 5 April 1958.

147. See *Kommunist Tadžikistana*, 17 August 1965 (no. 192), p. 2; *Kazachst. Pravda*, 17 January 1965, p. 4; *Sov. Litva*, 8 July 1967, p. 4; *Kommunist (Arm.)*, 13 January 1965 (no. 9), p. 2; *Kazachst. Pravda*, 27 July 1965, p. 4; *Zarja Vostoka*, 12 March 1966, p. 4.

148. *Kazachst. Pravda*, 17 January 1965, p. 4.

149. *CSP*, vol. 5 (New York, 1973), p. 84.

150. No general political explanation for the series of commemorations in Central Asia has been found. See Shapiro, 'Political Rehabilitation in Soviet Central Asian Party Organizations', pp. 3 and 199-209; see also Levytsky, *Stalinist Terror*, p. 23.

151. Shapiro, 'Rehabilitation Policy', pp. 156-63. She examines the rehabilitation of Ikramov, one of the victims from the show trial in 1938, and the relation between the latter's rehabilitation in 1957 and the rise of Muchitdinov, member of the party presidium from 1957 onwards. In the relevant speeches of Muchitdinov (*Pravda Vostoka*, 13 October 1956, pp. 4-5 and 28 December 1957, p. 4), the Uzbek victims were cleared from the accusation of 'nationalism and betrayal of the mother country'. In these, he mentioned a series of names of people affected, including their offices. In addition to rehabilitations of political functionaries, he specifically referred to rehabilitations of Uzbek literary men.

In general, we are dealing here with a restoration of the nationality of the native communists as a gesture towards the regional population. If, by following this course of action, Muchitdinov had merely wished to humour Khrushchev, both the relatively long series of names and the public reports on the rehabilitations would have been unnecessary. He could have made do with less. The effect of the Uzbek course, however, is that in the presidium Muchitdinov could act as a representative of the nationalities with a relatively liberal image.

152. See *Kommunist Tadžikistana*, 4 April 1964 (no. 80), p. 3; ibid., 30 May 1964 (no. 125), p. 3; ibid., 17 July 1965 (no. 284), p. 4; ibid., 21 August 1964 (no. 196), p. 2.

153. *Turkmen'skaja Iskra*, 7 July 1965 (no. 288), pp. 2 and 3.

154. K.H. Karpat, 'The Turkic Nationalities: Turkish-Soviet and Turkish-Chinese Relations' in W.O. McCagg and B.D. Silver (eds.), *Soviet Asian Ethnic Frontiers* (New York, 1979), pp. 133-5; B. Hayit, 'Tendenzen der Sowjetpolitik in Turkestan', *Osteuropa*, no. 14 (1964), p. 464.

155. Hayit, 'Tendenzen der Sowjetpolitik in Turkestan', p. 464.

156. *Pravda Vostoka*, 26 May 1966, p. 3.

157. *Turkmen'skaja Iskra*, 26 October 1967 (no. 252), p. 2.

158. *Izvestija*, 25 May 1966, p. 6, and 26 October 1967, p. 5 respectively.

159. *Pravda Vostoka*, 10 August 1967, p. 3.

160. *Kazachst. Pravda*, 26 December 1964, p. 2.

161. *Izvestia*, 12 January 1965, p. 6.
162. Neither Shapiro ('Political Rehabilitation in Soviet Central Asian Party Organizations', pp. 204-5) nor Levytsky (*Stalinist Terror*, p. 23) provide any further explanation.
163. Conquest, *Soviet Nationalities Policy in Practice* (London, 1967), pp. 58, 92, 95 and 97. The following persons were granted no public rehabilitation: Šumskij, Nuzratallev, Mdivani, Eskaraev, Kulumbetov, Sadvokasov, Mgaloblišvili, Isakeev, Urazbekov, Ajtakov, Chodžibaev, Gylling, Kruus, Andrezen and Sultan-Galiev. These are all top executives. The following people were publicly commemorated: Skrypnik, Torošelidze, Chodžaev, Ikramov, Musabekov, Goloded, Isaev, Rachimbaev, Šotemor, Atabaev and Achunbabaev. Conquest also mentions Ljubčenko and Červjakov, who had both been accused of bourgeois nationalism and had resorted to suicide. Both were rehabilitated.
164. *Pravda*, 25 January 1962; *Pravda Ukrainy*, 25 January 1962; *Rad'jans'ka Ukraina*, 25 January 1962.
165. D.M. Corbett, 'The Rehabilitation of Mykola Skrypnik', *Slavic Review*, no. 22 (1963), pp. 2 and 304-13.
166. See B. Lewytskyj, *Die Sowjetukraine 1944-1962* (Cologne, 1964), pp. 133-5. Omissions in Lewytskyj's survey of the case are the mentions of Skrypnik in *LES* (p. 719), an encyclopaedia edition which contains a biographical headword, and in a biographical note in *Istoričeskij Archiv*, no. 4 (1959), p. 54.
167. A.V. Snegov and E.S. Oslikovskaja, 'Za pravdivoe osveščenie istorii proletarskoj revoljucii', *Voprosy Istorii*, no. 3 (1956), pp. 138-45; A.V. Snegov, *Pravda*, 25 January 1962.
168. Relatively high-ranking officials were: Buačidze (Georgian divisional commander), Eremjan (Armenian people's commissar for finance), Šachbazi (people's commissar for public health in Azerbajdžan) and E.P. Berzin' (principal of Dal'stroj).
169. We are dealing here with Kosior and Bljucher (1969), Čubar' (1971), Antonov-Ovseenko and Voznesenskij (1977), Kuznecov, Krylenko and Šeboldaev (1975), Gorbunov, Rudzutak and Mirzojan (1977), Kedrov and Bubnov (1978), Dybenko and Kosior (1979), Bljucher, Šotman and Knorin (1980).
170. Except for two personalities who had been involved in the Leningrad affair: Voznesenskij and Kuznecov.
171. The cases of Antonov-Ovseenko and Bubnov, who had indeed belonged to oppositions, were discussed in pp. 89-90.
172. Cf. the approach to commemorations in the annual tear-off calendar, the means of mass propaganda *par excellence*. In the 1980 calendar, only those devoted stalinists who had not been purged until quite late were commemorated. See van Goudoever, 'De Sovjet scheurkalender 1980 en de politiek', pp. 642-8.
173. W.H. Roobol, 'De herwaardering van Stalin', *Internationale Spectator*, vol. 23, no. 14 (1969), pp. 1299-313; Medvedev, *Faut-il réhabiliter Staline?*
174. R.A. Medvedev, 'The Stalin Question' in S.F. Cohen, A. Rabinowitch and R. Sharlet (eds.), *The Soviet Union since Stalin* (London, 1980), pp. 46-9.
175. Cohen, 'The Stalin Question since Stalin', *An End to Silence*, pp. 45-7.
176. N.W. Heer, *Politics and History in the Soviet Union* (Cambridge, Mass., 1971), p. 78.
177. Ibid., p. 79.
178. I.S. Smirnov, 'Ob istočnikovedenij istorii KPSS', *VI*, no. 4 (1956), pp. 195-201.
179. Ja.T. Nikolaev, 'O besceremonnom obraščenii s memuarami starych bol'ševikov', *VI*, no. 4 (1956), pp. 139-41.
180. 'Vospominanija o V.I. Lenine', *VI*, no. 1 (1954), pp. 28-39.
181. *VI*, no. 10 (1954), p. 175.

182. F.L. Aleksandrov, 'Bor'ba Moskovich bol'ševikov za massy v period novogo revoljucionnogo pod'ema', *VI*, no. 7 (1954), p. 42.

183. *BSE²*, vol. 23; see also A.M. Gindin, 'Vice-predsedatel' II s''ezda partii', *VI KPSS*, no. 4 (1963), pp. 101-5.

184. Š.M. Levin, 'V.I. Lenin v Peterburge v 1905 g.', *VI*, no. 6 (1955), p. 4, and V.A. Timofeev, 'Bor'ba V.I. Lenina za sozyv III s''ezda RSDRP', *VI*, no. 4 (1955), p. 21.

185. I.I. Radčenko, 'Vospominanija o V.I. Lenine', *VI*, no. 4 (1955), pp. 37-44.

186. *Vospominanija o V.I. Lenine* (Moscow, 1954). This edition includes memoirs written by G.M. Kržižanovskij, C.S. Zelikson-Bobrovskaja, S.I. Gopner, E.D. Stasova, G.I. Petrovskij and others.

187. F.N. Kudrjavcev (ed.), *Vospominanija o V.I. Lenine. Annotirovannyj ukazatel' knig i žurnal'nych statej 1954-1961 gg.* (Moscow, 1963), pp. 8-9.

188. A.M. Sinicyn, 'Črezvyčajnye organy sovetskogo gosudarstva v gody velikoj otečestvennoj vojny', *VI*, no. 2 (1955), p. 41.

189. E.G. Bor-Ramenskij, 'Ob istočnikach i literature po istorii sovetskogo tyla v gody velikoj otečestvennoj vojny', *VI*, no. 12 (1955), p. 142.

190. *Radio Liberty Research*, 11 October 1974.

191. A.F. Trutneva, 'Kommunisty Moskvy–organizatory socialističeskogo sorevnovanija na mašinostroitel'nych predprijatijach (1946-1947 gg.)', *VI*, no. 1 (1956), p. 45.

192. *LES*, p. 466.

193. *Radio Liberty Research*, 2 July 1963.

194. *Radio Liberty Research*, 6 July 1978.

195. In November 1954 and February 1955 *Voprosy Istorii* published several articles on the issue of the Hungarian soviet republic without mentioning the name of Béla Kun. In April 1955, however, a contribution dealing with Lenin and the Hungarian revolt was published. In this, Kun was described as the 'head of the government of the Hungarian soviet republic at the time'. The article, moreover, quoted some of Lenin's criticisms of Kun, so that one cannot yet speak of a favourable context. The same article also criticised Varga through Lenin. See L. Réti, 'Lenin i Vengerskaja Sovetskaja Respublika', *VI*, no. 4 (1955), pp. 30-6. In November 1955, however, another article was published, signed by the Hungarian party leader M. Rákosi, which described the foundation of the Hungarian communist party:

> Béla Kun was the head of the communist party which was established on 20 November 1918. He was the organiser of the prisoners of war in Soviet Russia, where he maintained direct relations with Lenin. He was considered to be the most authoritative exponent of Lenin's views. Subsequently, however, it became evident that Béla Kun, as regards the solution to various important issues, adopted the opportunist line of action rather than Lenin's.

See M. Rákosi, 'Sozdanie KP Vengrii', *VI*, no. 11 (1955), pp. 47-8. Possibly, Rákosi wished to draw attention to Béla Kun so as to turn attention away from a public rehabilitation of Rajk. For a discussion of the Hungarian rehabilitations, see W.O. McCagg, 'After Rakosi: Disgrace and Rehabilitation', *Survey*, no. 40 (1962), pp. 124-32.

196. 'Ob izučenii istorii istoričeskoj nauki', *VI*, no. 1 (1956), p. 4.

197. Ibid., p. 11.

198. 'Vospominanija o partijnych s''ezdach', *VI*, no. 2 (1956), pp. 15-16, and S.N. Kanev, 'Partijnye massy v bor'be za edinstvo RKP(b) v period profsojuznoj diskussii (1920-1921 gg.)', *VI*, no. 2 (1956), pp. 17-21.

199. See *Partijnaja Žizn'*, no. 23 (1956), quoted in *Current Digest of the Soviet Press*, vol. 9, p. 2. In addition, see L.E. Holmes, 'Soviet Rewriting of 1917: The Case of A.S. Shliapnikov', *Slavic Review*, vol. 38, no. 2 (1979), pp. 224-42.

200. V.I. Beljaeva and L.G. Gol'dfarb, 'Bor'ba zavodskich partijnych organizacii Ukrainy za vosstanovlenie černoj metallurgii v 1924-1925 godach', *VI*, no. 2 (1956), pp. 36 and 40.

201. N.P. Čaplin was one of Ordžonikidze's assistants in Transcaucasia and one of the leaders of the Komsomol. Ja.B. Gamarnik was the head of the political department in the army. He committed suicide in order not to get involved in the trial against Tuchačevskij. S.A. Lozovskij was temporarily removed from the party in 1918, while later on he was one of the union leaders; in 1952 he was purged in connection with the Crimea affair, an anti-Semitic purge of Jewish politicans and writers accused of forming a plan to detach the Crimea from the Soviet Union in 1952. As appears from a statement by Khrushchev, he was rehabilitated in 1956. See 'Krymskoe delo', *Socialističeskij Vestnik*, no. 5 (1957), translated in *Ost-Probleme*, no. 8 (1957), pp. 927-31.

202. 'XX s''ezd KPSS i zadači issledovanija istorii partii', *VI*, no. 3 (1956), pp. 4-5.

203. Ibid.

204. Ibid., p. 8.

205. Ruchimovič was honoured in the press only for his function in the economy. See *Ekon. Gazeta*, 1 September 1969, and *Soc. Industrija*, 11 October 1979.

206. E.I. Bugaev, 'Kogda utračivaetsja naučnyi podchod', *Partijnaja Žizn'*, no. 14 (1956), pp. 62-72.

207. Heer, *Politics and History*, pp. 87-8 and 98-9.

208. *Pravda*, 20 January 1957, and *Izvestija*, 20 January 1957. The first issue of *Voprosy Istorii KPSS* was published in January 1958.

209. 'S.M. Kirov na frontach graždanskoj vojny (1919-1920 g.)', *Ist. Arch.*, no. 4 (1956), pp. 61-2.

210. 'Pis'ma Ja.M. Sverdlova iz ssylki (1911-1916 g.)', *Ist. Arch.*, no. 4 (1956), p. 129.

211. M.G. Rosal', 'Bol'ševiki Gel'singforsa v dni revoljucii 1917 g. (mart-jul')', *Ist. Arch.*, no. 5 (1956), pp. 150-1.

212. *Diplomatičeskij slovar'*, 2nd edn, vol. 3, p. 213; *Diplomatičeskij slovar'*, 3rd edn, vol. 3, p. 422.

213. N.I. Podvojskij, 'V.I. Lenin v 1917 godu', *Ist. Arch.*, no. 6 (1956), p. 132.

214. Unlike those of the other members of the government mentioned here who had resigned, Miljutin's personal history in the party had been free of problems after 1918. Furthermore, he had been a member of the — still small — Central Committee since as early as April 1917 and was, therefore, a very prominent party man. Doubtless Miljutin had been rehabilitated before 1958.

215. 'Vospominanija učastnikov velikogo oktjabrja', *Ist. Arch.*, no. 5 (1957), pp. 186-220.

216. *Ot fevralja k Oktjabrju (iz anketa učastnikov Velikoj Oktjabr'skoj Socialističeskoj Revoljucii)* (Moscow, 1957).

217. *Vospominanija o V.I. Lenine* (3 vols., Moscow 1956-60).

218. The following people were mentioned: P.A. Danilov, N.P. Gorbunov, Ja.S. Ganecki, A.F. Il'in-Ženevskij, M.S. Kedrov, N.V. Krylenko, S.A. Lozovskij, A.P. Pinkevič, I.A. Pjatnickij, I.I. Radčenko, Ja.E. Rudzutak, V.G. Sorin and G.S. Sokolov.

219. *Short Course. The History of the Communist Party of the Soviet Union*, Dutch edn (Amsterdam, 1950), pp. 257-63.

220. *Istorija KPSS* (1959), p. 257; *Istorija KPSS* (1962), p. 268; *Istorija*

KPSS (1973), p. 243.
    221. *Istorija KPSS* (1959), p. 259; *Istorija KPSS* (1962), p. 271; *Istorija KPSS* (1973), p. 245.
    222. *Istorija KPSS* (1959), p. 260; *Istorija KPSS* (1962), p. 271; *Istorija KPSS* (1973), p. 245.
    223. BSE^2, vol. 24, p. 403.
    224. Headword 'Levyj uklon', BSE^2, vol. 24, p. 404.
    225. *SIE*, vol. 8, pp. 514-17; BSE^3, vol. 14, p. 244.
    226. *Istorija KPSS* (1962), p. 274; *Istorija KPSS* (1973), p. 248.
    227. Kutuzov, Tolokoncev and Šljapnikov had been included in the encyclopaedia *Granat* at the time. The biographical notes in Lenin, *PSS*, and in the records of the party congresses indicate that no rehabilitation had taken place. G.I. Mjasnikov had been expelled from the party in 1922 and had emigrated. In 1945 he returned to the Soviet Union and was immediately arrested. He has not been rehabilitated.
    228. *Gesch. KPdSU*, vol. 4, p. 100; BSE^3, vol. 21, p. 305; *SIE*, vol. 11, pp. 772-3.
    229. Kiselev in MSE^3 (vol. 4), Kubjak in *SIE* (vol. 8), Pravdin in BSE^3 (vol. 20). The latter two did not reappear in publications until the end of the sixties. The following, less important persons were also found, who were not rehabilitated: V.P. Bekrenev, G.I. Bruno, Žilin, N.V. Kopylov, A.M. Taškin, M.I. Čelysev, E.N. Ignatov and K.N. Orlov. For other adherents to the 'workers' opposition' see F. Kool (ed.), *Arbeiterdemokratie oder Parteidiktatur* (Olten, 1967) and R.V. Daniels, *The Conscience of the Revolution* (New York, 1960), p. 168. M.K. Vladimirov, referred to as a prominent member of the 'workers' opposition' in *SIE* (vol. 11, p. 772), died in 1925. Ju.Ch. Lutovinov, who committed suicide in 1924, was not mentioned in any work of reference.
    230. Milonov was mentioned only in *SIE* (vol. 9, p. 445).
    231. *Short Course* (Dutch edn), p. 300.
    232. BSE^3, vol. 12, p. 437; *SIE*, vol. 7, p. 502; *Diplomatičeskij slovar'*, 1st edn, vol. 1, pp. 807-8; *Diplomatičeskij slovar'*, 2nd edn, vol. 2, p. 81; *Diplomatičeskij slovar'*, 3rd edn, vol. 2, p. 79.
    233. Lenin's letters to Kollontaj were included in Lenin's complete works (4th edn, vol. 36). From 1958 onwards, a number of favourable articles were devoted to her, although this did not yet happen in the central daily papers. Her 90th and 100th birthdays were commemorated on a large scale in 1962 and 1972. During the commemoration of fifty years of diplomatic service, Kollontaj was mentioned in the list of diplomats from the earliest days (see *Pravda*, 31 December 1967). In this capacity, Kollontaj was the central character in a stage play (1966) and in a film (1967).
    234. A.M. Itkina, *Revoljucioner, tribun, diplomat, Očerk žizni A.M. Kollontaj* (Moscow, 1970), pp. 219f; A.M. Kollontaj, *Iz moej žizni i raboty. Vospominanija i dnevniki* (Moscow, 1974), p. 10.
    235. BSE^3, vol. 7, pp. 406-7; *SIE*, vol. 4, p. 851.
    236. The following persons were neither publicly nor formally rehabilitated: M.S. Boguslavskij, A.Z. Kamenskij, V.N. Maksimovskij, T.V. Sapronov, V.M. Smirnov, M.P. Tomskij and A.G. Šljapnikov.
    237. *Pjatnadcatyj s"ezd VKP(b)*, p. 370.
    238. *Short Course* (Dutch edn), p. 348.
    239. *Istorija KPSS* (1959), p. 402; *Istorija KPSS* (1962), p. 422; *Istorija KPSS* (1971), p. 384.
    240. *Istorija KPSS* (1959), p. 405; *Istorija KPSS* (1962), p. 424; *Istorija KPSS* (1971), p. 386.
    241. *Istorija KPSS* (1962), p. 425; *Istorija KPSS* (1971), p. 387.

242. *BSE¹*, vol. 46, pp. 670-3.
243. *BSE²*, vol. 34, pp. 365-6.
244. *SIE*, vol. 11, pp. 510-11; *BSE³*, vol. 20, pp. 486-7.
245. *Gesch. KPdSU*, vol, IV, part 1, pp. 603-6.
246. *Short Course* (Dutch edn), pp. 348-9; Daniels, *Conscience of the Revolution*, pp. 322-69.
247. *VI KPSS*, no. 12 (1965), memoirs of A.I. Mitrofanov, quoted in *Current Digest of the Soviet Press*, vol. 18, no. 12, II, p. 2.
248. *Pjatnadcatyj s"ezd VKP(b)*, p. 370.
249. See *BSE²*, vol. 43, pp. 301-2; *BSE³*, vol. 26, pp. 251-3; *SIE*, vol. 14, pp. 458-64, headword 'Trockizm'; B.N. Ponomarev, *Der Trotskismus — ein Werkzeug des Antikommunismus* (2 vols., Berlin, 1972); *Istoričeskij opyt bor' by KPSS protiv trockizma* (Moscow, 1975); V. Ivanov, *Bor' ba za edinstva* (Moscow, 1979), and the review in *Pravda*, 27 May 1979, p. 3; *Moskovskaja Pravda*, 27 May 1979.
250. See the concise biographies in Lenin, *PSS*.
251. In 1962, the Italian communist party (PCI) demanded that Trotsky's role in the revolution should be determined objectively. See *Radio Liberty Research*, 5 February 1962. In Yugoslavia, party members were advised to read I. Deutscher's biography of Trotsky. See *Kommunist* (Belgrade), 8 February 1977.
252. *Deutscher Zeitung*, 27-28 January 1962.
253. See, for instance, the references in *BSE³* (see note 249).
254. For a more detailed explanation, see Heer's first-rate analysis in *Politics and History* (pp. 28-9 and 213-16).
255. Shapiro, 'Soviet Historiography', pp. 75-6; discussion between W. Laqueur and M. Fainsod in J.L.H. Keep (ed.), *Contemporary History in the Soviet Mirror* (London, 1964), p. 40. In both cases, the person involved was mentioned in *Oktjabr'*.
256. Cf. the concise biographies in the editions of the party congresses. The charges appeared in *Geschichte der Sowjetunion* (Berlin, 1960), p. 498.
257. See Heer, *Politics and History*, p. 213.
258. The following persons were not rehabilitated: G.E. Zinov'ev, L.B. Kamenev, G.Ja. Sokol'nikov, G.E. Evdokimov, A.S. Kuklin, I.K. Naumov, G.I. Safarov, P.A. Zaluckij, I.P. Bakaev, A.D. Sarkis, S.V. Mračkovskij, E.A. Osovskij, G.L. Pjatakov, K.B. Radek, Ch.G. Rakovskij, T.V. Sapronov, I.T. Smilga, V.M. Smirnov, V.A. Ter-Vaganjan and L.D. Trotsky. The list was derived from *SIE*, vol. 10, p. 258; *Geschichte der KPdSU*, vol. 4, part 1, pp. 453, 498-500, 505 and 510.
259. Ešba was included in *SIE* (vol. 16); a biography was published in Moscow in 1967; in 1963, 1968, 1973 and 1980 respectively, *Zarja Vostoka* devoted an article to him. In *BSE³*, however, his name was not included as a headword.
260. M.M. Lasevič: see *Geroi Oktjabrja*, vol. 2 (Leningrad, 1967); *BSE³*, not included in *SIE*; *Ist. Arch.*, no. 4 (1958), p. 121, and no. 1 (1959), note p. 34, in which the biographical data show many gaps.
261. S.I. Kavtaradze: see *BSE³*, vol. 11, p. 124; *DS*, 1st, 2nd and 3rd edns; *Pravda*, 6 October 1965, and *Izvestija*, 6 October 1965. Cf. Conquest, *Great Terror*, pp. 119-20.

4 CASE-STUDIES

Introduction

The issue of the individual rehabilitations in the communist party of the Soviet Union is best illustrated by the study of individual cases. The significance of every aspect of a rehabilitation is then brought out. Each case of rehabilitation is in itself worthy of a separate study, as examining the entire biography of a rehabilitated historical personality makes it possible to obtain a well-founded judgement of the treatment of the case in the Soviet press and historiography after 1953.

The aim of this study is to examine the significance of the rehabilitations. For individual cases, we are dealing with the question of whether a rehabilitation is complete; of whether the person involved has been rehabilitated in all respects. This can be judged best by those people who are considered to have been fully rehabilitated in the literature. Consequently, some cases have been selected to which the Soviet press has devoted a great deal of attention. The case-studies deal with the most important party executive surviving the terror, G.I. Petrovskij, the versatile party man in numerous offices, A.S. Bubnov, and Marshal V.K. Bljucher.

G.I. Petrovskij

Biographical Introduction

On the front pages of *Pravda* and *Izvestija* of 6 May 1953 it was briefly announced that the presidium of the Supreme Soviet of the Soviet Union had decided 'to grant comrade G.I. Petrovskij the Order of the Red Banner of Labour on the occasion of his 75th birthday in recognition of his services to the Soviet state'.[1] The announcement was signed by K.E. Vorošilov on 28 April. Many observers have interpreted this fact as the outcome of a decision to rehabilitate Petrovskij. After all, he had been the only one to escape elimination after his removal as candidate member of the politburo. Since 1940, he had held the modest post of assistant

173

director of the Museum of the Revolution in Moscow. His name was merely mentioned in relation to the Fourth Duma to which he had belonged as a representative of the workers.[2] Moreover, the city which was named after him, Dnepropetrovsk, continued to be called this. But that was all. It is remarkable that, in addition to Petrovskij, the three other former members of the Bolshevik Duma faction survived the terror as well.[3] Petrovskij felt the survival as a subtle punishment. His work in the museum demanded glorification of Stalin and he had to act as his faithful servant before visitors. As colleagues disappeared and died around him, he had to live in hourly dread of arrest.[4] Both his sons were arrested. The elder died in camp, the younger was killed at the front after his release.

In his youth, Petrovskij, an ethnic Ukrainian and metal worker, had joined the revolutionary movement in Ekaterinoslav. He was recruited by I.V. Babuškin and P.A. Morozov, who had come from St. Petersburg to set up a social democratic organisation there. He is now considered to have become a party member in 1897, before the party officially existed. In 1905, he was one of the organisers of the Soviet of Ekaterinoslav. The curia (group of workers' voters) there appointed him representative in the fourth Duma (1912). In the same year, Petrovskij was co-opted on to the Central Committee of the Bolsheviks. Since then he had taken part in various party conferences, one of which was in Kraków, where Lenin then lived. After the outbreak of the First World War, the social democratic representatives were arrested and convicted. During the trial, Petrovskij, chairman of his faction, addressed the court. In February 1915, he was sent into exile to Turuchansk near the Enisej, together with Kamenev, among others.

Later, Petrovskij had to move further on, to Jakutsk, where, after the February revolution, he played his part as a revolutionary together with E.M. Jaroslavskij. After his return, he was transferred to the Ukraine to work in the areas of agitation and propaganda. After the October revolution, he was called back to Petrograd by Lenin to take part in the Soviet government as people's commissar for internal affairs (NKVD). Under Lenin's supervision he worked on the Constitution of the RSFSR, among other things. He also co-signed the decision about the Red Terror (10 September 1918), in which the Terror was intensified in reaction to the attempted murder of Lenin. In March 1919, however, he was appointed chairman of the Ukrainian Executive Com-

mittee. Petrovskij held this office for twenty years, combined with
the membership of the Ukrainian politburo (from 1920).

When the Soviet Union was formally constituted in 1922, he
became one of the co-chairman of the All-Russian Central
Executive Committee, a sort of vice-president of the state. In the
twenties, he rose in the central organisation of the party. Full
member of the Central Committee in 1921, as a supporter of
Stalin he became candidate member of the politburo in 1926.
Petrovskij never actively participated in any opposition in the
party, and he acted as a good stalinist during the industrialisation
and collectivisation. His remarkably constant position, comparable
to that of his chief, M.I. Kalinin, was discontinued at the end of
1938. At the time of the eighteenth party congress (1939),
Petrovskij was attacked, yet he was not expelled from the party.
Like the other still-living representatives of the Bolsheviks in the
Duma, he survived the terror.

After his public rehabilitation, Petrovskij continued his work in
the Museum of the Revolution. He did not return to any political
position in the central machinery or in the Ukraine. Nor was he
restored to the membership of the Central Committee. Petrovskij
was admitted to the twentieth party congress as a visitor, not as a
representative. Apparently, the ruling party leaders did not consider it to be appropriate to entrust him with any genuine political
office, nor even with a post of honour.

However, he was allowed to engage in some journalistic activity,
provided that it involved his memories.[5] His memories of Lenin,
for example, found their way into *Voprosy Istorii* (January 1954)
and were included in the collection which was later published.[6]
Together with other surviving old Bolsheviks from the earliest
days, among whom were V.A. Karpinskij and G.M. Kržižanovskij,
Petrovskij also contributed to the elaborate commemoration of
Lenin in April 1955 by writing an article on Lenin's methods of
government for *Pravda*.[7] After that, his memories could be found
whenever a ritual commemoration took place: fifty years of revolution of 1905, 35 years after the tenth party congress. From all
these publications, one may infer that Petrovskij was used in
publications as an old Bolshevik, a living monument. He had to
bear witness to the course of events and customs in the party in the
days of Lenin, for this was what the party needed.

The twentieth party congress implied no significant change in
Petrovskij's work. His biographers claim that he enthused over

Khrushchev's secret speech. In the romanticising style of such works, it is reported that, the night after Khrushchev's revelations, Petrovskij gave a full account to some of his intimate friends and told them about the terror, while he paid tribute to the victims, among them his son Petr.[8] Afterwards, Petrovskij actively participated in the propaganda campaign on behalf of the resolution of the congress. He signed a letter which was published by a large group of old Bolsheviks who were held in good esteem (including Stasova, Kržižanovskij and Gopner).[9] In this, they warmly approved of the general leninist line of the party. Most of the those who signed, including Petrovskij, were rewarded for their support with the Order of Lenin or the Red Banner of Labour.[10] Formally, these badges of honour were granted for activities in the revolution of 1905: rather late, considering its commemoration in 1955. The regime must have wished to benefit from an emphasis on the bond with the old Bolsheviks to demonstrate the continuity between Lenin's party and the present party. Their public activity was of great use to the restoration of faith in the party, which had been damaged by Stalin's actions.

The Lenin cult which now replaced the Stalin cult revived partly because of the endeavours of these old partisans. Petrovskij's activities after the congress to help to restore the so-called leninist norm of party life were considerable. He gave many lectures at universities and in factories, to peasants and artists, etc. Together with a group of old Bolsheviks, he was sent on a tour to Finland, Bulgaria and Romania (1956-7).[11] Furthermore, he wrote articles on Lenin and the decisions of the congress in such newspapers as *Pravda, Izvestija, Sovetskaja Rossija, Trud, Radians' ka Ukraina, Robitnicij Gazeta, Mlada Ukraina* and the press of Siberia and Jakutia. His memoirs were now published as a pamphlet. The topics of his contributions, however, continued to be limited to the year 1917 and the preceding period.[12]

After the twentieth congress, Petrovskij had been enlisted in the process of collecting material on behalf of the rehabilitations: 'he actively participated in judging the work of his comrades, the old Bolsheviks; he collected material on the prominent activists of the revolution'.[13] Much is made of this in biographies dealing with Petrovskij. He co-operated in the restoration of the reputation and the rehabilitation of many innocent victims of the Stalin era, both of communists and of those who were not members of the party. Above all, he also helped the relatives of victims who had filed petitions for rehabilitation. Moreover, he made himself available for writing requests to the juridical or party authorities. Petrovskij is supposed to have supported the petitioners and to have promoted the idea of 'rehabilitation'. This account of Petrovskij's life suggests the existence of a pressure group of old Bolsheviks on behalf of relatives of victims of the terror. One may indeed assume that this group has been able to make an important contribution to the rehabilitations, as long as the party did not object. Several examples can be offered.

Petrovskij helped Sonja Tabačnica Dal'njaja, an old Bolshevik agitator, to obtain a personal pension and have her party membership restored. More familiar are the names of others he helped: the relatives of his former Ukrainian colleagues. He assisted with the rehabilitations of the daughter of S.V. Kosior, the son of E.I. Jakir (Petr Jakir, later a well-known dissident), and the sons of V.Ja. Čubar' and E.I. Kviring. This virtually sums up all the information provided by his biographers.[14] It means that he occupied himself with less important cases, predominantly with people he knew well. But he did not work on these cases in any official capacity, so that his contribution may be considered as an initiative.

Rehabilitation

The conferring of the Order of the Red Banner of Labour in May 1953 has various aspects which deserve our attention. This order is not the highest honour which could be conferred upon people of prestige such as Petrovskij's before 1938. After Stalin's death, the Order of Lenin was again granted on a relatively large scale. The motivation for the conferment of the order was limited to mentioning Petrovskij's service to the state; his services to the party or to the revolutionary movement were consciously omitted.

When the same order was conferred upon Petrovskij in 1928, as well as when he was granted the Order of Lenin in 1938, the citation had been more extensive and complete, listing all the aspects of his work omitted later.[15] The level of homage in 1953 therefore fell short of completeness, so that one should in fact speak of a partial rehabilitation. None of the party leaders apparently knew how to proceed with Petrovskij's rehabilitation, for the customary public congratulations failed to materialise. A second problem regarding the conferment of the order was represented by the date of publication: 28 April. Petrovskij had already celebrated his 75th birthday on 4 February 1953. As he had still been a non-person at the time, the celebration passed unnoticed in the press. This, however, applied to a large number of cases. Furthermore, it would have been normal for the publication of the decision to grant the order to have taken place at once. Instead, this took more than a week: 6 May. Undoubtedly, there had been some squabbling among the party leaders, which would explain the postponement. In general, the earlier public rehabilitations, like those of the Kremlin doctors and of Michoëls, are attributed to Berija. Petrovskij's rehabilitation can be seen in the same perspective. Robert Conquest worked out the case in further detail and put this rehabilitation within a wider framework of the struggle for power. Without rejecting the possibility that Petrovskij's rehabilitation could have been a demonstrative sign of liberalisation, Conquest suggested that there may have been a design to have a leader or figure of high prestige at hand to attack Khrushchev's position in the Ukraine. The fall from power of Mel'nikov, the Ukrainian party secretary, was said to have been effected by Berija. As a representative of the era before Khrushchev, Petrovskij could then have served as successor. Conquest nonetheless advances the possibility of a coalition between Berija and Khrushchev. In that case, Petrovskij could at any rate have been used by Berija as 'a rod in pickle against Khrushchev'.[16] Although the argument is impressive, this interpretation, in our view, overshoots the mark. To allow Petrovskij to hold a public office would have involved a risk. After all, people with incriminating pasts have always been reminded of their pasts by the party. Even if Petrovskij's fall from power could be said to have been unjustified, the idea of 'no smoke without a fire' was widely held in party circles. If he held an official post any reference to the attack on Petrovskij during the eighteenth party congress could have placed him in an awkward position. During the 'silent destalinisation' before 1956, it was generally believed that the issue of the purges had to be dealt with without publicity. None of the former victims were appointed to politically significant offices after rehabilitation. When this indeed appeared to be possible in other Eastern European countries later (Gomulka, Kádár, Husák), this could happen only under extreme circumstances. There was no question of it happening in the Soviet Union.

The most plausible explanation is still that the presidium had decided to give a sign of being liberally inclined as regards the treatment of non-persons. The leaders wished to put on a humane face within the framework of the restoration of the position of the party instead of the personal dictatorship. In view of the sensitivity of the subject, such a decision did not need to be effected unanimously or without debate. The propagandistic usefulness of a rehabilitated old Bolshevik was certainly regarded as a component of the revival of the Lenin cult. Khrushchev's confidant Snegov suggested as much in his explanation of the conferment of the order: 'all knew that a real brother in arms of Lenin was alive and working'.[17]

The Petrovskij case was not totally isolated. It is worth while examining which of the other surviving prominent old Bolsheviks were singled out after Stalin's death. Of the members of the Central Committee as composed in 1912-21, the following were still alive in 1953: E.D. Stasova, M.K. Muranov, G.I. Petrovskij, I.S. Belostockij, as well as the rulers V.M. Molotov, K.E. Vorošilov and A.A. Andreev. Nothing more is known about Belostockij than his membership of this official body in 1912. However, Stasova and Muranov, who had both sunk into oblivion after 1938, were presented with the Order of Lenin (October 1953) for services to the communist party and the Soviet state.[18] The honour conferred upon D.Z. Manuil'skij and G.M. Kržižanovskij is to some extent comparable, although they did not experience demotion of status under Stalin until very late.[19] From 1954 onwards, old Bolsheviks were granted orders on a larger scale, usually 'for fifty years of public and political work and in recognition of services to the revolutionary movement'. In July and August this wave of veneration reached its climax when Vorošilov, as chairman of the presidium of the Supreme Soviet, arranged a formal reception and honoured L.A. Fotieva, P.I. Voedovin and N.N. Kolesnikova as 'veterans of the revolution'. For the time being, this represented the end of this act.[20] The design for 'rewarding old Bolsheviks' had apparently been fulfilled for 1954. Once more a sufficient number of living symbols of Lenin's party had been put in the limelight. One should not forget, incidentally, that such notorious purgers as L.M. Kaganovič, A.Ja. Vyšinskij and M.F. Škirjatov, too, were presented with orders of Lenin.[21]

Considering Petrovskij's Ukrainian background, it may be of importance to examine the significance of the conferment of the order as regards the reappearance of his name in Ukrainian publications. The fact itself was not mentioned in the Ukrainian press. In comparison, D.Z. Manuil'skij was congratulated at length when he was granted his order. He, however, had been a member of the Ukrainian politburo until 1952 and had not yet been forgotten.

The Ukrainian party secretary A.I. Kiričenko could have included Petrovskij in his speech on the occasion of the commemoration of the tercentennial unification with Russia. In relation to the beginning of the Ukrainian Soviet state, however, he only mentioned the familiar names of Stalin, Molotov, Sverdlov, Dzeržinskij, Frunze, Khrushchev, Vorošilov and Kaganovič.[22] Later on, Petrovskij was mentioned as a matter of course in the context of the commemoration of fifty years of Soviet Ukraine in 1967.[23] He was involved, but some time passed before this was realised. Furthermore, the name Petrovskij was mentioned only very casually in *Voprosy Istorii* in articles dealing with the Ukrainian–Russian unification.[24] Until 1956 he was not referred to as head of the Ukrainian state in a survey in the *Great Soviet Encyclopaedia* either.[25] All this indicates that the Ukrainian party did not bother about Petrovskij's rehabilitation.

Biographies

As early as in 1954 the name of G.I. Petrovskij was recorded as a headword in a work of reference[26] and this has since become common practice. He is usually referred to as a party and Soviet official, and sometimes also as one of the oldest members of the revolutionary labour movement. The Ukrainian encyclopaedia bestows some extra honour upon him by adding the quality 'excellent' (*vidatni*).[27] In the daily press an exhaustive biographical article was published only at the time of Petrovskij's death in 1958.[28] The first biographical pamphlet was published in the Ukrainian language in 1961, soon followed by detailed Russian biographies.[29] Commemorations of his birthday took place at length in 1963, 1968 and, to a lesser extent, in 1978.[30] A commemorative meeting was arranged in the Institute for Marxism–Leninism in 1968. Mikojan made a speech, while memories were revived by various old Bolsheviks. New, concise biographies were published in 1968 and 1970.[31] A monument in commemoration of G.I. Petrovskij was erected in Kiev in 1970.[32] A selection from his work was published in the Ukrainian language.[33] Those authors who ventured upon the biography of Petrovskij were often old Bolsheviks. A.V. Snegov repeatedly contributed to these publications. He was a well-known party man, who himself had been brought back from Kolyma by Khrushchev and who had been rehabilitated. After 1964, he still defended Khrushchev's line of action during meetings of historians in which controversial topics came up for discussion: the debate on the publication of a six-volume party history and the polemic regarding A. Nekrič's book *22 June 1941*. Snegov thus incurred his expulsion in 1971.[34]

Practically every biography of Petrovskij published before 1969 is for the largest part, some 60-70 per cent, devoted to the latter's activities before 1917. After that, even less attention was paid to the period in which Petrovskij held several prominent offices, some 10 per cent for each biography. There is hardly any further interest in his work after 1953, which was so much expatiated upon in 1963-4. The Ukrainian press, moreover, now takes the largest part in publications on Petrovskij.

Petrovskij is depicted in the biographies as a true adept of Lenin, as a man who himself was instructed by Lenin. The relation between the two men is illustrated by a large number of quotations from Petrovskij's memoirs in which he describes their meetings and introduces Lenin as a speaker. Lenin's influence can also be observed in the appointment of Petrovskij as people's commissar for internal affairs, and as delegate to the peace negotiations in Brest-Litovsk. In those days Petrovskij was supervised by Lenin and party secretary Sverdlov. Little more is reported about his work than that he followed the example of Lenin's wise methods. Petrovskij, in brief, is presented as a creation of Lenin, as a high but subordinate official who let himself be guided by his idol.

Petrovskij's relation to Stalin is discussed only in those biographies which were published in the final years of Khrushchev. He is then presented to the reader as one of the critics of Stalin at the seventeenth party congress in 1934. This is linked with the activities of Kaganovič and Berija, who are held responsible for concocting a charge against Petrovskij. Khrushchev, on the other hand, figures as the patron of Petrovskij.

Petrovskij's attitude towards the oppositions in the party is described in approving terms by his biographers. They emphasise that his promotion to candidate member of the Central Committee is the result of his support of Lenin's viewpoint in the peace negotiations in Brest-Litovsk. He is said to have been a fierce opponent of Trotsky in the twenties. The literature is less enthusiastic about Petrovskij's attitude towards the 'right opposition'. Contrasts with Bukharin, to be sure, are sometimes pointed out, but interest in this is minimal. On the one hand, this may have been the result of the minimalisation of the 'right-wing danger' (see the attempt to rehabilitate Bukharin); on the other hand, Petrovskij himself may have had 'right-wing' sympathies. This last aspect applied to his son Petr who belonged to the school of Bukharin and who was a prominent executive in the party organisation in Leningrad. Petr supported the Rjutin group in those years and was killed in the terror. He was rehabilitated solely through his son Leonid's unflagging efforts.[35]

Criticisms of the Past

Nevertheless, Petrovskij did not remain exempt from criticism in the biographies written before 1960. In the period before the revolution he had shown some inclination to collaborate with the Mensheviks. The Bolshevik Duma faction in which Petrovskij took part had — self-evidently — voted with the Mensheviks in favour of a general progressive formula in the declaration of policy and had declared itself against a demonstration of workers on the day of the inauguration of the Duma. Petrovskij had dissociated himself in public from earlier attacks on the Mensheviks. Lenin hereupon decided to intervene and summoned the entire faction to Kraków, where he was then living. From 26 December 1912 to 1 January 1913 a conference took place during which Lenin severely criticised the group and denounced them as over-credulous souls.[36]

The biographer Snegov seized this theme to expatiate upon the similarly incorrect position taken by Stalin in pronouncing himself in favour of a conciliatory and cautious policy towards the Mensheviks without harsh terms of abuse. In other respects, too, Stalin was criticised in the biography on Petrovskij.

Snegov criticised Petrovskij also for the latter's activities immediately after the February Revolution. Together with the Bolsheviks E.M. Jaroslavskij and S. Ordžonikidze, he collaborated with Mensheviks and postponed revolutionary tasks. Lenin's criticism of them was disdainful: 'Some revolutionaries you are indeed!'[37]

Another biographer nonetheless discovered a different quotation from Petrovskij which is supposed to indicate the latter's lucid views on the revolution, dated March 1917. It purports that Petrovskij expected a second, now socialist, revolution.

Such critical issues were no longer included in the biographical material after 1969. Stalin was no longer mentioned. Petrovskij could be shown in a favourable light and there had to be no references either to dissent or to incorrect positions adopted by Stalin.

In this case of rehabilitation of a prominent party and Soviet leader who had merely fallen into disgrace, those works devoted to Petrovskij exhibit substantial shortcomings. History is manipulated and used as part of a propaganda campaign.

No reliable information is supplied on Petrovskij's political activities, and as a person he remains altogether obscure. His rehabilitation after the death of Stalin took place in silence and was initially full of gaps. There was no question of restoration to any kind of office.[38]

A.S. Bubnov

Biographical Introduction

Andrej Sergeevič Bubnov (22 March (3 April) 1884-12 January 1940),[39] son of a small textile manufacturer and town councillor in Ivanovo–Voznesensk, ethnic Great Russian, studied agricultural sciences in Moscow for several years. As a 17-year-old he had taken part in the revolutionary movement in his birthplace. A Bolshevik from 1903, he frequently co-operated with M.V. Frunze. After the revolution of 1905 Bubnov chose the life of a professional revolutionary and met with the fate concomitant with it: he was arrested 13 times and was repeatedly exiled. As a representative of Ivanovo–Voznesensk, he attended the fourth (Stockholm, 1906) and sixth (London, 1907) party congresses. After that, he was employed in the party organisation in Moscow. From 1910 onwards Bubnov belonged to the leading group of Bolsheviks, as a member of the Bolshevik Centre in Russia (1910) and as a candidate member of the Central Committee (1912). He guided the work of the Bolshevik faction in the Fourth Duma and was part of the editorial staff of *Pravda*, which was founded in 1912. Immediately after the outbreak of the First World War, he opposed the war and was arrested; together with V.V. Kujbyšev he was exiled to Samara and subsequently to Turuchansk. Overtaken by the February revolution on their way to Siberia, both returned from exile. Bubnov was appointed a candidate member of the Central Committee in April, and a full member in July. He was now part of the party leadership. He was the only one to participate in both the military-revolutionary committee of the Soviet of Petrograd and the Bolshevik military-revolutionary centre for the guidance of the revolt. On behalf of the Central Committee he exercised control over the newspaper of the Bolshevik military organisation *Soldat*. In addition, Bubnov was a member of the politburo which the party had called into existence for the time being. During the revolution of October he was a member of the so-called field staff and a commissar for railway stations, an important post for the strategy of the revolt. Elected to the Soviet government on the board of the people's commissariat for traffic after the crisis, he was responsible for the railway system. At the end of November Bubnov was sent temporarily to the Ukraine to secure the transport which was necessary to the fight against Ataman Kaledin.

In the party Bubnov was a prominent, yet not very notable, character who followed and carried out Lenin's line of action. His contribution to the Central Committee was small, and focused upon formal matters. In 1918 he joined the so-called 'left communists', who were opposed to signing the peace with Germany, and acted as one of the leaders. This incurred a severe personal reprimand from Lenin at the seventh party congress (March 1918). Bubnov lost his seat on the Central Committee and was directed to the Ukraine. He was there installed in the national secretariat, the group of nine (*devjatka*), in preparation for the revolt in the Ukraine. When an organisation office for a first Ukrainian party congress was set up, Bubnov was appointed to it. In the organisation's paper, *Kommunist*, he published a series of articles on the revolt, which still reflected a left communist outlook. The left-wing party leaders in the Ukraine, including, among others, G.L. Pjatakov and Ch.G. Rakovskij, raised no objections: at the first conference of the Ukrainian Bolsheviks (July 1918) Bubnov became a member of the Central Committee and of the military-revolutionary committee. As official order number one, Bubnov and Pjatakov now called for a full-scale revolt, which came to naught and was labelled as incorrect by the central party leaders. They were criticised during the second Ukrainian party conference (October 1918). Bubnov was not re-elected and was sent to occupied Kiev to supervise the underground Bolshevik organisation together with S.V. Kosior. Thanks to the success he achieved there Bubnov's star once again began to rise: he was once more installed in the Ukrainian Central Committee (third Ukrainian party conference, in March 1919), while after that the All-Russian party, too, allowed him to enter the ranks of the Central Committee as a candidate member (eighth congress, March 1919). At the same time, he was also elected in the Ukraine to the politburo and to the military-revolutionary committee of the Ukrainian front.

People's commissar Trotsky, who visited the Ukraine in May 1919, deemed the composition of this committee to be too shaky. He advised that Antonov-Ovseenko, Podvojskij and Bubnov be removed from the committee.[40] Differences of perception regarding strategy form the background to these transfers. The fact that the left communists and the military opposition were strongly represented was also important. On Trotsky's advice Bubnov was sent to Ekaterinoslav to recruit workers for the front together with Pjatakov. After that, Bubnov was constantly kept on the move: in July he was on the military-revolutionary committee of the fourteenth army, whereas in August he was no longer part of it, 'painlessly' removed by Trotsky and transferred to the Ukrainian council for defence.[41]

The enormous pressure on the Ukrainian and southern fronts caused by Denikin's attack on Moscow entailed the deployment of all Ukrainian leaders in critical positions, so that Bubnov was assigned to several other tasks in 1919.

At the eighth conference of the party in December 1919, Bubnov was once more rebuked by Lenin, who criticised the attitude of Bubnov, Manuil'skij, Rakovskij and Drobnis towards the Borotbists (the National Left Socialist–Revolutionary Ukrainian Party) because they were unwilling to co-operate with them and also because they did not want to enter into a compromise with the peasants.[42] Lenin did not wish to annoy the middle peasants and the kulaks in the Ukraine. Here the left-wing position of the Ukrainian leaders once again became evident. The dissension was discussed at greater length at the ninth party congress (March 1920).[43] This time, too, Bubnov had a considerable share in the discussion. He accused the Central Committee of disregarding the advice given by the Ukrainian party, which made it easier for the Borotbists to increase their hold on the population. Bubnov also criticised the nomination policy of Moscow, which he had been subjected to himself, for causing disruption in the communist ranks.[44] Even though he did not yet belong to the opposition of the democratic centralists at this congress, the core of his objections is cast in the same mould as that of the Decists.

The party, however, was alert and Bubnov was summoned back

to Moscow at the beginning of 1920. He was not re-elected to the Central Committee, indeed he became a member of the party bureau in Moscow, yet he was assigned the supervision of the textile works: a substantial demotion which, beyond doubt, induced him to join the Decists. He took part in the ninth party conference (September 1920) as one of the leaders of this opposition and criticised the organisational defects of the party secretariat (particularly Krestinskij), predominantly in the practical matter of not carrying out congress resolutions.[45] He had by then established a distinct reputation as trouble-maker; witness the comment by the workers' opposition leader S.P. Medvedev: 'as far as I know, Bubnov was always in opposition'.[46] At the subsequent, famous tenth congress, Bubnov continued these oppositional activities by advancing the resolution of the Decists. In relation to the most critical issue of the congress, the revolt in Kronštadt, he refrained from making a speech; Maksimovskij spoke on behalf of the Decists.[47] Bubnov left the congress and fought against the rebels with a rifle in his hands. Apart from the Order of the Red Banner, he thus also gained considerable credit from the party, which now trusted him once more. According to what he said himself, he opted in favour of the general policy and against oppositions. Bubnov was appointed to the military-revolutionary board of the Northern Caucasian military district and of the first cavalry army with Vorošilov and Budennyj. The Central Committee again installed him as a candidate member at the eleventh party congress (April 1922). The recently appointed secretary-general Stalin established Bubnov in his secretariat by appointing him chief of the agitprop department (May 1922). At the same time, he became a member of the board of the people's commissariat for education.

Above all, Bubnov had asserted himself as a practical man. He was no ideological genius, but he had proved he could stick to decisions once they had been taken or orders once they had been given. As for his oppositional activities, he had not taken initiatives, but had followed others. He was one of the leaders and exhibited a remarkably propagandistic proficiency through his lucid formulations. These activities had not been exceptional in the oppositional party climate in both the Ukraine and Moscow. Bubnov was a well-educated man and an intellectual, yet considering his practical disposition he did not act in the style of an intellectual. As he was very experienced as a political supervisor in the press and wrote a great deal himself, he was useful in an agitprop department. Politically vindictive towards Trotsky, he could be of great help to Stalin. His work in agitprop involved elaborating regulations for the press, and guidelines for educational programmes; he began to make use of the 'radio' medium for propaganda purposes. Despite his position as a guard of ideological purity Bubnov still had an odour of opposition about him. At the twelfth party congress (April 1923), an anonymous opposition pamphlet circulated which invited the oppositions to unite and to remove Zinov'ev, Kamenev and Stalin from the Central Committee. At the congress Zinov'ev summoned the unknown authors to introduce themselves, suggesting that the Decists were behind all this. Bubnov felt he was implicated and responded by sending a letter to the presidium (19 April 1923). He considered the pamphlet to be an anti-party programme and condemned every attempt at organised opposition as criminal. Bubnov believed that his conduct during the previous years had proved that he cared above all things for the unity of the party.[48] The congress confirmed him in his office (together with his colleagues in the party machinery — Molotov, Dzeržinskij and Kujbyšev).

In the light of this statement it is very surprising that Bubnov, albeit with some reservations, signed the 'platform of 46' (15 October 1923, written by Preobraženskij, Breslav and Serebrjakov). In this basically critical programme, which subsequently came to be stigmatised as 'Trotskyist', various oppositions came together. Even though Bubnov, together with a number of others, wrote that he did not agree entirely with the programme in matters of content and merely supported the practical proposition of the authors (i.e. to arrange a special conference to discuss the functioning of the party), his signature indicated that he was not averse to this kind of action.

This was a fairly naïve thing to do for a leader of agitprop. The party apparently deemed this to be unacceptable and removed him from that office, but it did not much resent Bubnov being dismissed: on the contrary, in January 1924 the plenary meeting of the Central Committee appointed him to be head of the political authority of the army (PUR) and a member of the military-revolutionary board of the Soviet Union. At the thirteenth party congress he even entered the orgburo (1924) and in 1925 he became one of the party secretaries (though only one year). This was a remarkable career for one of the '46'. In his new office as chief of the PUR he was the successor of co-signer Antonov-

Ovseenko, the Trotsky supporter who had continued his independent and provocative activities. Bubnov had probably bowed to
the party and acknowledged his mistake soon after October 1923.
In reaction to Preobraženskij's accusation 'Which hand do you use
to write your present articles?', Bubnov replied in January 1924: 'I
always use one and the same hand ... Furthermore I think it is useful to say that I will use this hand to fight against all, also my most
intimate friends, if they slide down into a break with bolshevism.'[49]
Both Preobraženskij's sarcasm and the appointments in January
1924 indicate that Bubnov's relapse into the opposition was not
serious and lasted only a very short time.

As political army leader Bubnov was assigned to carry out the
military reforms upon which the Central Committee had decided
in the absence of Trotsky in January 1924. These were necessary
because of 'Trotsky's disorganising activity'. Bubnov worked on
this in his army office under supervision of Frunze, later on under
Vorošilov, and in his party offices under Stalin. The reforms aimed
at providing a permanent grip on the army for the party, a safety
device against an independent position of the military. The instru-
ment was the *edinonačalie*, one-head leadership. The current
system of military commanders who were assisted by political
commissars had to be replaced by a system in which the
commander controlled the activities of his unit in both a military
and a political sense. For the sake of the transition towards the
new system the commanders were initially going to continue to
receive political assistance. Although this system has never
materialised because of the antagonism between party and military
it provided a suitable lever to remove the oppositions from the
army. Bubnov was initially successful: the New Opposition
obtained hardly any footing in the military bodies. Nevertheless,
inside the political army leadership he was confronted with opposition from the military-political academies, which deemed the
military unsuited to political activity. There was powerful opposition in the Tolmačev Academy in Leningrad and in the
Belorussian military district (in short the Tolmačev-Belorussian
opposition).

In the course of 1927 the conflict in the political military bodies
became evident and was made public. In 1928-9 the Central Committee repeatedly deliberated upon the issue and concluded that
the readiness to fight of the Red Army had been endangered (July
1929).[50] Bubnov, who had apparently failed to carry out instruc-

tions, was relieved from his assignment and was succeeded by Jan Gamarnik. Bubnov was appointed people's commissar for education of the Russian Federation (RSFSR) as successor of Lunačarskij (September 1929) and he criticised himself at the plenary session of the Central Committee in November 1929 (fully independently of the 'right opposition' which then fell from power). He kept his seats in the Central Committee and the orgburo. At the sixteenth party congress (1930) he confirmed his loyalty to party policy by severely denouncing both the left wing and the right wing.

In the framework of the cultural revolution it was the first task of the people's commissar to introduce general compulsory primary education, to expel the experiments of the twenties and to give strict guidance to educational institutions and programmes. Above all, the direct relation between theory and practice had to be indicated, to which end polytechnic education was extremely well suited. This aspect was emphasised in the biographies which were published under Khrushchev. 'Labour' as a school subject he deemed to be necessary, and he regretted its abolition by Stalin (1937). Together with the vice-secretary Krupskaja and other educationalists, Bubnov was opposed to this loosening of the relation between education and life, between theory and practice, which they felt to be necessary to build up socialist society.[51]

In addition to all these exacting offices, Bubnov regularly made time to engage in the study of party history. Several sketches by him had been published in *Pravda* as early as in 1920. The survey of the history of the party which he published in 1923 was reprinted four times. Of great importance was his standard work *The All-Russian Communist Party (Bolsheviks)*, which was published as volume 11 of the *Great Soviet Encyclopaedia* in 1930 and which was published individually afterwards.[52]

Little is known about Bubnov's end. He and his Ukrainian colleague V.P. Zatonskij were not admitted to the plenary session on 10-12 October 1937 because they did not have the special permits that were required for this meeting.[53] Bubnov returned to his office to resume his work, until the *dežurnaja* (the caretaker) came to inform him that his removal from his post had been announced on the radio at midnight. Bubnov explained that the party knew what it was doing and, according to a biographer in 1964 who admired his self-control and faith in the party, he commented: 'Please continue your work.'[54] The next day he handed over his work to his successor, P. A. Turkin.

Thereupon a notice of dismissal was published in the press: 'he failed to carry out his assignment and systematically unsettled the educational work, despite the enormous help given to him by the Soviet government'.[55] After several days he was arrested and falsely accused, but he refused categorically to plead guilty. He had become a victim of the arbitrariness in the period of the personality cult, as it was described euphemistially in the biographical data of the sixties. The date of his death, 12 January 1940, is confirmed by every Soviet work of reference. The cause of his death, execution, was not referred to until the twenty-second party congress, by KGB chairman Šelepin, who observed that Bubnov had been brought to trial by Stalin, Molotov and Kaganovič and had been executed.[56]

As far as Bubnov's family is concerned, nothing is known about his wife Marija Konstantinova Mjasnikova, who had been arrested and had probably died before 1956 as well. His two children were arrested in 1944; we know nothing about his son German, but his daughter Elena survived the terror, was rehabilitated and was allowed to contribute to the commemorative literature dealing with her father.

To sum up, these are the most prominent elements in Bubnov's biography: professional revolutionary before 1917; central and leading role during the October revolution; leader in the Ukraine during the Civil War; political chef of the Red Army; member of the government in the thirties; member of the Central Committee between 1922 and 1937; party historian; opposition leader of 'left communists' and Decists.

Oblivion

Before the purges all important Soviet works of reference, such as, to take just one example, the encyclopaedia *Granat*, had published articles on Bubnov.[57] In 1933, his 50th birthday had been effusively commemorated in the press.[58] After the report of his dismissal, however, nothing was heard about Bubnov in the Soviet press until 1956. His name was virtually ignored, and neither biographies nor encyclopaedic articles concerning him were published. His name was not mentioned when a number of important personalities were listed in relation to some party congress or other from the past.

Letters and telegrams by Lenin, which were published on a

limited scale in *Leninskij sbornik* and *Voennaja perepiska*, contained practically no names and certainly none of those who had been purged. Usually positions were mentioned without accompanying names. When in the text or in the address Bubnov's name had been mentioned in the file documents, it was omitted in the publication. A telegram to the chairman of the Ukrainian sovnarkom (the name of Rakovskij, to whom it was addressed, had been erased) instructed him to send the plenipotentiaries assigned to him to Charkov and Ekaterinoslav. The original text does not refer to 'plenipotentiaries', but to Pjatakov and Bubnov.[59] Bubnov's name did emerge in the collected works of Lenin, fourth edition, in a number of volumes which were published in 1950. The relevant passages occur in speeches and invariably contain criticisms by Lenin. However, no denigrating footnote was added, and the original text was even followed by the mention of Bubnov as *tovarišč*, comrade. Such presentations were common in this edition for others who had been purged.

Sometimes the silence on Bubnov was broken, particularly in those places where millions of communists were destined to learn the relevant text by heart: in the *Short Course, Kratkij kurs*, of the history of the party. Bubnov was mentioned in this as an Otzovist, the 'deviation' which intended to withdraw the Bolshevik faction from the Duma in 1908-9. Bubnov was mentioned here as the last person in a series which included Bogdanov, Lunačarskij, Aleksinskij and Pokrovskij. In this case, too, we may well have our doubts: the literature does not confirm it, although it is theoretically possible that Bubnov belonged to the Otzovists if one considers his presence in Moscow in 1908 and his presumable participation in the conference there (May 1908), where the deviation in question is assumed to have manifested itself. We do not have any information on Bubnov's position there. Nor do we have any information on attacks by Lenin on the Otzovism in which Bubnov is mentioned. Further research is required here. In addition, Bubnov was accused of holding a 'semi-Menshevik' point of view, which he was supposed to have entertained since February 1917 together with his colleagues in Moscow Kamenev, Rykov and Nogin.[60] This seems highly unlikely. Bubnov did not arrive in Moscow until April (after his return from Siberia he stayed in Samara for some time), and he opposed Kamenev and gave his full support to Lenin at the seventh party conference which began on 24 April in Petrograd.

The biographies from the sixties indicate unanimously that Bubnov made efforts to oppose association with the Mensheviks, though without supplying details on his position regarding the appreciation of the revolution or his attitude towards the Provisional Government. Here, too, further research into source materials is necessary.

Rehabilitation

We have no information on Bubnov's formal rehabilitation and posthumous restoration to party membership. Several publications merely mention the fact that he was rehabilitated after the twentieth party congress. For our more detailed investigation into the progress of Bubnov's rehabilitation we follow his name after its reappearance in the press, in source publications, works of reference, party histories, commemorative articles and commemorative meetings, as well as in biographies devoted to him.

The first biographies dealing with Bubnov were published in shortened form in the second half of 1957; the *Leningrad Handbook*, in mass edition, contains a biographical article. In addition, Bubnov's answers to an inquiry into his activities during the revolution dating from 1927 were published in a selection of interviews released both as a book and in *Istoričeskij Archiv*. A new edition of the work of Frunze, moreover, included a Bubnov biography in a footnote, the most detailed so far: more than two pages.[61]

Since 1957, biographical articles have been included in all the important encyclopaedias, honourable mentions have emerged in the party histories, memoirs dealing with Bubnov have been published, his work has been reprinted, his birthday has been commemorated, etc. For an accurate assessment of this rehabilitation it is essential to review these publications. The description under the headword 'Bubnov' in 1934 indicated that one was dealing with an 'important' (*krupnyj*) party and Soviet functionary. This qualification did not reappear. The adjective 'distinguished' (*vidnyj*) was used only in volume 51 of the *Great Soviet Encyclopaedia* (1958). The *Concise Soviet Encyclopaedia*, which was published at the same time, merely referred to a 'party and Soviet functionary', the description used in all other and subsequent encyclopaedias.[62]

The exact date of Bubnov's death was mentioned for the first time in 1958. The *Historical Encyclopaedia* is the only work of reference to mention the fact that he was purged: he was slandered and exposed to repression during the period of the personality cult of Stalin. He has been posthumously rehabilitated. As for the accuracy of the information on Bubnov's career, a large number of errors and omissions can be noticed.

It is remarkable, for instance, that such fundamental data as the precise periods in which he was part of the Central Committee are incorrect. This can be accounted for by the fact that Bubnov's published biography itself contained errors, while little or no source investigation was conducted by the encyclopaedists and one could not fall back on historical literature. Accuracy was not achieved until the seventies. In encyclopaedic articles on oppositions, Bubnov is mentioned only in the context of left-wing and military oppositions.

The new edition of the history of the communist party of the Soviet Union, several chapters of which were published in *Kommunist* in October 1958, included only a few names of historical Soviet personalities. The subsequent editions (1962, 1969, 1972) were hardly more detailed in this respect. Some more information on Bubnov was provided by the later editions after 1969. Additional data were supplied by the comprehensive six-volume party history, which has not yet been completed. Basically, however, all editions share the same points of interest in Bubnov. Bubnov's pre-revolutionary work in particular received honourable mention. Furthermore, he was presented in several series of names of noteworthy figures as one of the prominent Bolsheviks to have returned from exile, as belonging to the new party ranks that had risen during the Civil War (which is quite peculiar, as he was already a candidate member of the Central Committee in 1912). None of the accusations from the *Kratkij kurs* were repeated. On the contrary, after 1969 Bubnov was commended for his fight against Menshevism. Of his oppositional activities only his 'left communism' is mentioned and, in the six-volume edition, his Ukrainian aberrations. There were no references to Decism, nor to the 'platform of 46'. The reader, then, must have some difficulty noticing that (after 1969) his change dating from the end of 1923 is actually mentioned and that his fight against Trotskyism is commended.

On Bubnov's important offices after 1922 only the comprehensive six-volume edition offers some information, which again does not concentrate upon Bubnov individually and which is limited to mentioning his name in lists. The fact that Bubnov was important can be noticed by the reader when his name is presented in the lists of prominent party functionaries, which until today has been included in the brief surveys.

The issue of the personality cult and the rehabilitations came up for discussion once again at the twenty-second party congress. The chief of the KGB, A.N. Šelepin, made an elaborate speech directed against Kaganovič, Molotov and Malenkov, and in which he mentioned various names of victims. Bubnov was among them: Postyšev, Kosior, Ejche, Rudzutak, Čubar', Krylenko, Unšlicht and Bubnov had been brought to court. They belonged to a large group of comrades who, on the orders of Stalin, Molotov and Kaganovič, had been sent for trial before the Military Court in November 1937. Most of them, among whom the ones just mentioned, were executed.[63] No further information is provided on the differences between the dates of death of those mentioned or on the motives for mentioning these victims specifically.

Although in 1956 Bubnov was not yet mentioned in specialised historical works, his name re-emerged in the important source editions which were approved in the middle of 1956 and which were published at the end of the year. In the new edition of Lenin's telegrams from the Civil War, *Voennaja perepiska*, Bubnov's name was once again specifically mentioned.[64] In addition, a contribution by him was published in a collection of memoirs dealing with the revolution.[65] Publications like these, similar to the publication of memories of Lenin in this period, are works which are relevant to the level of the rehabilitations. The party leaders would not tolerate the publication of memoirs of a denounced or convicted person in these collections. The right to approve memoirs which were devoted to Lenin, after all, was explicitly restricted to the Institute for Marxism–Leninism.

All these memoirs were published in voluminous mass editions. In our view, historical figures who had formerly been purged and whose memoirs were published in these collections have been rehabilitated. Although no short biographies indicative of such rehabilitations have as yet been included in the relevant works, the evidence is given by the series of biographies published in *Memories of Lenin*, volume 2 (1957): the memoirs in volume 1 are by party members who were held in esteem. On this line of argument Bubnov's contribution to the collection of memories of the revolution in Petrograd is indicative of his rehabilitation, which must therefore have taken place before July 1956. *Izvestija*, moreover, considered it necessary to point out in the advertisement for the book that memories of old Bolsheviks were included, followed by a series of names of persons formerly purged or forgotten, including Bubnov.[66]

The extent to which writings of the person involved were republished represents an important criterion of the level of rehabilitation. These, to an even greater extent than the memories of Lenin or of the revolution, reflect the ideas and the political line of the person rehabilitated, which are then once again in circulation. This entails a careful examination of the tenability of these earlier statements in the light of the current party line. Bubnov's work, or, rather, selections from his work, were republished quite soon: one volume concerning the Red Army and one about education.[67]

As a result of the publication of his military writings, *Krasnaja Zvezda* devoted a lengthy article to Bubnov and his work, in which he was characterised as an 'important party–, state– and military-political activist'. The article did not criticise Bubnov, nor did it contain criticisms of the work under discussion, but it made no comments on his end either. It is remarkable that both in the article in *Krasnaja Zvezda* and in the preface to the collection a great deal of attention was paid to the relation between Bubnov and Frunze, which is also evident in the collection itself.[68] Bubnov's actual work in the army, particularly the introduction of the *edinonačalie*, the one-head leadership and the accompanying reorganisation of the army, therefore occupied a somewhat less prominent position than could be expected on the basis of these extremely essential activities. Bubnov's work, so to speak, emerged in the wake of the renewed interest in Frunze. If the republication had gone no further than this, one could only conjecture a pressure group of militaries and old Bolsheviks acting as a driving force behind Bubnov's rehabilitation. However, the republication of his work on education, predominantly official speeches from the thirties, causes surprise. In those days Bubnov did not have an easy time because of the dismantling of polytechnic education which he, like his assistant people's commissar Krupskaja, regarded as the basis of education. Krupskaja's work, however, was reprinted in full so that the motive for this interest in the work of both of them cannot but lie in the educational policy under Khrushchev. The close relation between theory and practice, which had to take shape especially at polytechnical schools, was involved here.

At the time, both collections of Bubnov's work, including the biographies which were supplemented, considerably enlarged the range of information on Bubnov because they supplied a lot of data on the period of his life after the Civil War, which until then had been dealt with in a few sentences. With this, the actual rehabilitation, his historical work excepted, is complete in 1959. The party, however, was interested only in those parts of his work which fitted in with the policy of its own days, of Khrushchev.

Commemorations

In 1933, the people's commissar for education of the RSFSR Bubnov was congratulated at great length on his 50th birthday, as was usual with prominent leaders. A whole page was devoted to him, and more or less elaborate congratulations were sent to him by all major party bodies and those party bodies with whom he was felt to have been associated in the past. Krupskaja and Kržižanovskij provided articles on his personality. In short, in this way Bubnov, too, had a share in the personality cult and the glorification.

Comparable to this homage was the commemoration of his 80th birthday in 1963. The list of the extremely diverse daily papers and periodicals which devoted articles to him was very impressive. 'Unwavering communist, pupil and brother in arms of Lenin, belonging to the glorious elect group of proletarian revolutionaries', sums up the epitheta ornantia; truly a public rehabilitation. The commemorative articles for once did not avoid referring to his tragic end by reporting that he had become a victim of arbitrariness and unfounded accusations.

The commemoration of Bubnov had a distinctly educational function. He was depicted as an example, as an excellent organiser who could act humanely and independently of bureaucracy, and who did not spare himself in self-criticism. Furthermore, we are presented with a view of a romantic revolutionary past behind the executive Bubnov. Bubnov's alleged resistance to the personality cult of Stalin is pointed out with great emphasis by the biographers. Berija is presented in this context as a villain, while Khrushchev, Švernik and Vorošilov are depicted as benevolent spirits. The fact that Bubnov had taken part in a dissident faction in the party is interpreted as a token of tolerance of the party. In spite of everything he had been trusted and employed in prominent offices. Bubnov's oppositional activity, the most delicate element in his biography, is not always referred to in the commemorative articles and when this happened, as in *Pravda*, attention is proudly called to his bold action against the Trotskyist opposition, or, as regards his service in the agitprop department, reference is made to his unflagging leninist loyalty, as in the educational journal *Narodnoe Obrazovanie.*

In addition to reports on his activities in the Ukraine, the army and education, his work as a historian was mentioned in various papers as well. Bubnov was regarded as an important, authoritative party historian who fought against objectivism. He was quoted as having said about himself: 'the proletarian revolutionary who takes up the pen of the historian is duty-bound to be an active fighter for leninism'.[69] The full, actual rehabilitation of Bubnov, by Soviet standards, has thus finally been completed. However, there is a fairly important restriction which we should bear in mind. Whenever Bubnov's oppositional activity comes up for discussion it is described in such abstract and covert terms that the reader cannot discover the actual meaning of this opposition. There are even biographical articles which do not mention this aspect at all. It is precisely this which forms an element of a full rehabilitation. No sympathetic commentaries could possibly be given on dissident activities because this would be tantamount to criticising Lenin. Any rehabilitation of oppositional activity would be equal to betraying the doctrine. In this light, it is amusing to observe that practically all biographical sketches of Bubnov include quotations from Lenin. In 1920, the great leader had once described Bubnov as 'the experienced party comrade Bubnov'. This rather trivial qualification can be found in numerous places, completely isolated from its context: we are, in fact, dealing here with a cynical passage from Lenin's criticisms of Bubnov as the leader of the opposition of the democratic centralists.[70]

Among the authors of the commemorative articles, one comes across several old Bolsheviks, a few of Bubnov's former assistants, and his daughter Elena Andreevna, as well as a number of unidentified writers. For the most important article of all, published in *Pravda*, the responsibility lies with the chief editorial staff, for this contribution has not been signed. Here, too, as in the case of the customary commemorative meetings which were organised by the Institute for Marxism–Leninism, the Museum for the Revolution, etc., it appears that old Bolsheviks quite often were selected to write commemorative articles.

Despite this considerable interest in Bubnov in 1963, five years later no more than one or two unimportant publications were devoted to him. It was not until 1974 (Bubnov's real date of death had in the meantime apparently registered in the press) that his (90th) birthday was again commemorated in *Pravda*.[71] This contribution had now been signed by the historian Lebedev, and included a brief and sketchy survey which presented Bubnov as a consistent fighter for the party and for leninism. No further information has been published in the Soviet press.

Biographies

The favourable commemoration of Bubnov was also confirmed in biographical works. Four short studies about his life were published in mass editions, two of which were by a national publishing house, one by a federal republican company, and one by local publishers. The two Muscovite biographies of *Politizdat*, published in 1964 and 1978 respectively, display several vast differences: in size (80 *v.* 412 pages), in circulation (70,000 *v.* 300,000 copies), and in type of biography (documentary *v.* romanticised story).[72] While in the biography of 1964 the reader is presented with a reasonably proportionate arrangement of the various periods in Bubnov's life, 96 per cent of the edition of 1978 is devoted to his life up to and including the October revolution. The latter edition is part of a series, *Ardent Revolutionaries*, in which only biographical stories about nineteenth-century revolutionaries and extremely eminent Bolsheviks are included. The authors, Binevič and Serebrjanskij, are two renowned commemorators of Bubnov in the military press of 1963. They are Bubnov's former assistants from the military machinery. The author of the 1978 edition, Gerasimov, is described as a 'historian–literary scholar', but is otherwise totally unknown. The local biography by Gorbunov, which is also a story though not without some serious research, was published in Yaroslavl in 1967 (2nd edition, 15,000 copies)[73] and is likewise devoted to the young revolutionary Bubnov, which is not illogical in view of the local character of this edition. Of considerable interest is the republic edition, published in the Ukrainian language, in Kiev (1965, 50,000 copies).[74] Not only is half of the edition devoted to Bubnov's activities in the Ukraine, which fills up a fairly large gap in our information on Bubnov, but this edition is also structurally well balanced. The author of this work, curiously enough, is the famous historian A.V. Licholat, who, ten years earlier, had still been a thoroughly stalinist writer.[75] Although he does not put forward any strong accusations against Bubnov, Licholat is the one biographer who plays the schoolmaster wherever Bubnov is supposed to have been remiss. Nevertheless, he manages to follow the trend in such a way that the reader gets a favourable impression of Bubnov's activities in the Ukraine.

All in all, we may argue that the essential biographies about Bubnov were published at the end of the Khrushchev era or shortly after and that the later editions merely deal with Bubnov as a revolutionary. It is important to note that the Ukrainian publishers provided a biography as well, as it were laying claim to the Ukrainian part in Bubnov's history, which, for that matter, was limited to the Civil War.

The number of distinguished heroes of the revolution in the Ukraine, however, is not particularly impressive. For many of them, some blemish has continued to spoil their commemoration. Leaders like Pjatakov and Rakovskij are still in disfavour, so that, in order to have at least some heroic biographies at our disposal, we have to fall back on approved political personalities, even if they have less status in the Ukraine. And in Bubnov's case we are not even dealing with an ethnic Ukrainian!

V.K. Bljucher

Biographical Introduction

The peasant's son Vasilij Konstantinovič Bljucher (19 November 1890-9 November 1938) was born in Barščinka (Yaroslavl government).[76] One of his ancestors in serfdom had been nicknamed by his master after the Prussian general Blücher, which explains the origin of the name. Despite many theories to the contrary, there is nothing mysterious about it: Bljucher was simply a Great Russian.

Active as a metal worker, he was arrested during a strike and convicted as an instigator, and spent the years 1910-13 in prison. Called up at the outbreak of the First World War, Bljucher served as a soldier and a non-commissioned officer. After being gravely wounded in 1915, which entailed a full year of recovery[77] — the story goes that he ended up in the mortuary twice — he was invalided out of the army. He joined the Bolsheviks in 1916 and served as a worker in various places, eventually in Samara. After

the February revolution he was assigned by the local party committee there to rejoin the army as a volunteer and to act as an
agitator among the soldiers. He was a member of the military-
revolutionary committee in Samara in October 1917 which was
supervised by V.V. Kujbyšev. After the Bolshevik revolution, the
committee sent him to Čeljabinsk with a detachment to join battle
with Hetman Dutov. Bljucher became the head of the military-
revolutionary committee in this town.

From Čeljabinsk he headed the Red Guards regiment in the
battle of Orenburg, which was captured by the Bolsheviks. However, the revolt of the Czechoslovak legion left the troops in an
untenable position because they were now surrounded by the
Czechs and Dutov's cossacks. Bljucher decided to break out with a
group of 10,000 partisans from the southern Urals and managed to
break through the encirclement northwards, covering 1,500
kilometres in 40 days to join the Eastern Front in Kungun
(August-September 1918). This raid won him considerable fame.
The 'proletarian commander' was the first to receive the Order of
the Red Banner, which had only just been introduced. There is an
apocryphal story which says that, in the report which dealt with
Bljucher, his feat was compared to Suvorov's expedition through
the Alps.[78] After that, as the commander of the 30th and then the
51st division of the 3rd army under R.I. Berzin, he fought against
the troops of Admiral Kolčak, near Perm, Vjatka and Tobolsk.

From March 1920, Bljucher had sole command of his division,
that is to say, he was not assisted by a political commissar. In the
autumn of 1920, he was put under the command of Frunze with
the 51st division where he helped to destroy the last bastion of
Vrangel' on the Crimea. With his troops he defended Kachovka in
the operation Perekop, the White 'Verdun'. After that, Bljucher
served as the garrison commander of the town and district of
Odessa for a few months.

In June 1921 he was sent to the pseudo-independent Soviet
republic of the Far East to replace R.I. Ejche as Minister of War
and Supreme Commander. In this capacity he participated in the
conference of Dairen. His most important activities included the
fight against the White Baron Ungern-Šternberg and the expulsion
of the Japanese troops. He gained new fame by the storming of
Voločaevka. After completion of this task and the abolition of the
Republic of the Far East (July 1922), he was charged with various
special assignments by the Supreme Military Council and was in

command of, among others, the first army corps in Petrograd. In the autumn of 1925, Bljucher was posted to Canton to advise Sun Jat-sen as head of the Soviet military mission, together with the political adviser M.M. Borodin. Here Bljucher came to be known by the name of General Galin (or Dzja-lin).

He had a large share in the reorganisation of the armed forces and the training of officers at the military academy of the Kvo Min Tang in Whampoa. After the death of Sun (1925), he was temporarily recalled. In his report to the party leadership he forewarned against Chiang Kai-sjek, whom he did not trust.[79] Back in China in 1926, he co-operated in the preparation and execution of the Northern Expedition. When Chiang turned against the communists and the collaboration with the Soviet Union was ended, Bljucher returned and for some time served as second-in-command in the Ukraine.

In 1929 Bljucher was again given an important assignment in Siberia, this time as the Supreme Commander of the Special Far East Army, which was put into action in 1929 against the Chinese take-over of the Chinese Eastern railway in Manchuria. He received a triumphant welcome when he returned to Moscow. He was the first to receive the newly introduced Order of the Red Star and he delivered a speech of greetings on behalf of the Red Army at the sixteenth party congress (1930).[80] According to an unconfirmed rumour, he had been invited by the Syrcov opposition to participate in a new government as people's commissar for war.[81]

From 1929 to 1938, Bljucher was in office in the Far East, where it was primarily his task to keep the Japanese forces, which had invaded Manchuria, out of Russian territory. Also a member of the Executive Committee of the province of the Far East, he expanded his office into a veritable governorship in Chabarovsk.

At the seventeenth party congress Bljucher was appointed candidate member of the Central Committee and made a speech in which he emphasised the perils of Japanese expansion.[82] In 1935, he was one of the five generals who were promoted to the new rank of marshal.

During the great purge, Bljucher, too, had to prove his loyalty to the party. He was summoned to Moscow to serve as a judge during the so-called trial against Tuchačevskij (June 1937). His absence in Chabarovsk was used by the new chief of the political department of the army, L.Z. Mechlis, to effect a reorganisation in the Far East. Through this Bljucher was robbed of his trusted seconds-in-command. He was himself put in an honourable yet lonely position as chief of the new blanket army organisation there, at the Far Eastern Front. He also received a second Order of Lenin.

His position, however, had been undermined, and his personal power now belonged to the past. In the spring of 1938, he defeated the Japanese near Lake Chasan, but he was subsequently criticised because of the heavy losses. Whereas Stalin had, if necessary, protected him in earlier days, this did not now happen. He signed his last order on 18 August 1938. Sent on leave to Soči together with his family, Bljucher was arrested on 22 October 1938. Berija is said to have interrogated him personally. He was accused of having been a spy for the Japanese since 1921. The marshal refused to confess. He died during interrogation in the Lefortovo prison on 9 November 1938.[83]

Bljucher's family, his brother and even his first wife were arrested. His under-age daughter, moreover, was imprisoned between 1950 and 1954.[84] A son, V.V. Bljucher, fought in the Second World War; he was not decorated for bravery because his father had been one of the purged. This was rectified in 1964 by granting him an order.[85]

In the West, Bljucher was regarded as a mysterious character for a long time: the general who had no past.[86] This was reinforced by his insignificant past as a worker, his German name and its historical meaning, the secret assignment in China and his Chinese pseudonym, as well as a lack of biographical information on him.

Oblivion

The press mentioned neither Bljucher's arrest nor his death. His name vanished altogether from publications: he was not even mentioned in a negative context. The party history, *Kratkij kurs*, discussed the Civil War without mentioning him and could easily ignore Bljucher, for he had held no prominent post in the party. Up until 1957, the *Great Soviet Encyclopaedia* avoided mentioning his name under the headwords which described his major feats: Voločaevka, Perekop and Kachovka.[87]

Rehabilitation

In 1955 Bljucher's case and possibly his rehabilitation were given serious consideration inside the presidium. During Khrushchev's and Bulganin's visit to Tito, they informed their host that the evidence against Bljucher had at the time been fabricated — indicative of a formal rehabilitation.[88] Two years later, Bljucher was the first military victim of Stalin to receive a public rehabilitation.

This happened in an article entitled 'Worker, Soldier, General', which was published on 10 August 1957 in the daily paper of the Ministry of Defence, *Krasnaja Zvezda.*[89] The author, V. Rušaev, had been head of staff alongside Bljucher for some time during the Civil War. He emphasised the plain social background of the marshal. The author paid most attention to the glorious expedition through the Urals in 1918. In a nutshell he mentioned Bljucher's share in the victories of Perekop, Voločaevka and Chasan.

The remaining biographical information was extremely brief and incomplete: only Bljucher's most important offices were listed, without providing any information on their significance. The reader was kept uncertain as to Bljucher's ultimate fate: his death could be read between the lines. No information was given on his demise, for the article concludes by commenting that the career of the 'legendary commander' had been illustrious.

The significance of this public rehabilitation was that Bljucher's name fully reappeared in publications afterwards. Henceforth he is once again qualified as a 'hero'. In an article in *Komsomol'skaja Pravda* two weeks later, for instance, the ex-officer A.I. Todorskij, once purged but rehabilitated while he was still alive, mentioned Bljucher, Tuchačevskij and Putna in the same breath as heroes.[90] In the historical press his date of death was mentioned casually, in a footnote.[91] Also in August 1957, the important fiftieth volume of the *Great Encyclopaedia* was sent to the press, including various mentions in lists of army commanders under the entries of party history and armed forces.[92] One is not surprised, then, to find a biography including a photograph in volume 51 of this edition in 1958, as well as in the *Concise Encyclopaedia* published in the same year, in which his precise date of death is mentioned for the first time.[93] From that point Bljucher once again took up a prominent place in the press: the amount of literature and the number of times he is mentioned are enormous. In that very year a biographical pamphlet was published in Blagoveščensk in the Far East.[94]

In 1960, a fairly detailed biography was published, which was written by V.V. Dušen'kin, a former assistant of Bljucher who had also written several articles about him in the press.[95] This short book went through three editions until 1964 and reflects the

gradual process of public rehabilitation by its inclusion of a growing number of names of purged victims such as Vacetis and Berzin.

Fitting in with the design to write more about the marshals and
generals, *Izvestija* devoted a long article to Bljucher in 1962 to
commemorate the grant of an order to him on 11 May 1919.[97]
This was a very trivial event indeed to be used to commemorate
him, the more so because no space was given to the reason for
granting the order. It was evidently a motive for writing about
Bljucher, which also occurred with other high-ranking military
victims in that same year.

This article, however, introduced a subsequent stage of rehabilitation: a distinct increase in the amount of interest in the marshal.
A postage stamp carrying his portrait was issued. Films were made
and presented, with such remarkably cynical and harrowing titles
as 'Heroes don't die'. A drama including, among others, the
character of Bljucher in a leading role even touched upon the issue
of the purges.[98] Finally, a collection of Bljucher's essays and
speeches was published.[99]

In addition to the biographies and memoirs devoted to Bljucher,
a number of studies were published which deal with specific
aspects of his life and which can be divided into two fields of
interest: the Civil War and, in particular, the famous raid and his
activities in China from 1924 to 1927. This last theme is interesting
in the light of Russian–Chinese relations. It is striking that
Bljucher's efforts in China are presented as an important contribution to the Chinese revolution and as a sign of Russian sympathy
towards the Chinese people.[100] The impression is given that the
present Chinese are ungrateful. The fact that Bljucher's role is put
forward in this context may be explained by the fact that he is not
involved as such in Stalin's mistakes in Chinese policy through his
warnings against Chiang.

The repercussions of the contemporary relations between the
Soviet Union and China express themselves in the total lack of
documents from the period between 1924 and 1927 in the edition
of Bljucher's work in 1963.[101] Apparently, publishing possibly
delicate historical material was felt to be undesirable. In 1970, on
the other hand, when the conflict between the Soviet Union and
China had reached the level of an armed battle, various short
studies about the activities of the Soviet advisers in China during
the twenties were published.[102]

In the literature dealing with Bljucher much is made of his

simple social background: the common working-class youth who becomes a soldier and who, thanks to the Bolshevik revolution, actually finds himself carrying a marshal's baton in his knapsack. Bljucher's political acumen is frequently stressed and he is described as an example of *edinonačalie*, one who is competent both as a military and as a political functionary.[103]

Because of his spectacular feats during the Civil War and the fight against Japan, Bljucher's commemoration may well be used for legend creation.

As he had never belonged to any opposition, a rehabilitation without restrictions was possible. Nevertheless, it still took quite some time before his biography was completed. Bljucher's activities represented a delicate matter in the context of international relations. Beyond doubt, all information regarding his person was classified.[104] In the case of Bljucher, too, the meddlings of the party resulted in the emergence of gaps in his biography and in the new editions of his work.

Notes

1. *Pravda*, 6 May 1953, p. 1; *Izvestija*, 6 May 1953, p. 1.

2. *BSE²*, vol. 5, p. 535.

3. We are dealing here with A.E. Badaev, M.K. Muranov and F.N. Samojlov. See Conquest, *Great Terror*, pp. 631 and 807, and A.B. Ulam, *Stalin. The Man and his Era* (New York, 1973), pp. 439-40.

4. Petrovskij was not removed from the party. He participated in the ninth party conference of the Soviet district in Moscow in March 1950. See G.I. Petrovskij, *Vibrani statti i promovi* (Kiev, 1974), p. 412. Furthermore, when it was announced in 1953 that he had been granted his order he was described as 'comrade', a term which is reserved for party members only. According to Roj Medvedev (*Let History Judge*, pp. 295 and 308), who conducted a number of interviews with friends of Petrovskij, Stalin deliberately decided upon this punishment. Khrushchev claimed that he had saved Petrovskij. See A.I. Mel'cin, 'Spodviznik Lenina', *VI KPSS*, no. 2 (1963), p. 98.

5. For Petrovskij's biography, see Bega and Aleksandrov, *Petrovskij*; in addition, *Serdce, otdannoe ljudjam. Rasskaz o žizni i dejatel'nosti G.I. Petrovskogo* (Moscow, 1964). A.V. Snegov acted as the leader of the group of authors.

6. *VI*, no. 1 (1954), pp. 34-42. *Vospominanija o V.I. Lenine* (1st edn, Moscow, 1954; 2nd edn, Moscow, 1955). For a complete survey of Petrovskij's contributions to the commemorations of Lenin, see *Vospominanija o V.I. Lenine. Annotirovannyj ukazatel' knig i žurnal'nych statej 1954-1961 gg.* (Moscow, 1963).

7. G.I. Petrovskij, 'Pod rukovodstvom velikogo vozdja', *Pravda*, 20 April 1955, p. 2.

8. Bega, *Petrovskij*, p. 309; *Serdce*, p. 186.

9. *Pravda*, 10 March 1956.

10. We are dealing here with a large-scale reward for 442 old Bolsheviks. See

Vedomosti Verchovnogo Soveta SSSR, no. 7 (31 March 1956), pp. 180-204.
    11. Bega, *Petrovskij*, pp. 309-11; *Serdce*, pp. 186-9.
    12. *Serdce*, p. 186; A.F. Melenevs'kij and G.M. Kurij, *G.I. Petrovskij* (Kiev, 1968), p. 290; Petrovskij, *Velikoe načalo (vospominanija starogo bol' sevika)* (Moscow, 1957); Petrovskij, *Veliki roki* (Kiev, 1957); Petrovskij, *Z revoljuciinoho minuloho* (Kiev, 1958).
    13. A.I. Mel'cin, 'Spodviznik Lenina', *VI KPSS*, no. 2 (1963), p. 98.
    14. Bega, *Petrovskij*, pp. 310-11; *Serdce*, p. 189.
    15. See *Pravda* and *Izvestija*, 4 February 1928 and 4 February 1938. In addition, see *Izvestija*, 9 February 1938, p. 1, and 28 February 1938, p. 1.
    16. Conquest, *Power and Policy*, pp. 211-13.
    17. *Serdce*, p. 185; cf. Shapiro, 'Rehabilitation Policy', p. 104.
    18. M.K. Muranov: Order of Lenin, *Izvestija*, 29 November 1953, p. 1; E.D. Stasova: Order of Lenin, *Izvestija*, 15 October 1953, p. 1.
    19. See *Izvestija*, 9 October 1953, p. 1, and 15 October 1953, p. 1.
    20. Ibid., 5 August 1954, p. 1. In 1954, the following old Bolsheviks were granted an Order of Lenin or the Order of the Red Banner of Labour (the date of publication in *Izvestija* is mentioned in parentheses): V.N. Sokolov (9 February); S.I. Gopner (12 February); S.V. Golujatko (2 April); N.A. Emeljanov (18 April); K.T. Sverdlova (4 June); V.A. Radus-Zen'kovic (20 June); C.S. Bobrovskja-Zelikson (3 July); L.A. Fotieva (28 July); P.I. Voevodin (29 July); N.N. Kolesnikova (31 July); S.N. Martikjan (3 August); A.I. Ostroumov (17 August); K.K. Dizjulis (18 August); S.M. Tetin (19 August); S.V. Nosov (26 August); N.O. Kučmenko (28 August); A.I. Blinnikov (30 August); S.Ch. Kasym-Chodzaev (21 September); V.D. Bonč-Bruevič (10 November). Of these, S.N. Martikjan had been released from camp shortly before. See Shapiro, 'Rehabilitation Policy', p. 104.
    21. See *Izvestija*, 15 August 1953, p. 1, 10 December 1953, p. 1, and 22 November 1953, p. 1.
    22. *Pravda*, 23 May 1954, pp. 2-4; *Izvestija*, 23 May 1954, pp. 2-4.
    23. Melenevs'kij, *Petrovskij*, p. 295.
    24. Petrovskij was mentioned in *VI*, no. 4 (1954), pp. 97-8, *VI*, no. 5 (1954), p. 10, and *VI*, no. 3 (1955), p. 25. Although the general theme of the articles could easily have served as a motive, he was not referred to in *VI*, no. 5 (1954), pp. 19-31 and in *VI*, no. 10 (1954), p. 146. In both cases, only Petrovskij's activities in the Ukraine have been looked for.
    25. *BSE²*, vol. 44, p. 94.
    26. *ES²*, vol. 2, p. 645. There are gaps in the biographical data in the article; in particular his senior positions in the party are missing.
    27. *URE*, vol. 11, pp. 121-2.
    28. *Pravda*, 10 January 1958, p. 4; *Izvestija*, 10 January 1958, p. 5.
    29. *G.I. Petrovskij* (Kiev, 1961); Bega, *Petrovskij*; *Serdce*.
    30. See the daily press about 4 February, Petrovskij's birthday.
    31. Melenevs'kij, *Petrovskij*; L. Klučnik and B. Zav'jalov, *G.I. Petrovskij* (Moscow, 1970).
    32. *Izvestija*, 8 May 1970, p. 6. At the same time, monuments were erected for both Kosior and Čubar'. All this happened in the context of the 100th birthday commemoration of Lenin.
    33. Petrovskij, *Vibrani statti i promovy*.
    34. A. Nekritsch and P. Grigorenko, *Genickschuss: Die Rote Armee am 22. Juni 1941* (Vienna, 1969), pp. 190-201; *Političeskij Dnevnik*, vol. 1, p. 304.
    35. *BSE³*, vol. 19, p. 488; L.P. Petrovskij, *P. Petrovskij* (Alma Ata, 1974; L. Petrovskij, 'Al'batros revoljucii', *Moskovskij Komsomolec*, 8 January 1980. I have not been able to find either of the latter two publications in the libraries consulted. See also *Političeskij Dnevnik*, vol. 1, p. 529.

36. *Serdce*, p. 61.
37. Ibid., p. 118.
38. In a rather curious article, C. Duevel ('The Hundredth Anniversary of the All-Ukrainian Starosta', *Radio Liberty Research*, 17 February 1978), considers the possibility that the name of the city of Dnepropetrovsk, named after Petrovskij, might be changed into Brežnevsk.
39. The precise date of birth is given by G.I. Gorbunov (*Orlinyj vzlet*, 2nd edn, (Yaroslavl, 1967), p. 10), and also by A. Rodin ('Ob utočnenijach v biografii A.S. Bubnova', *Voenno-istoričeskij Žurnal*, no. 4 (1979), pp. 74-5). In works of reference and commemorative articles in the press until 1973-4, Bubnov's date of birth was considered to be 6 April 1883 (new style). The cause of this variation is Bubnov himself, who since 1908 had given a false age to deceive the police and had stuck to it. Reports in the western press claiming that he was still alive in 1956 are incorrect. See *Süddeutsche Zeitung*, 23 March 1956, and *Studies in Comparative Communism*, vol. 2 (1969), no. 1, p. 142.
40. J.M. Meyer (ed.), *Trotsky Papers 1917-1922* (The Hague, 1964-71), vol. 1, pp. 416-17 and 430-1.
41. Ibid., pp. 638-9.
42. Lenin, *PSS*, 5th edn, vol. 39, pp. 370-1.
43. Ibid., vol. 40, p. 266.
44. *Devjatyj s"ezd RKP(b)*, pp. 58-60 and p. 133.
45. *Devjataja konferencija RKP(b)*, p. 238.
46. Ibid., p. 175.
47. *Desjatyj s"ezd RKP(b)*, pp. 135, 243 and note p. 878.
48. *Dvenadcatyj s"ezd RKP(b)*, p. 238.
49. V.P. Erasov, *Navsegda, do konca. Povest' ob Andree Bubnova* (Moscow, 1978), p. 407.
50. Ju.P. Petrov, *Partijnoe stroitel'stvo v sovetskoj armii i flote* (Moscow, 1964), pp. 171-2, 189-95, 238-44 and 258-71. See also A. Binevič and Z. Serebrjanskij, 'Slavnyj syn kommunisticeskoj partii', *Voenno-istoričeskij Žurnal*, no. 3 (1963), p. 41.
51. G.S. Prozorov, 'Vydajuščijsja dejatel' sovetskogo prosveščenija', *Sovetskaja Pedagogika*, no. 4 (1963), pp. 92-101; Z. Rabkin, 'Boevoj narkom kul'turnogo fronta', *Narodnoe Obrazovanie*, no. 5 (1963), pp. 73-81.
52. *BSE¹*, vol. 11, pp. 7-544.
53. A.V. Licholat, *A.S. Bubnov na Ukraini* (Kiev, 1965), p. 125.
54. A.I. Binevič and Z.L. Serebrjanskij, *Andrej Bubnov* (Moscow, 1964), p. 79.
55. *Pravda*, 13 October 1937, p. 6.
56. Others (D. Romanovskij, 'Narodnyj komissar', *Izvestija*, 6 April 1963, p. 4) reported that Bubnov had died in prison.
57. V.I. Nevskij, *Materialy dlja biografičeskogo slovarja social-demokratov, v stupivšich v rossijskoe rabočee dviženie za period ot 1880 do 1905 g.* (Moscow, 1923), pp. 106-9; *Dejateli revoljucionnogo dvizenija v Rossii. Biobibliografičeskij slovar'*, vol. 5, pp. 519-26; *BSE¹*, vol. 7, pp. 763-4; *Dejateli Sojuza Sovetskich Socialističeskich Respublik i Oktjabr'skoj revoljucii*, vol. 1, pp. 47-52 (is the same as *Granat*, vol. 41, p. 1).
58. *Pravda*, 6 April 1933, pp. 1, 3 and 6.
59. *Leninskij sbornik*, vol. 34 (Moscow, 1942), p. 152; Lenin, *PSS*, vol. 50, p. 326.
60. *Short Course* (Dutch edn), pp. 162 and 218.
61. *LES*, pp. 453-4; *Ist. Arch.*, no. 5 (1957), pp. 188-91; *Ot fevralja k oktjabrju*, pp. 61-6; M.V. Frunze, *Izbrannye proizvedenija* (Moscow, 1957), p. 443 and note p. 444.

62. *BSE²*, vol. 51, p. 43; *MSE³*, vol. 1, pp. 1258-9.
63. *CSP*, vol. 4, p. 181.
64. V.I. Lenin, *Voennaja perepiska* (Moscow, 1956), pp. 134-5, 145 and 150; cf. the 1966 edition (pp. 168 and 189) as well as *Leninskij sbornik* (vol. 34, pp. 153 and 171) for differences.
65. A.S. Bubnov, 'Lenin v oktjabr'skie dni'', *Oktjabr'skoe vooružennoe vosstanie v Petrograde. Vospominanija aktivnych učastnikov revoljucii* (Leningrad, 1956), pp. 17-19.
66. *Izvestija*, 2 November 1956, p. 3.
67. A.S. Bubnov, *Stat'i reči o narodnom obrazovanii* (Moscow, 1959); A.S. Bubnov, *O Krasnoj Armii. Sbornik* (Moscow, 1958).
68. *Krasnaja Zvezda*, 16 August 1958.
69. I.V. Stavickij, 'Vidnyj dejatel' partii i gosudarstva'', *VI KPSS*, no. 4 (1963), p. 112.
70. Lenin, *PSS*, 5th edn, vol. 42, p. 36.
71. *Pravda*, 3 April 1974, p. 6.
72. Binevič, *Bubnov*; Erasov, *Navsegda, do konca*.
73. Gorbunov, *Orlinyj vzlet*. The author had written an article for *Sovetskaja Rossija* at the time of the commemoration of Bubnov in 1963.
74. Licholat, *Bubnov*.
75. See pp. 37-41 and 141-149.
76. Up to and including 1969, the year 1889 was held to be Bljucher's year of birth. Since then, the year 1890 has been mentioned consistently in publications.
77. V.V. Dušen'kin, *Ot soldata do maršala* (Moscow, 1960), pp. 5 and 6.
78. Ibid., 3rd edn, p. 64; Dušen'kin, 'Proletarskij maršal', *Krasnaja Zvezda*, 19 November 1969, p. 4; 'V. K. Bljucher na frontach graždanskoj vojny', *Ist. Arch.*, no. 1 (1958), pp. 76-88.
79. J. Erickson, *The Soviet High Command: A Military-Political History, 1918-1941* (London, 1962), p. 231.
80. *Šestnadcatyj s"ezd*, pp. 13-14.
81. Roman Gul' (Roman Goul), *Vorošilov, Budennyj, Bljucher, Kotovskij* (Berlin, 1932), pp. 123-5.
82. *Semnadcatyj s"ezd*, pp. 629-31.
83. Dušen'kin, *Ot soldata*, 3rd edn, p. 221.
84. *Leningradskaja Pravda*, 4 October 1964; *New York Times*, 7 October 1964.
85. *Pravda*, 19 July 1964, p. 6, 25 July 1964, p. 2.
86. Gul', *Bljucher*, p. 123. The biography of Bljucher in works of reference about 1930 is incomplete as far as the 1920s are concerned, and contains no reference to his stay in China. See *BSE¹*, vol. 6, pp. 537-8; *MSE²*, vol. 1.
87. Erickson, *Soviet Command*, p. 499.
88. *New York Times*, 14 August 1957, informed by the Belgrade correspondent Harrison Salisbury.
89. V. Rusaev, 'Rabocij, soldat, polkovodec', *Krasnaja Zvezda*, 10 August 1957, p. 3.
90. A. Todorskij, 'Vo slavy Rodiny', *Komsomol'skaja Pravda*, 23 August 1957, p. 2.
91. *Ist. Arch.*, no. 5 (1957), p. 197; *Ot fevralja k oktjabrju*, p. 400.
92. *BSE²*, vol. 50, pp. 219, 260, 419 and 424.
93. Ibid., vol. 51, p. 39; *MSE³*, vol. 1, p. 1073.
94. V.P. Malysev and A.T. Jakimov, *Maršal Sovetskogo Sojuza Bljucher* (Blagoveščensk, 1958).
95. Dušen'kin, *Ot soldata*.
96. Ibid., 3rd edn, pp. 65-7. Other new names are Gološčekin, Ejdeman and

Kork. In the 3rd edition, however, the name of Vorošilov is mentioned only occasionally (cf. 1st edn, pp. 102 and 111, 3rd edn, pp. 178 and 190-1). Furthermore, in the 1st edition (pp. 108-9) a telegram by Stalin (dated 7 November 1929) is quoted which is no longer included in the 3rd edition (pp. 184-5).

97. V. Dušen'kin, 'Proletarskij maršal', *Izvestija*, 11 May 1962, p. 6. See *Krasnaja Zvezda*, 4 April 1962 (p. 3), in which the readers asked for more information on Tuchačevskij, Bljucher, Jakir, Uborevič, Kork, Egorov and Ejdeman.

98. *Pravda*, 13 August 1963, p. 4; *Sovetskaja Kul'tura*, 16 March 1965, p. 2; *Izvestija*, 14 November 1965, p. 5; *Trud*, 6 July 1966, p. 3; *Sovetskoe Kino*, 4 November 1967, p. 3. A postage stamp carrying his portrait was issued on 27 November 1962. He shared this honour with Vavilov (1961 and 1977), Tuchačevskij (1963), Steklov (1963 and 1977), Gamarnik (1964), Sejfullin (1964), Jakir (1966), Gaj (1969), Ikramov (1968), Postyšev (1968), Dybenko (1969), Kosior (1969) and Bauman (1973). I am indebted to Dr Z.R. Dittrich for this philatelic information.

99. V.K. Bljucher, *Stat'i i reči* (Moscow, 1963).

100. 'Iz istorii severnogo pochoda nacionalno-revoljucionnoj armii Kitaja', *Ist. Arch.*, no. 4 (1959), p. 101; Dušen'kin, *Ot soldata*, pp. 99-101 and 115.

101. Bljucher, *Stat'i*.

102. M.I. Kazanin, *V stabe Bljuchera. Vospominanija o Kitajskoj revoljucii 1925-1927 godov* (Moscow, 1966); *Vidnye sovetskie kommunisty-učastniki Kitajskoj revoljucii* (Moscow, 1970); A.I. Kartunova, *Bljucher v Kitae 1924-1927 gg.* (Moscow, 1970, 2nd enlarged edn, Moscow, 1979).

103. Dušen'kin, *Ot soldata*, p. 41; ibid., 3rd edn, p. 222; Kartunova, *Bljucher*, p. 50; *Vidnye kommunisty*, p. 41.

104. In 1963, V. Nikitin (*Literaturnaja Gazeta*, 22 February 1964) wanted to write about Bljucher, but he could find no information in the official files. What he did find was a manuscript written by K. Paustovskij in 1938, which contained a biography of the general. Nikitin thought that this had not been published, but the library of the International Institute of Social History in Amsterdam includes K.G. Paustovskij's *B.C. Blücher* (Barcelona, 1938). Actually, in 1960 such a biographical outline was published: K. Paustovskij, 'Vasilij Bljucher', *Polkovodcy graždanskoj vojny* (Moscow, 1960). *Novy Mir* (no. 2 (1962), pp. 178-83) contained the criticism that even Paustovskij had not succeeded in building up a 'living portrait'.

CONCLUSIONS

A full rehabilitation of victims of the terror is conceivable only if the *right of rehabilitation* is enshrined in a separate law. Otherwise the arbitrariness so characteristic of the terror might also manifest itself when rehabilitation is carried out. A second prerequisite is an independent jurisdiction which cannot be ruled by the party. A law of rehabilitation would have to contain the following elements: juridical rehabilitation in the form of a revision of sentence including an unequivocal explanation of the grounds for acquittal. The juridically rehabilitated person or his relatives would also have to be legally entitled to social rehabilitation, restoration to former office or to an office of the same standing, compensation for loss of income and confiscated property, pension rights, a regulation for expenses made on account of poor health, and compensation. Naturally rehabilitated people should be free to choose a place of residence, and the rehabilitation should be announced in the daily press.

In Czechoslovakia, the regime long retained its stalinist leanings. This explains the approach to the amnesties and the issue of the rehabilitations before 1968. The conditionality written into the regulations reflected a great deal of uncertainty and fear. The party leadership was apprehensive of a decline in the dominant social position of the party and their own personal positions. Any step on behalf of the victims of the terror was dangerous and had to be reversible, hence the conditionality mentioned.

When at the end of 1967 liberalisation could no longer be avoided and the stalinist party leader A. Novotný was replaced, an attempt was made to catch up on the backlog. The Prague Spring represented a spontaneous wave of liberalisation. The intellectuals reverted to humanistic ideals and wondered how they themselves had been able to have faith in stalinism and why they had been capable of commending the terror. They acted, as it were, as the nation's conscience and fulfilled the traditional social-political role of literary people in their country.

The relative freedom of the press which they had secured in 1968 made it possible to bring up the issue of the terror in public. In the communist party, this was reflected by the institution of a committee which had to examine the course of events during the terror and the rehabilitations. The committee presented a report which contained a number of far-reaching recommendations to revise the political customs of the party to make them agree with general humanitarian standards. The party had almost accepted the proposals.

This development, however, was cut off by the invasion in August 1968 and the subsequent 'normalisation'. The ultimate result of the rehabilitations was fairly poor. The fact that, during the period of destalinisation and liberalisation, such far-reaching measures towards rehabilitation could be taken, especially in Czechoslovakia, can be accounted for by the democratic traditions of the country. These turned out to be so powerful that even during the Interbellum, when authoritarian governments were established in all the remaining Eastern European countries, the Czechoslovak democracy continued to operate. Even after a full generation of communist administration, the memory of this past had not been lost, because a strong class of citizens and intelligentsia did not allow itself to be wiped out as bearers of a democracy in which a keen sense of justice was fully developed.

The history of the rehabilitations in Czechoslovakia forms an interesting addition to our knowledge of rehabilitations inside the Soviet Union. The *conditionality* which could be observed in various Czechoslovak regulations before 1968 also appears to have manifested itself in the Soviet Union, at least in some cases. Only a few people have given evidence of this in *samizdat*. We have too little information to justify drawing cast-iron conclusions. Yet, from comparing the Soviet Union with Czechoslovakia, we may infer that in the Soviet Union, too, *actual* conditionality in amnesty, release and rehabilitation is highly probable. Although the communist party of the Soviet Union took a giant step forward towards redressing injustice, it has come nowhere near the Czechoslovak developments in 1968. Characteristic of the formal rehabilitations in the Soviet Union is the total *lack of publicity*. It is highly questionable whether those who were released were actually familiar with the rights they could lay claim to. We may also doubt whether these were known by the authorities which could be appealed to. The existing regulations had been designed to restore justice in exceptional cases and did not serve to redress large-scale injustice. We have been able to retrieve very little information on these regulations and their application.

In the years between 1953 and 1956, there was often no question at all of social rehabilitation for those released prisoners

who were faced with a so-called 'minus', that is, who were pro-
hibited from settling in a number of places. In principle, housing
arrangements were limited to the town where the arrest had taken
place. Financial compensation for those who were acquitted after
revision of the sentence proved to be totally inadequate, and
totally unrelated to possible claims for loss of income or pension,
let alone for compensation. Relatives could make no claim whatsoever on any compensation for themselves, even though they frequently suffered administrative punishment and were undoubtedly
discriminated against.

It is probable that the revision of sentences was frequently
settled rapidly. A number of released prisoners, beyond doubt,
have benefited from this, but a number of them have been treated
unjustly. The revisions turned out to produce two types of results:
acquittal because no indictable offence had been committed, or
acquittal because there was not enough evidence. From a debate
among Soviet lawyers, it appears that the predominant feeling is
that in both cases the innocence is indisputable. Even so, there are
also lawyers who — we think, rightly — argue that acquittal on
account of lack of sufficient evidence does not indicate that the
person involved is completely innocent.

The formal rehabilitations took place mainly in the second half
of the fifties. It is quite remarkable that in the sixties no change at
all was effected in the approach to this aspect of rehabilitation. The
party, after all, waged a press campaign against the personality cult
and the terror in 1963 and 1964. There was no accompanying
development in the juridical field through which shortcomings of
earlier rehabilitations could be redressed. One may compare the
Prague Spring, where the entire course of events was administered
anew, this time by statute. Nothing like this happened inside the
Soviet Union. This underlines the political nature of the press campaign mentioned. The communist party persistently refuses to deal
with formal rehabilitations in a consistent manner, without apply-
ing political norms. This represents a *crucial* shortcoming.

After Stalin's death, the party exerted itself first and foremost to
release those who were personally known to the party leaders, and
concerned itself with party executives. Large-scale releases of
people in the camps and prisons did not follow until three years
later, while many others saw their 'minus' punishment repealed. In
this study, the number of camp survivors who were now restored
to their rights has been estimated at 2 million. As the number of

victims of the terror is estimated at millions and millions of people, this is a shockingly low number. Millions of people have not survived the terror. Strictly speaking, the communist party has acknowledged as much by maintaining *silence* about the releases.

When the communist party faced up to the problem of the terror and the rehabilitations, the issue was handed over in the first instance to those persons in the party leadership who were to a high degree co-responsible for the terror. This happened in both Czechoslovak and Soviet history: Barák, Berija and Molotov initiated the rehabilitations. In the Soviet case, the struggle for power in the party turned out favourably for the prisoners in the camps. Because of Molotov's defeat, both the large-scale releases and a significant change of course of the party in the policy of rehabilitations were possible. Despite the large number of shortcomings mentioned here, things could have been worse had Molotov triumphed over Khrushchev.

Reinstatement in the communist party has been a strictly political and ideological affair. The charges used at the time to have party members convicted have played no part in decisions upon reinstatement in the party. The complete political histories of those involved, on the other hand, have been important. As for cases of opposition in the twenties, favourable decisions were reached only in exceptional cases. The selection of victims of the show trials was conducted in the same fashion. The faithful stalinists were reinstated in the party, whereas the former opposition, except in one or two cases, continued to be excluded.

It is highly probable that these exceptional cases of rehabilitation in categories which were in fact unqualified can be accounted for by the obstinacy with which the relatives of the victims have constantly harassed the regime and kept pestering it for rehabilitation. The politburo was the only official body which could decide upon such important matters. The debates inside this administrative body, which undoubtedly flared up each time these petitions had to be considered, upset the usual routine, so that in such cases the party leaders eventually gave in. This, however, did not always happen.

No public rehabilitation was possible without formal rehabilitation and reinstatement in the party. There is, however, no further connection between these two forms of rehabilitation. Until 1962, the biographical articles provided only incidental, indefinite information on the downfall and rehabilitation of the victims involved.

The national press did not join in, with the exception of the journal of the Ministry of Defence *Krasnaja Zvezda*. The military machinery had suffered a severe blow during the terror in the thirties. The glory of the Red Army could not be praised when the majority of its heroes were non-persons. The public rehabilitations in this period, furthermore, were basically confined to several federal republics. There is no demonstrable link between these publications and changes in the party of the regional party leadership. The public rehabilitations in these federal republics rather served to restore the national identity and the specific recognisability of the party in the past. Such a restoration was necessary in the Baltic republics in particular, which, relatively speaking, showed the largest number of publications; the party leadership there had been wiped out completely during the great purge.

This varied picture of public rehabilitations in the federal republics is the result of the liberties that could be taken by the party secretaries at this level of administration. They formed part of the politics of Khrushchev, who had allied himself to the party secretaries of the federal republics in order to consolidate his power. The federal republics were granted some freedom of action within certain limits prescribed by Moscow.

The background of the independent proceedings of the federal republics in the domain of public rehabilitations is formed by the necessity of presenting good national leaders who were at the same time good communists. Bolshevism had hardly taken root in the nationalities during the revolution, so that national Bolshevik leaders are few in number. A number of them had already been removed from the party on account of bourgeois nationalism in the twenties, and these national communists were not permitted rehabilitation. Others kept their positions in the thirties as stalinists: this small group was obliterated during the period of the terror. A number of these victims, however, were rehabilitated.

In order to keep the non-Russian nationalities in line with the mainstream of the Soviet state without exerting the straightforward pressure of physical terror, allowances had to be made for national identities. National feelings, however, may be excited only if they are linked with relations with the Soviet Union as a whole and with the communist party. Useful in this respect is the publication of biographies of national communist heroes, provided that these were also known as faithful stalinists. In addition, this end was also served by the publication of biographies of Russian communists or communists of ethnic origins different from those of the national population. These contributions had to display the warm feelings of the other nations.

There is seldom any demonstrable direct relation between public rehabilitations and the struggle for power inside the party leadership, although this link is clear in the case of the so-called 'anti-party group' in 1957. In many cases of public rehabilitation, there is probably some connection with disputes among the party leaders, but this is difficult to prove. Quarrels about the rehabilitations, furthermore, are perfectly imaginable during the stage of formal rehabilitation. Various prominent party functionaries had already been formally rehabilitated long before they were publicly rehabilitated. The policy in Czechoslovakia in the fifties clearly showed how little information came out, while a great deal of political scheming was taking place behind the scenes.

As Stalin and the terror were openly attacked during its course, the twenty-second party congress marked a turning point in the public rehabilitations. Various speakers expatiated upon the execution of the terror in their provinces and mentioned examples of victims. The idea was to get the Chinese party to understand that it pursued the wrong course by holding on to the policies of Stalin. China was itself not directly criticised. The conflict between Moscow and Beijing had not yet come to a head. Therefore the 'anti-party group' and Albania were attacked. Supporters of the views of Molotov were thus warned at the same time not to turn away from the party line of destalinisation.

After the party congress, a press campaign against the terror was initiated, in which biographical articles on the victims were used as illustrations. This campaign assumed large-scale dimensions in the years 1963 and 1964. As appeared from Soviet as well as Czechoslovak sources, it was set up to point out the dangers of the personality cult to the Chinese party. The cult of Mao Ze-dong could possibly degenerate into a system of terror, victimising the party itself. The Chinese communist party had to follow the example of the Soviet party to prevent its own downfall. By using these tactics, the communist party of the Soviet Union hoped to settle the dispute with China to its own advantage.

It sometimes happens that the name of a victim is mentioned incidentally in the press or in some publication or other. It is of no importance to the progress of the rehabilitation of the person involved when the latter is mentioned in the daily or in the periodical press. In such a case we are dealing with an informal rehabilitation. In an official party history, both of the national party and of the parties of the federal republics, however, such an incidental reference does indicate a formal rehabilitation and reinstatement in the party. Yet such a reference does not guarantee the emergence of commemorative articles in the press, or recording in an encyclopaedia. Because, moreover, such incidental mentions in official histories are not attended with further information on the person in question, we do not think it is accurate to describe such a case as a public rehabilitation. This description should be applied to biographical press articles.

By and large, the role of historians in the process of rehabilitation has been limited to carrying out party resolutions. There is no question of any daring initiative in public rehabilitations. The cautious attempt of the editorial staff of *Voprosy Istorii* to adopt Khrushchev's policy of destalinisation in 1956 was made under the political protection of members of the presidium, probably of Khrushchev and Mikojan. It did not result in any remarkable new initiatives. The reason that historians are remiss lies in the notion of the communist party that historiography is a form of propaganda, which demands strict supervision. Historians who concern themselves with the history of the twentieth century and the Soviet history, as a result, do not pursue their studies with the scientific thirst for knowledge required. Those who feel themselves to be true historians prefer to seek work in earlier Russian history, and even then suffer ample inconvenience from party arrogance in this field.

Soviet society has not recovered from the effects of the Great Terror. It is beyond the power of the communist party to redress the balance of justice. The phenomenon of the rehabilitations in the fifties and sixties had to create the impression that the party had fundamentally changed its attitude towards the terror. The emphasis with which the party insists it has overcome the effects of the terror and the assertive nature of the official statements indicating that all cases of injustice have been revised, however, contrast sharply with the actual facts.

It has now become evident in an historical perspective that the party did not wish to be reminded of the terror. This is indicated by the small number of commemorative articles dealing with prominent victims during the past fifteen years, and by the meagre contents of such articles when they are concerned with victims of the terror. The official party histories and the commemorations of

Stalin cover up the terror by supplying deliberately trivial information in obscure and euphemistic terms. This could not have
been symbolised more clearly than by the raising of Stalin's bust at
his grave, eight years after his corpse had been removed from the
Mausoleum. Such a symbol has intrinsic meaning for a party which
sets such great store by ritual and liturgy. In contrast to what had
been suggested by the absence of the bust, it is now no longer
obvious that the Soviet leader Stalin was supposed to have done
something wrong. The past has been neutralised and the next
generation of Soviet executives will no longer have any knowledge
of the terror of Stalin.

One must look for the motives for the activities of the party
functionaries in the relation between party and terror. From the
first days of the Bolshevik regime up to the present the terror has
served as an accepted means of preserving power. Party executives
are accustomed to the phenomenon of terror. The party, after all,
does not give its officials moral, humanitarian instruction. Its
materialistic ethics postulate the power of the party as the only
standard, by which all actions of the executives and even of the
entire population are judged. The issue of the terror is examined
exclusively from a political angle: when and to what extent is the
terror expedient?

In its attacks upon the terror the Soviet press, too, presents a
'good' alternative to the enforcement of terror: the working
methods of Iron Feliks, i.e. Dzeržinskij, leader of the Čeka when
the Soviet power was established. Dzeržinskij, after all, did not
persecute members of the party (at least not systematically) and in
this he showed the 'proper' moral attitude!

The party's familiarity with the terror led to delay in the completion of rehabilitations. On the one hand, the party wished to rid
itself of the image that its power was based exclusively upon the
use of terror, but, on the other, it was extremely hesitant to
rehabilitate those who had once, no matter when, been known to
be opposed to the party line. Where precisely can the dividing line
be drawn between 'avowed' and 'silent' opponents? All thinking of
the party officials, trained in systematic purging, is based upon the
notion that the party is infallible. To them, it is difficult to accept
that party members can be prosecuted by the party itself without
any justification at all.

In Stalin's days, the entire communist party had been suffused
with a powerful sense of absolute loyalty. Regardless of his status

or his past, any party executive who was promoted knew that he could be purged. The Great Terror in the thirties and the permanent high level of terror in the subsequent years brought about a type of party official characterised by *blind loyalty* and implicit conformism. These new officials are used to carrying out orders. Their image of the past is determined by the precepts of the party. They know better than to dissent, lest they are overtaken by the 'truth', that is, lest they are purged.

This total obedience does not dissolve when a dictator dies. Such loyalty, moreover, no longer merely concentrates upon personalities, but also upon the entire *nomenklatura* — the Soviet elite — which closes ranks whenever its position is endangered. Khrushchev's fall from power serves as a case in point, because his policy threatened the officials personally. The *nomenklatura* proves to be hypersensitive with respect to the image of the party. Even the smallest damage to this image is feared to lead to loss of face — which is then felt to be a loss of prestige, something a party that claims nothing but success cannot afford. This is why the party leaders wish to forget about the past of Stalin's terror. Raking up the past may cause damage to the elite. The policy of rehabilitation is curbed by a *fear of the past.*

Russian social and intellectual developments provide the ultimate explanation for this disparaging treatment of the victims of the terror. The Russian sense of justice has been suppressed by ages of serfdom. There was no middle class which had its own position between the nobility and the agricultural population: hence, there was no question of any independent action towards the nobility and the state. No legal protection for individuals ever emerged. Humanitarian thinking, in terms of a constitutional state which protects the rights and interests of its individual subjects, could not prosper. Furthermore, intellectual life in the Soviet Union is largely determined by the question of its relation to the autocracy, and the question of support for, or resistance against, the system of government. As yet, there has been no room for contemplation on the position of individuals in society. The developments in the beginning of the twentieth century, when a middle class began to manifest itself and the autocracy began to be dismantled by degrees, had no time to mature. The October revolution established the supremacy of the communist party which, in accordance with Russian autocratic traditions, arrested the genesis of an individualistic sense of justice.

APPENDIX A   COMPUTATION OF THE NUMBER OF PEOPLE RESTORED TO CIVIL RIGHTS DURING LIFE

The number of people restored to civil rights during life in the period 1954-8 can be computed as follows. The computation is based upon the fact that those involved were entitled to vote again. Through the publication of the results, the precise total number of the electorate at the time of the elections for the Supreme Soviet in 1954 and in 1958 is known to us.[1] The increase in the electorate in this period (13,085,509 people) should be approximately the same as the demographic increase in the number of people entitled to vote, that is, the increase in the number of people over 18.

Assuming that a large number of people had the right to vote restored, this has to result in an extra increase in the number of the electorate. They include, at any rate, those people who were released from the camps and prisons, who lived in exile and/or who had received additional punishment involving the loss of civil rights. Those who had been sent away to permanent settlement (*specpereselency*) are not included in this computation, because this group retained the right to vote.[2]

The demographic increase in the number of people entitled to vote involves the group of new voters (those who had reached the age of 18 since the elections in 1954), minus the number of deceased who had been entitled to vote. One can only deduce the data from the census in 1959 and from the rates of mortality. These inevitable extrapolations have brought about a substantial error in the computation, and the sources, moreover, are not very reliable. The value of the result of the computation will be discussed below.

Our most important source of demographic information is the official census, which gives us the situation on 15 January 1959. The data on the numbers of people are given in five-year age groups. Table A.1 presents the data of those age groups relevant to the computation.[3]

219

Table A.1: 1959 Census

Age Group	Number of People
0-4	24,334,000
5-9	22,029,000
10-14	15,337,000
15-19	16,471,000
20-24	20,343,000
25-29	18,190,129
30 and upwards	92,122,871
Total	208,827,000

New Voters

The age group which had not yet voted in 1954 and which participated in the elections for the first time in 1958 includes those who,
in 1958, reached the ages of 19, 20, 21 and 22 respectively, as well
as a number of those who reached the age of 18 before the
elections. Those 22-year-olds who had already voted in 1954,
because they had reached the age of 18 before the elections, must
be subtracted from the number of new voters in 1958.

The computation of the cohorts of 19-, 20-, 21-, 22- and 18-
year-olds in 1958 is based upon the demographic situation as
reflected by the census of 15 January 1959. As no more accurate
data are available, it is assumed that, in principle, these cohorts are
spread out evenly over the age groups of five years.

The number of 20-, 21- and 22-year-olds is therefore constantly
assessed at $^1/_5$ of 20,343,000 (see Table A.1), i.e. 4,068,600
people for each cohort. These groups together amount to three
times this number, i.e. 12,205,800 people.

The number of 19-year-olds can be computed somewhat more
accurately. The age group from 15 to 19 years old comprises, as
appears from the census, a number of 16,471,000 people. The
statistical annual of 1959 provides a number of 14,675,000 people
for the age group between 16 and 19 years old.[4] Assuming that
here, too, the cohorts are spread out evenly, the total number of
19-year-olds is $^1/_4$ of 14,675,000, i.e. 3,668,750 people. The total
number of 19-, 20-, 21- and 22-year-olds, then, is 15,874,550
people.

We now have to compute the numbers of those 18-year-olds
who had already voted in 1958 and those 22-year-olds who had

already voted in 1958. Both in 1954 and in 1958, the elections took place in the middle of March, and those who had reached the age of 18 two weeks or more before the elections were allowed to participate for the first time. In 1958, the number of 18-year-olds is assumed to be the same as the number of 19-year-olds, i.e. 3,668,750 people. Between 1 January and 1 March, $\frac{1}{6}$ of this number had reached the age of 18, assuming an even spreading here too: $\frac{1}{6}$ of 3,668,750 people equals 611,458 people. In 1958, the number of 22-year-olds amounted to 4,068,000 people. Disregarding the minor death rate of this age group, we use this number as the basis of the number of 18-year-olds in 1954: $\frac{1}{6}$ of this adds up to a number of 678,000 people. We have to subtract the number of 18-year-olds participating in 1954 from the total number. The difference, 678,000 minus 611,458, is 66,542, and is subtracted from the total number of new voters: 15,874,550 minus 66,542 equals 15,808,008 people.

The Number of Deaths of those Entitled to Vote, between 1954 and 1958

The number of those entitled to vote who died between 1954 and 1958 must be subtracted from the number of new voters in 1958. The total mortality rates for the population in these years are known to us, and are presented in Table A.2. We are dealing exclusively with those deceased who were entitled to vote. The number of deceased under 18 must be subtracted from the mortality rates for the entire population. For this we need to know the mortality rates related to the various age groups, which are known for 1959.[5]

Table A.2: Mortality Rates in the Soviet Union, 1954-9

Year	Mortality Rate (per thousand)	Total Population (millions)	Total Number of Deceased
1954	8.8	191.0	1,680,000
1955	8.2	194.4	1,594,080
1956	7.6	197.9	1,504,040
1957	7.8	201.4	1,570,920
1958	7.2	204.9	1,475,280
1959	7.6	208.8	1,586,880

Source: *Narodnoe Chozjajstvo 1972* (Moscow, 1972).

The number of deceased 18- and 19-year-olds is subtracted from the result of Table A.3. Assuming that we are dealing with an even spreading of mortality over the age group of 15- to 19-year-olds, we shall take this number to be $\frac{2}{5}$ of 21,412, i.e. 8,565 people. The total number of deceased under 18 in 1959, therefore, is 323,689 minus 8,565, i.e. 315,124 people.

No such specification is possible for the period from 1954 up to and including 1958. For these years, only the total mortality rates are available. It is assumed that proportionately the number of deceased under 18 and the total number of deceased in the period 1954-8 does not differ from that in 1959. The proportion can be computed on the basis of the results of Tables A.2 and A.3. The total of deceased in 1959 is 1,586,880. The number of deceased under 18 is 315,124. In 1959, the number of deceased over 18, that is, those entitled to vote, is 1,586,880 minus 315,124, i.e. 1,271,756. The number of deceased over 18 and the total number are in the ratio of 1,271,756 to 1,586,880, i.e. a ratio of 0.8015.

Through multiplication of the total numbers by 0.8015, we now apply this ratio to the total mortality rates for the years 1954-8.

The result of Table A.4 must be corrected, because the number of deceased should be computed for the period between March

Table A.3: Mortality Rates for the Age Groups under 19 in 1959

Age Group	Specific Mortality (per thousand)	Total Number in Each Age Group	Number of Deceased
0-4	11.9	24,334,000	265,775
5-9	1.1	22,029,000	24,232
10-14	0.8	15,337,000	12,270
15-19	1.3	16,471,000	21,412
Total			323,689

Table A.4: Mortality Rates for the Age Groups over 18, 1954-7

Year	Total Number of Deceased	Number of Deceased over 18
1954	1,680,800	1,347,161
1955	1,594,080	1,277,655
1956	1,504,040	1,205,488
1957	1,570,920	1,259,092
Total		5,089,396

1954 and March 1958 rather than for the calendar years 1954-7. The number of deceased over 18 in 1958 is 1,475,280 multiplied by 0.8015, i.e. 1,182,437. For the months January and February, the number in this group is ⅙ of 1,182,437, i.e. 197,073. The number of deceased over 18 in 1954 is 1,347,161 multiplied by ⅙, i.e. 224,527. The difference is 27,454. This number must be subtracted from the total number of deceased over 18 (see result in Table A.4). The end result, then, is 5,089,396 minus 27,454, i.e. 5,061,942.

Result

The total number of new voters minus the number of those deceased results in an increase in the total number of the electorate between 1954 and 1958. The sum total of the new voters is 15,808,008 people, and the number of those voters who died between March 1954 and March 1958 was computed at 5,061,942. The demographic increase is 15,808,008 minus 5,061,942, i.e. 10,746,066.

The official specification of the electorate in 1958 indicated an increase of 13,085,509 voters since 1954. The difference between the actual number of participants in the elections and the number which, on the basis of the demographical computation, could be expected to take part is 13,085,509 minus 10,746,066, i.e. 2,339,443 people. As such demographic factors as emigration and immigration are negligible in the Soviet Union during the fifties, only rehabilitations can account for this number of voters.[6]

As stated above, the computation is not entirely accurate. The most conspicuous source of error can be found in the computation made in the section on 'New Voters'. It can be argued that the number of new 19-year-old voters is greater than computed here. In determining the number of 19-year-olds, after all, we used the average number in the age group 16-19 years as a basis. The 16- and 17-year-olds were born in 1942 and 1941 respectively, those years of war which showed decreasing birth rates. The number of 19-year-olds is probably almost the same as the number of 20-year-olds, a difference of approximately 400,000 people. Let us assume the actual number of 19-year-olds is 4,068,600. The difference between this number and the one used in the computation is 4,068,600 minus 3,668,750, i.e. 399,850. This number causes the difference between the actual number of voters and the demographic computation to be smaller. We assume this to be realistic, and consequently the number of rehabilitated can be computed at 2,339,443 minus 399,850, i.e. 1,939, 593, that is to say, almost 2 million people. Because of our deficient sources, this number of 2 million people restored to civil rights can only be regarded as a rough indication.

Notes

1. *Pravda* and *Izvestija*, 18 March 1954, p. 1: 120,750,816 voters; *Pravda* and *Izvestija*, 19 March 1958, p. 1: 133,836,325 voters.
2. *Postanovlenie C.I.K.* of 16 October 1937, in *Sbornik normativnych aktov (1917-1959)*, p. 310. I should like to thank Dr G.P. van den Berg in Leiden for pointing out this exception. Cf. also Nekrič, *Punished Peoples*, p. 141, and Geilke, 'Rechtsfragen', p. 129.
3. *Itogi vsesojuznoj perepisi naselenija 1959 g.*, vol. 1 (Moscow, 1962).
4. *Narodnoe Chozjajstvo 1959* (Moscow, 1960), p. 11.
5. *Narodnoe Chozjajstvo 1962* (Moscow, 1963), p. 31.
6. Cf. the use of data of the elections for demographic purposes in C. Verceil's 'Essai sur l'évolution démografique de l'URSS', *Population*, vol. 13, no. 2 *bis* (1958), pp. 29-76.

APPENDIX B LIST OF PUBLIC POSTHUMOUS REHABILITATIONS IN THE FORM OF CONCISE BIOGRAPHIES IN THE SOVIET PRESS AND ENCYCLOPAEDIAS

The list is arranged in accordance with the Russian alphabet in order to facilitate retracing the names. All names published in national encyclopaedias between 1956 and 1980 have been included. Names published in encyclopaedias of the federal republics are mentioned only if they come to light in random tests and have not been examined systematically.

In the encyclopaedia which is mentioned first, the name of the person involved was published for the first time. After that, additional, and possibly also earlier, mentions are recorded.

The list furthermore refers to initiative articles. Commemorations are indicated only by year of appearance. The articles in question can be found by consulting the indexes of *Letopis' Gazetnych Statej* in the years mentioned.

Finally, the list refers to articles in the historical press between 1956 and 1980.

Averin, V. K.	*URE*
Agamal'jan, R. M.	*Kommunist (Arm.)* 5 February 1964
Adamovič, E. M.	*URE*
Adamovič I. A.	*BeISE, Granat, Sov. Beloruss* 23 February 1965
Ajtakov, N.	*SIE, Granat, BSE¹, BSE³*
Ajtiev, A.	*KSE, Kazachst. Pravda* 2 November 1963
Akulov, I. A.	*MSE³, URE, USE, BSE³, Izvestija* 12 April 1963
Aleksandrovskij, S. S.	*DS², DS³*
Alekseev, N. A.	*USE, BSE¹, Sov. Patriot* 23 February 1977
Aliev, B.	*Bak. Rab.* 19 April 1975
Alichanjan, G. S.	*Kommunist (Arm.)* 29 December 1977

225

Alksnis, Ja. I.	*MSE³, USE, BSE³, Krasn. Zv.* 27 January 1962
Amelin, M. P.	*USE, Voenno-ist.* 1964/7
Ammosov, M. K.	*BSE³, Sov. Ross.* 26 December 1967
Amosov, I. K.	*USE*
Anaškin, I. I.	*Bak. Rab.* 13 November 1965, commemorations 1970, 1980
Anvarov, S.	*Komm. Tadžik.* 6 August 1964
Anvel't, Ja. Ja.	*SIE, BSE³, ENE, Sov. Est.* 18 April 1956, *VIKPSS* 1964/4, commemorations 1957, 1959, 1964, 1969
Angaretis, Z. I.	*SIE, BSE¹, BSE³, BeISE, Sov. Litva* 14 June 1956, *Ist. SSSR* 1967/5, commemorations 1957, 1967, 1972
Andronnikov, V. N.	*BSE³, USE*
Antipov, N. K.	*LES, Granat, BSE¹, BSE³, MSE³, ES³, Izvestija* 19 December 1964
Antonov-Ovseenko, V. A.	*LES, Granat, BSE¹, BSE², BSE³, SIE, SVE, MSE³, DS², DS³, Krasn. Zv.* 22 March 1963, *Voenno-ist.* 1963/3, commemorations 1965, 1973
Appoga, E. F.	*Krasn. Zv.* 1 December 1963
Aristov, M. L.	*BSE³*
Arisjan, L. E.	*Kommunist (Arm.)* 19 January 1963
Arosev, A. Ja.	*MSE³, Granat, BSE¹, BSE³, USE, Moskovsk. Pravda* 18 March 1967
Arustamov, L. A.	*Kommunist (Arm.)* 2 June 1976
Asatkin-Vladimirskij, A. N.	*BelSE*
Atabaev, K. S.	*BSE³, Izvestija* 26 October 1967, commemoration 1977
Atojan, A. T.	*Kommunist (Arm.)* 16 November 1960, commemorations 1965, 1975
Achundov, R. A.	*SIE, BSE³, Bak. Rab.* 13 January 1957, commemorations 1967, 1977
Ačkanov, G. P.	*SIE, BSE³, USE, Vodnyj Transport* 9 January 1962, commemoration 1975
Bazilevič, G. D.	*BSE³, USE, SVE, Voenno-ist* 1964/2
Bakiev, Ch.	*Komm. Tadžik* 21 August 1964, commemoration 1975

Bakunc, E. S.	*Kommunist (Arm.)* 31 August 1967
Bantke, S.	*Sov. Mold.* 12 September 1964
Barinov, M. V.	*Bak. Rab.* 15 October 1963, commemoration 1978
Baryšev, N. V.	*BSE³*
Bauman, K. Ja.	*URE, BSE³, USE, Sov. Latvija* 27 October 1957, *VIKPSS* 1967/12, commemorations 1962, 1972
Begge, K. M.	*Sov. Latvija* 2 December 1964
Bedija, E.	*Zarja Vostoka* 20 July 1971
Bejka, D. S.	*BSE³, Sov. Latvija* 14 August 1958
Bekzadjan, A. A.	*BSE³, Kommunist (Arm.)* 25 October 1957, commemoration 1971
Beloborodov, A. G.	*BSE³, Granat, BSE¹*
Belov, I. P.	*BSE³, SVE, Izvestija* 15 June 1963, *Voenno-ist.* 1963/6, 1966/3
Berzin', E. P.	*LME, Sov. Latvija* 7 February 1974
Berzin, R. I.	*SIE, BSE³, USE, SVE, BelSE, Krasn. Zv.* 19 February 1959, *Voenno-ist.* 1963/8
Berzin, Ja. A.	*MSE³, BSE¹, BSE³, SIE, DS³, USE, Sov. Latvija* 15 June 1958, *VIKPSS* 1981/10, commemorations 1965, 1971
Berzin, Ja. K.	*BSE³, USE, SVE, Krasn. Zv.* 13 November 1964, commemoration 1979
Blagonravov, G. I.	*LES, SIE, BSE³, Gudok* 27 January 1968, *Voenno-ist.* 1965/3
Blaževič, I. F.	*Sov. Litva* 25 September 1976, *Voenno-ist.* 1967/8
Blumental', F. L.	*Voenno-ist.* 1966/8
Bljucher, V. K.	*BSE², BSE¹, BSE³, SIE, MSE³, SVE, Krasn. Zv.* 10 August 1957, *Voenno-ist.* 1964/11, 1966/2, 1969/1, 1979/10, *VIKPSS* 1964/11, commemorations 1958, 1962, 1964, 1966, 1969, 1980
Bobinskij, S. Ja.	*BSE³*
Bogdanov, M. S.	*USE*
Bogdanov, P. A.	*BSE³, Granat, BSE¹*

Bokij, G. I.

LES, BSE¹, BSE³, MSE³, Sov. Latvija 20 September 1963, commemoration 1979

Bokis, G. G.

Sov. Latvija 20 September 1963

Borisenko, A. N.

Voenno-ist. 1964/6

Borodin, M. M.

BSE³, BSE¹, Moskovsk. Pravda 30 June 1964, commemorations 1974, 1979

Bor'jan, B. A.

BSE³, Kommunist (Arm.) 19 September 1962

Breslav, B. A.

BSE³, BSE¹, USE

Brjuchanov, N. P.

MSE³, Granat, BSE¹, BSE³, SIE, Izvestija 28 December 1963, commemorations 1968, 1978

Buačidze, F. M.

Zarja Vostoka 4 April 1975

Bubnov, A. S.

BSE², Granat, BSE¹, BSE³, SIE, SVE, Pravda 6 April 1963, *VIKPSS* 1963/4, *Voenno-ist.* 1963/3, *Ist. SSSR* 1967/6, commemoration 1978

Budzynskij, S.

SIE, BSE³

Buzdalin, S. F.

USE

Bulat, I. L.

URE, USE

Bulin, A. S.

Krasn. Zv. 1 February 1964, *Voenno-ist.* 1963/12

Buniat- Zade, D. Ch.

Bak. Rab. 8 April 1959, commemoration 1968

Vajner, V. Ja.

Voenno-ist. 1969/8

Vajnuch-Vajnjarch, D. A.

Voenno-ist. 1969/8

Vakman, R. Ja.

ENE, Sov. Est. 13 October 1957, commemorations 1969, 1974

Valeckij, G.

BSE³, BSE¹, SIE

Varejkis, I. M.

SIE, BSE¹, BSE³, USE, Pravda 18 September 1964, *VIKPSS* 1963/11, commemorations 1966, 1969, 1974

Varskij, A. E.

MSE³, BSE¹, BSE³, SIE

Vasilenko, M. I.

SIE, BSE³, USE, SVE

Vacetis, I. I.

MSE³, Granat, BSE¹, BSE³, SIE, SVE, Sov. Latvija 21 February 1958, *Voenno-ist.* 1962/4

Veger, E. I.

URE, USE, Pravda Ukr. 20 September 1964

Vejs, E.	*LME, Sov. Latvija* 23 December 1958
Velibekov, B. K.	*Bak. Rab.* 14 January 1959, commemoration 1974
Velikanov, M. D.	*SIE, BSE³, SVE, Krasn. Zv.* 22 November 1963, commemoration 1973
Vellekov, Č.	*Turkmen. Iskra* 19 June 1965
Verchovskij, A. I.	*SIE, BSE¹, BSE³, SVE*
Vesnik, Ja. I.	*Krasn. Zv.* 21 August 1964
Viktorov, M. V.	*SIE, BSE³, USE, SVE*
Vilčinskas, I.	*MLTE, Sov. Litva* 14 November 1973
Voznesenskij, N. A.	*LES, BSE², BSE³, SIE, SVE, Leningr. Pravda* 30 November 1963, *VIKPSS* 1963/6 *VI* 1963/6, commemoration 1973
Volkovič, D. I.	*Sov. Belorussija* 4 April 1965
Voskanov, G. K.	*USE, Sov. Moldav.* 25 December 1971, *Voenno-ist.* 1969/12, commemoration 1976
Voskanov, R. A.	*Kommunist (Arm.)* 10 August 1969
Voskanjan, G. K.	*Kommunist (Arm.)* 21 December 1966
Gaven, Ju. P.	*BSE³, USE*
Gavro, L. M.	*USE, SVE, Pravda Ukr.* 30 December 1964, *Voenno-ist.* 1969/12
Gadžiev, M. G.	*Bak. Rab.* 21 December 1966, commemoration 1976
Gaj, G. D.	*SIE, BSE¹, BSE³, USE, SVE, Krasn. Zv.* 14 March 1961, *Voenno-ist.* 1969/12, commemorations 1962, 1965, 1967, 1977
Gajlit, Ja. P.	*Krasn. Zv.* 26 May 1964, *Voenno-ist.* 1964/5
Galler, L. M.	*MSE³, BSE³, SIE, Voenno-ist.* 1963/3
Galling, A. K.	*Voenno-ist.* 1969/12
Gamarnik, Ja. B.	*BSE², BSE¹, BSE³, SIE, MSE³, ES³, SVE, Krasn. Zv.* 13 April 1962,

	VIKPSS 1964/6, *Voenno-ist.* 1964/5, commemorations 1964, 1974
Ganeckij, Ja. S.	*BSE², Granat, Dejateli, BSE¹, BSE³, SIE, MSE³, DS³, Izvestija* 14 March 1964, *VIKPSS* 1964/3, commemorations 1969, 1979
Gar'kavyj, I. I.	*SIE, BSE³, USE, SVE, Sov. Moldav.* 17 September 1963, commemoration 1978
Gastev, A. K.	*KLE, BSE¹, BSE³, USE, Trud* 13 May 1965, commemoration 1975
Gejn, K. V.	*Moskovsk. Pravda* 19 February 1976
Gekker, A. I.	*SIE, BSE³, USE, SVE, Kommunist (Arm..)* 16 May 1978, *Voenno-ist.* 1966/5
Germanovič, M. Ja.	*Voenno-ist.* 1965/11, 1969/12
Geurkov, A. G.	*Zarja Vostoka* 17 March 1967
Gikalo, N. F.	*SIE, BSE³, SVE, Sov. Torgovlja* 28 September 1957, commemoration 1977
Gittis, V. M.	*SIE, BSE¹, BSE³, SVE*
Glagolev, V. P.	*SIE*
Glebov-Avilov, N. P.	*SIE, Dejateli, Granat, BSE¹, BSE³, SVE*
Gogoberidze, L. D.	*SIE, BSE³, Zarja Vostoka* 27 April 1966, commemorations 1968, 1976
Golikov, A. G.	*Voenno-ist.* 1969/12
Goloded, N. M.	*ES³, SIE, BSE¹, BSE³, Sov. Belorus.* 22 May 1964, commemoration 1974
Gološčekin, F. I.	*SIE, BSE¹, BSE³, Sov. Rossija* 11 March 1976, *VIKPSS* 1964/8
Gorbačev, B. S.	*SVE, Voenno-ist.* 1966/7
Gorbunov, N. P.	*BSE³, BSE¹, Sov. Rossija* 25 December 1966, *Ist. SSSR* 1968/5
Gordon, L. M.	*Voenno-ist.* 1969/12
Gorjačev, E. I.	*Voenno-ist.* 1969/12
Gramp, A. N.	*Komsomols. Pravda* 15 November 1964
Gribov, S. E.	*Voenno-ist.* 1965/7, 1966/7
Grin'ko, G. F.	*URE, BSE¹, BSE³*

Gruodis, I.	*MSE³, MLTE, Sov. Litva* 8 December 1967
Grjaznov, I. K.	*SIE, BSE³, Krasn. Zv.* 10 August 1967, *Voenno-ist.* 1963/2
Grzelszczak, F. Ja.	*SIE, BSE³*
Gusejnov, M. D.	*SIE, BSE³, Bak. Rab.* 7 March 1964
Danilov, P. A.	*Vospominanija o V. I. Lenine* (1957)
Daniševskij, K. Ch.	*LME, SIE, BSE¹, BSE³, SVE, Sov. Latvija* 24 September 1957, *Voenno-ist.* 1969/6
Daškevič, P. V.	*BSE³*
Daštojan, R.P.	*Kommunist (Arm.)* 30 December 1969, commemoration 1979
Degot', V. A.	*VIKPSS* 1965/6
Deribas, T. D.	*BSE³, Krasn. Zv.* 11 October 1963
Džabiev, G. P.	*Bak. Rab.* 8 September 1964, commemoration 1979
Džakupov, S.	*Kazachst. Pravda* 17 January 1965
Džandosov, U.	*Kazachst. Pravda* 20 February 1964, commemoration 1979
Dovlatov, I. I.	*Bak. Rab.* 24 February 1967, commemoration 1977
Dogadov, A. I.	*BSE³, Granat, BSE¹*
Dodobaev, B.	*Komm. Tadžik.* 29 November 1964
Drabavičiute, A.	*MLTE, Sov. Litva* 4 June 1968, commemoration 1973
Dubovoj, I. N.	*URE, BSE³, Krasn. Zv.* 27 March 1963, *Voenno-ist.* 1966/9, commemoration 1966
Dušenov, K. I.	*SVE, Voenno-ist.* 1965/7
Dybenko, P. E.	*LES, Granat, BSE¹, BSE², BSE³, SIE, MSE³, SVE, Komsomolsk. Pravda* 15 June 1957, *Voenno-ist.* 1964/1, 1965/10, 1966/7, commemorations 1963, 1964, 1969, 1979
D'jakov, T. M.	*Komm. Tadžik.* 17 August 1965, commemoration 1967
Egorov, A. I.	*BSE², BSE¹, BSE³, SIE, MSE³, SVE, Krasn. Zv.* 6 January 1963, *Voenno-ist.* 1963/11, 1966/4, 1973/10,

	commemoration 1965
Egorova, E. N.	*BSE³, Sov. Latvija* 22 March 1964, commemoration 1967
Enukidze, A. S.	*URE, SIE, BSE¹, BSE³, Granat, Pravda* 19 May 1962, *VIKPSS* 1967/5, commemorations 1967, 1977
Erbanov, M. N.	*SIE, BSE¹, BSE³, Pravda* 12 March 1964, commemoration 1979
Eremjan, V. A.	*Kommunist (Arm.)* 5 September 1975
Zjavkin, F. M.	*Izvestija* 25 November 1964
Žandosov, O. K.	*KSE*
Žgenti, T. G.	*SIE, BSE³, Zarja Vostoka* 7 February 1967, commemoration 1977
Žloba, D. P.	*MSE³, BSE¹, BSE³, SIE, SVE, Krasn. Zv.* 14 February 1958, *Voenno-ist.* 1965/2, commemoration 1967
Zarifjan, M. G.	*Kommunist (Arm.)* 11 June 1976
Zatonskij, V. P.	*SIE, Granat, BSE¹, BSE³, Pravda Ukr.* 9 August 1963, *VIKPSS* 1963/9, commemorations 1968, 1978
Zelenskij, I. A.	*BSE³, Granat, BSE¹, Pravda Vostoka* 25 February 1970
Zotov, S. A.	*SIE*
Zof, V. I.	*MSE³ Granat, BSE¹, BSE³, SIE, SVE*
Ibragimov, G.	*MSE³, KLE, BSE¹*
Ivanenko, G. V.	*Pravda Ukr.* 12 November 1963
Ivanov, V. I.	*Pravda Vostoka* 20 July 1963, commemoration 1973
Ikramov, A.	*MSE³, BSE¹, BSE³, SIE, Pravda* 9 April 1964, commemorations 1968, 1978
Il'drym, Č. I.	*Bak. Rab.* 10 July 1958, commemoration 1980
Il'in-Ženevskij, A. F.	*ES, BSE¹, BSE³, SIE*
Isaev, U. D.	*KSE, Kazachstan. Pravda* 8 September 1960, commemoration 1965

Islamov, A. I.	*Pravda Vostoka* 28 February 1967
Ismajlov, I.	*Komm. Tadžik.* 30 May 1964
Israfilbekov, M.	*Bak. Rab.* 28 October 1972
Kabakov, I. D.	*BSE³, BSE¹, Sov. Rossija* 21 November 1971
Kabulov, I. Ju.	*Kazachstan. Pravda* 25 March 1964
Kavtaradze, G. D.	*Zarja Vostoka* 29 July 1965
Kazanskij, E. S.	*BSE³, SVE, Voenno-ist.* 1966/1 and 4
Kakurin, N. E.	*SIE, BSE³*
Kalmanovič, M. I.	*BSE³, BelSE*
Kalmykov, B. E.	*BSE², BSE¹, BSE³, SIE, MSE³, Izvestija* 24 October 1963, commemorations 1964, 1973
Kalmykov, M. V.	*Voenno-ist.* 1968/12
Kal'van, I. I.	*SVE, Voenno-ist.* 1966/11
Kamenev, S. S.	*BSE², Granat, BSE³, SIE, MSE³, ES³, SVE, Pravda Ukr.* 21 August 1959, *Voenno-ist.* 1966/2 and 3
Kaminskij, G. N.	*SIE, BSE³, Sov. Belorus.* 14 August 1963, *VIKPSS* 1965/11, commemorations 1965, 1967
Kanatčikov, S. I.	*BSE³, Literaturn. Gazeta* 11 April 1979
Kangelari, V. A.	*Krasn. Zv.* 31 July 1963
Karaev, A. A.	*Bak. Rab.* 7 June 1966, commemoration 1976
Karaev, A. K.	*Voenno-ist.* 1966/6
Karagezjan, A. N.	*Kommunist (Arm.)* 29 September 1970
Karachan, L. M.	*DS², DS³, SIE, Granat, BSE³, Kommunist (Arm.)* 2 February 1964, commemoration 1979
Kartvelišvili, L. I.	*SIE, BSE³, Pravda Ukr.* 30 April 1966, commemorations 1970, 1980
Kas'jan, S. O.	*BSE³, Kommunist (Arm.)* 28 January 1966, commemoration 1976
Kachiani, M. I.	*Zarja Vostoka* 19 December 1971
Kachojan, A. S.	*Kommunist (Arm.)* 27 February 1964, commemoration 1974
Kаširin, I. D.	*VI* 1966/9

Kaširin, N. D.	*SIE, BSE³, SVE, KSE, Voenno-ist.* 1966/4
Kvantiliani, E. A.	*Zarja Vostoka* 15 May 1969
Kviring, E. I.	*SIE, Granat, BSE¹, BSE³, Pravda* 13 September 1963, *VIKPSS* 1963/10, commemoration 1968
Kvjatek, K. F.	*Voenno-ist.* 1966/3
Kedrov, M. S.	*MSE³, BSE¹, BSE³, SVE, Krasn. Zv.* 24 February 1963, *Voenno-ist.* 1963/2, *VIKPSS* 1963/11, commemorations 1964, 1978
Kernovič, K.	*Sov. Litva* 11 March 1977
Kil'berg, A. M.	*Sov. Eston.* 28 October 1962
Kireev, G.P.	*SVE, Voenno-ist.* 1965/1
Kiselev, A. S.	*MSE³, Granat, BSE¹, BSE³, SIE, Izvestija* 11 March 1964, commemorations 1969, 1979
Klestov, N. S.	*BSE³*
Klimenko, I. E.	*Pravda Ukr.* 8 September 1971
Knorin, V. G.	*SIE, BSE³, Sov. Latvija* 31 July 1957, *VIKPSS* 1965/8, commemorations 1965, 1970, 1975
Knjagnickij, P. E.	*SVE*
Kovtjuch, E. I.	*BSE², BSE³, SIE, MSE³, SVE, Krasn. Zv.* 21 May 1965, *Voenno-ist.* 1966/11, commemoration 1970
Kogan, E. S.	*Moskovsk. Pravda* 11 October 1966
Kodackij, I. F.	*Leningr. Pravda* 1 July 1973
Kožanov, I. K.	*SIE, BSE³, SVE, Voenno-ist.* 1964/8
Koževnikov, S. N.	*Voenno-ist.* 1966/9
Kolotilov, N. N.	*BSE³*
Kolčanovskij, N. P.	*DS³*
Komarov, N. P.	*BSE³, Leningr. Pravda* 23 December 1976
Korbutjak, V. Ju.	*Pravda Ukr.* 28 November 1963
Kork, A. I.	*MSE³, BSE³, SIE, Sov. Estonija* 15 October 1958, *Voenno-ist.* 1962/7, 1966/4, 1967/7, commemorations 1962, 1965, 1967, 1970
Kornjušin, T. D.	*URE*
Korostelev, A. A.	*BSE³, KSE, Učitel' naja Gazeta* 11

	October 1962
Kosarev, A. V.	*BSE², BSE¹, BSE³, SIE, MSE³,* *Pravda* 14 November 1963, *VIKPSS* 1963/11
Kosior, S. V.	*BSE², Granat, BSE¹, BSE³, SIE, MSE³, ES³, SVE, Pravda Ukr.* 9 July 1958, *VIKPSS* 1964/11, commemorations 1964, 1969, 1979
Kostanjan, A. A.	*Kommunist (Arm.)* 28 July 1967, commemoration 1970
Kostrzeva, V.	*BSE², BSE³, MSE³*
Kocjubinskij, Ju. M.	*BSE³, SVE, Pravda Ukr.* 7 December 1966
Kraval', I. A.	*BSE³*
Krapivjanskij, N. G.	*Voenno-ist.* 1964/12
Krasikov, P. A.	*LES, BSE¹, BSE³, SIE, MSE³, Izvestija* 8 October 1970, *VIKPSS* 1963/7
Krasnoščekov, A. M.	*BSE³*
Krestinskij, N. N.	*URE, SIE, Granat, BSE³, Izvestija* 27 October 1963, *Lenin PSS* vols. 37, 44
Krinickij, A. I.	*BSE³, Sel'skaja Žizn'* 9 September 1964, *VIKPSS* 1964/12, commemoration 1974
Krumina, G. I.	*Sov. Rossija* 8 February 1964
Krumin', G. I.	*Sov. Latvija* 22 July 1964
Krumin', Ja. M.	*SIE, BSE³, Sov. Latvija* 25 September 1964, commemoration 1974
Krylenko, N. V.	*LES, Granat, BSE¹, BSE², BSE³, SIE, SVE, Sov. Sport* 12 November 1960, *Voenno-ist.* 1964/11 and 12, *VIKPSS* 1965/5, *VI* 1975/5, commemorations 1964, 1965, 1975
Kubjak, N. A.	*SIE, BSE³, Leningr. Pravda* 29 July 1971
Kuznecov, A. A.	*LES, BSE², BSE³, SIE, MSE³, Pravda* 20 February 1965, commemoration 1975
Kuznecov, P. M.	*Kommunist (Arm.)* 20 January 1966,

Lencman, Ja. D.	*SIE, BSE³, Sov. Latvija* 1 September 1957, commemorations 1966, 1971
Leščenko, D. I.	*SIE, Pravda* 21 January 1966
Lobov, S. S.	*BSE³*
Lozovskij, S. A.	*BSE², Granat, BSE¹, BSE³, SIE, URE, Izvestija* 29 March 1963, *VIKPSS* 1967/7, commemorations 1968, 1978
Loktionov, A. D.	*SVE, Voenno-ist.* 1963/8
Lominadze, V. V.	*BSE³, Zarja Vostoka* 15 June 1977
Lomov-Oppokov, G. I.	*SIE, Granat, BSE³, Ekonom. Gazeta* 9 February 1963, commemorations 1968, 1978
Longva, R. V.	*Voenno-ist.* 1966/7
Ludri, I. M.	*BSE³*
Lukašin, S. L.	*Kommunist (Arm.)* 13 January 1965, commemoration 1975
Ljubimov, I. E.	*SIE, BSE³, SVE*
Ljubovič, A. M.	*SIE, BSE³*
Ljubčenko, P. P.	*BSE³, Pravda Ukr.* 19 January 1967, commemoration 1977
Mad'jar, L. I.	*BSE³*
Majorov, M. M.	*SIE, BSE³, Pravda Ukr.* 10 January 1965, commemoration 1970
Maksimov, K. G.	*Moskovsk. Pravda* 26 June 1964
Malenkov, G. M.	*ENE, BSE²*
Malyšev, S. V.	*Sov. Torgovlja* 19 July 1977
Mamedbekov, K. G.	*BSE³*
Mamikonjan, V. A.	*Kommunist (Arm.)* 14 February 1968
Manžara, D. I.	*Pravda Vostoka* 11 November 1965, commemoration 1975
Mancev, D. E.	*BSE³*
Masančin, M.	*KSE, Sov. Kirgizija* 13 July 1965, commemoration 1975
Medvedev, A. V.	*URE, Pravda Ukr.* 22 March 1969
Meženinov, S. A.	*SIE, BSE³*
Mežlauk, V. I.	*MSE³, BSE³, SIE, SVE, Pravda* 20 February 1963, *VIKPSS* 1963/2, commemoration 1973
Mežlauk, I. I.	*SIE, BSE³, SVE, Izvestija* 14

	October 1971
Mezis, A. I.	*Krasn. Zv.* 2 September 1964, *Voenno-ist.* 1964/8
Mel'ničanskij, G. N.	*BSE³, Granat*
Mechonošin, K. A.	*LES, SIE, BSE³, SVE, Sov. Rossija* 30 October 1964, *Voenno-ist.* 1964/10
Mikeladze, A. N.	*Zarja Vostoka* 12 March 1966
Milonov, Ju. K.	*SIE*
Milč, L. R.	*Pravda Ukr.* 10 March 1967
Miljutin, V. P.	*SIE, BSE³, Izvestija* 1 December 1964
Mirzabekjan, A. M.	*Kommunist (Arm.)* 26 June 1965
Mirzabekjan, T. K.	*Bak. Rab.* 22 March 1966
Mirzojan, L. I.	*BSE³, Kazachstan. Pravda* 23 November 1958, *VIKPSS* 1965/1, commemorations 1967, 1977
Mirring, R.	*ENE*
Miršarapov, M.	*Pravda Vostoka* 24 February 1968
Mif, P. A.	*BSE³, VI* 1972/2
Michajlov, V. M.	*BSE³*
Molotov, V. M.	*ENE, Granat, BSE¹, BSE², BSE³, SVE, DS¹, LTE, SES, BelSE, Lenin PSS* vols. 44, 52
Morozov, M. V.	*Pravda Vostoka* 6 September 1978
Mostovenko, P. N.	*SIE, BSE³, Sov. Moldavija* 9 May 1976
Muklevič, R. A.	*SIE, BSE³, SVE, Voenno-ist.* 1965/11
Muralov, A. I.	*SIE, BSE³, Sov. Rossija* 21 June 1966
Musabekov, G. M.	*SIE, Granat, BSE³, Bak. Rab.* 26 July 1958, commemorations 1968, 1978
Mchitarjan, V.	*Kommunist (Arm.)* 29 July 1965
Myrzagaliev, M. K.	*KSE*
Mjasnikov, A. F.	*Voenno-ist.* 1966/1
Nagovicyn, I. A.	*SIE, BSE³*
Nazaretjan, A. M.	*BSE³, Pravda* 17 November 1964, commemorations 1967, 1969
Nanejšvili, V. I.	*Bak. Rab.* 26 March 1968,

	commemoration 1978
Narimanov, M. A.	*Bak. Rab.* 22 July 1965, commemoration 1977
Nauekajtis, K.	*Sov. Litva* 11 March 1976
Nevskij, V. I.	*LES, Granat, BSE³, SIE, MSE³, SVE, Leningr. Pravda* 18 May 1957, *VIKPSS* 1966/5, 1967/11, 1976/5, commemorations 1965, 1966
Nejman, K. A.	*Sov. Latvija* 21 May 1963
Nemcov, N. M.	*SIE, Moskovsk. Pravda* 29 April 1964
Netupskajte, Ja. A.	*MLTE, Sov. Litva* 29 October 1967
Novickij, F. F.	SIE, BSE³
Norvidas, F.	*MLTE, Sov. Litva* 27 May 1973
Nosov, I. P.	*BSE³, Sov. Rossija* 31 August 1963
Nuridžanjan, A. S.	*Kommunist (Arm.)* 25 December 1966
Nurmakov, N.N.	*KSE, Kazachstan. Pravda* 25 April 1965, commemoration 1975
Nurpejsov, S.	*Kazachstan. Pravda* 23 February 1964
Odincov, A. V.	*Pravda* 10 November 1964
Okulov, A. I.	*KLE, SVE*
Okunev, G. S.	*Voenno-ist.* 1965/7
Onufriev, I. A.	*SVE*
Oras, P. Ju.	*Sov. Estonija* 14 April 1963
Orachelašvili, M. D.	*BSE², Granat, BSE³, SIE, Pravda* 10 June 1963, *VIKPSS* 1971/5, commemorations 1971, 1973
Orachelašvili-Mikeladze, M. P.	*Pravda Vostoka* 17 November 1967, commemoration 1977
Orlov, V. M.	*MSE³, BSE³, SIE, SVE, Voenno-ist.* 1965/6
Osenjan, Š. A.	*Kommunist (Arm.)* 19 April 1966
Osepjan, G. A.	*Krasn. Zv.* 1 August 1964, *Voenno-ist.* 1963/7, commemoration 1964
Osepjan, Ch.	*Kommunist (Arm.)* 21 April 1961
Osinskij-Obolenskij, V. V.	*SIE, Granat, BSE³*
Pavlov, A. V.	*SIE, BSE³, SVE, Voenno-ist.* 1966/10

Pavlunovskij, I. P.	*BSE³*
Panceržanskij, E. S.	*BSE³, SVE, Voenno-ist.* 1968/6
Paskuckij, N. A.	*BSE³, Turkmen. Iskra* 27 May 1964
Pauker, A.	*BSE³*
Pašukanis, E. B.	*BSE³*
Pegel'man, Ch. G.	*SIE, BSE³, ENE, Sov. Estonija* 19 June 1957, commemorations 1960, 1965, 1975
Perfil'ev, E. L.	*Pravda Vostoka* 13 June 1968
Pestkovskij, S. S.	*BSE³, Granat, KSE*
Peters, Ja. Ch.	*SIE, BSE³, SVE, Sov. Latvija* 5 April 1958, commemoration 1976
Peterson, A. D.	*SIE, BSE³*
Peterson, R. A.	*Sov. Latvija* 20 January 1967
Petin, N. N.	*SIE, BSE³, SVE, Krasn. Zv.* 14 May 1976, *Voenno-ist.* 1969/4
Petrov, S. P.	*Sov. Rossija* 17 October 1964
Petrovskij, L. G.	*BSE³, SVE*
Petrovskij, P. G.	*BSE³, Moskovsk. Komsomolec* 8 January 1980
Pečak, K. Ja.	*LME, Sov. Latvija* 23 June 1962, commemoration 1972
Peče, Ja. Ja.	*SIE*
Pilackaja, O. V.	*BSE³, Moskovsk. Pravda* 31 July 1964
Piljar, R.	*Sov. Litva* 8 August 1975
Piontkovskij, S. A.	*SIE, BSE³*
Pismanik, G. E.	*Sov. Belorus.* 23 February 1965
Plau, D.	*ENE, Sov. Est.* 18 June 1976
Plešakov, M. G.	*Bak. Rab.* 9 April 1965, commemoration 1966
Pogosjan, O. A.	*Kommunist (Arm.)* 20 November 1960, commemoration 1967
Pozern, B. P.	*LES, SIE, BSE³, ES³*
Polonskij, V. I.	*BSE³, Trud* 18 June 1963, commemorations 1966, 1973
Polujan, D. V.	*Turkmen. Iskra* 7 December 1965
Polujan, Ja. V.	*SIE, BSE³, Sov. Rossija* 7 May 1969
Popkov, P. S.	*LEs, BSE³*
Popov, N. N.	*SIE, BSE³, Pravda Ukr.* 9 January 1971

Popok, I. A.

BSE³, Turkmen. Iskra 20 September 1964, commemoration 1974

Postyšev, P. P.

BSE², BSE³, SIE, MSE³, SVE, Sov. Patriot 29 December 1957, *Pravda Ukr.* 23 September 1958, commemorations 1962, 1967

Pravdin, A. G.

BSE³, Gudok 4 February 1970

Pramnek, E. K.

BSE³, Sov. Latvija 1 June 1958, commemoration 1960

Primakov, V. M.

MSE³, BSE³, SIE, SVE, Krasn. Zv. 16 May 1962, *Voenno-ist.* 1967/12, commemorations 1967, 1968, 1977

Pruknjak, E.

SIE

Ptucha, V. V.

BSE³

Pugačev, S. A.

SIE, SVE, Krasn. Zv. 28 February 1964, *Voenno-ist.* 1964/2

Putna, V. K.

MSE³, BSE³, SIE, SVE, Sov. Litva 21 February 1958, *Voenno-ist.* 1963/4, 1967/2, commemorations 1968, 1969, 1973

Pylaev, G. N.

BSE³

Pjatnickij, I. A.

BSE², BSE³, SIE, MSE³, Pravda 30 January 1962, commemoration 1972

Radžabov, S.

Kommunist Tadžik. 1 November 1967

Radčenko, A. F.

URE

Radčenko, I. I.

LES, BSE³, SIE, Komsomolsk. Pravda 24 October 1964, commemoration 1974

Rajk, L.

SIE, Pravda 30 March 1956

Raskol'nikov, F. F.

Granat, Leningrad. Pravda 15 January 1964, *VIKPSS* 1963/12, *Voenno-ist.* 1964/3, *Lenin PSS* vols. 35, 50

Rasulzade, A. G.

Bak. Rab. 24 November 1964

Rattel', N. I.

BSE³, SVE

Raudmec, I. I.

ENE, Sov. Estonija 16 October 1957

Rachimbaev, A.R.

BSE³, Kommunist Tadžik. 14 July 1966, commemoration 1969

Rachmanov, G.

Bak. Rab. 19 December 1962

Rovio, G. S.	*Sov. Rossija* 7 November 1964
Rogov, M. I.	*BSE³, Granat, Moskovsk. Pravda* 10 November 1970
Rogovskij, N. M.	*Voenno-ist.* 1963/11
Rozybakiev, A.	*KSE, Pravda* 2 March 1968, commemoration 1977
Rojzenman, B. A.	*BSE³*
Rudzutak, Ja. E.	*BSE², Granat, BSE³, SIE, MSE³, Sov. Latvija* 25 October 1956, *VIKPSS* 1963/4, commemorations 1962, 1964, 1967, 1969, 1977
Rumjancev, I. P.	*BSE³*
Ruchimovič, M. L.	*SIE, BSE³, Ekonom. Gazeta* 1 September 1969, commemoration 1979
Ryvkin, O. L.	*SIE, BSE³*
Ryskulov, T. R.	*BSE³, KSE, Kazachstan. Pravda* 29 December 1964, *VIKPSS* 1965/ 12, commemorations 1965, 1974
Rjazanov, D. B.	*BSE³, Granat*
Rjastas, O. I.	*SIE, BSE³, ENE, Sov. Estonija* 20 August 1957, commemorations 1965, 1970
Sabanin, A. V.	*DS³*
Sablin, Ju. V.	*SIE, BSE³, Voenno-ist.* 1965/8
Sadaev, D. S.	*Sov. Kirgizija* 7 July 1968
Sadatjan, G. A.	*Kommunist (Arm.)* 4 January 1975
Said-Galiev, S. G.	*BSE³, VIKPSS* 1964/2
Sarkisov, S. A.	*URE*
Svanidze, A. S.	*SIE*
Svanidze, N. S.	*Zarja Vostoka* 21 March 1965
Svečin, A. A.	*SIE, SVE, Voenno-ist.* 1965/10
Svečnikov, M. S.	*BSE³, SVE, Voenno-ist.* 1967/7
Sviderskij, F. I.	*BSE³*
Sviridov, I. A.	*Krasn. Zv.* 14 February 1964
Svistun, P. I.	*VI* 1966/2
Segizbaev, S.	*SIE, BSE³, KSE, Pravda Vostoka* 10 August 1967, commemorations 1974, 1979
Sedjakin, A. I.	*BSE³, SVE, Krasn. Zv.* 28 November 1963, *Voenno-ist.* 1963/11

Sejfullin, S.	*MSE³, BSE³, KSE*
Serbičenko, A. K.	*URE, Granat, Pravda Ukr.* 24 November 1970, commemoration 1980
Serdič, D. F.	*SIE, Voenno-ist.* 1966/8
Serebrovskij, A. P.	*MSE³, BSE³, URE, Granat, Bak. Rab.* 5 January 1960, commemorations 1964, 1974, 1977, 1980
Sijak, I. M.	*Pravda Ukr.* 24 November 1963
Skvirskij, B. E.	*DS², DS³*
Skobelev, M. I.	*SIE, BSE³*
Skrypnik, N. A.	*LES, BSE³, SIE, URE, Pravda* 25 January 1962, commemoration 1972
Slavin, I. E.	*Voenno-ist.* 1964/3
Slánský, R.	*BSE³*
Sklac'ka, O. V.	*URE*
Smirnov, A. P.	*BSE³, Granat*
Smirnov, G. I.	*Ekonom. Gazeta* 13 April 1963
Smirnov, P. A.	*SVE*
Smorodin, P. I.	*LES, BSE³, SIE, Moskovsk. Komsomolec* 28 July 1964, commemoration 1967
Snesarev, A. E.	*SIE, SVE, Krasn. Zv.* 25 August 1974, *Voenno-ist.* 1965/2
Sokolovskaja, S. I.	*SIE, BSE³*
Sollogub, N. V.	*SVE*
Solov'ev, V. I.	*BSE³*
Soms, K. P.	Sel'skaja Žizn' 18 September 1964
Sorin, V. G.	*VIKPSS* 1965/1
Sorokin, Ja. V.	*Krasn. Zv.* 20 March 1963
Stambolcjan, A. A.	*Kommunist (Arm.)* 26 October 1965, commemoration 1976
Stark, L. N.	*DS², DS³*
Staryj, G. I.	*SIE, BSE³, ESM, Sov. Moldavija* 9 December 1965, commemorations 1970, 1975, 1980
Steklov, Ju. M.	*SIE, Granat, BSE³, Izvestija* 27 August 1963, commemoration 1973

Steckij, A. I.	*BSE³*
Stomonjakov, B. S.	*DS², DS³*
Strievskij, K. K.	*BSE³, Moskovsk. Pravda* 2 October 1975, commemoration 1980
Stroganov, V. A.	*Pravda Ukr.* 24 December 1978
Strod, I. Ja.	*BSE³, SVE, Sov. Latvija* 5 March 1963, *Voenno-ist.* 1963/4, 1967/2, commemoration 1964
Sulimov, D. E.	*SIE, BSE³*
Sultanzade, A. S.	*SIE*
Sultanov, G.	*SIE, Bak. Rab.* 26 May 1964, commemorations 1966, 1969, 1979
Sultanova, A. M.	*Bak. Rab.* 23 October 1965, commemoration 1976
Suchomlin, K. V.	URE, Pravda Ukr. 22 May 1966
Syrba, K.	*Sov. Moldavija* 19 February 1974
Syrcov, S. I.	*BSE³*
Sytin, P. P.	*SVE, Voenno-ist.* 1970/8
Tairov, V. Ch.	*Kommunist (Arm.)* 12 July 1967
Tarnogorodskij, N. P.	*BSE³*
Tarchanov, O. S.	*SIE*
Tatarov, I. L.	*SIE*
Tatimov, M.	*KSE, Kazachstan. Pravda* 4 April 1964
Tacho-Godi, A. A.	*BSE³*
Tašev, K.	*Kommunist Tadžik.* 29 November 1964
Tejter, E.	*Sov. Estonija* 7 February 1976
Teodorovič I. A.	*SIE, BSE³, Granat, Sel'skaja žizn'* 26 October 1966, commemoration 1975
Teplov, N. P.	*BSE³*
Ter-Vartanjan, A. E.	*Kommunist (Arm.)* 1 November 1960, commemoration 7 May 1974
Ter-Gabrieljan, S. M.	*MSE³, BSE³, Kommunist (Arm.)* 20 October 1960, commemorations 1961, 1966, 1976
Ter-Simonjan, D. A.	*Kommunist (Arm.)* 28 August 1960, commemorations 1965, 1975
Terleckij, E. P.	*BSE³*
Togoev, D. N.	*SIE, BSE³*

Tolpygo, B. V.	*Kommunist Tadžik.* 29 September 1964
Toporkov, A. S.	*Izvestija* 22 July 1962
Torošelidze, M. G.	*Zarja Vostoka* 13 June 1970, commemoration 1980
Trilisser, M. A.	*BSE³*
Trifonov, V. A.	*MSE³, BSE³, Krasn. Zv.* 18 December 1963
Trojanker, B. U.	*Krasn. Zv.* 28 May 1965
Tuberik, K.	*ENE, Sov. Estonija* 27 April 1972
Tuchačevskij, M.N.	*LES, Granat, BSE², BSE³, SIE, MSE³, SVE, Izvestija* 29 December 1961, *Voenno-ist.* 1961/7, 1963/2, 4 and 12, 1964/2, 1973/2, commemorations 1962, 1963, 1968, 1973
Tjurjakulov, N. T.	*BSE³*
Uborevič, I. P.	*BSE², BSE³, SIE, MSE³, Sov. Litva* 6 October 1961, *VIKPSS* 1966/1, *Voenno-ist.* 1962/9, 1966/2, commemorations 1962, 1966, 1967, 1969, 1971, 1976
Ugarov, A. I.	*URE, SIE, BSE³*
Ugarov, F. Ja.	*LES, Granat*
Unšlicht, I.S.	*BSE², Granat, BSE¹, BSE³, SIE, MSE³, ES³, Sov. Litva* 18 December 1964, *VIKPSS* 1964/7, 1965/4, *Voenno-ist.* 1964/12, commemorations 1969, 1979
Uralov, S. G.	*SIE, BSE³*
Urickij, S. P.	*Krasn. Zv.* 2 March 1965
Uchanov, K. V.	*BSE², BSE¹, BSE³, SIE, Sov. Rossija* 23 September 1966
Ušakov, K. P.	*Voenno-ist.* 1967/2
Fedin, A. F.	*Kommunist Tadžik.* 3 September 1957, commemoration 1963
Fed'ko, I. F.	*MSE³, BSE¹, BSE³, SIE, Krasn. Zv.* 9 July 1957, *Voenno-ist.* 1962/6, 1966/2, 1967/6, commemorations 1958, 1959, 1962, 1967, 1969, 1972, 1977

Figatner, Ju. P.	*SIE, BSE³, Izvestija* 22 February 1964, commemoration 1979
Fomin, V. V.	*BSE³, Vodnyj Transport* 2 April 1964
Frumkin, M. I.	*SIE, Granat, BSE¹, BSE³*
Chavkin, S. T.	*BSE³*
Chalatov, A. B.	*MSE³, Granat, BSE¹, BSE³, SIE, Kommunist (Arm.)* 3 June 1960, commemoration 1964
Chalepskij, I. A.	*SIE, BSE¹, BSE³, Krasn. Zv.* 2 July 1963
Chandžjan, A. G.	*BSE², BSE³, Kommunist (Arm.)* 31 January 1961, commemorations 1966, 1971
Chataevič, M. M.	*BSE³, ES³, BSE¹, VIKPSS* 1963/6
Chachan'jan, G. D.	*SIE, BSE¹, BSE³, Kommunist (Arm.)* 21 September 1967, *Voenno-ist.* 1965/12, 1966/2, commemorations 1967, 1971, 1975
Chačiev, A. M.	*Kommunist (Arm.)* 23 January 1975
Chvesin, T. S.	*MSE³, BSE³*
Chinčuk, L. M.	*SIE, BSE¹, BSE³*
Chitarov, R. M.	*Kommunist (Arm.)* 9 March 1963
Chodžaev, N.	*Pravda Vostoka* 17 February 1967
Chodžaev, F.	*SIE, Granat, BSE¹, BSE³, Izvestija* 25 May 1966, commemorations 1966, 1971, 1976
Chumarjan, A. Ch.	*Zarja Vostoka* 20 January 1965, commemoration 1975
Civcivadze, I. V.	*BSE³, BSE¹, Zarja Vostoka* 20 March 1966, commemoration 1971
Cichon, A. M.	*BSE³, BSE¹*
Čaplin, N. P.	*BSE², BSE³, SIE, URE, Pravda* 19 December 1962, commemoration 1964
Červjakov, A. G.	*SIE, Granat, BSE¹, BSE³*
Černjavskij, V. I.	*URE*
Černjak, R. I.	*MSE³, Kommunist (Arm.)* 3 April 1969
Čubar', V. Ja.	*LES, Granat, BSE¹, BSE², BSE³, SIE, MSE³, URE, ES³, Pravda Ukr.*

	1 July 1958, commemorations 1961, 1966, 1971
Čuvyrin, M. E.	*URE, Pravda Ukr.* 9 January 1973
Čudov, M. S.	*LES, BSE¹, BSE², BSE³, SIE, Leningrad. Pravda* 5 September 1973
Čumbalov, M. M.	*Kazachstan. Pravda* 24 April 1964
Čuckaev, S. E.	*SIE, Granat, BSE¹, BSE³*
Šaverdjan, D. A.	*SIE, BSE³, Kommunist (Arm.)* 6 January 1960, commemorations 1962, 1966
Šarangovič, V. F.	*BelSE*
Šatov, V. S.	*SIE, BSE³, KSE, Kazachstan. Pravda* 26 December 1967
Šachbazi, T.	*Bak. Rab.* 15 July 1972
Šachmuradov, A. S.	*Kommunist (Arm.)* 9 May 1964
Šachsuvarjan, A. A.	*Kommunist (Arm.)* 17 October 1963, commemorations 1968, 1978
Šacht, E. G.	*Krasn. Zv.* 21 November 1964
Šackin, L. A.	*SIE, BSE³*
Šeboldaev, B. P.	*BSE², BSE¹, BSE³, SIE, MSE³, Kommunist (Arm.)* 30 May 1965, commemoration 1975
Šifres, A. L.	*Voenno-ist.* 1969/1
Šmidt, V. V.	*LES, Granat, BSE¹, BSE³, SIE*
Šmidt, D. A.	*URE*
Šorin, V. I.	*MSE³, BSE¹, BSE³, SIE, Krasn. Zv.* 21 September 1960, *Voenno-ist.* 1966/4, commemoration 1962
Šotemore, Š.	*SIE, BSE³, Kommunist Tadžik.* 4 April 1964
Šotman, A. V.	*LES, BSE¹, BSE³, SIE, URE, Sov. Litva* 15 June 1963, commemorations 1965, 1970
Štern, G. M.	*URE, SIE, BSE³*
Štrauch, E. M.	*BSE³, Sov. Eston.* 21 January 1976
Šumjackij, B. Z.	*SIE, Granat, BSE¹, BSE³, DS², DS³, Sov. Kul'tura* 12 November 1976
Ejdeman, R. P.	*BSE², BSE¹, BSE³, SIE, MSE³, Sov. Patriot.* 18 April 1962, *VIKPSS* 1964/12, *Voenno-ist.* 1963/7, commemorations 1965, 1975

Ejche, R. I.	*BSE², BSE¹, BSE³, SIE, MSE³, Sov. Latvija* 14 February 1957, *VIKPSS* 1965/7, commemorations 1963, 1965, 1968, 1970
Eliava, Š. Z.	*SIE, Granat, BSE¹, BSE³, Zarja Vostoka* 29 September 1963, commemorations 1964, 1965, 1968, 1973
Erznkjan, A. A.	*Kommunist (Arm.)* 13 May 1969, commemoration 1979
Efendiev, B. I.	*Kommunist (Arm.)* 23 May 1973
Efendiev, S. M.	*MSE³, BSE³, SIE, Bak. Rab.* 26 May 1957, commemorations 1967, 1977
Ešba, E. A.	*SIE, Zarja Vostoka* 29 March 1963, commemorations 1968, 1973, 1980
Juzefovič, I. S.	*SIE, BSE¹, BSE³*
Jurenev, K. K.	*SIE, Granat, BSE¹, BSE³, DS², DS³*
Jusifzade, A. B.	*Bak. Rab.* 11 May 1966
Jakir, I. E.	*BSE², BSE¹, BSE³, SIE, URE, Izvestija* 6 February 1962, *Voenno-ist.* 1962/5 and 12, 1963/12, 1966/10, 1967/2, commemorations 1963, 1966, 1971, 1976
Jakovenko, V. G.	*SIE, BSE¹, BSE³, Ist. SSSR* 1969/3
Jakovlev, Ja. A.	*BSE², Granat, BSE¹, BSE³, SIE, ES³, URE, MSE³, Sel'skaja Žijn'* 19 June 1966, commemoration 1976
Jakovleva, V. N.	*SIE, Granat, BSE¹, BSE³*
Janson, N. M.	*BSE³, ENE, BSE¹, Sov. Eston.* 10 December 1972

APPENDIX C   LIST OF PROMINENT PARTY
EXECUTIVES NOT PUBLICLY REHABILITATED

Reinstatement in the party is indicated by an asterisk. Arrangement
in accordance with the Russian alphabet.

Avilov, B. V.	*BSE[1]*
Amosov, A.M.*	*BSE[1]*, Lenin *PSS* 52
Amosov, P. N.	*BSE[1]*
Al'skij, A. O.	*BSE[1]*, Lenin *PSS* 44
Angarskij, N. S.*	*BSE[1]*, Lenin *PSS* 31
Anikst, A. M.*	*BSE[1]*, Lenin *PSS* 52
Asfendiarov, S. D.	*BSE[1]*
Aussem, V. Ch.	*BSE[1]*
Aussem, O. Ch.	*Granat, BSE[1]*
Bažanov, V. M.*	*BSE[1]*, Lenin *PSS* 50
Bakaev, I. P.	*BSE[1]*
Balickij, V. A.	*BSE[1]*
Belen'kij, G. Ja.*	*Granat, BSE[1]*, Lenin *PSS* 49
Bicenko, A. A.	*BSE[1]*
Bogolepov, D. P.*	*BSE[1]*, Lenin *PSS* 50
Boguslavskij, M. S.	*Granat, BSE[1]*, Lenin *PSS* 42
Bronskij, M. G.*	*BSE[1]*, Lenin *PSS* 30
Brykov, A. P.*	*BSE[1]*, Lenin *PSS* 53
Bujko, A.M.*	*BSE[1]*, *Odinnadcatyj s' ezd*, 812
Bumažnyj, E. O.*	*BSE[1]*, *Sed'maja konferencija*, 376
Bukharin, N. I.	*Granat, BSE[1]*, Lenin *PSS* 27, 30, 34
Vajnštejn, A. I.	*Granat, BSE[1]*
Vasil'čenko, S. F.*	*BSE[1]*, Lenin *PSS* 50
Golubev, I. M.*	*BSE[1]*, Lenin *PSS* 39
Gubel'man, M. I.	*BSE[1]*
Dermanis, V.	*BSE[1]*
Dimanštejn, S. M.	*BSE[1]*
Domskij, G. G.	*BSE[1]*, Lenin *PSS* 49
Dosser, Z. N.*	*BSE[1]*, Lenin *PSS* 52
Drobnis, Ja. N.	*Dejateli, Granat, BSE[1]*, Lenin *PSS* 39
Evdokimov, G. E.	*BSE[1]*, *Vos' moj s' ezd*, 567
Evrejnov, N. N.	*BSE[1]*

Ežov, N. I.	No mention
Enukidze, T. T.*	*BSE¹*, Lenin *PSS* 53
Žerve, B. O.	*BSE¹*
Zaks, S. M.	*BSE¹*, Lenin *PSS* 48
Zaluckij, P. A.	*BSE¹*, Lenin *PSS* 44
Zinov'ev, G. E.	*Granat, BSE¹*, Lenin *PSS* 17, 27, 30
Il'in, N. I.	*BSE¹*
Kaganovič, M. M.	*BSE¹*
Kaktyn', A. M.*	*BSE¹*, Lenin *PSS* 53
Kamenev, L. B.	*Granat*, Lenin *PSS* 10, 26, 44
Kutuzov, I. I.*	*Granat*, Lenin *PSS* 43
Leplevskij, G. M.*	*Granat*, Lenin *PSS* 54
Lorenc, I. L.*	*Granat*, Lenin *PSS* 50
Muralov, N. I.	*Granat*, Lenin *PSS* 50
Poskrebyšev, A. N.	*BSE¹*
Preobraženskij, E. A.	*Granat*, Lenin *PSS* 42
Pjatakov, G. L.	*Granat*, Lenin *PSS* 27
Radek, K. B.	*Granat*, Lenin *PSS* 26
Rakovskij, Ch. G.	*Granat*, Lenin *PSS* 26
Rykov, A. I.	*Granat*, Lenin *PSS* 10
Sapronov, T. V.	*Granat*, Lenin *PSS* 39
Serebrjakov, L. P.	*Granat*, Lenin *PSS* 42
Smilga, I. T.	*Granat*, Lenin *PSS* 32
Smirnov, I. N.	*Granat*, Lenin *PSS* 44
Sokol'nikov, G. Ja.	*Granat*, Lenin *PSS* 34
Sosnovskij, L. S.	*Granat*, Lenin *PSS* 37
Tolokoncev, A. F.*	*Granat, Odinnadcatyj s'' ezd*, 853
Tomskij, M. P.	*Granat*, Lenin *PSS* 17
Trotsky, L. D.	*Granat*, Lenin *PSS* 7, 34, 48
Uglanov, N. A.	*Granat*, Lenin *PSS* 52
Ustinov, A. M.*	*Granat*, Lenin *PSS* 31
Fenigštejn-Doleckij, Ja. G.	*BSE¹*, Lenin *PSS* 35
Filatov, N. A.	*BSE¹*
Frumkina, M. Ja.	*BSE¹*
Chodorovskij, I. I.*	*BSE¹*, Lenin *PSS* 45
Chotimskij, V. I.*	*BSE¹*, *Odinnadcatyj s'' ezd*, 857
Šklovskij, G. I.	*BSE¹*, Lenin *PSS* 47
Šljapnikov, A. G.	*Granat*, Lenin *PSS* 26
Ejsmont, N. B.*	*Granat*, Lenin *PSS* 51
Epštejn, M. S.	*BSE¹*
Jagoda, G. G.	*BSE¹*, Lenin *PSS* 54

	1956	1957	1958	1959	1960	1961	1962	1963	1964	1965	1966	1967
Bakinskij Rabočij	-/-	2/2	2/2	2/2	1/1	-/-	1/1	1/3	4/9	4/5	5/7	-/5
Ekonom. Gazeta	-/-	-/-	-/-	-/-	-/-	-/-	-/-	2/2	-/1	-/-	-/-	-/-
Gudok	-/-	-/-	-/-	-/-	-/-	-/-	-/-	-/-	-/2	-/-	-/-	-/1
Izvestija	-/-	-/-	-/-	-/-	-/-	1/1	2/12	7/15	6/15	0/4	1/1	1/3
Kazachst Pravda	-/-	-/-	1/1	-/-	1/1	-/-	-/-	1/3	6/7	2/3	-/-	1/2
Kommunist (Arm.)	-/-	1/1	-/-	-/-	8/8	2/3	1/3	3/6	5/9	5/9	5/9	4/13
Komm. Tadžik.	-/-	1/1	-/-	-/-	-/-	-/-	-/-	-/4	7/12	1/2	1/1	1/4
Komsomols Pravda	-/-	1/1	-/-	-/-	-/-	-/-	-/1	-/7	1/5	-/2	-/1	-/2
Krasnaja Zvezda	-/-	2/2	1/1	1/1	1/1	1/3	3/6	12/18	9/14	3/5	-/2	1/7
Leningrads Pravda	-/-	1/1	-/-	-/-	-/-	-/-	-/1	1/2	1/4	-/3	-/-	-/-
Literaturn Gazeta	-/-	-/-	-/-	-/-	-/-	-/-	-/1	-/1	-/1	-/-	-/-	-/-
Literaturn Rossija	-/-	-/-	-/-	-/-	-/-	-/-	-/-	-/1	-/1	-/-	-/-	-/1
Moskovsk Pravda	-/-	-/-	-/-	-/-	-/-	-/-	-/-	-/1	4/9	-/-	1/1	1/2
Pravda	-/-	-/-	-/-	-/-	-/-	-/-	4/7	5/10	4/11	1/2	-/3	-/2
Pravda Ukrainy	-/-	-/-	3/3	1/1	-/-	-/-	-/5	4/10	3/7	1/2	3/6	3/6
Pravda Vostoka	-/-	-/-	-/-	-/-	-/-	-/-	-/-	1/7	-/5	2/2	-/1	3/5

	1956	1957	1958	1959	1960	1961	1962	1963	1964	1965	1966	1967
Sel'skaja Žizn'	–/–	–/–	–/–	–/–	–/–	–/–	–/–	–/–	2/2	–/–	2/3	–/–
Sov. Belorussija	–/–	–/–	–/–	–/–	–/–	–/–	–/–	1/2	1/4	3/5	–/–	–/–
Sov. Estonija	1/1	5/6	1/1	–/1	–/–	–/–	–/–	1/3	–/2	–/2	–/2	–/1
Sov. Kirgizija	–/–	–/–	–/–	–/–	–/–	–/–	–/1	–/2	–/3	1/1	–/–	–/–
Sov. Kul'tura	–/–	–/–	–/–	–/–	–/–	–/–	–/–	–/–	–/1	–/–	–/–	–/–
Sov. Latvija	1/1	5/5	7/7	–/1	–/1	1/1	1/5	3/9	4/10	–/4	–/1	1/3
Sov. Litva	1/1	–/1	1/1	–/–	–/–	1/1	–/1	1/5	1/3	–/1	–/3	2/4
Sov. Moldavija	–/–	–/–	–/–	–/1	–/–	–/–	–/–	1/3	1/6	1/2	–/2	–/4
Sov. Patriot	–/–	–/–	–/2	–/–	–/–	–/–	1/1	–/–	–/–	–/–	–/1	–/–
Sov. Rossija	–/–	–/–	–/–	–/–	–/–	–/–	–/3	–/5	4/10	1/3	2/3	1/2
Sov. Torgovlja	–/–	1/1	–/–	–/–	–/–	–/–	–/–	–/1	–/–	–/–	–/–	–/–
Sov. Sport	–/–	–/–	–/–	–/–	1/1	–/–	–/–	–/–	–/–	–/1	–/–	–/–
Trud	–/–	–/–	–/–	–/–	–/–	–/–	–/1	1/2	–/3	1/1	–/–	–/5
Turkm. Iskra	–/–	–/–	–/–	–/–	–/–	–/–	–/–	–/2	2/3	2/2	–/–	–/1
Učitel Gazeta	–/–	–/–	–/–	–/–	–/–	–/–	2/2	–/1	–/–	–/–	–/–	–/–
Vodnyj Transport	–/–	–/–	–/–	–/–	–/–	–/–	1/2	–/–	1/2	–/–	–/1	–/–
Zarja Vostoka	–/–	–/–	–/–	–/–	–/–	–/–	–/–	3/7	–/4	3/5	4/6	4/5
Total	3/3	19/21	16/18	4/7	12/14	6/10	16/52	48/131	66/165	31/66	24/54	23/78

	1968	1969	1970	1971	1972	1973	1974	1975	1976	1977	1978	1979	1980
Bakinskij Rabočij	1/3	–/1	–/2	–/1	2/2	–/1	–/2	1/2	–/4	–/6	–/4	–/2	–/3
Ekonom. Gazeta	–/1	1/1	–/–	–/–	–/–	–/1	–/–	–/–	–/–	–/–	–/–	–/–	–/–
Gudok	1/1	–/–	1/1	–/–	–/–	–/1	–/–	–/–	–/–	–/–	–/–	–/–	–/–
Izvestija	–/3	–/4	1/1	1/3	–/2	–/1	–/3	–/–	–/1	–/2	–/2	–/–	–/–
Kazachst. Pravda	–/–	–/1	–/–	–/–	–/–	–/–	–/1	–/2	–/1	–/2	–/1	–/2	–/–
Kommunist (Arm.)	1/3	3/4	–/4	1/4	–/–	1/3	–/2	3/11	2/5	1/7	1/3	1/4	–/–
Komm. Tadžik.	–/–	–/2	–/–	–/–	–/–	–/–	–/–	–/1	–/–	–/2	–/–	–/–	–/1
Komsomols. Pravda	–/–	–/–	–/–	–/1	–/–	–/1	–/–	–/–	–/–	–/1	–/–	–/–	–/1
Krasnaja Zvezda	–/1	–/3	–/–	–/1	–/–	–/2	1/2	–/2	1/3	–/5	–/–	–/2	–/2
Leningrads. Pravda	–/–	–/1	–/–	1/1	–/–	2/2	–/1	–/1	1/1	–/–	–/1	–/1	–/1
Literaturn. Gazeta	–/–	–/–	–/–	–/–	–/–	–/–	–/–	–/–	–/–	–/–	–/–	–/–	–/–
Literaturn. Rossija	–/1	–/–	–/–	–/–	–/–	–/–	–/–	–/–	–/–	–/1	–/1	1/1	–/–
Moskovsk. Komsom.	–/–	–/–	–/–	–/–	–/–	–/–	–/–	–/–	–/–	–/–	–/–	–/–	1/1
Moskovsk. Pravda	–/–	–/–	1/2	–/–	–/2	–/1	–/1	1/1	1/1	–/2	–/–	–/1	–/1
Pravda	1/1	–/2	–/–	–/1	–/2	–/1	–/1	1/1	1/1	–/3	–/2	–/2	–/3
Pravda Ukrainy	–/2	–/2	1/3	2/3	–/1	1/1	–/1	–/3	–/1	–/3	1/3	–/2	–/2
Pravda Vostoka	2/4	–/1	1/1	–/1	–/–	–/–	–/1	–/1	–/2	–/1	1/3	–/1	–/1
Sel'skaja Žizn'	–/–	–/–	–/–	–/1	–/–	–/–	–/1	–/1	–/1	–/–	–/–	–/–	–/–
Social. Industrija	–/–	–/–	–/–	–/–	–/–	–/–	–/1	–/1	–/1	–/–	–/2	–/1	–/–
Sov. Belorussija	–/–	–/1	–/1	–/–	–/–	–/1	–/1	–/1	–/–	–/2	–/2	–/1	–/2
Sov. Estonija	–/1	–/4	–/2	–/–	2/2	–/–	–/1	–/1	3/4	–/1	–/1	1/1	–/–
Sov. Kirgizija	1/1	–/–	–/–	–/–	–/–	–/1	–/2	–/2	–/–	–/–	–/–	–/1	–/–

	1968	1969	1970	1971	1972	1973	1974	1975	1976	1977	1978	1979	1980
Sov. Kul'tura	—/—	—/—	—/—	—/—	—/—	—/—	—/—	—/—	—/—	—/—	—/—	—/2	—/—
Sov. Latvija	—/1	—/—	—/3	—/2	—/1	—/1	1/2	—/—	—/1	—/1	—/—	—/—	—/—
Sov. Litva	1/2	—/3	—/—	—/1	—/2	2/4	—/2	—/1	2/2	1/3	—/1	—/1	—/1
Sov. Moldavija	—/1	—/2	—/1	1/4	—/1	—/2	1/3	—/3	1/4	—/2	—/2	—/—	—/1
Sov. Patriot	—/—	—/—	—/—	—/—	—/—	—/—	—/—	—/—	—/—	—/1	—/—	—/—	—/—
Sov. Rossija	—/—	1/1	—/3	1/1	—/—	—/1	—/3	—/—	1/2	—/1	—/1	—/2	—/—
Sov. Torgovlja	—/—	—/—	—/—	—/—	—/—	—/—	—/—	—/—	—/—	1/1	—/—	—/—	—/—
Sov. Sport	—/—	—/—	—/—	—/—	—/—	—/—	—/—	—/1	—/—	—/—	—/—	—/—	—/—
Turkm. Iskra	—/—	—/—	—/—	—/—	—/—	—/—	—/1	—/1	—/—	—/1	—/—	—/—	—/—
Učitel. Gazeta	—/—	—/—	—/—	—/1	—/—	—/—	—/—	—/—	—/—	—/—	—/—	—/—	—/—
Vodnyj Transport	—/—	—/1	—/1	—/—	—/—	—/—	—/1	—/1	—/—	—/1	—/1	—/—	—/—
Zarja Vostoka	—/5	1/1	1/2	3/5	—/—	—/4	—/1	1/1	—/2	1/4	—/4	—/—	—/3
Total	8/31	6/35	6/27	10/31	4/13	6/28	3/28	6/37	12/35	4/51	3/26	3/26	1/22

BIBLIOGRAPHY

Publications in the Soviet Union and Eastern Europe

Encyclopaedias

BelSE	Belaruskaja Saveckaja Encyklapedyja (Minsk, 1969-75)
BSE¹	*Bol'saja Sovetskaja Enciklopedija* 1st edn (Moscow, 1926-47)
BSE²	*Bol'saja Sovetskaja Enciklopedija*, 2nd edn (Moscow, 1948-60)
BSE³	*Bol'saja Sovetskaja Enciklopedija*, 3rd edn (Moscow, 1970-8)
Dejateli	*Dejateli revoljucionnogo dviženija v Rossii. Biobibliografičeskij slovar', vol 5, Social-demokratov 1880-1904* (Moscow, 1931)
DS¹	*Diplomatičeskij slovar'*, 1st edn (Moscow, 1948-50)
DS²	*Diplomatičeskij slovar'*, 2nd edn (Moscow, 1960-4)
DS³	*Diplomatičeskij slovar'*, 3rd edn (Moscow, 1971-3)
ENE	*Eesti Nougude Entsüklopeedia* Tallinn, (1968-76)
Granat	*Enciklopedičeskij slovar' Russkogo bibliografičeskogo instituta 'Granat'*, vol. 41, parts 1-3 (Moscow, 1927-9)
ES²	*Enciklopedičeskij slovar'* (Moscow, 1953-5)
ES³	*Enciklopedičeskij slovar'* (Moscow, 1963-4)
ESM	*Enciklopedija Sovetike Moldovenjaske* (Kišinev, 1970-8)
KLE	*Kratkaja Literaturnaja Enciklopedija* (Moscow, 1962-72)
KSE	*Kazak Sovet Enciklopedijasy* (Alma-Ata, 1972-)
LES	*Leningrad. Enciklopedičeskij spravočnik* (Moscow-Leningrad, 1957)
LME	*Latvijas PSR Maza Enciklopedija* (Riga, 1967-72)
LTE	*Lietuviskoj Tarybiné Enciklopedija* (Vil'na, 1978-81)
MLTE	*Mazoji Lietuviskoji Tarybiné Enciklopedija* (Vil'na, 1966-75)
MSE¹	*Malaja Sovetskaja Enciklopedija*, 1st edn (Moscow, 1928-31)
MSE²	*Malaja Sovetskaja Enciklopedija*, 2nd edn (Moscow, 1933-47)
MSE³	*Malaja Sovetskaja Enciklopedija*, 3rd edn (Moscow, 1958-60)
Nevskij	V. Nevskij, *Materialy dlja biografičeskogo slovarja social-demokratov, vstupivšich v rossijskoe raboćee dvizenie za period ot 1880 do 1905 g.* (Moscow-Petrograd, 1923)
SES	*Sovetskij Enciklopedičeskij Slovar'* (Moscow, 1980)
SIE	*Sovetskaja Istoričeskaja Enciklopedija* (Moscow, 1961-76)
SVE	*Sovetskaja Voennaja Enciklopedija* (Moscow, 1976-80)
URE	*Ukrainska Rad'jans'ka Enciklopedija* (Kiev, 1959-65)
USE	*Ukrainskaja Sovetskaja Enciklopedija* (Kiev, 1978-)

Press

Bakinskij Raboćij (Bak. Rab.)
Bjulleten' Verchovnogo Suda SSSR (BVS SSSR)
Československý Časopis Historický (Prague)
Ekonomičeskaja Gazeta
Gudok
Istoričeskie Zapiski
Istoričeskij Archiv (Ist. Arch.)
Istorija SSSR (Ist. SSSR)
Izvestija
Kazachstanskaja Pravda

Kommunist
Kommunist (Armenii)
Kommunist Tadžikistana
Komsomol'skaja Pravda
Krasnaja Zvezda (Krasn. Zv.)
Leningradskaja Pravda
Letopiś Gazetnych Statej
Letopiś Žurnal'nych Statej
Literaturnaja Gazeta
Literaturnaja Rossija
Moskovskaja Pravda
Moskovskij Komsomolec
Narodnoe Obrazovanie
Novyj Mir
Partijnaja Žizn'
Politika (Prague)
Pravda
Pravda Ukrainy
Pravda Vostoka
Rabočaja Gazeta
Rudé Právo (Prague)
Sbírka Zákonu Ceskoslovenskó Socialistické Republiky (Sb. Zak.) (Prague)
Sel'skaja Žizn'
Socialističeskaja Industrija
Socialističeskaja Zakonnosť
Sovetskaja Belorussija
Sovetskaja Estonija
Sovetskaja Justicija
Sovetskaja Kirgizija
Sovetskaja Kuľtura
Sovetskaja Latvija
Sovetskaja Litva
Sovetskaja Moldavija (Sov. Mold.)
Sovetskaja Pedagogika
Sovetskaja Rossija
Sovetskaja Torgovlja
Sovetskij Patriot
Sovetskij Sport
Sovetskoe Gosudarstvo i Pravo
Sudebnaja Praktika Verchovnogo Suda SSSR (SP)
Trud
Trybuna Ludu (Warsaw)
Turkmen'skaja Iskra
Učiteľskaja Gazeta
Vedomosti Verchovnogo Soveta SSSR (VVS SSSR)
Vodnyj Transport
Voenno-istoričeskij Žurnal (Voenno-ist.)
Voprosy Istorii (VI)
Voprosy Istorii Kommunističeskoj Partii Sovetskogo Sojuza (VI KPSS)
Zarja Vostoka
Z Pola Walki (Warsaw)

Literature and Source Publications

Abramov, A. *U Kremlevskoj steny* (Moscow, 1974)

Ajrapetjan, G.A. *Legendarnyj Gaj* (Moscow, 1965)
—— *Komkor Chachanjan* (Erevan, 1970)
Aktivnye borcy za Sovetskuju vlast' v Azerbajdžane (Baku, 1957)
Anikeev, V.V. *Dejatel' nost' C. K. RKP(b) v 1918-1919 godach. Chronika sobytij*
    (Moscow, 1976)
Antonov-Ovseenko, V.A. *V revoljucii* (Moscow, 1957)
Archangel'skij, V. P. *Smorodin* (Moscow, 1974)
Astachova, N. and Cellarius, E. *Tovarišč Ol'ga* (Moscow, 1969) (O.V. Pilackaja)
Babenko, P.M. *I.E. Jakir* (Moscow, 1964)
Bacinskij, P.P. *P. P. Ljubčenko* (Kiev, 1970)
—— *Kviring, V.E.* and Perel'man, M.B. *E.I. Kviring* (Moscow, 1968)
Bagaev, B. *B. Šumjackij* (Krasnojarsk, 1974)
Barančenko, V. *Gaven* (Moscow, 1967)
Bega, F.F. and Aleksandrov, V.G. *Petrovskij* (Moscow, 1963)
Berchin, I.B. *Voennaja reforma v SSSR (1924-25 gg.)* (Moscow, 1958)
Bereznoj, A.F. and Smirnov, S.V. *Bojcy revoljucii. Sotrudniki bol'ševistskoj
    pečati. Biobibliografičeskij spravočnik* (Leningrad, 1969)
Binevič, A.I. and Serebrjanskij, Z.L. *Andrej Bubnov* (Moscow, 1964)
Blinov, A.S. *I. Akulov* (Moscow, 1967)
Bljucher, V.K. *Stat' i i reči* (Moscow, 1963)
Boldyrev, V.A. (ed.) *Naučno-praktičeskij komentarij k ugolovno-processual'nomu
    kodeksu RSFSR* (Moscow, 1963)
Bondarevskaja, T.P. *A. V. Šotman* (Moscow, 1963)
Borcy za sčast'e narodnoe (Kazan', 1967)
Bubnov, A.S. *1924 God v voennoj stroitel'stve* (Moscow, 1925)
—— *Voevaja podgotovka i političeskaja rabota* (Moscow, 1927)
—— *Graždanskaja vojna, partija i voennoe delo. Sbornik statej* (Moscow, 1928)
—— *V.K.P.(b)* (Moscow-Leningrad, 1931)
—— *O Krasnoj Armii. Sbornik* (Moscow, 1958)
—— *Stat' i i reči o narodnom obrazovanii* (Moscow, 1959)
Chasanov, K. *Tovarišč Akmal'. O žizni i dejatel'nosti A.I. Ikramova* (Tashkent,
    1970)
Chodzaev, F. *Izbrannye trudy* (Tashkent, 1970-3)
Daniševskij, J.K. *Biobibliografija* (Riga, 1964)
Desjatyj s''ezd RKP(b). Mart 1921 g. Stenografičeskij otčet (Moscow, 1963)
Devjataja Konferencija RKP(b). Sentjabr' 1920 goda. Protokoly (Moscow, 1972)
Devjatyj s''ezd RKP(b). Protokoly (Moscow, 1960)
D'jakov, B. *Povest' o perežitom* (Moscow, 1966)
Dmitrevskij, V.I. *Pjatnickij* (Moscow, 1971)
—— *Desjat' stupeni k pobede. Ob O.A. Pjatnickoj* (Moscow, 1976)
Donesenija komissarov Petrogradskogo voenno-revoljucionnogo komiteta, ed.
    G.A. Belov (Moscow, 1957)
Drobizev, V. and Dumova, N. *V. Ja Čubar'* (Moscow, 1963)
Dubinskij, I. *Primakov* (Moscow, 1968)
Dubinskij, I.M. *Kavkaskie druz'ja Il'ica* (Tbilisi, 1970)
Dubinskij, I.V. *Naperekor vetram* (Moscow, 1964) (I.E. Jakir)
Dubinskij-Muchadze, I.M. *Ordžonikidze* (Moscow, 1963)
Dušen'kin, V. *Ot soldata do maršala* (Moscow, 1960) (V.K. Bljucher)
—— *Proletarskij maršal* (Moscow, 1973) (V.K. Bljucher)
Dvadcat' vtoroj s''ezd KPSS, 17-31 oktjabrja 1961 goda. Stenografičeskij otčet
    (Moscow, 1962)
Dvadcatyj s''ezd KPSS, 14-15 fevralja 1956 goda. Stenografičeskij otčet (Moscow,
    1956)
Dvenadcatyj s''ezd RKP(b). 17-25 aprelja 1923 goda (Moscow, 1968)

Dzidzarija, G. A. *Efrem Ešba* (Moscow, 1957)
Enciklopedičeskij slovar' pravovych znanij (Moscow, 1965)
Erasov, V. P. *Navsegda, do konca. Povest' ob Andree Bubnova* (Moscow, 1978)
Etapy bol'sogo puti. Vospominanija o grazdanskoj vojne (Moscow, 1963)
Frunze, M. V. *Izbrannye proizvedenija* (Moscow, 1957)
Geroi graždanskoj vojny, ed. T. Gladkov (Moscow, 1963)
Geroi Oktjabrja (Leningrad, 1967)
Geroi Oktjabrja (Moscow, 1967)
Geschichte der Kommunistischen Partei der Sowjetunion (Berlin, 1974)
Geschichte der Sowjetunion (Berlin, 1960)
Gheorghiu-Dej, Gh. *Articole si cuvintari 1961-1962* (Bucharest, 1963)
Gindin, A. M and Gindin, G. M. *S Leninym v serdce (žizn' P. Krasikova)* (Moscow, 1968)
Gorbunov, G. *Orlinyj vzlet* (Yaroslavl, 1967) (A. S. Bubnov)
Gorlov, V. P. *Geroičeskij pochod* (Moscow, 1963) (E. I. Kovtjuch)
Isanov, A. I. *F. Chodžaev* (Tashkent, 1972)
Istorija i istoriki. Istoriografija istorii SSSR. Sbornik statej (Moscow, 1965)
Istorija Kommunističeskoj Partii Sovetskogo Sojuza (Ist. KPSS)
   2nd edn (Moscow, 1959)
   rev. 2nd edn (Moscow, 1962)
   3rd edn (Moscow, 1969)
   4th edn (Moscow, 1971)
   5th edn (Moscow, 1976)
   6th edn (Moscow, 1982)
Istorija Vsesojuznoj Kommunističeskoj Partii (Bol'ševikov), Kratkij kurs pod redak ciej komissii C.K. VKP(b) Odobren C.K. VKP(b) 1938 goda (Moscow, 1946)
Itkina, A. M. *Revoljucioner, tribun, diplomat. Očerk žizni A. M. Kollontaj* (1st edn, Moscow, 1964; 2nd edn, 1970)
Itogi vsesojuznoj perepisi naselenija 1959 g. (Moscow, 1962)
Jakir, I. E. *Vospominanija o graždanskoj vojne* (Moscow, 1957)
—— *Komandarm Jakir. Vospominanija druzej i soratnikov* (Moscow, 1963)
Jakutov, V. D. *N. M. Goloded* (Minsk, 1981)
Jestřáb, M. and Hladil, V. *Soudní rehabilitace. Komentár k zákonu c. 82/1968 Sb. o soudní rehabilitaci* (Prague, 1969)
Junga, E. S. *Put' matrosa. Rasskaz o Pavle Dybenko* (Moscow, 1958)
Juridičeskij slovar' (Moscow, 1956)
Kameneva, N. S. *Put' polkovodca (Vospominanija ob otce)* (Kiev, 1982)
Karenin, A. *S. M. Efendiev* (Baku, 1963)
Kartunova, A. I. *V. K. Bljucher v Kitae 1924-1927 gg. Dokumentirovannyj očerk. Dokumenty* (1st edn, Moscow, 1970; 2nd edn, Moscow, 1979)
Kazanin, M. I. *V štabe Bljuchera. Vospominanija o Kitajskoj revoljucii 1925-1927 godov* (Moscow, 1966)
Ključnik, L. and Zav'jalov, B. *G. I. Petrovskij* (Moscow, 1970)
Kollantaj, A. M. *Izbrannye stat'i i reči* (Moscow, 1972)
—— *Iz moej žizni i raboty. Vospominanija i dnevniki* (Moscow, 1974)
Kolotov, V. V. *Nikolaj Alekseevic Voznesenskij* (Moscow, 1974)
—— and Petrovicev, G. A. *N. A. Voznesenskij (1903-1950). Biografičeskij očerk* (Moscow, 1963)
Kommandarm krylatych (Riga,1973) (Ja. I. Alksnis)
Komissary (Moscow, 1967)
Kommunisticeskaja Partija Sovetskogo Sojuza v rezoljucijach i resenijach s"ezdov, konferencij i plenumov Central'nogo Komiteta, vols. 6-9 (Moscow, 1971-2)
Kommunisty. Sbornik (Moscow, 1976)
Kondrat'ev, N. D. *Maršal Bljucher* (Moscow, 1965)

—— *Na linii ognja* (Moscow, 1974) (I.F. Fed'ko)
Korobejnikov, I.I. and Tanjaev, A.P. *A. Dogadov* (Kazan' 1971)
Korol'ov, B. and Levin, V. *M.M. Majorov* (Kiev, 1969)
Kosarev, A.V. *Sbornik vospominanii* (Moscow, 1963)
Krastin', Ja. and Berzin's, V. *Glavnokomandujuščij vsemi vooruzennymi silami*
   respubliki I.I. Vacietis. Sbornik dokumentov (Riga, 1978)
Krivov, T.S. *V Leninskom stroju* (Moscow, 1973)
Krylenko, N.V. *Sudebnye reči. Izbr.* (Moscow, 1964)
Kuznecov, N.G. *Na dalekom meridiane* (Moscow, 1966) (G.M. Štern)
Kuznecov, N.V. *V.G. Knorin* (Minsk, 1979)
Laduchin, V.N. *V.I. Šorin* (Kalinin, 1960)
Lappo, D.D. *I. Varejkis* (Moscow, 1966)
Latysskie revoljucionnye dejateli (Riga, 1958)
Lebedinskij, V.G. and Kalenov, Ju. A. *Prokurorskij nadzor v SSSR* (Moscow,
   1957)
Lenin, V.I. *Sočinenija*, 4th edn (Moscow, 1941-67)
—— *Voennaja perepiska (1917-1920)*, ed. A.E. Antonov (Moscow, 1956)
—— *Polnoe Sobranije Sočinenij*, 5th edn (Moscow, 1958-65) (*PSS*)
—— *Voennaja perepiska, 1917-1922 gg.* (Moscow, 1966)
Leninskij Sbornik XXXIV (Moscow 1942)
Leonov, I.T. *G.N. Kaminskij* (Moscow, 1967)
Licholat, A.V. *Razgrom nacionalističeskoj kontrrevoljucii na Ukraine 1917-1922*
   gg. (Moscow, 1954)
—— *A.S. Bubnov na Ukraini* (Kiev, 1965)
Lozecko, A.B. *G. Kaminskij. Dokumental'naja povest'* (Moscow, 1966)
Makasov, A.V., Rudnickij, V.A. *Š. Šotemor* (Dusanbe, 1964)
Malyšev, V.P. and Jakimov, A.T. *Maršal Sovetskogo Sojuza Bljucher*
   (Blagoveščensk, 1958)
Marjagin, G.A. *Postyšev* (Moscow, 1965)
Mel'čin, A.I. *Stanislav Kosior* (Moscow, 1964)
Melenevs'kij, A.F. and Kurij, G.M. *G.I. Petrovskij* (Kiev, 1968)
Mil'čakov, A.I. *Pervoe desjatiletie. Zapiski veterana komsomola* (Moscow, 1965)
Morozov, V. *V.P. Zatonskij* (Kiev, 1967)
Mriščuk, D.V. *G.I. Staryj, 1880-1937* (Kiev, 1974)
Muchamedzanov, M.M. *Molodez'i revoljucija* (Moscow, 1972) (L.A. Šackin)
Musabekov, G.M. *Izbrannye stat'i i reči* (2 vols., Baku, 1960)
Mužestvennye borcy za delo kommunizma. Sbornik statej (Tashkent, 1957)
Narodnoe Chozjajstvo 1959 (Moscow, 1960)
Narodnoe Chozjajstvo 1962 (Moscow, 1963)
Narodnoe Chozjajstvo 1972 (Moscow, 1972)
Nikulin, L. *Tuchačevskij* (Moscow, 1963)
Očerki istorii Kommunističeskoj Partii Gruzii, ed. V.G. Esajasvili (2 vols., Tbilisi,
   1957-63)
Očerki istorii Kommunističeskoj Partii Moldavii (Kišinev, 1964)
Očerki istorii Kommunističeskoj Partii Ukrainy (Kiev, 1961)
Odinnadcatyj s"ezd RKP(b). Mart-aprel' 1922 g. Stenografičeskij otčet (Moscow,
   1961)
Oktjabr'skoe vooruzennoe vosstanie v Petrograde. Vospominanija aktivnych
   učastnikov revoljucii (Leningrad, 1956)
Oni borolis' za vlast' sovetov (Novosibirsk, 1970)
Oni služili narodu (Kujbysev, 1968)
Ot fevralja k Oktjabrju (iz anketa učastnikov Velikoj Oktjabr'skoj Socialističeskoj
   Revoljucii) (Moscow, 1957)
Packorija, V.A. *Š. Eliava* (Tbilisi, 1974)

Pankov, D. V. *Komkor Ejdeman* (Moscow, 1965)
Partija šagaet v revoljuciju (1st edn, Moscow, 1964; 2nd edn, Moscow, 1969)
Petrov, Ju. P. *Voennye komissary v gody graždanskoj vojny (1918-1920 gg.)*
    (Moscow, 1956)
—— *Partijnoe stroitel' stvo v sovetskoj armii i flote* (Moscow, 1964)
G.I. Petrovskij (Kiev, 1961)
Petrovskij, G. I. *Veliki roki* (Kiev, 1957)
—— *Velikoe načalo* (Moscow, 1957)
—— *Z revoljucionnoho minuloho* (Kiev, 1958)
—— *Vibrani statti i promovi* (Kiev, 1974)
Petrovskij, L. P. *P. Petrovskij* (Alma Ata, 1974)
Pjatnadcatyj s″ ezd VKP(b). Stenografičeskij otčet (Moscow, 1962)
Pjatnickij, I. A. *Izbrannye vospominanija i stat' i* (Moscow, 1969)
Pjatyj (Londonskij) s″ ezd RSDRP. Aprel' -mai 1907 goda. Protokoly (Moscow,
    1963)
Plotnikov, I. F. *Desjat' tysjac geroev. Legendarny rejd ural'skich partizan vo glave s
    V. K. Bljucherom* (Moscow, 1967)
Polkovodcy graždanskoj vojny (Moscow, 1960)
Ponomarew, P. N. *Der Trotskismus – ein Werkzeug des Antikommusismus* (2 vols.,
    Berlin, 1972)
Popov, A. S. *Trud, talant, doblest'* (Moscow, 1972) (M. N. Tuchačevskij)
Poslancy partii, Vospominanija, ed. N. F. Brycev and I. L. Obertas (Moscow, 1967)
Postyšev, P. P. *Graždanskaja vojna na vostoke Sibiri (1917-1922 gg.).
    Vospominanija* (Moscow, 1957)
—— *Iz prošlogo. Rasskazy i očerki* (Moscow, 1958)
Prí rucní slovnik k dejinám KSC (Prague, 1964)
Protokoly Central' nogo Komiteta RSDRP(b). Avgust 1917-fevral' 1918 (Moscow,
    1958)
Putna, V. K. *Vostočnyj front* (Moscow, 1969)
Rachunov, R. D. *Peresmotr prigovorov i opredelenij v prezidiumach sudov*
    (Moscow, 1956)
Rakitin, A. V. *Imenem revoljucii (Očerki o V. A. Antonove-Ovseenko)* (Moscow,
    1965)
—— *Antonov-Ovseenko. Dokumenty biografičeskij očerk* (Leningrad, 1975)
Revoljutcionery Prikam' ja (Perm', 1966)
Ribos, E. Ju. *P. P. Postyšev. Biografičeskij očerk* (Moscow, 1962)
Rivlin, A. L. *Peresmotr prigovorov v SSSR* (Moscow, 1958)
Salechov, M. I. and Gorelik, Ja. M. *Tovariš Jan (Naris pro Jana Borisovica
    Gamarnika)* (Kiev, 1963)
Salechov, N. I. *Ja. B. Gamarnik* (Moscow, 1964)
Samojlo, A. A. *Dve žizni* (Leningrad, 1963) (M. S. Kedrov)
—— and Sbojčakov, M. I. *Poučitel' nyj urok* (Moscow, 1962) (I. P. Uborevič)
Savost'janov, V. I. and Egorov, P. Ja. *Komandarm pervogo ranga* (Moscow, 1966)
    (I. P. Uborevič)
Sbojčakov, M. I., Cybov, S. I. and Čistjakov, N. F. *M. S. Kedrov* (Moscow, 1969)
*Sbornik normativnych aktov po sovetskomu ispravitel' no-trudovomu pravu
    (1917-1959 gg.). Istorija zakonodatel' stva,* ed. P. M. Losev and G. I. Ragulin
    (Moscow, 1959)
*Sbornik postanovlenij plenuma i opredelenij kollegij
    Verchovnogo Suda SSSR po voprosam ugolovnogo procesa 1946-1962 gg.*
    (Moscow, 1964)
Sbornik postanovlenij plenuma Verchovnogo Suda SSSR 1924-1963 gg. (Moscow,
    1964)
Sbornik postanovlenij plenuma Verchovnogo Suda SSSR 1924-1970 gg. (Moscow,

1970)
Sbornik zakonov i ukazov prezidiuma Verchovnogo Soveta SSSR (1938-jul'-1956 gg.) (Moscow, 1956)
Sbornik zakonov i ukazov prezidiuma Verchovnogo Soveta SSSR 1938-1967) (3 vols., Moscow, 1968-71)
Sed' maja (aprel' skaja) vserossijskaja konferencija RSDRP(b).
Petrogradskaja konferencija RSDRP(b). Aprel' 1917 goda (Moscow, 1958)
Sed' moj ekstrennyj s"ezd RKP(b) mart 1918 goda. Stenografičeskij otčet (Moscow, 1962)
Šejnis, Z. S. *Soldaty revolucii* (Moscow, 1981)
Semnadcatyj s"ezd VKP(b). Stenografičeskij otčet (Moscow, 1934)
Serce, otdannoe ljudjam. Rasskaz o žizni i dejatel' nosti G. I. Petrovskogo, ed. A. V. Snegov *et al.* (Moscow, 1964)
Šestnadcataja konferencija VKP(b). Aprel' 1929 goda. Stenografičeskij otčet (Moscow, 1962)
Šestnadcatyj s"ezd VKP(b). Stenografičeskij otčet (Moscow, 1930)
Šestoj s"ezd RSDRP(b). Avgust 1917 g. Protokoly (Moscow, 1958)
S"ezdy Sovetov sojoznych i avtonomnych sovetskich socialističeskich respublik. Sbornik dokumentov (7 vols., Moscow, 1959-65)
Simonjan, M. *Žizn' dlja revoljucii* (Moscow, 1962) (N. V. Krylenko)
Simonov, E. D. *Čelovek mnogich versin* (Moscow, 1969) (N. V. Krylenko)
Snesarev, A. E. *Žizn' i naucnaja dejatel' nost'* (Moscow, 1973)
Soldaty partii (Moscow, 1971)
Soratniki V. I. Lenina — organizatory profsojuzov SSSR (Moscow, 1970)
Šotman, A. V. *Zapiski starogo bol'ševika* (Leningrad, 1963)
Spravočnik partijnogo rabotnika, vol. 1- (Moscow, 1961-)
Stasova, E. D. *Slavnye bol'sevicki* (Moscow, 1958)
—— *Vospominanija* (Moscow, 1969)
Steklov, Ju. M. *Vospominanija i publicistika* (Moscow, 1965)
—— *Izbrannoe* (Moscow, 1973)
Stranicy slavnoj istorii. Vospominanija o 'Pravda' 1912-1917 gg. (Moscow, 1962)
Todorskij, A. I. *Maršal Tuchačevskij* (Moscow, 1963)
Trinadcatyj s"ezd RKP(b), maj 1924 goda. Stenografičeskij otčet (Moscow, 1963)
Trukan, G. A. *Jan Rudzutak* (Moscow, 1963)
Tuchačevskij, M. N. *Izbrannye Proizvedenija* (2 vols., Moscow, 1964)
—— *Maršal Tuchačevskij. Vospominanija druzej i soratnikov* (Moscow, 1965)
Uborevič, I.P. *Komandarm Uborevič. Vospominanija druzej i soratnikov* (Moscow, 1964)
Ugolovno-processual'nyj Kodeks RSFSR (Moscow, 1953) (*UPK*)
Ugolovnyj kodeks RSFSR (Moscow, 1957)
Uistokov partii. Rasskazy o soratnikach V. I. Lenina (1st edn, Moscow, 1963; 2nd edn, Moscow, 1969)
Utkes, D. *Slavnye bol'ševiki* (Moscow, 1958)
Velikaja Oktjabr'skaja Socialističeskaja Revoljucija. Sbornik vospominanij (Moscow, 1957)
Vidnye sovetskie kommunisty-učastniki Kitajskoj revoljucii (Moscow, 1970)
Viktorov, L. *Podpol'scik, voin, čekist* (Moscow, 1963) (M. S. Kedrov)
Vneočerednoj dvadcatpervyj s"ezd KPSS 27 janvarja-5 fevralja 1959 goda. Stenografičeskij otčet (Moscow, 1959)
Vosemnadcatyj s"ezd VKP(b) 10-21 marta 1939. Stenografičeskij otčet (Moscow, 1939)
Vos'maja konferencija RKP(b). Dekabr' 1919 g. Protokoly (Moscow, 1961)
Vos'moj s"ezd RKP(b) mart 1919 goda. Protokoly (Moscow, 1959)
Vospominanija o G. I. Petrovskom (Moscow, 1978)

Vospominanija o V.I. Lenine, 1st edn (Moscow, 1954)
Vospominanija o V.I. Lenine, 2nd edn (Moscow, 1955)
Vospominanija o V.I. Lenine (3 vols., Moscow, 1956-60)
Vospominanija o V.I. Lenine (5 vols., Moscow, 1979-)
Vospominanija o V.I. Lenine. Annotirovannyj ukazatel' knig i žurnal'nych statej 1954-1961 gg., ed. F.N. Kudrjavcev (Moscow, 1963)
Vožaki Komsomola (1st edn, Moscow, 1965; 2nd edn, Moscow, 1974)
Za narodnoe delo (Dusanbe, 1970)
Za sovetskij Turkestan (Tashkent, 1963)
Za sovetskij Turkmenistan. Vospominanija učastnikov revoljucii i grazdanskoj vojny (Aschabad, 1963)
Zdanovič, S.F. *K. Bauman* (Moscow, 1967)
Žensciny russkoj revoljucii (Moscow, 1968)
Žensciny v revoljucii (Moscow, 1959)
Zigalov, 1. *Povest' o baltijskom matrose* (Moscow, 1973) (P.E. Dybenko)
Zinin, V.K. *Vernyj syn partii* (Erevan, 1966) (A.G. Chandžan)
Znamenoscy revoljucii (Tallinn, 1964)

Publications outside the Soviet Union and Eastern Europe

Periodicals

Absees
The American Slavic and East European Review
Bulletin der Internationalen Juristen-Kommission (IJK)
Bulletin d'informations. Commission pour la Vérité sur les crimes de Staline
Central Asian Review
Chronika. A Chronicle of Current Events
Le Contrat social
The Current Digest of the Soviet Press
Internationale Spectator
Kontinent (Russian and German editions)
Osteuropa
Osteuropa-Recht
Ost-Probleme
Pamjat'
Peking Review/Beijing Review
Političeskij Dnevnik 1964-1970 (Amsterdam, 1972-5). See also End to Silence
Posev
Problems of Communism
Radio Free Europe Research
Radio Liberty Research
Ruslandbulletin
Russian Review
Slavic Review
Soviet Studies
Soviet Studies. Information Supplement
Sowjet Studien
Spiegel Historiael
Studies in Comparative Communism
WGO — Die wichtigsten Gesetzgebungsakte in den Ländern Ost-, Südosteuropas und in den Ostasiatischen Volksdemokratien. Continued later on as *WGO*

Monatshefte Osteuropäisches Recht WQO — Wiener Quellenhefte zur Ostkunde. Reihe Recht (Vienna, 1958-67)

Books

Allilueva, S. *Only One Year* (London, 1969)
Antonov-Ovseenko, A. *Portret tirana* (New York, 1980)
—— *The Time of Stalin. Portrait of a Tyranny* (New York, 1981)
Arbeiterdemokratie oder Parteidiktatur, ed. F. Kool (Olten, 1967)
AS, A serial register of the Arkhiv Samizdata, ed. A. Boiter (Munich, 1972)
Bibliographie des deutschsprachigen Schrifttums zum Ostrecht (1945-1964), ed. C. Bussmann and W. Durchlaub (Trittau-Holst, 1969)
Biographic Directory of the USSR, compiled by the Institute for the Study of the USSR, Munich (New York, 1958)
Blanc, Y. and Kaisergruber, D. *L'affaire Boukharine ou Le recours de la mémoire* (Paris, 1979)
Borijs, J. *The Russian Communist Party and the Sovietization of Ukraine. A Study in the Communist Doctrine of the Self-determination of Nations* (Stockholm, 1960)
Brandt, C. *Stalin's Failure in China 1924-1927* (Cambridge, Mass., 1958)
Bukovsky, V. *To Build a Castle. My Life as a Dissenter* (London, 1978)
Carrère d'Encausse, H. 'Le XXème Congrès du PC de l'URSS', *Le Vingtième Congrès, Mythes et Realités de l'Europe de l'Est en 1956* (Paris, 1977)
Chalanov, V. '*Article 58*'. *Mémoires du prisonnier Chalanov* (Paris, 1969)
Chornovil, V. *The Chornovil Papers* (New York, 1968)
Coates, K. *The Case of Nikolai Bukharin* (Nottingham, 1978)
Cohen, S. F. *Bukharin and the Bolshevik Revolution. A Political Biography 1888-1938* (New York, 1973)
—— *An End to Silence, see End to Silence*
Conquest, R. *Power and Policy in the USSR. The Study of Soviet Dynastics* (London, 1961)
—— *Russia after Khrushchev* (New York, 1965)
—— *Soviet Nationalities Policy in Practice* (London, 1967)
—— *The Great Terror* (Harmondsworth, 1971)
Contemporary History in the Soviet Mirror, ed. J. L. H. Keep (London, 1964)
CSP: Current Soviet Policies, ed. Ch. Saikowski and L. Griulow
    vol 1, *The Nineteenth Party Congress* (New York, 1953)
    vol. 2, *The Twentieth Party-Congress* (New York, 1957)
    vol. 3, *The Twentyfirst Congress* (New York, 1960)
    vol. 4, *The Twentysecond Congress* (New York, 1962)
    vol. 5, *The Twentythird Congress* (New York, 1973)
Daniels, R. V. *The Conscience of the Revolution* (New York, 1960)
An End to Silence. Uncensored Opinion in the Soviet Union from Roy Medvedev's Underground Magazine Political Diary, ed. S. F. Cohen (New York, 1982)
Enteen, G. M. *The Soviet Scholar-Bureaucrat: M. N. Pokrovskii and the Society of Marxist Historians* (London, 1978)
Entstalinisierung. Der XX. Parteitag der KPdSU und seine Folgen, ed. R. Crusius and M. Wilke (Frankfurt-on-Main, 1977)
Erickson, J. *The Soviet High Command: A Military-Political History, 1918-1941* (London, 1962)
Fincke, M. *Die aufsichtliche Ueberprüfung rechtskräftiger Strafurteile im Sovjetrecht* (Herrenalb, 1966)
Fricke, K. W. *Warten auf Gerechtigkeit. Kommunistische Säuberungen und Rehabilitierungen. Bericht und Dokumentation* (Cologne, 1971)
Geilke, G. 'Rechtsfragen der Rückkehr zwangsausgeziedelter Bevölkerungen in

Länderen des Ostblocks' in *Das Recht auf die Heimat*, vol. 3, ed. K. Rabl
    (Munich, 1959)
Ginzburg, E. *Into the Whirlwind* (Harmondsworth, 1968)
—— *Krutoj maršrut. Tjur' ma-lager' ssylka*, vol. 2 (Milan, 1979)
Gordon Skilling, H. *Czechoslovakia's Interrupted Revolution* (Princeton, 1976)
Goul, R. (Gul', R.) *Les grands chefs de l'armée soviétique* (Paris, 1935)
Griffith, W. E. *Albania and the Sino-Soviet Rift* (Cambridge, Mass., 1963)
Gul' R. *Vorošilov, Budennyj, Bljucher, Kotovskij* (Berlin 1932)
Hayit, B. *Sowjetrussische Orientpolitik am Beispiel Turkestans* (Cologne, 1962)
Heer, N. W. *Politics and History in the Soviet Union* (Cambridge, Mass., 1971)
Heinzig, D. *Sowjetische Militärberäter bei den Kuomintang 1923-27*
    (Baden-Baden, 1978)
Heller, M. and Nekrich, A. *Geschichte der Sowjetunion* (2 vols., Königstein, 1982)
*Judicial Statistics of the Czechoslovak SR as Contained in the Statistické ročenky
    CSSR 1968-1980* (Leiden, 1983)
Kaplan, K. *Dans les archives du Comité Central. 30 Ans de secrets du Bloc
    soviétique* (Paris, 1978)
Khrushchev, N. S. 'Secret speech' in *Current Soviet Policies*, vol. 2
Khrushchev Remembers, ed. S. Talbot (Boston, 1970)
Khrushchev. The Last Testament, ed. S. Talbot (London, 1974)
Kopácsi, S. *Die ungarische Tragödie. Wie der Aufstand von 1956 liquidiert wurde*
    (Stuttgart, 1979)
Koriakov, M. [M.] *Živija istorija 1917-1975* (Munich, 1977)
*Korte leergang. Geschiedenis van de Communistische Partij der Sowjet-Unie
    (Bolsjewiki). Korte leergang onder redactie van een commissie in het Centraal
    Comité van de Communistische Partij der Sowjet-Unie, goedgekeurd door het
    Centraal Comité* (Amsterdam, 1950)
Kusin, V. V. *From Dubček to Charter 77. A Study of 'Normalisation' in
    Czechoslovakia, 1968-1978* (Edinburgh, 1978)
Kuusinen, A. *Der Gott stürzt seine Engel* (Vienna, 1972)
Lazich, B. and Drachkovich, M. *Biographical Dictionary of the Komintern*
    (Stanford, Cal. 1973)
Lazitch, B. *Le Rapport Khrouchtchev et son histoire* (Paris, 1976)
Leonhard, W. *The Kremlin since Stalin* (London, 1962)
Levytsky, B. *The Stalinist Terror in the Thirties*, see *Stalinist Terror*
Lewytzkyj, B. *Die Sowjetukraine 1944-1962* (Cologne, 1964)
—— *Die KPdSU. Porträt eines Ordens* (Stuttgart, 1967)
—— *Die Marschälle und die Politik. Eine Untersuchung über den Stellenwert des
    Militärs innerhalb des sowjetischen Systems seit dem Sturz Chruschtschews*
    (Cologne, 1971)
—— *The Uses of Terror. The Soviet Secret Service 1917-1970* (London, 1971)
—— *Politische Opposition in der Sowjet Union. Analyse und Dokumentation*
    (Munich, 1972)
Löbl, E. and Pokorný, D. *Die Revolution rehabilitiert ihre Kinder. Hinter den
    Kulissen des Slánský-Prozesses* (Vienna, 1968)
London, A. *Ich gestehe. Der Prozess um Rudolf Slansky* (Hamburg, 1970)
Lubachko, I.S. *Belorussia under Soviet Rule 1917-1957* (Lexington, Mass., 1972)
Maloumian, A. *Les fils du Goulag* (Paris, 1976)
Mandelštam, N. *Mémoires* (Amsterdam, 1971)
—— *Tweede Boek* (Amsterdam, 1973)
Medvedev, R. A. *Faut-il réhabiliter Staline?* (Paris, 1969)
—— *Let History Judge. The Origins and Consequences of Stalinism* (London,
    1971)
—— *K sudu istorii. Genezis i posledstvija Stalinizma*, 2nd edn (New York, 1974)

—— *Political Essays* (Nottingham, 1976)
—— *On Stalin and Stalinism* (Oxford, 1979)
—— *Bukharin. The Last Years* (New York, 1980)
—— *Khrushchev* (Oxford, 1982)
—— and Z. A. *A Question of Madness* (London, 1971)
—— , —— *Khrushchev. The Years in Power* (New York, 1976)
Medwedjew, Sh. A. *Der Fall Lysenko. Eine Wissenschaft kapituliert* (Hamburg, 1971)
Meissner, B. *Das Ende des Stalin-Mythos. Die Ergebnisse des 20. Parteikongresses des KPdSU* (Frankfurt-on-Main, 1956)
Monatshefte für Osteuropaïsches Recht (WGO). Gesamtregister für die Jahrgänge 1958-1978, ed. G. Geilke (Hamburg, 1982)
Moroz, V. *Among the Snows* (London, 1971)
—— *Boomerang. The Works of Valentyn Moroz*, ed. Ya. Bihun (Baltimore, 1974)
Nachrichten aus der CSSR. Dokumentation der Wochenzeitung 'Literárni listy' des Tschechoslowakischen Schriftstellerverbandes Prag, Februar-August 1968, ed. J. Skvorecký (Frankfurt-on-Main, 1968)
Nekrič, A. [M.] *Otreši̇̀s ot stracha. Vospominanija istorika* (London, 1979)
—— *The Punished Peoples. The Deportation and Fate of Soviet Minorities at the End of the Second World War* (New York, 1978)
Nekrich, A. *Geschichte der Sowjetunion, see M. Heller and A. Nekrich*
Nekritsch, A. and Grigorenko, P. *Genickschuss: Die Rote Armee am 22 Juni 1941* (Vienna, 1969)
Nord, L. *Maršal M. N. Tuchachevskij* (Paris, 1978)
Olickaja, E. *Moi vospominanija* (Frankfurt-on-Main, 1971)
Pelikan, J. *Pervertierte Justiz* (Vienna, 1972)
Piller-rapport, see Das unterdrückte Dossier
Politiceskij Dnevnik 1964-1970 (2 vols., Amsterdam, 1972-5)
Polonsky, A. and Drukier, B. *The Beginnings of Communist Rule in Poland, December 1943-June 1945* (London, 1980)
Quellen und Schrifttum des Strafrechts, H.-H. Jescheck and K. H. A. Löffler, vol. 1: *Europa* (Munich, 1972)
Rechtswörterbuch, C. Creinfelds (Munich, 1968)
Reddaway, P. (ed.) *Uncensored Russia, see Uncensored Russia*
Reshetar, J. S. *The Ukrainian Revolution, 1917-1920. A Study in Nationalism* (Princeton, 1952)
Rigby, T. H. *Communist Party Membership in the USSR 1917-1967* (Princeton, 1968)
Romanian History 1848-1918. Essays from the First Dutch–Romanian Colloquium of Historians Utrecht 1977, ed. A. P. van Goudoever (Groningen, 1979)
Sakharov, A. D. *Sakharov Speaks* (London, 1974)
Samizdat Register, 2 vols., R. A. Medvedev (London, 1977-81)
Shapiro, J. 'Rehabilitation Policy and Political Conflict in the Soviet Union 1953-1964', unpublished PhD thesis Columbia University, 1967 (University Microfilms, Ann Arbor, Mich, 1977)
Short Course. The History of the CPSU, see Korte leergang
Slanska, J. *De Waarheid over Mijn Man* (Leiden, 1969)
Slusser, R. M. *The Berlin Crisis of 1961. Soviet–American Relations and the Struggle for Power in the Kremlin, June-November 1961* (Baltimore, 1973)
Solschenizyn, A. I. *Der Archipel Gulag 1918-1956. Versuch einer künstlerischen Bewältigung* (3 vols., Berne, 1974-6)
Solzhenitzyn, A. I. *Cancer Ward* (Harmondsworth, 1971)
Solzhenitsyn. A Documentary Record ed. L. Labedz (Harmondsworth, 1972)

Soviet Asian Ethnic Frontiers, ed. W. O. McCagg and B. D. Silver (New York, 1979)

Soviet Leaders, ed. G.W. Simmonds (New York, 1967)

The Soviet Police System, ed. R. Conquest (London, 1968)

The Soviet Union since Stalin, ed. S. F. Cohen, A. Rabinowitch and R. Sharlet (London, 1980)

Das Staatsangehörigkeitsrecht der Sowjetunion einschliesslich der geschichtsverfassungsrechtlichen Entwicklung der wichtigsten Gebietseinheiten und Völkerschaften. Sammlung geltender Staatsangehörigkeitsgesetze, vol. 25, ed. G. Geilke (Frankfurt-on-Main, 1969)

Stalinism. Essays in Historical Interpretation, ed. R. C. Tucker (New York, 1977)

The Stalinist Terror in the Thirties. Documentation from the Soviet Press, ed. B. Levytsky (Stanford, Cal., 1974)

Suda, Z. *Zealots and Rebels. A History of the Ruling Communist Party of Czechoslovakia* (Stanford, Cal., 1980)

Tatu, M. *Power in the Kremlin. From Khrushchev to Kosygin* (New York, 1969)

Tökés, R. L. *Béla Kun and the Hungarian Soviet Republic* (Stanford, Cal., 1967)

Trotsky Papers 1917-1922, ed. J. M. Meyer (The Hague, 1964-71)

Das Tschechoslowakische Strafgesetzbuch vom 12. Juli 1950 (in der Fassung vom 22. Dezember 1956), ed. E. Schmied, 2nd edn (Berlin, 1958)

The Ukraine, 1917-1921: A Study in Revolution, ed. T. Hunczak (Cambridge, Mass., 1977)

Ulam, A. B. *Stalin. The Man and his Era* (New York, 1973)

Uncensored Russia. The Human Rights Movement in the Soviet Union. The Annotated Text of the Unofficial Moscow Journal 'A Chronicle of Current Events', nos. 1-11, ed. P. Reddaway (London, 1972)

Das unterdrückte Dossier. Bericht des ZK des KPTsch über politische Prozesse und 'Rehabilitierungen' in der Tschechoslowakei 1949-1968 (the *Piller-rapport*), ed. J. Pelikán (Vienna, 1970)

Le Vingtième Congrès, Mythes et réalités de l'Europe de l'Est en 1956, Colloquium, Paris, 6 March 1976 (Paris, 1977)

Who was Who in the USSR (Metuchen, NJ, 1972)

Windsor, P. and Roberts, A. *Czechoslovakia 1968. Reform, Repression and Resistance* (London, 1969)

INDEX OF NAMES

SUBJECT INDEX

For Product Safety Concerns and Information please contact our EU
representative GPSR@taylorandfrancis.com
Taylor & Francis Verlag GmbH, Kaufingerstraße 24, 80331 München, Germany

www.ingramcontent.com/pod-product-compliance
Lightning Source LLC
Chambersburg PA
CBHW060154280326
41932CB00012B/1759